Lecture Notes in Computer Science 9476

Commenced Publication in 1973
Founding and Former Series Editors:
Gerhard Goos, Juris Hartmanis, and Jan van Leeuwen

More information about this series at http://www.springer.com/series/7410

Michael Reiter · David Naccache (Eds.)

Cryptology and Network Security

14th International Conference, CANS 2015
Marrakesh, Morocco, December 10–12, 2015
Proceedings

 Springer

Editors
Michael Reiter
Department of Computer Science
UNC Chapel Hill
Chapel Hill, NC
USA

David Naccache
Départment d'Informatique
Ecole Normale Supérieure
Paris
France

ISSN 0302-9743   ISSN 1611-3349   (electronic)
Lecture Notes in Computer Science
ISBN 978-3-319-26822-4   ISBN 978-3-319-26823-1   (eBook)
DOI 10.1007/978-3-319-26823-1

Library of Congress Control Number: 2015954619

LNCS Sublibrary: SL4 – Security and Cryptology

Springer Cham Heidelberg New York Dordrecht London

Printed on acid-free paper

Springer International Publishing AG Switzerland is part of Springer Science+Business Media
(www.springer.com)

Preface

These proceedings contain the papers accepted for presentation at the 14th International Conference on Cryptology and Network Security, held in Marrakesh, Morocco, during December 10–12, 2015. A total of 12 full papers and six short papers were accepted by a Program Committee of 42 experts in the areas of network security and cryptology. Full papers were accompanied by a 30-minute presentation at the meeting, and short papers were allowed 20 minutes.

The reviewing period began immediately after the submission deadline of June 19, 2015. Papers received an average of 3.5 reviews each, with a minimum of three and a maximum of six. After reviews were submitted, the merits of each paper were debated by the reviewers via the conference reviewing website; no face-to-face Program Committee meeting was held. Notifications of acceptance or rejection were sent to authors on August 28, 2015.

In addition to these papers, the conference featured two invited keynote presentations. Andrew Clark, Visiting Professor at the Information Security Group, Department of Mathematics, Royal Holloway University of London, delivered a keynote lecture entitled "Finding Evidence in the Internet of Everything" on the first day of the conference. Gilles Barthe, Research Professor at the IMDEA Software Institute, presented "Towards High-Assurance Cryptographic Implementations" on the second day of the conference.

We are grateful to the authors of all papers submitted to the conference; to the Program Committee members; to other colleagues who assisted the Program Committee in reviewing for the conference, including Vincenzo Iovino, Jean Lancrenon, Florian Lugou, Yanjiang Yang, Tsz Hon Yuen, and Yongjun Zhao; to our invited speakers; and to the Steering Committee and General Chair of the conference.

October 2015

Michael Reiter
David Naccache

Organization

General Chair

Anas Abou El Kalam   IGS-IPI, France

Program Committee Chairs

David Naccache   École Normale Supérieure, France
Michael K. Reiter   University of North Carolina at Chapel Hill, USA

Organizing Chair

Jean Philippe Leroy   Institut de Poly-Informatique Groups IGS, France

Program Committee Members

Ludovic Apvrille   Télécom ParisTech, France
Feng Bao   Hauwei, China
Sasha Boldyreva   Georgia Tech, USA
Stephen Checkoway   Johns Hopkins University, USA
Hao Chen   UC Davis, USA
Liqun Chen   HP Labs, UK
Sherman S.M. Chow   Chinese University Hong Kong, SAR China
Jean-Sebastien Coron   University of Luxembourg, Luxembourg
Manuel Costa   Microsoft Research, UK
George Danezis   University College London, UK
Eric Diehl   Sony Pictures Entertainment, USA
Itai Dinur   École Normale Supérieure, France
Tudor Dumitras   University of Maryland, College Park, USA
Aggelos Kiayias   University of Athens, Greece
Jean Louis Lanet   University of Limoges, France
Anja Lehmann   IBM Zurich, Switzerland
Tancrède Lepoint   CryptoExperts, France
Cristina Nita-Rotaru   University of Purdue, USA
Alina Oprea   RSA Labs, USA
Victor Patriciu   Military Technical Academy, Romania
Rene Peralta   NIST, USA
Benny Pinkas   Bar Ilan University, Israel
Christina Pöpper   Ruhr-Universität Bochum, Germany
Bart Preneel   Katholieke University Leuven, Belgium
Reza Reyhanitabar   EPFL, Switzerland

Mark Ryan	University of Birmingham, UK
Peter Y.A. Ryan	University of Luxembourg, Luxembourg
Ahmad-Reza Sadeghi	TU Darmstadt, Germany
Rei Safavi-Naini	University of Calgary, Canada
Damien Sauveron	University of Limoges, France
Emil Simion	Polytechnic University Bucharest, Romania
Thomas Souvignet	Gendarmerie Nationale, France
Rainer Steinwandt	Florida Atlantic University, USA
Willy Susilo	University of Wollongong, Australia
Mehdi Tibouchi	NTT Secure Platform Laboratories, Japan
Cristian Toma	Academic Economic Studies Bucharest, Romania
Ingrid Verbauwhede	Katholieke University Leuven, Belgium
Guilin Wang	Huawei, China
Ting-Fang Yen	DataVisor, USA
Lei Zhang	East China Normal University, China

Steering Committee

Yvo Desmedt	University of Texas, USA
Juan A. Garay	Yahoo! Labs, USA
Amir Herzberg	Bar Ilan University, Israel
Yi Mu	University of Wollongong, Australia
David Pointcheval	CNRS and ENS Paris, France
Huaxiong Wang	Nanyang Technical University, Singapore

Local Arrangements Committee

Imane Bouij-Pasquier	ENSA Marrakech, Morocco
Youssef Bentaleb	CMRPI, Morocco
Jean Philippe Leroy	IGS-IPI, France
Hicham Medroumi	ENSEM, Morocco
Steeve Augoula	Artimia, France
M. Ouabiba de Montfort	Artimia, France
Chary Meryem	AB Sec, Morocco
Larbi Bessa	IGS-IPI, France
Jean Marie Mahé	IGS-IPI, France
Benhadou Siham	ENSEM, Morocco
Youssef Saoubou	ENSEM - IGS-IPI, France
Ismail Rachdaoui	ENSEM - IGS-IPI, France
Mounia EL Anbal	ENSEM - IGS-IPI, France
Raja Mouachi	SFFSM
Abdeljalil Agnaou	ENSA, Morocco
Sanaa Ibjaoun	ENSA - University Valanciennes, France

Contents

Secure Multi-party Computation

Cryptography and VPNs

Internet of Things and Privacy

PUDA – Privacy and Unforgeability for Data Aggregation

Iraklis Leontiadis[(✉)], Kaoutar Elkhiyaoui, Melek Önen, and Refik Molva

EURECOM, Sophia Antipolis, France
{iraklis.leontiadis,kaoutar.elkhiyaoui,melek.onen,refik.molva}@eurecom.fr

Abstract. Existing work on secure data collection and secure aggregation is mainly focused on confidentiality issues. That is, ensuring that the untrusted Aggregator learns only the aggregation result without divulging individual data inputs. In this paper however we consider a malicious Aggregator which is not only interested in compromising users' privacy but also is interested in providing bogus aggregate values. More concretely, we extend existing security models with the requirement of *aggregate unforgeability*. Moreover, we instantiate an efficient protocol for private and unforgeable data aggregation that allows the Aggregator to compute the sum of users' inputs without learning individual values and constructs a proof of correct computation that can be verified by any third party. The proposed protocol is provably secure and its communication and computation overhead is minimal.

1 Introduction

With the advent of *Big Data*, research on privacy preserving data collection and analysis is culminating as users continuously produce data which once aggregated becomes very valuable. Often scenarios regarding data analysis involve an Aggregator which collects individual data from multiple (independent) users to compute useful statistics, these statistics are generally forwarded to Data Analyzers whose role is to extract insightful information about the entire user population. Various motivating examples for the aforementioned generic scenario exist in the real-world:

- The analysis of different user profiles and the derivation of statistics can help recommendation engines provide targeted advertisements. In such scenarios a service provider would collect data from each individual user (i.e.: on-line purchases), thus acting as an Aggregator, and compute an on-demand aggregate value upon receiving a request from the advertisement company. The latter will further infer some statistics acting as a Data Analyzer, in order to send the appropriate advertisements to each category of users.
- Data aggregation is a promising tool in the field of healthcare research. Different types of data, sensed by body sensors (eg. blood pressure), are collected on a large scale by Aggregators. Health scientists who act as Data Analyzers

© Springer International Publishing Switzerland 2015
M. Reiter and D. Naccache (Eds.): CANS 2015, LNCS 9476, pp. 3–18, 2015.
DOI: 10.1007/978-3-319-26823-1_1

infer statistical information from these data without accessing the individual inputs (for privacy reasons). An aggregate value computed over a large population would give very useful information for deriving statistical models, evaluating therapeutic performance or learning the likelihood of upcoming patients' diseases.

Unfortunately, existing solutions only focus on the problem of data confidentiality and consider the Aggregator to be *honest-but-curious*: the Aggregator wants to discover the content of each individual data, but performs the aggregation operation correctly. In this paper we consider a more powerful security model by assuming a malicious Aggregator: The Aggregator may provide a bogus aggregate value to the Data Analyzer. In order to protect against such a malicious behavior, we propose that along with the aggregate value, the Aggregator provides a proof of the correctness of the computation of the aggregate result to the Data Analyzer. For efficiency reasons, we require that the Data Analyzer verifies the correctness of the computation without communicating with users in the system.

The underlying idea of our solution is that each user encrypts its data according to Shi *et al.* [17] scheme using its own secret encryption key, and sends the resulting ciphertext to the untrusted Aggregator. Users, also homomorphically tag their data using two layers of randomness with two different keys and forward the tags to the Aggregator. The latter computes the sum by applying operations on the ciphertexts and derives a proof of computation correctness from the tags. The Aggregator finally sends the result and the proof to the Data Analyzer. In addition to ensuring obliviousness against the Aggregator and the Data Analyzer (i.e. neither the Data Analyzer nor the Aggregator learns individual data inputs), the proposed protocol assures *public verifiablity*: any third party can verify the correctness of the aggregate value.

To the best of our knowledge we are the first to define a model for *Privacy and Unforgeability for Data Aggregation* (**PUDA**). We also instantiate a **PUDA** scheme that supports:

- A multi-user setting where multiple users produce personal sensitive data without interacting with each other.
- Privacy of users' individual data.
- Public verifiability of the aggregate value.

2   Problem Statement

We are envisioning a scenario whereby a set of users $\mathbb{U} = \{\mathcal{U}_i\}_{i=1}^n$ are producing sensitive data inputs $x_{i,t}$ at each time interval t. These individual data are first encrypted into ciphertexts $c_{i,t}$ and further forwarded to an untrusted Aggregator $\mathcal{A}$. Aggregator $\mathcal{A}$ aggregates all the received ciphertexts, decrypts the aggregate and forwards the resulting plaintext to a Data Analyzer $\mathcal{DA}$ together with a cryptographic proof that assures the correctness of the aggregation operation, which in this paper corresponds to the *sum* of the users' individual data.

An important criterion that we aim to fulfill in this paper is to ensure that Data Analyzer $\mathcal{DA}$ verifies the correctness of the Aggregator's output without compromising users' privacy. Namely, at the end of the verification operation, both Aggregator $\mathcal{A}$ and Data Analyzer $\mathcal{DA}$ learn nothing, but the value of the aggregation. While homomorphic signatures proposed in [4, 10] seem to answer the verifiability requirement, authors in those papers only consider scenarios where a single user generates data.

In the aim of assuring both individual user's privacy and unforgeable aggregation, we first come up with a generic model for privacy preserving and unforgeable aggregation that identifies the algorithms necessary to implement such functionalities and defines the corresponding privacy and security models. Furthermore, we propose a concrete solution which combines an already existing privacy preserving aggregation scheme [17] with an additively homomorphic tag designed for bilinear groups.

Notably, a scheme that allows a malicious Aggregator to compute the sum of users' data in privacy preserving manner and to produce a proof of correct aggregation will start by first running a setup phase. During setup, each user receives a secret key that will be used to encrypt the user's private input and to generate the corresponding authentication tag; the Aggregator $\mathcal{A}$ and the Data Analyzer $\mathcal{DA}$ on the other hand, are provided with a secret decryption key and a public verification key, respectively. After the key distribution, each user sends its data encrypted and authenticated to Aggregator $\mathcal{A}$, while making sure that the computed ciphertext and the matching authentication tag leak no information about its private input. On receiving users' data, Aggregator $\mathcal{A}$ first aggregates the received ciphertexts and decrypts the sum using its decryption key, then uses the received authentication tags to produce a proof that demonstrates the correctness of the decrypted sum. Finally, Data Analyzer $\mathcal{DA}$ verifies the correctness of the aggregation, thanks to the public verification key.

2.1 PUDA Model

A **PUDA** scheme consists of the following algorithms:

- **Setup**$(1^\kappa) \to (\mathcal{P}, \mathsf{SK_A}, \{\mathsf{SK}_i\}_{\mathcal{U}_i \in \mathbb{U}}, \mathsf{VK})$: It is a randomized algorithm which on input of a security parameter κ, this algorithm outputs the public parameters $\mathcal{P}$ that will be used by subsequent algorithms, the Aggregator $\mathcal{A}$'s secret key $\mathsf{SK_A}$, the secret keys SK_i of users $\mathcal{U}_i$ and the public verification key VK.
- **EncTag**$(t, \mathsf{SK}_i, x_{i,t}) \to (c_{i,t}, \sigma_{i,t})$: It is a randomized algorithm which on inputs of time interval t, secret key SK_i of user $\mathcal{U}_i$ and data $x_{i,t}$, encrypts $x_{i,t}$ to get a ciphertext $c_{i,t}$ and computes a tag $\sigma_{i,t}$ that authenticates $x_{i,t}$.
- **Aggregate**$(\mathsf{SK_A}, \{c_{i,t}\}_{\mathcal{U}_i \in \mathbb{U}}, \{\sigma_{i,t}\}_{\mathcal{U}_i \in \mathbb{U}}) \to (\mathsf{sum}_t, \sigma_t)$: It is a deterministic algorithm executed by the Aggregator $\mathcal{A}$. It takes as inputs Aggregator $\mathcal{A}$'s secret key $\mathsf{SK_A}$, ciphertexts $\{c_{i,t}\}_{\mathcal{U}_i \in \mathbb{U}}$ and authentication tags $\{\sigma_{i,t}\}_{\mathcal{U}_i \in \mathbb{U}}$, and outputs the sum sum_t of the values $\{x_{i,t}\}_{\mathcal{U}_i \in \mathbb{U}}$ in cleartext and a proof σ_t of correctness for sum_t.

– **Verify**$(VK, t, \text{sum}_t, \sigma_t) \rightarrow \{0, 1\}$: It is a deterministic algorithm that is executed by the Data Analyzer $\mathcal{DA}$. It outputs 1 if Data Analyzer $\mathcal{DA}$ is convinced that proof σ_t corresponds to the sum $\text{sum}_t = \sum_{\mathcal{U}_i \in \mathbb{U}} \{x_{i,t}\}$, where $x_{i,t}$ are individual data inputs at time interval t of user $\mathcal{U}_i$; and 0 otherwise.

2.2 Security Model

In this paper, we only focus on the adversarial behavior of Aggregator $\mathcal{A}$. The rationale behind this, is that Aggregator $\mathcal{A}$ is the only party in the protocol that sees all the messages exchanged during the protocol execution: Namely, Aggregator $\mathcal{A}$ has access to users' ciphertexts. It follows that by ensuring security properties against the Aggregator, one by the same token, ensures these security properties against both Data Analyzer $\mathcal{DA}$ and external parties.

In accordance with previous work [11,17], we formalize the property of *Aggregator obliviousness*, which ensures that at the end of a protocol execution, Aggregator $\mathcal{A}$ only learns the sum of users' inputs and nothing else. Also, we enhance the security definitions of data aggregation with the notion of *aggregate unforgeability*. As the name implies, aggregate unforgeability guarantees that Aggregator $\mathcal{A}$ cannot forge a valid proof σ_t for a sum sum_t that was not computed correctly from users' inputs (i.e. cannot generate a proof for $\text{sum}_t \neq \sum x_{i,t}$).

Aggregator Obliviousness. *Aggregator Obliviousness* ensures that when users $\mathcal{U}_i$ provide Aggregator $\mathcal{A}$ with ciphertexts $c_{i,t}$ and authentication tags $\sigma_{i,t}$, Aggregator $\mathcal{A}$ cannot reveal any information about individual inputs $x_{i,t}$, other than the sum value $\sum x_{i,t}$. We extend the existing definition of *Aggregator Obliviousness* (cf. [11,13,17]) so as to capture the fact that Aggregator $\mathcal{A}$ not only has access to ciphertexts $c_{i,t}$, but also has access to the authentication tags $\sigma_{i,t}$ that enable Aggregator $\mathcal{A}$ to generate proofs of correct aggregation.

Similarly to the work of [11,17], we formalize *Aggregator obliviousness* using an indistinguishability-based game in which Aggregator $\mathcal{A}$ accesses the following oracles:

– $\mathcal{O}_{\text{Setup}}$: When called by Aggregator $\mathcal{A}$, this oracle initializes the system parameters; it then gives the public parameters $\mathcal{P}$, the Aggregator's secret key SK_A and public verification key VK to $\mathcal{A}$.
– $\mathcal{O}_{\text{Corrupt}}$: When queried by Aggregator $\mathcal{A}$ with a user $\mathcal{U}_i$' s identifier uid_i, this oracle provides Aggregator $\mathcal{A}$ with $\mathcal{U}_i$'s secret key denoted SK_i.
– $\mathcal{O}_{\text{EncTag}}$: When queried with time t, user $\mathcal{U}_i$'s identifier uid_i and a data point $x_{i,t}$, this oracle outputs the ciphertext $c_{i,t}$ and the authentication tag $\sigma_{i,t}$ of $x_{i,t}$.
– $\mathcal{O}_{\text{AO}}$: When called with a subset of users $\mathbb{S} \subset \mathbb{U}$ and with two time-series $\mathcal{X}_{t^*}^0 = (\mathcal{U}_i, t, x_{i,t}^0)_{\mathcal{U}_i \in \mathbb{S}}$ and $\mathcal{X}_{t^*}^1 = (\mathcal{U}_i, t, x_{i,t}^1)_{\mathcal{U}_i \in \mathbb{S}}$ such that $\sum x_{i,t}^0 = \sum x_{i,t}^1$, this oracle flips a random coin $b \in \{0, 1\}$ and returns an encryption of the time-serie $(\mathcal{U}_i, t, x_{i,t}^b)_{\mathcal{U}_i \in \mathbb{S}}$ (that is the tuple of ciphertexts $\{c_{i,t}^b\}_{\mathcal{U}_i \in \mathbb{S}}$ and the corresponding authentication tags $\{\sigma_{i,t}^b\}_{\mathcal{U}_i \in \mathbb{S}}$.

Aggregator $\mathcal{A}$ is accessing the aforementioned oracles during a learning phase (cf. Algorithm 1) and a challenge phase (cf. Algorithm 2). In the learning phase, $\mathcal{A}$ calls oracle $\mathcal{O}_{\mathsf{Setup}}$ which in turn returns the public parameters $\mathcal{P}$, the public verification key VK and the Aggregator's secret key $\mathsf{SK_A}$. It also interacts with oracle $\mathcal{O}_{\mathsf{Corrupt}}$ to learn the secret keys SK_i of users $\mathcal{U}_i$, and oracle $\mathcal{O}_{\mathsf{EncTag}}$ to get a set of ciphertexts $c_{i,t}$ and authentication tags $\sigma_{i,t}$.

In the challenge phase, Aggregator $\mathcal{A}$ chooses a subset $\mathbb{S}^*$ of users that were not corrupted in the learning phase, and a challenge time interval t^* for which it did not make an encryption query. Oracle $\mathcal{O}_{\mathsf{AO}}$ then receives two time-series $\mathcal{X}_{t^*}^0 = (\mathcal{U}_i, t^*, x_{i,t^*}^0)_{\mathcal{U}_i \in \mathbb{S}^*}$ and $\mathcal{X}_{t^*}^1 = (\mathcal{U}_i, t^*, x_{i,t^*}^1)_{\mathcal{U}_i \in \mathbb{S}^*}$ from $\mathcal{A}$, such that $\sum x_{i,t^*}^0 = \sum_{\mathcal{U}_i \in \mathbb{S}^*} x_{i,t^*}^1$. Then oracle $\mathcal{O}_{\mathsf{AO}}$ flips a random coin $b \xleftarrow{\$} \{0,1\}$ and returns to $\mathcal{A}$ the ciphertexts $\{c_{i,t^*}^b\}_{\mathcal{U}_i \in \mathbb{S}^*}$ and the matching authentication tags $\{\sigma_{i,t^*}^b\}_{\mathcal{U}_i \in \mathbb{S}^*}$.

At the end of the challenge phase, Aggregator $\mathcal{A}$ outputs a guess b^* for the bit b.

We say that Aggregator $\mathcal{A}$ succeeds in the Aggregator obliviousness game, if its guess b^* equals b.

Algorithm 1. Learning phase of the obliviousness game

$(\mathcal{P}, \mathsf{SK_A}, \mathsf{VK}) \leftarrow \mathcal{O}_{\mathsf{Setup}}(1^\kappa);$
// $\mathcal{A}$ executes the following a polynomial number of times
$\mathsf{SK}_i \leftarrow \mathcal{O}_{\mathsf{Corrupt}}(\mathsf{uid}_i);$
// $\mathcal{A}$ is allowed to call $\mathcal{O}_{\mathsf{EncTag}}$ for all users $\mathcal{U}_i$
$(c_{i,t}, \sigma_{i,t}) \leftarrow \mathcal{O}_{\mathsf{EncTag}}(t, \mathsf{uid}_i, x_{i,t});$

Algorithm 2. Challenge phase of the obliviousness game

$\mathcal{A} \rightarrow t^*, \mathbb{S}^*;$
$\mathcal{A} \rightarrow \mathcal{X}_{t^*}^0, \mathcal{X}_{t^*}^1;$
$(c_{i,t^*}^b, \sigma_{i,t^*}^b)_{\mathcal{U}_i \in \mathbb{S}^*} \leftarrow \mathcal{O}_{\mathsf{AO}}(\mathcal{X}_{t^*}^0, \mathcal{X}_{t^*}^1);$
$\mathcal{A} \rightarrow b^*;$

Definition 1 (Aggregator Obliviousness). *Let* $\Pr[\mathcal{A}^{\mathbf{AO}}]$ *denote the probability that Aggregator $\mathcal{A}$ outputs $b^* = b$. Then an aggregation protocol is said to ensure Aggregator obliviousness if for any polynomially bounded Aggregator $\mathcal{A}$ the probability* $\Pr[\mathcal{A}^{\mathbf{AO}}] \leq \frac{1}{2} + \epsilon(\kappa)$, *where ϵ is a negligible function and κ is the security parameter.*

Aggregate Unforgeability. We augment the security requirements of data aggregation with the requirement of *aggregate unforgeability*. More precisely, we assume that Aggregator $\mathcal{A}$ is not only interested in compromising the privacy of users participating in the data aggregation protocol, but is also interested in tampering with the sum of users' inputs. That is, Aggregator $\mathcal{A}$ may sometimes have an incentive to feed Data Analyzer $\mathcal{DA}$ erroneous sums. Along these

---

Algorithm 3. Learning phase of the aggregate unforgeability game

---

$(\mathcal{P}, \mathsf{SK}_\mathsf{A}, \mathsf{VK}) \leftarrow \mathcal{O}_{\mathsf{Setup}}(1^\kappa)$;
// $\mathcal{A}$ executes the following a polynomial number of times
// $\mathcal{A}$ is allowed to call $\mathcal{O}_{\mathsf{EncTag}}$ for all users $\mathcal{U}_i$
$(c_{i,t}, \sigma_{i,t}) \leftarrow \mathcal{O}_{\mathsf{EncTag}}(t, \mathsf{uid}_i, x_{i,t})$;

Algorithm 4. Challenge phase of the aggregate unforgeability game

---

$(t^*, \mathsf{sum}_{t^*}, \sigma_{t^*}) \leftarrow \mathcal{A}$

---

lines, we define *aggregate unforgeability* as the security feature that ensures that Aggregator $\mathcal{A}$ cannot convince Data Analyzer $\mathcal{DA}$ to accept a bogus sum, as long as users $\mathcal{U}_i$ in the system are honest (i.e. they always submit their correct input and do not collude with the Aggregator $\mathcal{A}$).

In compliance with previous work [7,10] on homomorphic signatures, we formalize *aggregate unforgeability* via a game in which Aggregator $\mathcal{A}$ accesses oracles $\mathcal{O}_{\mathsf{Setup}}$ and $\mathcal{O}_{\mathsf{EncTag}}$. Furthermore, given the property that anyone holding the public verification key VK can execute the algorithm Verify, we assume that Aggregator $\mathcal{A}$ during the unforgeability game runs the algorithm Verify by itself.

As shown in Algorithm 3, Aggregator $\mathcal{A}$ enters the *aggregate unforgeability* game by querying the oracle $\mathcal{O}_{\mathsf{Setup}}$ with a security parameter κ. Oracle $\mathcal{O}_{\mathsf{Setup}}$ accordingly returns public parameters $\mathcal{P}$, verification key VK and the secret key SK_A of Aggregator $\mathcal{A}$. Moreover, Aggregator $\mathcal{A}$ calls oracle $\mathcal{O}_{\mathsf{EncTag}}$ with tuples $(t, \mathsf{uid}_i, x_{i,t})$ in order to receive the ciphertext $c_{i,t}$ encrypting $x_{i,t}$ and the matching authenticating tag $\sigma_{i,t}$, both computed using user $\mathcal{U}_i$'s secret key SK_i. Note that for each time interval t, Aggregator $\mathcal{A}$ is allowed to query oracle $\mathcal{O}_{\mathsf{EncTag}}$ for user $\mathcal{U}_i$ only once. In other words, Aggregator $\mathcal{A}$ cannot submit two distinct queries to oracle $\mathcal{O}_{\mathsf{EncTag}}$ with the same time interval t and the same user identifier uid_i. Without loss of generality, we suppose that for each time interval t, Aggregator $\mathcal{A}$ invokes oracle $\mathcal{O}_{\mathsf{EncTag}}$ for all users $\mathcal{U}_i$ in the system.

At the end of the *aggregate unforgeability* game (see Algorithm 4), Aggregator $\mathcal{A}$ outputs a tuple $(t^*, \mathsf{sum}_{t^*}, \sigma_{t^*})$. We say that Aggregator $\mathcal{A}$ wins the *aggregate unforgeability* game if one of the following statements holds:

1. $\mathsf{Verify}(\mathsf{VK}, t^*, \mathsf{sum}_{t^*}, \sigma_{t^*}) \to 1$ and Aggregator $\mathcal{A}$ never made a query to oracle $\mathcal{O}_{\mathsf{EncTag}}$ that comprises time interval t^*. In the remainder of this paper, we denote this type of forgery **Type I Forgery**.
2. $\mathsf{Verify}(\mathsf{VK}, t^*, \mathsf{sum}_{t^*}, \sigma_{t^*}) \to 1$ and Aggregator $\mathcal{A}$ has made a query to oracle $\mathcal{O}_{\mathsf{EncTag}}$ for time t^*, however the sum $\mathsf{sum}_{t^*} \neq \sum_{\mathcal{U}_i} x_{i,t^*}$. In what follows, we call this type of forgery **Type II Forgery**.

Definition 2 (Aggregate Unforgeability). *Let* $\Pr[\mathcal{A}^{\mathbf{AU}}]$ *denote the probability that Aggregator $\mathcal{A}$ wins the* aggregate unforgeability *game, that is, the probability that Aggregator $\mathcal{A}$ outputs a* **Type I Forgery** *or* **Type II Forgery** *that will be accepted by algorithm* Verify.

An aggregation protocol is said to ensure aggregate unforgeability if for any polynomially bounded aggregator $\mathcal{A}$, $\Pr[\mathcal{A}^{\mathbf{AU}}] \leq \epsilon(\kappa)$, where ϵ is a negligible function in the security parameter κ.

3 Idea of our PUDA Protocol

- A *homomorphic encryption* algorithm that allows the Aggregator to compute the sum without divulging individual data.
- A *homomorphic tag* that allows each user to authenticate the data input $x_{i,t}$, in such a way that the Aggregator can use the collected tags to construct a proof that demonstrates to the Data Analyzer $\mathcal{DA}$ the correctness of the aggregated sum.

Concisely, a set of non-interacting users are connected to personal services and devices that produce personal data. Without any coordination, each user chooses a random tag key tk_i and sends an encoding $\overline{\mathsf{tk}}_i$ thereof to the key dealer. After collecting all encoded keys $\overline{\mathsf{tk}}_i$, the key dealer publishes the corresponding public verification key VK. This verification key is computed as a function of the encodings $\overline{\mathsf{tk}}_i$. Later, the key dealer gives to each user in the system an encryption key ek_i that will be used to compute the user's ciphertexts. Accordingly, the secret key of each user SK_i is defined as the pair of tag key tk_i and encryption key ek_i. Finally, the key dealer provides the Aggregator with secret key SK_A computed as the sum of encryption keys ek_i and goes off-line.

Now at each time interval t, each user employs its secret key SK_i to compute a ciphertext based on the encryption algorithm of Shi *et al.* [17] and a homomorphic tag on its sensitive data input. When the Aggregator collects the ciphertexts and the tags from all users, it computes the sum sum_t of users' data and a matching proof σ_t, and forwards the sum and the proof to the Data Analyzer. At the final step of the protocol, the Data Analyzer verifies with the verification key VK and proof σ_t the validity of the result sum_t.

Thanks to the homomorphic encryption algorithm of Shi *et al.* [17] and the way in which we construct our homomorphic tags, we show that our protocol ensures *Aggregator Obliviousness*. Moreover, we show that the Aggregator cannot forge bogus results. Finally, we note that the Data Analyzer $\mathcal{DA}$ does not keep any state with respect to users' transcripts be they ciphertexts or tags, but it only holds the public verification key, the sum sum_t and the proof σ_t.

4 PUDA Instantiation

Let $\mathbb{G}_1, \mathbb{G}_2, \mathbb{G}_T$ be three cyclic groups of large prime order p and g_1, g_2 be generators of $\mathbb{G}_1, \mathbb{G}_2$ accordingly. We say that e is a bilinear map, if the following properties are satisfied:

1. *bilinearity*: $e(g_1^a, g_2^b) = e(g_1, g_2)^{ab}$, for all $g_1, g_2 \in \mathbb{G}_1 \times \mathbb{G}_2$ and $a, b \in \mathbb{Z}_p$.
2. *Computability*: there exists an efficient algorithm that computes $e(g_1^a, g_2^b)$ for all $g_1, g_2 \in \mathbb{G}_1 \times \mathbb{G}_2$ and $a, b \in \mathbb{Z}_p$.

3. *Non-degeneracy*: $e(g_1, g_2) \neq 1$.

To encrypt users' data homomorphically, we employ the *discrete logarithm* based encryption scheme of Shi *et al.* [17]:

4.1 Shi-Chan-Rieffel-Chow-Song Scheme

- **Setup**(1^κ): Let $\mathbb{G}_1$ be a group of large prime order p. A trusted key dealer $\mathcal{KD}$ selects a hash function $H : \{0,1\}^* \to \mathbb{G}_1$. Furthermore, $\mathcal{KD}$ selects secret encryption keys $ek_i \in \mathbb{Z}_p$ uniformly at random. $\mathcal{KD}$ distributes to each user $\mathcal{U}_i$ the secret key ek_i and sends the corresponding decryption key $SK_A = -\sum_{i=1}^n ek_i$ to the Aggregator.
- **Encrypt**($ek_i, x_{i,t}$): Each user $\mathcal{U}_i$ encrypts the value $x_{i,t}$ using its secret encryption key ek_i and outputs the ciphertext $c_{i,t} = H(t)^{ek_i} g_1^{x_{i,t}} \in \mathbb{G}_1$.
- **Aggregate**($\{c_{i,t}\}_{i=1}^n, \{\sigma_{i,t}\}_{i=1}^n, SK_A$): Upon receiving all the ciphertexts $\{c_{i,t}\}_{i=1}^n$, the Aggregator computes: $V_t = (\prod_{i=1}^n c_{i,t})H(t)^{SK_A} = H(t)^{\sum_{i=1}^n ek_i} g_1^{\sum_{i=1}^n x_{i,t}} H(t)^{-\sum_{i=1}^n ek_i} = g_1^{\sum_{i=1}^n x_{i,t}} \in \mathbb{G}_1$. Finally $\mathcal{A}$ learns the sum $sum_t = \sum_{i=1}^n x_{i,t} \in \mathbb{Z}_p$ by computing the discrete logarithm of V_t on the base g_1. The sum computation is correct as long as $\sum_{i=1}^n x_{i,t} < p$.

The above scheme is efficient as long as the plaintext values remain in a small range so as to the discrete logarithm computation during **Aggregate** algorithm is fast.

4.2 PUDA Scheme

In what follows we describe our **PUDA** protocol:

- **Setup**(1^κ): $\mathcal{KD}$ outputs the parameters $(p, g_1, g_2, \mathbb{G}_1, \mathbb{G}_2, \mathbb{G}_T)$ for an efficient computable bilinear map $e : \mathbb{G}_1 \times \mathbb{G}_2 \to \mathbb{G}_T$, where g_1 and g_2 are two random generators for the multiplicative groups $\mathbb{G}_1$ and $\mathbb{G}_2$ respectively and p is a prime number that denotes the order of all the groups $\mathbb{G}_1, \mathbb{G}_2$ and $\mathbb{G}_T$. Moreover secret keys $a, \{tk_i\}_{i=1}^n$ are selected by $\mathcal{KD}$. $\mathcal{KD}$ publishes the verification key $VK = (vk_1, vk_2) = (g_2^{\sum_{i=1}^n tk_i}, g_2^a)$ and distributes to each user $\mathcal{U}_i \in \mathbb{U}$ the secret key $g_1^a \in \mathbb{G}_1$, the encryption key ek_i and the tag key tk_i through a secure channel. Thus the secret keys of the scheme are $SK_i = (ek_i, tk_i, g_1^a)$. After publishing the public parameters $\mathcal{P} = (H, p, g_1, g_2, \mathbb{G}_1, \mathbb{G}_2, \mathbb{G}_T)$ and the verification key VK, $\mathcal{KD}$ goes off-line and it does not further participate in any protocol phase.
- **EncTag**($t, SK_i = (ek_i, tk_i, g_1^a), x_{i,t}$): At each time interval t each user $\mathcal{U}_i$ encrypts the data value $x_{i,t}$ with its secret encryption key ek_i, using the encryption algorithm, described in Sect. 4.1, which results in a ciphertext

$$c_{i,t} = H(t)^{ek_i} g_1^{x_{i,t}} \in \mathbb{G}_1$$

$\mathcal{U}_i$ also constructs a tag $\sigma_{i,t}$ with its secret tag key (tk_i, g_1^a):

$$\sigma_{i,t} = H(t)^{tk_i} (g_1^a)^{x_{i,t}} \in \mathbb{G}_1$$

Finally $\mathcal{U}_i$ sends $(c_{i,t}, \sigma_{i,t})$ to $\mathcal{A}$.

- **Aggregate**($\mathsf{SK_A}, \{c_{i,t}\}_{\mathcal{U}_i \in \mathbb{U}}, \{\sigma_{i,t}\}_{\mathcal{U}_i \in \mathbb{U}}$): Aggregator $\mathcal{A}$ computes the sum $\mathsf{sum}_t = \sum_{i=1}^{n} x_{i,t}$ by using the **Aggregate** algorithm presented in Sect. 4.1. Moreover, $\mathcal{A}$ aggregates the corresponding tags as follows:

$$\sigma_t = \prod_{i=1}^{n} \sigma_{i,t} = \prod_{i=1}^{n} H(t)^{\mathsf{tk}_i} (g_1^a)^{x_{i,t}} = H(t)^{\sum \mathsf{tk}_i} (g_1^a)^{\sum x_{i,t}}$$

$\mathcal{A}$ finally forwards sum_t and σ_t to data analyzer $\mathcal{DA}$.

- **Verify**($\mathsf{VK}, t, \mathsf{sum}_t, \sigma_t$): During the verification phase $\mathcal{DA}$ verifies the correctness of the computation with the verification key $\mathsf{VK} = (\mathsf{vk}_1, \mathsf{vk}_2) = (g_2^{\sum \mathsf{tk}_i}, g_2^a)$, by checking the following equality:

$$e(\sigma_t, g_2) \stackrel{?}{=} e(H(t), \mathsf{vk}_1) e(g_1^{\mathsf{sum}_t}, \mathsf{vk}_2)$$

Verification correctness follows from bilinear pairing properties:

$$
\begin{aligned}
e(\sigma_t, g_2) &= e(\prod_{i=1}^{n} \sigma_{i,t}, g_2) = e(\prod_{i=1}^{n} H(t)^{\mathsf{tk}_i} g_1^{a x_{i,t}}, g_2) \\
&= e(H(t)^{\sum_{i=1}^{n} \mathsf{tk}_i} g_1^{a \sum_{i=1}^{n} x_{i,t}}, g_2) \\
&= e(H(t)^{\sum_{i=1}^{n} \mathsf{tk}_i}, g_2) e(g_1^{a \sum_{i=1}^{n} x_{i,t}}, g_2) \\
&= e(H(t), g_2^{\sum_{i=1}^{n} \mathsf{tk}_i}) e(g_1^{\sum_{i=1}^{n} x_{i,t}}, g_2^a) \\
&= e(H(t), g_2^{\sum_{i=1}^{n} \mathsf{tk}_i}) e(g_1^{\mathsf{sum}_t}, g_2^a) \\
&= e(H(t), \mathsf{vk}_1) e(g_1^{\mathsf{sum}_t}, \mathsf{vk}_2)
\end{aligned}
$$

5 Analysis

5.1 Aggregator Obliviousness

Theorem 1. *The proposed solution achieves Aggregator Obliviousness in the random oracle model under the decisional Diffie-Hellman (DDH) assumption in $\mathbb{G}_1$.*

Due to space limitations the proof of Theorem 1 can be found in the full version [14].

5.2 Aggregate Unforgeability

We first introduce a new assumption that is used during the security analysis of our **PUDA** instantiation. Our new assumption named hereafter LEOM is a variant of the LRSW assumption [16] which is proven secure in the generic model [18] and used in the construction of the CL signatures [5].

The oracle $\mathcal{O}_{\mathsf{LEOM}}$ first chooses a and k_i, $1 \leq i \leq n$ in $\mathbb{Z}_p^*$. Then it publishes the tuple $(g_1, g_2^{\sum_{i=1}^{n} k_i}, g_2^a)$. Thereafter, the adversary picks $h_t \in \mathbb{G}_1$ and makes queries $(h_t, i, x_{i,t})$ for $1 \leq i \leq n$ to the $\mathcal{O}_{\mathsf{LEOM}}$ oracle which in turn replies with $h_t^{k_i} g_1^{ax_{i,t}}$ for $1 \leq i \leq n$.

The adversary is allowed to query the oracle $\mathcal{O}_{\mathsf{LEOM}}$ for different h_t with the restriction that it cannot issue two queries for the same pair (h_t, i).

We say that the adversary breaks the LEOM assumption, if it outputs a tuple $(z, h_t, h_t^{\sum_{i=1}^n k_i} g_1^{az})$ for a previously queried t and $z \neq \sum_{i=1}^n x_{i,t}$.

Theorem 2. *(LEOM Assumption) Given the security parameter κ, the public parameters $(p, e, \mathbb{G}_1, \mathbb{G}_2, g_1, g_2)$, the public key $(g_2^a, g_2^{\sum_{i=1}^n k_i})$ and the oracle $\mathcal{O}_{\mathsf{LEOM}}$, we say that the LEOM assumption holds iff:*

For all probabilistic polynomial time adversaries $\mathcal{A}$, the following holds:

$$\Pr[(z, h_t, \sigma_t) \leftarrow \mathcal{A}^{\mathcal{O}_{\mathsf{LEOM}}(.)} : z \neq \sum_{i=1}^n x_{i,t} \wedge \sigma_t = h_t^{\sum_{i=1}^n k_i} g_1^{az}] \leq \epsilon_2(\kappa)$$

Where ϵ_2 is a negligible function.

We show in our analysis that a **Type I Forgery** implies breaking the BCDH assumption and that a **Type II Forgery** implies breaking the LEOM assumption.

Theorem 3. *Our scheme achieves aggregate unforgeability against a* **Type I Forgery** *under* BCDH *assumption in the random oracle model.*

Theorem 4. *Our scheme guarantees aggregate unforgeability against a* **Type II Forgery** *under the* LEOM *assumption in the random oracle model.*

Due to space limitations, the security evidence of the LEOM assumption and proofs for Theorems 3 and 4 are deferred to Appendix A and B.

5.3   Performance Evaluation

In this section we analyze the extra overhead of ensuring the *aggregate unforgeability* property in our **PUDA** instantiation scheme. First, we consider a theoretical evaluation with respect to the mathematical operations a participant of the protocol be it user, Aggregator or Data Analyzer has to perform to ensure public verifiablity. That is, the computation of the tag by each user, the proof by the Aggregator and the verification of the proof by the Data Analyzer. We also present an experimental evaluation that shows the practicality of our scheme.

To allow the Data analyzer to verify the correctness of computations performed by an untrusted Aggregator, the key dealer distributes to each user $g_1^a, \mathsf{tk}_i \in \mathbb{G}_1$ and publishes $g_2^a, g_2^{\sum_{i=1}^n \mathsf{tk}_i} \in \mathbb{G}_2$, which calls for one exponentiation in $\mathbb{G}_1$ and $1 + n$ in $\mathbb{G}_2$. At each time interval t each user computes $\sigma_{i,t} = H(t)^{\mathsf{tk}_i}(g_1^a)^{x_{i,t}} \in \mathbb{G}_1$, which entails two exponentiations and one multiplication in $\mathbb{G}_1$. To compute the proof σ_t, the Aggregator carries out $n - 1$ multiplications in $\mathbb{G}_1$. Finally the data analyzer verifies the validity of the aggregate sum by checking the equality: $e(\sigma_t, g_2) \stackrel{?}{=} e(H(t), \mathsf{vk}_1)e(g_1^{\mathsf{sum}_t}, \mathsf{vk}_2)$, which

Table 1. Performance of tag computation, proof construction and verification operations. l denotes the bit-size of the prime number p.

Participant	Computation	Communication
User	$2\text{EXP} + 1\text{MUL}$	$2 \cdot l$
Aggregator	$(n-1)\text{MUL}$	$2 \cdot l$
Data analyzer	$3\text{PAIR} + 1\text{EXP} + 1\text{MUL} + 1H\!ASH$	-

asks for three pairing evaluations, one hash in $\mathbb{G}_1$, one exponentiation in $\mathbb{G}_1$ and one multiplication in $\mathbb{G}_T$ (see Table 1). The efficiency of **PUDA** stems from the constant time verification with respect to the number of the users. This is of crucial importance since the Data Analyzer may not be computationally powerful.

We implemented the verification functionalities of **PUDA** with the Charm cryptographic framework [1,2]. For pairing computations, it inherits the PBC [15] library which is also written in C. All of our benchmarks are executed on Intel® $\text{Core}^T M$ i5 CPU M 560 @ 2.67GHz × 4 with 8GB of memory, running Ubuntu 12.04 32bit. Charm uses 3 types of asymmetric pairings: MNT159, MNT201, MNT224. We run our benchmarks with these three different types of asymmetric pairings. The timings for all the underlying mathematical group operations are summarized in Table 3. There is a vast difference on the computation time of operations between $\mathbb{G}_1$ and $\mathbb{G}_2$ for all the different curves. The reason is the fact that the bit-length of elements in $\mathbb{G}_2$ is much larger than in $\mathbb{G}_1$.

As shown in Table 2, the computation of tags $\sigma_{i,t}$ implies a computation overhead at a scale of milliseconds with a gradual increase as the bit size of the underlying elliptic curve increases. The data analyzer is involved in pairing evaluations and computations at the target group independent of the size of the data-users.

6 Related Work

In [12] the authors presented a solution for verifiable aggregation in case of untrustworthy users. The solutions entails signatures on commitments of the

Table 2. Computational cost of **PUDA** operations with respect to different pairings.

Operation \ Pairings	MNT159	MNT201	MNT224
Tag	1.2 ms	1.8 ms	2.2 ms
Verify	28.3 ms	42.7 ms	53.5 ms

Table 3. Average computation overhead of the underlying mathematical group operations for different type of curves.

Op. \ Curve	MNT159	MNT201	MNT224
HASH in $\mathbb{G}_1$	0.139 ms	0.346 ms	0.296 ms
HASH in $\mathbb{G}_2$	25.667 ms	41.628 ms	48.305 ms
MUL in $\mathbb{G}_1$	0.004 ms	0.0006 ms	0.006 ms
MUL in $\mathbb{G}_2$	0.040 ms	0.051 ms	0.054 ms
MUL in $\mathbb{G}_T$	0.012 ms	0.015 ms	0.016 ms
EXP in $\mathbb{G}_1$	0.072 ms	0.092 ms	0.099 ms
EXP in $\mathbb{G}_2$	0.615 ms	0.757 ms	0.784 ms
PAIR	7.077 ms	10.674 ms	13.105 ms

secret values with non-interactive zero knowledge proofs, which are verified by the Aggregator. Hung-Min *et al.* [19] employed aggregate signatures in order to verify the integrity of the data, without addressing confidentiality issues for a malicious Aggregator. In [6], authors proposed a solution which is based on homomorphic message authenticators in order to verify the computation of generic functions on outsourced data. Each data input is authenticated with an authentication tag. A composition of the tags is computed by the cloud in order to verify the correctness of the output of a program P. Thanks to the homomorphic properties of the tags the user can verify the correctness of the program. The main drawback of the solution is that the user in order to verify the correctness of the computation has to be involved in computations that take exactly the same time as the computation of the function f. Backes *et al.* [3] proposed a generic solution for efficient verification of bounded degree polynomials in time less than the evaluation of f. The solution is based on *closed form efficient* pseudorandom function PRF. Contrary to our solution both solutions do not provide individual privacy and they are not designed for a multi-user scenario.

Catalano *et al.* [8] employed a nifty technique to allow single users to verify computations on encrypted data. The idea is to re-randomize the ciphertext and sign it with a homomorphic signature. Computations then are performed on the randomized ciphertext and the original one. However the aggregate value is not allowed to be learnt in cleartext by the untrusted Aggregator since the protocols are geared for cloud based scenarios.

In the multi-user setting, Choi *et al.* [9] proposed a protocol in which multiple users are outsourcing their inputs to an untrusted server along with the definition of a functionality f. The server computes the result in a privacy preserving manner without learning the result and the computation is verified by a user that has contributed to the function input. The users are forced to operate in a *non-interactive* model, whereby they cannot communicate with each other. The underlying machinery entails a novel proxy based oblivious transfer protocol, which along with a fully homomorphic scheme and garbled circuits allows for verifiability and privacy. However, the need of fully homomorphic encryption and garbled circuits renders the solution impractical for a real world scenario.

7   Concluding Remarks

In this paper, we designed and analyzed a protocol for privacy preserving and unforgeable data aggregation. The purpose of the protocol is to allow a data analyzer to verify the correctness of computation performed by a malicious Aggregator, without revealing the underlying data to either the Aggregator or the data analyzer. In addition to being provably secure and privacy preserving, the proposed protocol enables *public verifiability* in *constant time*.

Acknowledgments. We thank the anonymous reviewers for their suggestions for improving this paper. The research leading to these results was partially funded by the FP7-USERCENTRICNETWORKING european ICT project under the grant number 611001.

A   Security Evidence for the **LEOM** Assumption

In this section we provide security evidence for the hardness of the new LEOM assumption by presenting bounds on the success probabilities of an adversary $\mathcal{A}$ which presumably breaks the assumption. We follow the theoretical *generic group model* (GGM) as presented in [18]. Namely under the GGM framework an adversary $\mathcal{A}$ has access to a black box that conceptualizes the underlying mathematical group $\mathbb{G}$ that the assumption takes place. $\mathcal{A}$ without knowing any details about the underlying group apart from its order p is asking for encodings of its choice and the black box replies through a random encoding function ξ_c that maps elements in $\mathbb{G}_c \rightarrow \{0,1\}^{\lceil \log_2 p \rceil}$ to represent element in $\mathbb{G}_c, c \in [1, 2, T]$.

Theorem 5. *Suppose $\mathcal{A}$ is a polynomial probabilistic time adversary that breaks the* LEOM *assumption, making at most q_G oracle queries for the underlying group operations on $\mathbb{G}_1, \mathbb{G}_2, \mathbb{G}_T$ and the $\mathcal{O}_{\mathsf{LEOM}}$ oracle, all counted together. Then the probability ϵ_2 that $\mathcal{A}$ breaks the* LEOM *assumption is bounded as follows:*

$$\epsilon_2 \leq \frac{(q_G)^2}{p}.$$

Due to space limitations we include the proof in the full version [14].

B   Aggregate Unforgeability

Theorem 3. *Our scheme achieves* Aggregate Unforgeability *for a* **Type I Forgery** *under* BCDH *assumption in the random oracle model.*

Proof. We show how to build an adversary $\mathcal{B}$ that solves BCDH in $(\mathbb{G}_1, \mathbb{G}_2, \mathbb{G}_T)$. Let g_1 and g_2 be two generators for $\mathbb{G}_1$ and $\mathbb{G}_2$ respectively. $\mathcal{B}$ receives the challenge $(g_1, g_2, g_1^a, g_1^b, g_1^c, g_2^a, g_2^b)$ from the BCDH oracle $\mathcal{O}_{\mathsf{BCDH}}$ and is asked to output $e(g_1, g_2)^{abc} \in \mathbb{G}_T$. $\mathcal{B}$ simulates the interaction with $\mathcal{A}$ in the **Learning** phase as follows:

Setup:

– To simulate the $\mathcal{O}_{\mathsf{Setup}}$ oracle $\mathcal{B}$ selects uniformly at random $2n$ keys $\{\mathsf{ek}_i\}_{i=1}^n$, $\{\mathsf{tk}_i\}_{i=1}^n \in \mathbb{Z}_p$ and outputs the public parameters $\mathcal{P} = (\kappa, p, g_1, g_2, \mathbb{G}_1, \mathbb{G}_2)$ the verification key $\mathsf{VK} = (\mathsf{vk}_1, \mathsf{vk}_2) = (g_2^{b \sum_{i=1}^n \mathsf{tk}_i}, g_2^a)$ and the secret key of the Aggregator $\mathsf{SK}_A = -\sum_{i=1}^n \mathsf{ek}_i$.

Learning Phase

– $\mathcal{A}$ is allowed to query the random oracle H for any time interval . $\mathcal{B}$ constructs a $H - \mathtt{list}$ and responds to $\mathcal{A}$ query as follows:
   1. If query t already appears in a tuple H-tuple$\langle t : r_t, \mathsf{coin}(t), H(t) \rangle$ of the $H - \mathtt{list}$ it responds to $\mathcal{A}$ with $H(t)$.

2. Otherwise it selects a random number $r_t \in \mathbb{Z}_p$ and flips a random coin $\xleftarrow{\$} \{0,1\}$. With probability π, $\mathsf{coin}(t) = 0$ and $\mathcal{B}$ answers with $H(t) = g_1^{r_t}$. Otherwise if $\mathsf{coin}(t) = 1$ then $\mathcal{B}$ responds with $H(t) = g_1^{cr_t}$ and updates the $\mathtt{H-list}$ with the new tuple $H\text{-tuple}\langle t : r_t, \mathsf{coin}(t), H(t)\rangle$.

– Whenever $\mathcal{A}$ submits a query $(t, \mathsf{uid}_i, x_{i,t})$ to the $\mathcal{O}^{\mathcal{A}}_{\mathsf{EncTag}}$, $\mathcal{B}$ responds as follows:

1. $\mathcal{B}$ calls the simulated random oracle, receives the result for $H(t)$ and appends the tuple $H\text{-tuple}\langle t : r_t, \mathsf{coin}(t), H(t)\rangle$ to the $\mathtt{H-list}$.
2. If $\mathsf{coin}(t) = 1$ then $\mathcal{B}$ stops the simulation.
3. Otherwise it chooses the secret tag key tk_i where $i = \mathsf{uid}_i$ to be used as secret tag key from the set of $\{\mathsf{tk}_i\}$ keys, chosen by $\mathcal{B}$ in the **Setup** phase.
4. $\mathcal{B}$ sends to $\mathcal{A}$ the tag $\sigma_{i,t} = g_1^{r_t \mathsf{btk}_i} g_1^{a x_{i,t}} = H(t)^{\mathsf{btk}_i} g_1^{a x_{i,t}}$, which is a valid tag for the value $x_{i,t}$. Notice that $\mathcal{B}$ can correctly compute the tag without knowing a and b from the BCDH problem parameters g_1^a, g_1^b.
5. $\mathcal{B}$ chooses also a secret encryption key $\mathsf{ek}_i \in \{\mathsf{ek}_i\}_{i=1}^n \in \mathbb{Z}_p$ and computes the ciphertext as $c_{i,t} = H(t)^{\mathsf{ek}_i} g_1^{x_{i,t}}$. The simulation is correct since $\mathcal{A}$ can check that the sum $\sum_{i=1}^n x_{i,t}$ corresponds to the ciphertexts given by $\mathcal{B}$ with its decryption key $\mathsf{SK}_A = -\sum_{i=1}^n \mathsf{ek}_i$, considering the adversary has made distinct encryption queries for all the n users in the scheme at a time interval t.

Now, when $\mathcal{B}$ receives the forgery $(\mathsf{sum}_t{}^*, \sigma_t{}^*)$ at time interval $t \neq t^*$, it continues if $\mathsf{sum}_t{}^* \neq \Sigma_t$. $\mathcal{B}$ first queries the H-tuple for time t^* in order to fetch the appropriate tuple.

– If $\mathsf{coin}(t^*) = 0$ then $\mathcal{B}$ aborts.
– If $\mathsf{coin}(t^*) = 1$ then since $\mathcal{A}$ outputs a valid forged $\sigma_t{}^*$ at t^*, it is true that the following equation should hold:

$$e(\sigma_t{}^*, g_2) = e(H(t^*), \mathsf{vk}_1) e(g_1^{\mathsf{sum}_t{}^*}, \mathsf{vk}_2)$$

which is true when $\mathcal{A}$ makes n queries for time interval t^* for distinct users to the $\mathcal{O}^{\mathcal{A}}_{\mathsf{EncTag}}$ oracle during the **Learning** phase. As such $\sigma_t{}^* = g_1^{cr_t b \sum \mathsf{tk}_i} g_1^{a \mathsf{sum}_t{}^*}$. Finally $\mathcal{B}$ outputs:

$$e\left(\left(\frac{\sigma_t{}^*}{g_1^{a\mathsf{sum}_t{}^*}}\right)^{\frac{1}{r_t \sum \mathsf{tk}_i}}, g_2^a\right) = e\left(\left(\frac{g_1^{cr_t b \sum \mathsf{tk}_i} g_1^{a\mathsf{sum}_t{}^*}}{g_1^{a\mathsf{sum}_t{}^*}}\right)^{\frac{1}{r_t \sum \mathsf{tk}_i}}, g_2^a\right) =$$

$$e\left((g_1^{cr_t b \sum \mathsf{tk}_i})^{\frac{1}{r_t \sum \mathsf{tk}_i}}, g_2^a\right) = e(g_1^{bc}, g_2^a) = e(g_1, g_2)^{abc}$$

Let $\mathcal{A}^{\mathbf{AU1}}$ be the event when $\mathcal{A}$ successfully forges a **Type I forgery** σ_t for our **PUDA** protocol that happens with some non-negligible probability ϵ'. event_0 is the event when $\mathsf{coin} = 0$ in the learning phase and event_1 is the event when $\mathsf{coin} = 1$ in the challenge phase. Then $\Pr[\mathcal{B}^{\mathsf{BCDH}}] = \Pr[\mathsf{event}_0]\Pr[\mathsf{event}_1]\Pr[\mathcal{A}^{\mathbf{AU2}}] = \pi(1 - \pi)^{q_H - 1}\epsilon'$, for q_H random oracle queries with the probability $\Pr[\mathsf{coin}(t) = 0] = \pi$. As such we ended up in a contradiction assuming the hardness of the BCDH assumption and finally $\Pr[\mathcal{A}^{\mathbf{AU1}}] \leq \epsilon_1$, where ϵ_1 is a negligible function.

Theorem 4. *Our scheme guarantees aggregate unforgeability against a* **Type II Forgery** *under the* LEOM *assumption.*

Proof (Sketch). Here we show how an adversary $\mathcal{B}$ breaks the LEOM assumption by using an Aggregator $\mathcal{A}$ that provides a **Type II Forgery** with a non-negligible probability. Notably, adversary $\mathcal{B}$ simulates oracle $\mathcal{O}_{\mathsf{Setup}}$ as follows: It first picks secret encryptions keys $\{\mathsf{ek}_i\}_{i=1}^n$ and sets the corresponding decryption key $\mathsf{SK}_A = -\sum_{i=1}^n \mathsf{ek}_i$. Then, it forwards to $\mathcal{A}$ the public parameters $\mathcal{P} = (p, g_1, g_2, \mathbb{G}_1, \mathbb{G}_2)$, the public key $(\mathsf{vk}_1, \mathsf{vk}_2) = (g_2^{\sum_{i=1}^n k_i}, g_2^a)$ of the $\mathcal{O}_{\mathsf{LEOM}}$ oracle and the secret key $\mathsf{SK}_A = -\sum_{i=1}^n \mathsf{ek}_i$.

Afterwards, when adversary $\mathcal{B}$ receives a query $(t, \mathsf{uid}_i, x_{i,t})$ for oracle $\mathcal{O}_{\mathsf{EncTag}}$, adversary $\mathcal{B}$ calls oracle $\mathcal{O}_{\mathsf{LEOM}}$ with the pair $(h_t = H(t), i, x_{i,t})$. Oracle $\mathcal{O}_{\mathsf{LEOM}}$ accordingly returns $h_t^{k_i} g_1^{a x_{i,t}}$ and adversary $\mathcal{B}$ outputs $\sigma_{i,t} = h_t^{k_i} g_1^{a x_{i,t}}$. Note that if we define the tag key tk_i of user $\mathcal{U}_i$ as k_i, then the tag $\sigma_{i,t} = h_t^{k_i} g_1^{a x_{i,t}}$ is computed correctly.

Eventually with a non-negligible advantage, Aggregator $\mathcal{A}$ outputs a **Type II Forgery** $(t^*, \mathsf{sum}_{t^*}, \sigma_{t^*})$ that verifies:

$$e(\sigma_{t^*}, g_2) = e(H(t^*), \mathsf{vk}_1) e(g_1^{\mathsf{sum}_{t^*}}, \mathsf{vk}_2)$$

where t^* is previously queried by Aggregator $\mathcal{A}$ and $\mathsf{sum}_{t^*} \neq \sum_{i=1}^n x_{(i,t^*)}$.

It follows that $\mathcal{B}$ breaks the LEOM assumption with a non-negligible probability by outputting the tuple $(H(t^*), \mathsf{sum}_{t^*}, \sigma_{t^*})$. This leads to a contradiction under the LEOM assumption. We conclude that our scheme guarantees *aggregate unforgeability* for a **Type II Forgery** under the LEOM assumption.

References

1. Akinyele, J.A., Green, M., Rubin, A.D.: Charm: a tool for rapid cryptographic prototyping. http://www.charm-crypto.com/Main.html
2. Akinyele, J.A., Green, M., Rubin, A.D.: Charm: a framework for rapidly prototyping cryptosystems. IACR Cryptology ePrint Archive, 2011:617 (2011). http://eprint.iacr.org/2011/617.pdf
3. Backes, M., Fiore, D., Reischuk, R.M.: Verifiable delegation of computation on outsourced data. In: ACM Conference on Computer and Communications Security, pp. 863–874 (2013)
4. Boneh, D., Gentry, C., Lynn, B., Shacham, H.: Aggregate and verifiably encrypted signatures from bilinear maps. In: EUROCRYPT, pp. 416–432 (2003)
5. Camenisch, J.L., Lysyanskaya, A.: Signature schemes and anonymous credentials from bilinear maps. In: Franklin, M. (ed.) CRYPTO 2004. LNCS, vol. 3152, pp. 56–72. Springer, Heidelberg (2004)
6. Catalano, D., Fiore, D.: Practical homomorphic MACs for arithmetic circuits. In: Johansson, T., Nguyen, P.Q. (eds.) EUROCRYPT 2013. LNCS, vol. 7881, pp. 336–352. Springer, Heidelberg (2013)
7. Catalano, D., Fiore, D., Warinschi, B.: Homomorphic signatures with efficient verification for polynomial functions. In: Garay, J.A., Gennaro, R. (eds.) CRYPTO 2014, Part I. LNCS, vol. 8616, pp. 371–389. Springer, Heidelberg (2014)

8. Catalano, D., Marcedone, A., Puglisi, O.: Authenticating Computation on Groups: New Homomorphic Primitives and Applications. In: Sarkar, P., Iwata, T. (eds.) ASIACRYPT 2014, Part II. LNCS, vol. 8874, pp. 193–212. Springer, Heidelberg (2014)

9. Choi, S.G., Katz, J., Kumaresan, R., Cid, C.: Multi-client non-interactive verifiable computation. In: Sahai, A. (ed.) TCC 2013. LNCS, vol. 7785, pp. 499–518. Springer, Heidelberg (2013)

10. Freeman, D.M.: Improved security for linearly homomorphic signatures: a generic framework. In: Fischlin, M., Buchmann, J., Manulis, M. (eds.) PKC 2012. LNCS, vol. 7293, pp. 697–714. Springer, Heidelberg (2012)

11. Joye, M., Libert, B.: A scalable scheme for privacy-preserving aggregation of time-series data. In: Sadeghi, A.-R. (ed.) FC 2013. LNCS, vol. 7859, pp. 111–125. Springer, Heidelberg (2013)

12. Kursawe, K., Danezis, G., Kohlweiss, M.: Privacy-friendly aggregation for the smart-grid. In: Fischer-Hübner, S., Hopper, N. (eds.) PETS 2011. LNCS, vol. 6794, pp. 175–191. Springer, Heidelberg (2011)

13. Leontiadis, I., Elkhiyaoui, K., Molva, R.: Private and dynamic time-series data aggregation with trust relaxation. In: Gritzalis, D., Kiayias, A., Askoxylakis, I. (eds.) CANS 2014. LNCS, vol. 8813, pp. 305–320. Springer, Heidelberg (2014)

14. Leontiadis, I., Elkhyaoui, K., Önen, M., Molva, R.: Private and unforgeable data aggregation. IACR Cryptology ePrint Archive (2015). http://eprint.iacr.org/2015/562.pdf

15. Lynn, B.: The stanford pairing based crypto library. http://crypto.stanford.edu/pbc

16. Lysyanskaya, A., Rivest, R., Sahai, A., Wolf, S.: Pseudonym systems. In: Heys, H., Adams, C. (eds.) Selected Areas in Cryptography. LNCS, vol. 1758, pp. 184–199. Springer, Berlin Heidelberg (2000)

17. Shi, E., Chan, T.-H.H., Rieffel, E.G., Chow, R., Song, D.: Privacy-preserving aggregation of time-series data. In: NDSS (2011)

18. Shoup, V.: Lower bounds for discrete logarithms and related problems. In: Fumy, W. (ed.) EUROCRYPT 1997. LNCS, vol. 1233, pp. 256–266. Springer, Heidelberg (1997)

19. Sun, H.-M., Lin, Y.-H., Hsiao, Y.-C., Chen, C.-M.: An efficient and verifiable concealed data aggregation scheme in wireless sensor networks. In: International Conference on Embedded Software and Systems, ICESS 2008, pp. 19–26, July 2008

A Security Framework for Internet of Things

Imane Bouij-Pasquier[1]([✉]), Anas Abou El Kalam[1], Abdellah Ait Ouahman[1],
and Mina De Montfort[2]

[1] UCA - ENSA, Marrakesh, MOROCOO
imane.pasquier@gmail.com
[2] Société ARTIMIA, Reims, France

Abstract. As we move towards the Internet of Things (IoT), the number of sensors deployed around the world is growing at a rapid pace. There is a huge scope for more streamlined living through an increase of smart services but this coincides with an increase in security and privacy concerns, therefore access control has been an important factor in the development of IoT.

This work proposes an authorization access model called SmartOr-BAC built around a set of security and performance requirements. This model enhances the existing OrBAC (Organization-based Access Control) model and adapts it to IoT environments. SmartOrBAC separates the problem into different functional layers and then distributes processing costs between constrained devices and less constrained ones and at the same time addresses the collaborative aspect with a specific solution. We also apply SmartOrBAC to a real example of IoT and demonstrate that even though our model is extensive, it does not add additional complexity regarding traditional access control model.

1 Introduction

Today we are seeing a shift in our conception of Internet towards a global network of "smart objects", which we can call the Internet of Things (IoT). This shift is expected to accelerate during the coming years [1,2] due to a fall in hardware costs, internet's technological maturity and the swift development of communication technology. This will lead to a smooth assimilation of these smart objects into the Internet, which will in turn enable mobile and widespread access. Areas that are expected to be directly affected include healthcare [3,4], supply chain management [5], transport systems [6], agriculture and environmental monitoring [7,8], life at home and more, as we move towards "smart homes" [9–11] and the next generation of "smarter cities" [12].

This extension and proliferation of technology will certainly change our live, but will also present security and privacy challenges [13–15], since unexpected information leaks and illegitimate access to data and physical systems could have a high impact on our lives. Moreover, malicious modifications or denial of service may also cause damage in the context of IoT. This is why the implementation of an access control mechanism that respects both the character of and the

© Springer International Publishing Switzerland 2015
M. Reiter and D. Naccache (Eds.): CANS 2015, LNCS 9476, pp. 19–31, 2015.
DOI: 10.1007/978-3-319-26823-1_2

constraints on, smart objects in the IoT environment, is imperative. In this paper we address one of the most relevant security issues – authorization and access control – in the context of distributed, cross-domain systems that consist of resource constrained devices not directly operated by humans. In particular, we focus on the problem where a single constrained device is communicating with several other devices from different organizations or domains. Based on OrBAC [16] access control model, our "Smart OrBAC" proposal is specifically designed for IoT environments. It in fact takes the main features of IoT into account and facilitates a distributed-centralized approach where authorization decisions are based on local conditions, and in this way offers context-aware access control.

The reminder of the paper is organized as follows. Section 2 gives an overview of the literature and discusses the important access control models currently existing in the IoT environment. Afterwards Sect. 3 presents the background needed to understand our new work. The SmartOrBAC access control model is then detailed in Sect. 4 followed in Sect. 5 by a brief description of the implementation. Finally, in Sect. 6, we conclude the paper and present our perspectives.

The main contributions of this work can be outlined as follows:

– Abstraction layers design regarding the specificities of IoT devices.
– SmartOrBAC, our access control model for IoT.
– Collaborative protocol managing in IoT.
– Applying SmartOrBAC to an IoT case study and showing that it does not present additional complexity.

2   Related Work

Zhang and Gong proposed in [17] the UCON model taking into consideration flexibility and heterogeneity in an IoT distributed environment. However, UCON is a conceptual model only, and thus it does not give details on the implementation of the monitoring process. This approach is still not practical.

The CAPBAC model is implemented in a centralized approach in [18] where the proposed framework is based on a central Policy Decision Point (PDP) which handles authorization decisions. Whereas the implementation of capability-based access control in IoT is considered in [19] with an entirely distributed approach without intervention of central entities. The limits of both a purely centralized approach and fully distributed approach will be detailed later on in this paper (see 3.2 Main architectures for IoT access control).

The Capability-based Context-Aware Access Control (CCAAC) [20] is a delegation model based on a federated vision of IoT [21], where a central entity in each domain is in charge of authorizing a delegation request from a delegator, and making the decision about granting it to the delegate. However, this vision does not make use of technologies specifically designed for constrained highly context dependent environments such as IoT. Furthermore, the technical requirements in the constrained environment of the different actors involved in the proposed delegation mechanism are missing from this study.

Seitz et al. present in [22] an authorization framework based on XACML [23]. Evaluating XACML policies is too heavy-weight for constrained devices; therefore most of the authorization process is externalized. In order to convey the authorization decision from the external point to the device, an assertion is encoded in JSON [24] and is sent to the end-device (i.e., sensor or constrained device). The end-device takes responsibility for local conditions verification. However, this study does not give information about the central component involved neither about its management within the organization. Also, this proposal is bound to the use of XACML, which is not specifically designed for use in constrained devices.

3 Background

In this section we provide a brief description of some of the core concepts that make up our scheme. First of all, we give in this section an overview of the OrBAC access control model and its benefits over other commonly accepted models. We then propose an overview of the main approaches and trends to provide access control process in IoT scenarios based on the architecture taxonomy proposed in [25].

3.1 Organization-Based Access Control Model (OrBAC)

The Organization-Based Access control model (OrBAC) introduces the concept of organization as a structured group of active entities, in which subjects play specific roles. An activity is a group of one or more actions, a view is a group of one or more objects and a context is a specific situation.

Actually, the Role entity is used to structure the link between the Subjects and the Organizations. The Empower (org, r, s) relationship (or predicate) means that org employs subject s in role r. In the same way, the objects that satisfy a common property are specified through views, and activities are used to abstract actions.

In security rules, permissions are expressed as Permission (org, r, v, a, c), obligations and prohibitions are defined similarly. Such an expression is interpreted as: in the context c, organization org grants role r the permission to perform activity a on a view v.

As rules are expressed only through abstract entities, OrBAC is able to specify the security policies of several collaborating and heterogeneous organizations. Moreover, OrBAC takes the context (e.g., specific situations, time and location constraints) into account. However, despite the several advantages of OrBAC, it is not completely adapted to IoT. In particular, OrBAC is not able to manage collaboration-related aspects. In fact, as OrBAC security rules have the Permission (org, r, v, a, c) form, it is not possible to represent rules that involve several independent organizations. Furthermore, it is impossible to associate permissions to entities belonging to other partner-organizations (or to sub-organizations). As a result, if we can assume that OrBAC provides a framework for expressing the security policies of several organizations, it is unfortunately only adapted to centralized structures and does not cover the distribution, collaboration and interoperability needs when it comes to cross-domain services as it is the case in IoT scenarios.

In order to overcome the limitations listed above, we suggest, on one hand, to extend OrBAC to include collaboration-related and context aware concepts, and on the other hand, we construct an IoT adapted framework with a new architecture articulated around four functional layers. The resulting framework is called "SmartOrBAC".

3.2   Main Architectures for IoT Access Control

This section gives an overview of the most commonly used approaches to provide access control in IoT scenarios highlighting their main advantages and drawbacks:

- **Centralized Architecture:** The access control process is externalized into a central entity responsible for the authorization processing and thus, the end-devices (i.e., sensors, actuators) play a limited role and the access control process is located within a non-constrained entity. It follows that the use of standard security protocols normally used in the traditional Web is not restricted. Nonetheless, in IoT scenarios, contextual information is of great importance, while in a centralized architecture, access control decisions are not based on such local information related to the end-device.
- **Distributed Approach:** The access control process is located in the end-devices. An advantage of this approach is that end-devices act smartly, and are autonomous. Moreover it allows real time contextual information to become central to the authorization decision. However, this approach means that each device must be capable of handling authorization processes and having adequate resources which makes it inappropriate for resource-constrained devices.
- **Centralized-distributed Approach:** The end-devices participate partially in the access control decisions. This approach is motivated by the importance of taking into account the context of the end-device while making the decision. It allows the use of standard technologies to perform the authorization process. Nevertheless the transmission of the contextual information to a central entity may cause delays and the value acquired by the end-device will not be the same at the time of making the authorization decision.

In our proposal, we choose to design our access control based on the centralized-distributed approach. But unlike other proposals that use this approach, each separate group of components will have a central authorization engine (rather than just having one of these engines centrally performing all the authorization processes). The selection process that determines which entity will act as this engine depends on the contextual properties of the nodes in its group. The aim of this is to make the access control mechanism more time efficient by facilitating a smoother exchange of information between the end device and the authorization engine (see Fig. 1). This vision is made possible by the fact that in a constrained environment, not all the devices are at the same level of constraint [27–31]. In almost every WSN, less constrained nodes exist, and thus the central authorization server in charge of an area can be implemented on one of them. For more understanding, the next section gives an overview of the different actors involved in the proposed architecture and their properties.

4   SmartOrBAC

This section provides a detailed description of the key aspects of our proposal. We begin with an explanation of the most relevant features of our abstraction layers design followed by an overview of the main aspects of our collaborative solution. Then we present our version of the distributed-centralized architecture and give a structured expression of the *context* concept. Finally we apply our proposal on a typical IoT healthcare scenario.

Before going into details, we first identify the following actors [26]:

- **Resource Server (*RS*):** an entity which hosts and represents a Resource that might contain sensor or actuator values or other information;
- **Resource Owner (*RO*):** the principal that owns the resource and controls its access permissions;
- **Client (*C*):** an entity which attempts to access a resource on a Resource Server;
- **Client Owner (*CO*):** the principal that owns the Client and controls permissions concerning authorized representations of a Resource.

Consequently, in a basic scenario, *C* wants to access *R* located on *RS*. It follows logically that, *C* and / or *RS* are constrained.

4.1   SmartOrBAC Abstraction Layers

The SmartOrBAC architecture proposes, among others, a model based on a partitioning of the access control process into functional layers depending on the capabilities offered on each one. This approach is directly inspired by the fact that each device is constrained to a different level; they are in fact not all uniformly constrained. Note that the term "constrained node" is used according to the RFC 7228 [27].

While processing access control related tasks each layer assists the one below when needed. Note that the authentication process details are out the scope of this study. Only authorization aspects are treated. Four layers are introduced:

Constrained Layer. One or both of *C* and *RS* are presumed to be located in a constrained node, but despite this, must perform access control related tasks. We thus consider that either of them may be unable to manage complex tasks while processing authorization requests. In addition, nodes do not always have permanent network connectivity. That's why both of C and RS are considered to be constrained layer actors.

In order to address the limitations present in this layer, a less constrained device is associated to each area of constrained devices. This centric entity is defined by the upper layer called less-constrained layer (see Fig. 1).

Less Constrained Layer. To relieve constrained layer actors from conducting computationally intensive tasks, another layer is introduced. Each group of constrained layer actors is bound to a less constrained layer actor that belongs to the same security domain (see Fig. 1). This link is configured by the entity in charge of the device (see below Organization layer). We call this central element the "Client Authorization Engine" (CAE), on the client side, and Resource Authorization Engine (RAE) on the resource side.

The CAE belongs to the same security domain as C. It assists C in determining if RS is an authorized source for R by obtaining authorization information and supporting C in handling the authorization process.

The RAE belongs to the same security domain as R and RS. It assists RS in determining the correct permissions of C on the requested resource R. RAE obtains authorization information and supports RS in handling the authorization process.

Organization Layer. In the real world, C and R are under the control of some physical entities. These entities are commonly called ROr "Resource Organization" and COr "Client Organization" (see Fig. 2). In order to keep close to

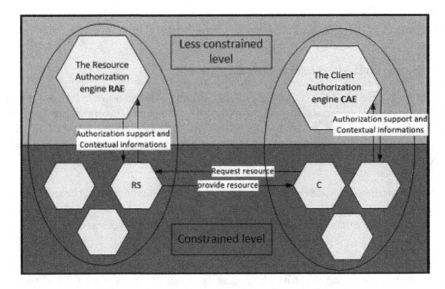

Fig. 1. Constrained and less constrained layers defined according to a centralised-distributed approach

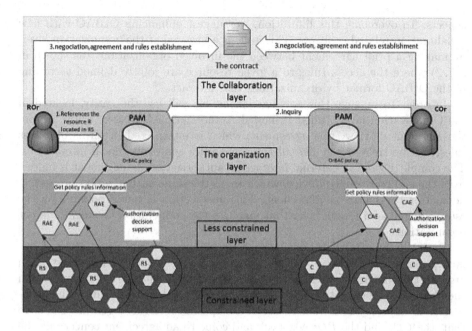

Fig. 2. Management of cross domain requirement in IoT environment

reality and to the OrBAC environment, we represent this entity by Organizations. Thus, each organization specifies the security policy for its devices and structures them in security domains.

The client organization COr is in charge of the entity proceeding to the resource request and thus, must specify security policies for C, including with whom C is allowed to communicate. This means that COr has to define authorized sources for a resource R. COr also configures C and CAE in order to make them belong to the same security domain.

The resource Organization ROr belongs to the same security domain as R and RS. ROr is in charge of R and RS and thus, must specify the authorization policies for R and decides with whom RS is allowed to communicate. That means that ROr has to configure if and how an entity with certain attributes is allowed to access R. ROr also configures RS and RAE in order to make them belong to the same security domain.

Subsequently, on the client side, COr defines authorized sources for R, and on the Resource side, ROr configures if and how an entity can access R. In orders to do this, ROr and COr must have already agreed on the terms of such a service and on how to organize and structure this collaboration. An agreement is passed between the two entities before this interaction takes place (see below Collaboration layer: a cross domain access control).

Collaboration Layer: A Cross Domain Access Control. As seen above, the OrBAC access model does not handle the collaborative interaction aspects. To overcome this limitation, we suggest enhancing OrBAC with new collaboration related concepts. This issue is addressed at the organization layer, by making a prior agreement between the involved organizations (as shown in Fig. 2) where the access rules to a given resource are jointly defined according to the OrBAC format by organizations that interact.

In order to manage this new agreement, we will use the entity, located in the Organization layer, called Principal Authorization Manager "PAM". From the RS point of view, this agreement, which is interpreted in terms of access rules, will be treated just like all the other rules concerning local interactions. The complexity of the external interaction authorization management is hidden from the end constrained device, which keeps the same authorization processing no matter the nature of the client. This abstraction is made possible by the establishment of a fourth layer that manages the cooperation between different organizations.

Basically, SmartOrBAC begins with the publication and negotiation of collaboration rules as well as the corresponding access control rules. First, each organization determines which resources it will offer to external partners, and then references them into the PAM. At this point, other organizations can contact it to express their wish to use these specific referenced resources. To do that, the COr and the ROr negotiate and come to an agreement concerning the use of the resource R. Then, they establish a contract and jointly define security rules concerning access to R. The COr's and ROr's exchange format and the contract aspect will be discussed in a future paper. In the rest of this section, let us focus on access control rules. These rules are registered – according to an OrBAC format – in the PAM of both organizations. Parallel to this, COr creates locally a "virtual resource" called R_image which represents (the remote) R in the client organization side. Then COr adds a rule in its OrBAC policy base to define which entities can invoke R_image (see Figs. 2 and 3).

4.2   Enhancing OrBAC for Context Awareness

Unlike traditional services where the concept of context is limited to a finite set of use cases, in the IoT environment, the concept is getting wider by taking on an ambient character in order to allow services taking into account the contextual information collected in real time by the different sensors [20]. The Context used in defining the SmartOrBAC rule is a set of contexts (C_{Set}) with different types (C_{Type}). The type of context can be a concrete property such as time or location, but also security related context such as authentication and trust level. In order to take the context into account in the access control decision, each of the context types has to be evaluated with a certain constraint (C_{Const}).

The overall context definition in SmartOrBAC can be expressed with the following notation:

$$\text{TYPES} \in \{authLevel, trustLevel, time, location \dots\} \tag{1}$$

$$C_{Set} = \{C_{Type(1)}, C_{Type(2)}, \dots, C_{Type(n)}\} \tag{2}$$

$$\text{Where } C_{Type(1)}, C_{Type(2)}, \ldots, C_{Type(n)} \text{ in TYPES} \tag{3}$$
$$C_{Const} = < C_{Type(i)} > < OP > < VALUE >$$

where OP is a logical operator, i.e., OP $\in \{>, <, \geq, \leq, =, \neq\}$, and VALUE is a specific value of C_{Type}. Finally, we define C as a set of context constraints C_{Const}

$$C = \{C_{Const(1)}, C_{Const(2)}, \ldots, C_{Const(n)}\} \tag{4}$$

4.3 Scenario

In order to illustrate SmartOrBAC, we apply the different concept detailed above in a typical healthcare scenario [28,29].

Assume that John, a man with a heart condition, has opted for an assisted living service that is provided by a medical center. John uses a device that monitors his heart rate and his position; his home is also equipped with multiple sensors and actuators (temperature sensor, humidity sensor, luminosity sensor...). In case of a cardiac arrest the heart monitor automatically sends an alarm to an emergency service, transmitting John's current location.

A doctor, who monitors John's health remotely from the medical center, receives an alarm that John has fainted. An ambulance is instructed to go to assist John. A smart driving application is used by the ambulance to reach John's home as quickly as possible.

The situation requires the interaction of the following organizations: "smart home of John", "the medical center", "the ambulance", and "the police department for traffic jams monitoring".

First of all, each of these organizations determines which device's re-sources it will offer to external partners. At this stage, we find in the *PAM* of John's smart home's organization resources such as the heart monitor resource. The medical center organization makes an inquiry to the *PAM*. As soon as the target resource is found, the negotiation phase begins between the *ROr* of the smart home and the *COr* of the medical center. The resulting contract is then transcript in terms of authorization rules regarding the OrBAC format for both of the medical center and smart home of John. More precisely, if the agreement between the two organizations is: *"Assigned doctor from medical center have the permission to remotely actuate the implanted cardioverter defibrillator from the heart monitor device in the heart attack emergency context"*, the *ROr* of Smart home should:

– have (or create) a rule that grants the permission to a certain role (e.g., *Doctor*) to actuate the heart monitor: *Permission(smart home, Doctor, vital equipement, Actuating, Cheart_attack_Emergency)*. Note that, from John's smart home's point of view, every user playing the *"Doctor"* role will have this permission;
– create a "virtual user" noted *v_user_doctor* that represents the medical center for its use of the implanted cardioverter defibrillator (see Fig. 3);
– add the following *Empower(smart home, v_user_doctor, Doctor)* association to its rule base. This rule grants the user medical center's doctor the right to play the Doctor role.

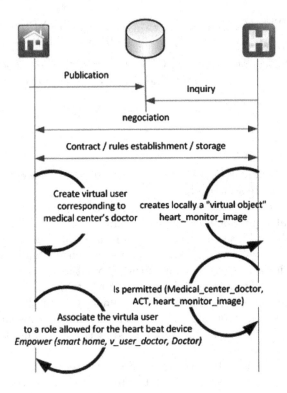

Fig. 3. Virtual user and virtual object in SmartOrBAC

In parallel, the *COr* of the medical center creates locally a "virtual object" *heart_monitor_image* which represents the (remote) implanted device (the resource made available by John's Smart Home), and adds a rule in its OrBAC base to define which of the medical center's roles can invoke *heart_monitor_image* to use the real heart monitor. Let's assume that the assisted living dispositive is a set of different devices (sensors and actuators) with different capabilities. We also assume that the specific device *RS* of heart monitoring that the medical center tries to access is located in the constrained layer, such as the client device *C* used by the doctor in the medical center. The link between the *RS* and its corresponding *RAE* located in the less constrained layer has already been configured by the *ROr* of John's smart home. The same applies for the *CAE* and *C* that have been already configured by the *COr* of medical center.

Before the doctor's device *C* in the medical center sends an actuating request to the heart monitoring device *RS*, it asks the corresponding *CAE* in the medical center for assistance in order to determine if the local image of *RS* (*heart_monitor_image*) is an authorized source.

At this moment, *CAE* starts evaluating the authorization policy rules, using as object the *heart_monitor_image*. Note that at this level, the external nature of the heart monitor device is unknown. Then, if information about policy rules is needed, a request is sent to the *PAM* of the medical center. Once this process is completed, if *RS* is an allowed source, an actuating request is directly sent to the heart monitoring device.

Once the request is received, the authorization decision process begins on the smart home organization side. For that, the device sends an authorization process request, with contextual information, to the corresponding *RAE* in John's smart home. The latter evaluates the authorization decision regarding authorization rules in John smart home's *PAM* especially those detailed above where the subject is *v_user_doctor*. The result is sent to *RS* which, in turn, sends an access response to the doctor's device.

5 Implementation

The transmissions between the different entities included in our Framework (*C/RS, C/CAE, RS/RAE*) are done via the CoAP [30] protocol (Constrained Application Protocol), which is a specialized Web transfer protocol that is intended for use in resource-constrained Internet devices. Like HTTP, CoAP is based on the wildly successful REST model: servers make resources available under a URL, and clients access these resources using methods such as GET, PUT, POST and DELETE.

Since the XML representation is too verbose for efficient transmission over limited channels, we use JSON-based notation for our authorization requests and responses. In fact JSON [24] (JavaScript Object Notation) is a lightweight data-interchange format that efficiently reduces the size of the transmitted messages between *C* and *RS* devices and optimizes the processing time.

The device part of our framework (especially *C* and *RS*) was implemented on an example platform: the Arduino Mega 2560 board3. This board features a 16 MHz processor, 256 kB of Flash Memory, 8 kB of SRAM, and 4 kB of EEPROM. We choose this board in order to test our approach on the lowest performance of the end constrained devices. The board was programmed in Java using a custom implementation of the CoAP protocol stack and the assertions were wrapped in JSON format using the standard Java API (javax.json.*).

6 Conclusion

Our SmartOrBAC access model is specifically designed for the IoT environment and it is conceived through an abstraction layer design that makes use of a deep understanding of the IoT paradigm as it is used in the real world. For these smart services, contextual information is a leading element in decision making therefore only a real-time consideration of this information will achieve smartness. For this reason, we enhanced the "context" notion (originally present in OrBAC) in order to fit the IoT requirements.

Understanding that users belonging to an organization need to dynamically access resources controlled by other organizations we also extended our model with specific collaborative mechanisms where the same OrBAC security policy can be used for local as well as external access. In this way, SmartOrBAC improves the management of the security policy and reduces considerably its complexity.

In our future work, we will explore how to make the SmartOrBAC model more effective and we will go deeper in the study of the negotiation process and the e-contract format. Finally, another relevant research line related to this work is the consideration for additional privacy enhancement through techniques such as the use of pseudonyms or anonymous assertions.

References

1. European Commission: Internet of things in 2020 road map for the future. Working Group RFID of the ETP EPOSS, Technical report (2008)
2. Guillemin, P., Friess, P.: Internet of things strategic research roadmap. The Cluster of European Research Projects, Technical report (2009)
3. Istepanian, R.S.H., Jara, A., Sungoor, A., Philips, N.: Internet of things for M-health applications (IoMT). In: Proceedings of the 1st AMA IEEE Medical Technology Conference on Indi-vidualized Healthcare, IEEE, Washington, USA (2010)
4. Jara, A., Zamora, M., Skarmeta, A.: An internet of things-based personal device for di-abetes therapy management in ambient assisted living (AAL). Pers. Ubiquit. Comput. **15**(4), 431–440 (2011)
5. Chaves, L.W.F., Decker, C.: A survey on organic smart labels for the internet-of-things. In: 2010 Seventh International Conference on Networked Sensing Systems (INSS), pp. 161–164 (2010)
6. Santa, J., Zamora-Izquierdo, M.A., Jara, A.J., Skarmeta, A.F.: Telematic platform for in-tegral management of agricultural/perishable goods in terrestrial logistics. Comput. Electron. Agric. **80**, 31–40 (2012)
7. Burrell, J., Brooke, T., Beckwith, R.: Vineyard computing: sensor networks in agricul-tural production. IEEE Pervasive Comput. **3**(1), 38–45 (2004)
8. Radu, V.: Stochastic Modeling of Thermal Fatigue Crack Growth. Applied Condition Monitoring, vol. 1. Springer, Heidelberg (2015)
9. Gungor, V., Sahin, D., Kocak, T., Ergut, S., Buccella, C., Cecati, C., Hancke, G.: Smart grid and smarthomes: key players and pilot projects. IEEE Ind. Electron. Mag. **6**(4), 18–34 (2012)
10. Kovatsch, M., Weiss, M., Guinard, D.: Embedding internet technology for home automation. In: 2010 IEEE Conference on Emerging Technologies and Factory Automation (ETFA), pp. 1–8. Bilbao, Spain, IEEE (2010)
11. Helal, S., Mann, W., El-Zabadani, H., King, J., Kaddoura, Y., Jansen, E.: The gator tech smart house: a programmable pervasive space. Computer **38**(3), 50–60 (2005)
12. Castro, M., Jara, A., Skarmeta, A.: Smart lighting solutions for smart cities. In: Proceedings of the 27th International Conference on Advanced Information Networking and Applications Workshops (WAINA 2013), Barcelona, Spain, pp. 1374–1379. IEEE (2013)
13. Miorandi, D., Sicari, S., Pellegrini, F., Chlamtac, I.: Internet of things: vision, applications & research challenges. Ad Hoc Netw. **10**(7), 1497–1516 (2012)
14. Sundmaeker, H., Guillemin, P., Friess, P., Woelffle, S.: Vision and challenges for realising the internet of things. Eur. Comm. Inf. Soc. Media (2010)
15. Atzori, L., Iera, A., Morabito, G.: The internet of things: a survey. Comput. Netw. **54**(15), 2787–2805 (2010)

16. Kalam, A.A.E., Baida, R.E., Balbiani, P., Benferhat, S., Cuppens, F., Deswarte, Y., Miege, A., Saurel, C., Trouessin, G.: Organization based access control. In: 4th IEEE Workshop on Policies for Distributed Systems and Networks (pOLICY). pp. 120–134. Italy, 4–6 July 2003

17. Zhang, G., Gong, W.: The research of access control based on UCON in the internet of things. J. Softw. **6**(4), 724–731 (2011)

18. Gusmeroli, S., Piccione, S., Rotondi, D.: A capability-based security approach to manage access control in the internet of things. Math. Comput. Modell. **58**(5–6), 1189–1205 (2013)

19. Hernndez-Ramos, J., Jara, A.J., Marin, L., et al.: Distributed capability-based access control for the internet of things. J. Internet Serv. Inf. Secur. **3**(3/4), 1–16 (2013)

20. Bayu, B., Mahalle, P.N., Prasad, N.R., Prasad, R.: Capability-based access control delegation model on the federated IoT network. In Proceedings of the 15th International Symposium on Wirless Personal Multimedia Communications (WPMC 2012), Taipei, China, pp. 604–608. IEEE (2012)

21. Prasad, R. (ed.): My personal Adaptive Global NET (MAGNET). Signals and Communication Technology Book. Springer, Netherlands (2010)

22. Seitz, L., Selander, G., Gehrmann, C.: Authorization framework for the internet-of-things. In: 14th IEEE International Symposium and Workshops on a World of Wireless, Mobile and Multimedia Networks (WoWMoM 2013), Madrid, Spain, pp. 1–6. IEEE (2013)

23. Moses, T.: Extensible Access Control Markup Language (XACML) Version 2.0 (2005)

24. Crockford, D.: RFC 4627: The application/json media type for javascript object notation (2006)

25. Roman, R., Zhou, J., Lopez, J.: On the features and challenges of security and privacy in distributed internet of things. Comput. Netw. **57**(10), 2266–2279 (2013)

26. Gerdes, S., Seitz, L., Selander, G., Bormann, C.: An architecture for authorization in constrained environments. IETF, Draft (2015)

27. Bormann, C., Ersue, M., Keranen, A.: Terminology for constrained-node networks. IETF RFC 7228 (2014)

28. Memon, M., Wagner, S.R., Pedersen, C., Beevi, F., Hansen, F.O.: Ambient assisted living healthcare frameworks, platforms, standards, and quality attributes. Sensors **14**, 4312–4341 (2014)

29. Dohr, A., Modre-Opsrian, R., Drobics, M., Hayn, D., Schreier, G.: The internet of things for ambient assisted living. In: 2010 Seventh International Conference on Information Technology: New Generations (ITNG), pp. 804–809 (2010)

30. Shelby, Z., Hartke, K., Bormann, C.: Constrained application protocol (CoAP) IETF RFC 7252 (2014)

31. Mainetti, L., Patrono, L., Vilei, A.: Evolution of wireless sensor networks towards the internet of things: a survey. In: 19th International Conference on Software, Telecommunications and Computer Networks (SoftCOM), IEEE (2011)

Privacy-Aware Authentication
in the Internet of Things

Hannes Gross[1]([⊠]), Marko Hölbl[2], Daniel Slamanig[1], and Raphael Spreitzer[1]

[1] Graz University of Technology, Inffeldgasse 16a, 8010 Graz, Austria
{hannes.gross,daniel.slamanig,raphael.spreitzer}@iaik.tugraz.at
[2] University of Maribor, Smetanova Ulica 17, 2000 Maribor, Slovenia
marko.holbl@um.si

Abstract. Besides the opportunities offered by the all-embracing Internet of Things (IoT) technology, it also poses a tremendous threat to the privacy of the carriers of these devices. In this work, we build upon the idea of an RFID-based IoT realized by means of standardized and well-established Internet protocols. In particular, we demonstrate how the Internet Protocol Security protocol suite (IPsec) can be applied in a privacy-aware manner. Therefore, we introduce a privacy-aware mutual authentication protocol compatible with restrictions imposed by the IPsec standard and analyze its privacy and security properties. With this work, we show that privacy in the IoT can be achieved without proprietary protocols and on the basis of existing Internet standards.

Keywords: Internet of Things · Privacy · Privacy-aware authentication · EPC Gen2 · RFID · IPsec · IKEv2

1 Introduction

The Internet of Things (IoT), in particular the secure and privacy-aware integration of RFID tags into the Internet, is a demanding area of research. Motivated by the tight integration and interconnection of objects to share information autonomously via the Internet, research on security and privacy issues has gained increasing attention. More specifically, if the corresponding information is not protected properly, it can be misused to track RFID tags. For instance, RFID tags that respond with their ID to requests from any (malicious) reader easily allow anyone to track the corresponding carrier. Hence, privacy-aware authentication aims for the authentication of RFID tags, but only authentic counterparts, e.g., genuine clients or backends, are able to identify RFID tags.

Thereby privacy-aware authentication is not as strong as anonymous authentication (e.g., [2,5]), which even hides tag identities from genuine readers. However, while anonymous authentication is only reasonable within specific applications and often *not* even desired, privacy-aware authentication should be

---

The full version of this extended abstract is available in the IACR Cryptology ePrint Archive.

© Springer International Publishing Switzerland 2015
M. Reiter and D. Naccache (Eds.): CANS 2015, LNCS 9476, pp. 32–39, 2015.
DOI: 10.1007/978-3-319-26823-1_3

considered as *absolutely necessary* in the IoT in order to prevent malicious readers or other external entities from tracking RFID tags.

Even though privacy aspects of RFID protocols have gained increasing attention, e.g., proposals of tag-authentication protocols [16,18] and RFID privacy models [9,10,18] for the theoretical investigation of these protocols, so far mostly proprietary solutions have been considered. However, proprietary solutions impede the establishment of an RFID-based IoT for the following reasons: (1) many of these "light-weight" protocols are in fact insecure. (2) a seamless integration into the existing Internet environment is not possible, since different communication protocols between tags, readers, and the actual Internet are employed.

Contribution. In this paper we evaluate existing Internet security protocols regarding their suitability for privacy-aware authentication protocols. Based on this investigation, we advance the idea of an IoT based on IPsec by designing a privacy-aware mutual authentication protocol which is standard conform.[1] Finally, we compare the performance to proprietary protocols.

2   Internet Security Protocols

There are two predominant technologies to secure the communication over the Internet, namely the Transport Layer Security protocol (TLS) [7] and the Internet Protocol Security protocol suite (IPsec) [13]. While TLS is integrated in the Transport Layer of the OSI protocol stack and is therefore visible for applications, IPsec has the advantage of being transparent for application-layer protocols. Consequently, IPsec is closer to the physical layer, which has the advantage of less overhead in terms of additional headers added by upper-layer protocols. This is especially important, as minimizing the communication overhead is crucial for RFID tags. Note that multiple RFID tags usually share only one half-duplex communication channel and the communication speed is limited to a few kilo bits per second. Thus, IPsec seems to be preferable over TLS. However, for the sake of completeness, we still investigate the possible implementation of privacy-aware authentication in IPsec and TLS within the following paragraphs.

Privacy-Aware Authentication in IPsec and TLS. Besides secure and authenticated communication, one of the major issues of RFID tags is privacy. Thus, the question is whether or not privacy-aware authentication can be implemented by using the Internet standard protocols IPsec or TLS.

Comparing IPsec—respectively the Internet Key Exchange protocol (IKEv2) used by IPsec—and TLS, we observe that both protocols support symmetric authentication by means of a pre-shared secret (PSK) as well as asymmetric authentication via certificates. However, the way both protocols implement the key agreement and the authentication is different. In case of IKEv2, both

---

[1] In the full version of this paper we adapt the HPVP model [9] to prove the required properties of mutual authentication protocols following the IPsec standard.

communication parties establish a confidential and integrity-protected communication channel by means of a Diffie-Hellman (DH) key agreement and the authentication is then performed subsequently over the already encrypted channel. Hence, passive attackers cannot gain any information on eavesdropped authentication procedures. Active attackers, on the other hand, can exploit the fact that the tags need to claim their identity in order to prove it. Later, in Sect. 4 we demonstrate how to counteract such active attacks.

In contrast, TLS does not encrypt the communication until the authentication phase is finished. Even considering a passive attacker only, the identity of the involved parties cannot be protected as the identities are claimed in plaintext in the PSK setting of TLS. The same argument holds for the certificate-based authentication method. Hence, we conclude that privacy-aware authentication cannot be achieved by TLS alone.

Nevertheless, note that both protocols also support completely anonymous DH communication channels (without authentication). Based on such an anonymous DH channel, one could implement a privacy-aware authentication mechanism on the application layer (in a non-standard conform way). We do not consider this approach as a viable option. These arguments also hold for DTLS [17], which has been promoted for wireless sensor nodes in the IoT (e.g., [11,14]).

3   RFID Privacy Models

One of the first models for the privacy analysis in RFID systems has been proposed by Vaudenay [18]. Depending on the adversary's capabilities, Vaudenay defined different privacy notions (cf. [18]). A follow-up paper of Paise and Vaudenay [15] extended the model to also cover mutual authentication. However, Armknecht et al. [3,4] observed some issues of the aforementioned model and showed that mutual authentication and narrow-forward privacy (resp. narrow-strong privacy) cannot be achieved if tag corruption reveals both the static and the temporary/volatile memory (resp. the static memory only). Later on, Hermans et al. [9] presented a new model (HPVP) to overcome these issues. In particular, they claim that their model achieves the strongest notion of privacy (wide-strong privacy) in case the used public-key encryption scheme is IND-CCA2 secure.

In the full version of this paper we adapt the HPVP model for (IPsec-conform) mutual authentication and analyze the required properties (correctness, privacy, and security) of our privacy-aware authentication protocol proposed in Sect. 4.3.

4   IPsec-Conform Authentication

IPsec relies on the Internet Key Exchange protocol (IKEv2) for the negotiation of the security functionality and for the authentication of the involved parties. Thus, in order for a protocol to be IPsec-compatible it must precisely follow the message flow and data processing steps of IKEv2, which we sketch below.

The basic message flow between an initiator and a responder is as follows [12].

IKE_SA_INIT_REQ ↔ IKE_SA_INIT_RSP: These request/response messages are used to negotiate the cryptographic algorithms to be used subsequently and to exchange the initial DH parameters and nonces in order to derive the required key material. Hence, subsequent to these messages, the communication is already confidential and integrity protected.

IKE_AUTH_REQ ↔ IKE_AUTH_RSP: These request/response messages are used to authenticate both parties. Therefore, these messages are used to exchange the claimed identities along with an authentication value (either based on a PSK or a signature in case of certificate-based authentication).

4.1 IPsec Conformance of Existing Protocols

When looking at existing literature [6, 10] we observe that there are only very few mutual-authentication protocols that have been formally analyzed. To the best of our knowledge, only the PKC [18] and IBIHOP [16] meet these requirements, but do not conform to the flow of the messages exchanged in IKEv2. Hence, a privacy-aware authentication protocol that fits into IKEv2 still needs to be defined.

4.2 Possible Realizations

In general, privacy-aware authentication in the IKEv2 protocol could be realized for either a *tag-initiated* or a *backend-initiated* authentication scenario. However, when the tag initiates the IKEv2 protocol, then the IKEv2 message flow requires the tag to reveal its identity to an unauthenticated communication partner, which violates the privacy of the tag.

On the other hand, if the backend initiates the communication, a unique PSK per tag leads to the situation that the backend does not know for which of the tags to compute the authentication value ($AUTH$). A straightforward realization would thus be to use a PSK that is shared among all the tags, but this has the major drawback that one broken tag results in a broken system. As an alternative, a backend-first scenario could be realized by using certificates. Again, in a scenario where the tag starts the communication this would inevitably reveal the tag's identity. Nevertheless, if the backend initiates the protocol, the identity of the backend can be verified by first ensuring the validity of the certificate, and then checking the $AUTH$ value with the public-key of the backend. Only if both are valid, the tag continues the protocol execution by sending its response containing the identity claim, and the $AUTH$ value. The tag authentication can then either be certificate-based or PSK-based. Because the tag reveals its identity only after the backend was authenticated and the communication channel in the second protocol phase is already secured, this ensures that neither active nor passive attackers can identify specific tags.

However, the validation of certificates on the tag side, i.e., verifying the certificate chain up to a trusted root certificate, represents an enormous effort for a constrained RFID tag. Even if the tag uses PSK-based authentication and only a single backend certificate is used—and therefore no certificate chain needs to be verified—, at least the certificate as well as a signature must be verified on the tag side. A PSK-based authentication mechanism for both sides is thus the desired choice in terms of computational overhead.

Furthermore, in a typical IoT scenario, an RFID tag is usually the initiator of the conversation as the tag updates the backend with the information gathered from its environment. Thus, the resulting requirements for an IPsec-conform privacy-aware authentication are: (1) a tag-initiated protocol, and (2) the corruption of one tag should not lead to a broken system regarding the remaining tags. In the next section, we propose a new privacy-aware authentication protocol, which we analyze under an adapted HPVP model (cf. full version). In addition, it is compliant with the IKEv2 protocol, i.e., allows tag-initiated conversations, and uses PSK-based authentication on both sides.

4.3   IPsec-Conform Privacy-Aware Authentication

Figure 1 shows our IPsec-conform privacy-aware mutual authentication protocol, which relies on the Diffie-Hellman Integrated Encryption (DHIES) scheme [1]. Subsequently, we use the additive notation as in the elliptic curve setting for the description of our protocol. We denote by $\mathbb{G}$ the description of an additive group of prime order q with some fixed generator G.

DHIES Excursus. DHIES [1] is a public-key encryption scheme $\Pi_{DHIES} = $ (Gen, Enc, Dec). Here, the Gen algorithm generates a private key $k \xleftarrow{R} \mathbb{Z}_q$ and a public key $K \leftarrow k \cdot G$. The Enc algorithm takes the public key K and a message m. It computes an ephemeral public key $R \leftarrow r \cdot G$ for $r \xleftarrow{R} \mathbb{Z}_q$ and the secret DH value $P \leftarrow r \cdot K$. P is then used to derive two symmetric keys via a key-derivation function as $(k_{mac}, k_{enc}) \leftarrow \mathsf{KDF}(P)$. These keys are used to obtain $c \leftarrow \mathsf{SymEnc}_{k_{enc}}(m)$ using a symmetric encryption algorithm and to generate a tag as $t \leftarrow \mathsf{Mac}_{k_{mac}}(m)$ to authenticate the message (MAC-and-encrypt). Finally, Enc outputs the tuple (R, c, t). The Dec algorithm takes a secret key k and ciphertext (R, c, t). It computes the DH value $P = k \cdot R$. Then, the KDF is computed over P and the two keys k_{mac} and k_{enc} are used to decrypt c and to verify the tag t. If t is valid, it returns $m \leftarrow \mathsf{SymDec}_{k_{enc}}(c)$ and $\perp$ otherwise.

Our Protocol. Figure 1 omits the IPsec parameters (see [12] for details) that are not relevant for the properties of our protocol for brevity reasons. The setup of the backend generates a DHIES key pair $(k_B, K_B = k_B \cdot G)$. The setup of a tag generates a unique pre-shared secret key k_{PSK} for the tag, which is shared between the tag and the backend.

The protocol follows the notion of a tag-initiated challenge-response protocol to be compatible with the IPsec's IKEv2 protocol. Each tag contains the backend's public key K_B (the static DH parameter), which ensures that only the genuine backend (in possession of k_B) can decrypt the received data. The tag starts the protocol by generating a nonce N_T (of suitable bitsize κ) and the

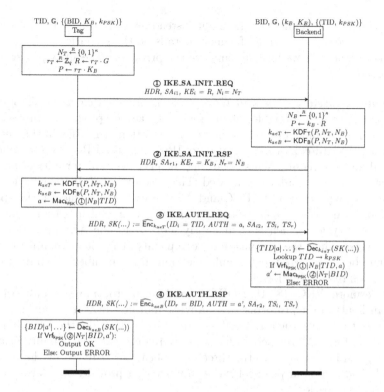

Fig. 1. IPsec-conform privacy-aware mutual authentication protocol

ephemeral DH parameter $R \leftarrow r_T \cdot G$ for $r_T \stackrel{R}{\leftarrow} \mathbb{Z}_q$. Based on the resulting shared secret $P = r_T \cdot k_B \cdot G$ and the nonces, the tag and the backend derive symmetric encryption and authentication keys for both sides by means of a KDF. In contrast to a single DHIES instance—and to fit into the IKEv2 protocol—, two separate key derivation functions (KDF_T and KDF_B) are used to derive the keys (k_{mac}, k_{enc}) for the tag and the backend, respectively. Instead of referring directly to the encryption or authentication keys, we use k_{ae*} for $*$ being T or B to denote these tuples. Furthermore, we denote by $\widehat{\mathsf{Enc}}_{k_{ae*}}$ that the symmetric encryption SymEnc and the Mac function of the DHIES is implicitly called such that $\widehat{\mathsf{Enc}}_{k_{ae*}}$ returns the tuple (c,t) under the key set k_{ae*}. The decryption $\widehat{\mathsf{Dec}}_{k_{ae*}}$ works analogously.

After the backend decrypted the tag's ID (TID), the corresponding PSK (k_{PSK}) is used to verify the tag authentication. Therefore, we use an additional PSK (k_{PSK}) for the authentication of both sides—by generating a and a', respectively. Hence, we define a protocol for tag-first authentication with an "implicit" backend-first authentication. Implicit backend-first authentication is achieved as only the genuine backend is able to decrypt the message containing the tag's ID that is required for the subsequent tag authentication. Note that readers function as pure routers in our IoT setting and solely bridge the IP packets between the tags and the backend. Such an IoT scenario has multiple untrusted readers, which are not directly modeled here but instead are only considered as possible adversaries (see Gross et al. [8] for more details on the scenario).

In the full version we formally analyze the privacy and security properties of our protocol.

Performance Evaluation and Comparison. As elliptic curve cryptography (ECC) is the most reasonable setting for public-key cryptography in resource-constrained environments, we assume an instantiation of DHIES in this setting. In [8], the standard-conform integration of IPsec into the EPC Gen2 standard is presented and the requirements regarding the cryptographic primitives and the implementation overhead are evaluated. They use the NIST P-192 elliptic curve and the AES algorithm. Both ECC and AES cores were designed for low-power applications. As these results show, one ECC scalar multiplication consumes around 700 k cycles, which is significantly more than one AES operation with only 1 k cycles. Thus, the computational complexity of a protocol mainly depends on the number of required scalar multiplications if the number of symmetric-key operations is reasonably low.

Furthermore, PKC [18], IBIHOP [16], and our protocol are the only privacy-aware authentication protocols that provide mutual authentication. However, in contrast to our protocol IBIHOP is less efficient and like the PKC it is not standard conform. More specifically, we only require two scalar multiplications on the tag's side compared to the three multiplications required by the IBIHOP protocol. Therefore, our protocol is the only one that provides standard-conform mutual authentication.

5   Conclusion

Building on the recent work in [8], that focused on the integration of IPsec into RFID tags, we proposed an IPsec-conform privacy-aware mutual authentication mechanism between RFID tags and clients on the Internet. Thereby, we further paved the way for an IoT that is based on well-established standards. Our privacy-aware authentication does not reveal sensitive information like IDs unless the tag is assured to communicate with a genuine backend. Consequently, we reduce privacy concerns of carriers of RFID tags since undesired disclosure of sensitive information is prevented.

Acknowledgements. We would like to thank the anonymous reviewers for their valuable comments. This work has been supported by the Austrian Science Fund (FWF) under the grant number TRP251-N23 (Realizing a Secure Internet of Things - ReSIT), the FFG research program SeCoS (project number 836628) and by EU HORIZON 2020 through project PRISMACLOUD (GA No. 644962).

References

1. Abdalla, M., Bellare, M., Rogaway, P.: The oracle Diffie-Hellman assumptions and an analysis of DHIES. In: Naccache, D. (ed.) CT-RSA 2001. LNCS, vol. 2020, pp. 143–158. Springer, Heidelberg (2001)

2. Armknecht, F., Chen, L., Sadeghi, A.-R., Wachsmann, C.: Anonymous authentication for RFID systems. In: Ors Yalcin, S.B. (ed.) RFIDSec 2010. LNCS, vol. 6370, pp. 158–175. Springer, Heidelberg (2010)
3. Armknecht, F., Sadeghi, A., Scafuro, A., Visconti, I., Wachsmann, C.: Impossibility results for RFID privacy notions. Trans. Comput. Sci. **11**, 39–63 (2010)
4. Armknecht, F., Sadeghi, A.-R., Visconti, I., Wachsmann, C.: On RFID privacy with mutual authentication and tag corruption. In: Zhou, J., Yung, M. (eds.) ACNS 2010. LNCS, vol. 6123, pp. 493–510. Springer, Heidelberg (2010)
5. Burmester, M., de Medeiros, B., Motta, R.: Anonymous RFID authentication supporting constant-cost key-lookup against active adversaries. IJACT **1**(2), 79–90 (2008)
6. Coisel, I., Martin, T.: Untangling RFID privacy models. J. Comput. Netw. Commun. **2013**, 710275:1–710275:26 (2013)
7. Dierks, T., Rescorla, E.: The Transport Layer Security (TLS) Protocol Version 1.2. RFC 5246 (2008)
8. Gross, H., Wenger, E., Martín, H., Hutter, M.: PIONEER—a prototype for the internet of things based on an extendable EPC Gen2 RFID tag. In: Sadeghi, A.-R., Saxena, N. (eds.) RFIDSec 2014. LNCS, vol. 8651, pp. 54–73. Springer, Heidelberg (2014)
9. Hermans, J., Pashalidis, A., Vercauteren, F., Preneel, B.: A new RFID privacy model. In: Atluri, V., Diaz, C. (eds.) ESORICS 2011. LNCS, vol. 6879, pp. 568–587. Springer, Heidelberg (2011)
10. Hermans, J., Peeters, R., Preneel, B.: Proper RFID privacy: model and protocols. IEEE Trans. Mob. Comput. **13**(12), 2888–2902 (2014)
11. Hummen, R., Shafagh, H., Raza, S., Voigt, T., Wehrle, K.: Delegation-based authentication and authorization for the IP-based internet of things. In: SECON, pp. 284–292. IEEE (2014)
12. Kaufman, C., Hoffman, P., Nir, Y., Eronen, P.: Internet Key Exchange Protocol Version 2 (IKEv2). RFC 5996 (Proposed Standard), Sept. 2010. Obsoleted by RFC 7296, updated by RFCs 5998, 6989
13. Kent, S., Seo, K.: Security Architecture for the Internet Protocol. RFC 4301 (2005)
14. Kothmayr, T., Schmitt, C., Hu, W., Brünig, M., Carle, G.: DTLS based security and two-way authentication for the internet of things. Ad Hoc Netw. **11**(8), 2710–2723 (2013)
15. Paise, R., Vaudenay, S.: Mutual authentication in RFID: security and privacy. In: ASIACCS, pp. 292–299. ACM (2008)
16. Peeters, R., Hermans, J., Fan, J.: BIHOP: proper privacy preserving mutual RFID authentication. In: RFIDSec Asia, pp. 45–56. IOS Press (2013)
17. Rescorla, E., Modadugu, N.: atagram Transport Layer Security Version 1.2. RFC 6347 (Proposed Standard), January 2012
18. Vaudenay, S.: On privacy models for RFID. In: Kurosawa, K. (ed.) ASIACRYPT 2007. LNCS, vol. 4833, pp. 68–87. Springer, Heidelberg (2007)

Password-Based Authentication

Security of Linear Secret-Sharing Schemes Against Mass Surveillance

Irene Giacomelli[1]([✉]), Ruxandra F. Olimid[2], and Samuel Ranellucci[1]

[1] Department of Computer Science, Aarhus University, Aarhus, Denmark
giacomelli@cs.au.dk
[2] Department of Computer Science, University of Bucharest,
Romania and Applied Cryptography Group, Orange, Bucharest, Romania

Abstract. Following the line of work presented recently by Bellare, Paterson and Rogaway, we formalize and investigate the resistance of linear secret-sharing schemes to mass surveillance. This primitive is widely used to design IT systems in the modern computer world, and often it is implemented by a proprietary code that the provider ("big brother") could manipulate to covertly violate the privacy of the users (by implementing Algorithm-Substitution Attacks or ASAs). First, we formalize the security notion that expresses the goal of big brother and prove that for any linear secret-sharing scheme there exists an undetectable subversion of it that efficiently allows surveillance. Second, we formalize the security notion that assures that a sharing scheme is secure against ASAs and construct the first sharing scheme that meets this notion.

Keywords: Linear secret-sharing · Algorithm-substitution attack · Mass surveillance · Kleptography

1 Introduction

The paper considers the possibility of mass surveillance by *algorithm-substitution attacks* (ASAs) against secret sharing. Secret-sharing generally refers to a method for splitting a secret into pieces (called *shares* of the secret) so that the secret can be reconstructed when a qualified set of shares are combined together (reconstruction property); on the other hand, unqualified sets of shares reveal no information about the original secret (privacy property). An ASA replaces the real sharing algorithm by a subverted version that allows a privileged party (*big brother*) to break privacy and reconstruct the secret from an unqualified sets of shares. Since secret sharing is widely used as building block for distributed protocols and systems, its insecurity against this kind of attack could have significant consequences. For example, big brother could mount ASA against a key backup system based on secret sharing, recover the private keys and break confidentiality (in order to maintain the same terminology as in the existing literature [1], we refer to this kind of scenario as *mass surveillance*).

© Springer International Publishing Switzerland 2015
M. Reiter and D. Naccache (Eds.): CANS 2015, LNCS 9476, pp. 43–58, 2015.
DOI: 10.1007/978-3-319-26823-1_4

Motivation. Applications for access control, key backup and recovery or secure storage systems sometimes implement proprietary piece of code to perform secret sharing [2–6]. Often, the security of the entire system relies on the privacy property of the underlying secret sharing scheme (e.g. access control systems grant permission only if a set of qualified shares are available for reconstruction). Therefore, mounting ASAs against such systems might lead to serious consequences: big brother can ruin access control, disclose private keys or learn secret data.

To exemplify, we focus on the scenario of long-term secure storage systems that use secret sharing to assure data confidentiality and availability. A client-side application runs a sharing algorithm to split data in share that are privately sent to a set of independent storage nodes, which can be located across different geographical and network areas, benefit of distinct protection mechanisms and even belong to various storage providers. To later access the stored data, the client application requests a qualified set of shares from several storage nodes and reconstructs. The architecture introduces multiple points of trust: reconstruction is possible only if the adversary breaks into several storage nodes and obtains a qualified set of shares; the architecture assumes no trust on individual storage providers, as no one can access the data using its own shares only. Now, suppose an undetectable ASA replaces the client-side application code with a subverted version designed by big brother that allows reconstruction from an unqualified sets of shares; if big brother is a storage provider, then it can perform surveillance by breaking the privacy property using the shares stored on its own servers; if big brother is an outsider, it can perform surveillance by only breaking into a few storage nodes, independently of the access structure. On the other hand, the client would like a guarantee that no ASAs will succeed, under the minimal detectability conditions.

Related Work. Kleptography was introduced by Young and Yung in the 90s to consider undetectable modifications to cryptosystems that deliberately provide trapdoor capabilities [7,8], as an extension to the existing notions of subliminal and convert channels [9,10]. Since then, kleptographic attacks have been designed for a wide range of cryptographic primitives and protocols. Despite the amount of work that has been done on the field, only recently Bellare, Paterson and Rogaway formalize the security notions in the settings of modern cryptography [1]. They set the terminology for ASAs (Asymmetric Substitution Attacks) and use a game-based approach to model both negative and positive results, i.e. when an adversary (big brother) can, respectively cannot perform surveillance without being detected. Their work focuses on symmetric encryption and highlights its impact on real-world systems. We follow their line of work, formalize and investigate the resistance of *linear secret-sharing* to mass surveillance. The security in this framework of other fundamental primitives has already been studied: see the recent work of Ateniese, Magri and Venturi [11] for a formal treatment of subversion-resilient signature schemes.

Table 1. Strong subversion and resilience modeling

	Strong subversion (big brother's goal)	Strong resilience (users' goal)
Detection algorithm	PK, $\mathcal{T}$; choose the secret	$\emptyset$; access SECRET oracle
Subverted algorithm	PK, $\mathcal{T}$	PK, SK, $\mathcal{T}$

Modeling and Results. We assume that big brother subverts the sharing scheme embedding in it a strategy $\mathcal{T}$ and an encryption key. Big brother aims for a strong form of subversion, that disallows users from detecting ASAs or gain his abilities to perform surveillance even in case of reverse engineering. So, we consider asymmetric ASAs, where big brother embeds into the code a public key PK and keeps the corresponding secret key SK private. In this strong surveillance model, the subverted algorithm has access to the public key PK and the strategy $\mathcal{T}$ and it remains undetectable by the users even if both PK and $\mathcal{T}$ are given to the detection algorithm (run by the users). We give additional power to the detection algorithm and allow it to choose the secret to be shared. This models big brother's goal to keep subversion hidden for all possible secrets and hence make the ASA undetectable. Following the strategy $\mathcal{T}$, big brother corrupts a set of unqualified parties and uses their shares to gain information about the secret. This is the framework we formalize in Sect. 3, where we also show our negative result: for any linear secret-sharing scheme there exists an undetectable subverted version of it that efficiently allows surveillance.

On the other hand, users aim for a strong form of resilience against surveillance, that allows detectability even if they only have black-box access to the subverted sharing algorithm. In this strong resilience model, the subverted algorithm can also be given access to the private key SK and it is detectable by users even if the detection algorithm is given nothing (except the inputs and outputs of the black-box). Symmetric ASAs suffice, as (PK, SK) can be seen a single secret key K embedded into the code; however, we maintain the asymmetric notation for continuity. We now disallow the detection algorithm to choose the secret to be shared and give it access to a SECRET oracle, reflecting that users should detect surveillance for sampled inputs. We formalize this framework in Sect. 4, where we also give the first construction of a linear secret-sharing scheme that is resilient against any efficient subversion. To obtain this positive result, we require that all the users give input to the sharing algorithm.

In contrast to [1], we consider strong forms of subversion and resilience to model the goals of big brother, respectively users and give the detection and subverted algorithms distinct capabilities. Similar to [1] (where big brother is not allowed to select the encryption key), we do not allow big brother to select the secret (Table 1). However, we discuss in Sect. 4 the settings that allow surveillance resilience when big brother is allowed to select the secret and show that our proposal remains secure under this settings.

2 Preliminaries

Let $\mathbb{F}$ be a finite field and $v \in \mathbb{F}^n$ a vector of n components; we denote by $v[i]$ its i-th component. We denote sampling uniformly at random a value x from a set X as $x \leftarrow X$ and assigning a value Y to a variable y as $y \leftarrow Y$.

2.1 Secret Sharing

Let n be the set of parties (e.g. the different storage nodes) $\mathcal{P} = \{P_1, \ldots, P_n\}$. A *secret sharing scheme* consists of two algorithms $\Pi = (\mathsf{Sh}, \mathsf{Rec})$ such that:

- the *sharing algorithm* Sh is a randomized algorithm that receives as input a secret s and outputs a vector of shares $S = (S[1], \ldots, S[n])$; We call *dealer* the entity that runs the algorithm on input s and that receives the output S. We assume that the sharing algorithm is connected by a bidirectional secure channel[1] with each players P_i, in such a way that the share $S[i]$ is securely sent to the player P_i.

  For any subset of players $A \subset \{P_1, \ldots, P_n\}$, let S_A be the vector of shares held by players in A, i.e. $S_A = (S[i])_{P_i \in A}$. A set $A \subset \{P_1, \ldots, P_n\}$ is called *unqualified* if the distribution of S_A is independent from s, while it is called *qualified* if the secret s is uniquely determined from S_A.
- the *reconstruction algorithm* Rec is a deterministic algorithm that receives as input a subset of shares S_A and outputs the value s if the set of shares corresponds to a qualified set of players; otherwise it outputs the special symbol $\perp$. We ask that the entire set of players $\{P_1, \ldots, P_n\}$ is always qualified.

The access structure of Π, Γ, is defined as the set of all $A \subset \{P_1, \ldots, P_n\}$ that are qualified and Γ_{min} is the set of the minimal qualified subsets, i.e. $\Gamma_{min} = \{B \in \Gamma \mid \nexists B' \subset B, B' \in \Gamma\}$. Let γ be the cardinality of the largest set in Γ_{min}, i.e. $\gamma = \max\{|B| \mid B \in \Gamma_{min}\}$ and let ρ the reconstruction threshold, i.e. the smallest integer such that every $A \subset \{P_1, \ldots, P_n\}$ of cardinality ρ is qualified.

Remark 1. In general, γ differs from the reconstruction threshold ρ. For example, let $n = 4$ and $\Gamma_{min} = \{\{P_2, P_3\}, \{P_2, P_4\}, \{P_3, P_4\}\}$. Then $\gamma = 2$, but $\rho = 3$. The inequality $\gamma \leq \rho$ always holds.

2.2 Linear Secret Sharing

Informally, a secret sharing scheme is called *linear* if the secret and the shares are elements of some vector spaces and the shares are computed as a linear function of the secret.

More precisely, given M a $n \times m$ matrix ($m > l$) with elements in $\mathbb{F}$, the Linear Secret-Sharing Scheme (LSSS) associated to M, $\Pi_M = (\mathsf{Sh}_M, \mathsf{Rec}_M)$, is defined

---

[1] By secure channel we mean an authenticated and private channel that is also subversion resilient, that is big bother can not implement surveillance over it. Using the results of [1,11] for encryption scheme and digital signature such a channel can be easily implemented.

in Construction 1. To share a secret $s = (s[1], \ldots, s[l]) \in \mathbb{F}^l$, the algorithm first forms a column vector $f \in \mathbb{F}^m$ where s appears in the first l entries and with the last d entries chosen uniformly at random and then computes $S = M \cdot f$. We will use π_l to denote the projection that outputs the first l coordinates of a vector, i.e. $\pi_l(f) = s$. Similarly, let $\pi^d(f)$ be the last d elements of f; hence, $\pi^d(f) = r$, where $d = m - l$.

$\mathsf{Sh}_M(s)$

$\quad r \leftarrow \mathbb{F}^d$

$\quad f^T \leftarrow (s, r)^T$

$\quad S \leftarrow M \cdot f$

$\quad$ return S

$\mathsf{Rec}_M(S_B)$

$\quad$ **if** B *is qualified* **then**

$\quad\quad s \leftarrow N_B \cdot S_B$

$\quad$ **else**

$\quad\quad s \leftarrow \perp$

$\quad$ return s

Construction 1: LSSS $\Pi_M = (\mathsf{Sh}_M, \mathsf{Rec}_M)$

Let m_i be the row i of M and m^i be the column i of M. If $B \subseteq \mathcal{P}$, then $M_B = (m_i)_{P_i \in B}$ denotes the matrix built from all rows m_i such that $P_i \in B$.

It easy to see that a player subset B is qualified if and only if there exists a $l \times |B|$ matrix N_B such that for any $f \in \mathbb{F}^d$, $N_B \cdot (M_B \cdot f) = \pi_l(f)$.

Remark 2. The inequality $\gamma > l$ always holds from the correctness of reconstruction and the usage of randomness ($d > 0$).

For the rest of the paper, we fix M and denote $\Pi_M = (\mathsf{Sh}_M, \mathsf{Rec}_M)$ by $\Pi = (\mathsf{Sh}, \mathsf{Rec})$ to simplify notation. See two examples of linear secret-sharing scheme in the full version of the paper [12].

3 Subverting Secret-Sharing

This section models big brother's $\mathcal{B}$ goal: to subvert the sharing algorithm Sh to an algorithm $\widetilde{\mathsf{Sh}}$ that allows him to perform surveillance, while it remains undetected under the strong subversion scenario (see Sect. 1).

Surveillance means that $\mathcal{B}$ compromises privacy and learns the secret (or part of it) from corrupting an unqualified set of parties. To do so, $\mathcal{B}$ can embed in the code a key and a strategy. The embedded key is used to favor $\mathcal{B}$ over other entities, by leaking information in encrypted form. In real life, $\mathcal{B}$ aims to keep decryption capabilities to itself even in case of reverse engineering the algorithm, so our definitions consider asymmetric ASAs ($\mathcal{B}$ embeds a public key PK in the code and keeps the corresponding secret key SK private). The strategy $\mathcal{T}$ defines the unqualified set of parties $\mathcal{B}$ must corrupt to break the privacy of the scheme. We expect that $\mathcal{B}$ embeds in the code and hence follows a strategy $\mathcal{T}$ that maximizes its chances to win (e.g. minimum number of parties, if all parties are equally susceptible to corruption or easy to corrupt parties otherwise).

Undetectability means that no efficient detection algorithm $\mathcal{U}$ that is not given the decryption key SK can distinguish between the real and the subverted sharing algorithm. In the absence of the undetectability condition, subversion is always possible: $\widetilde{\mathsf{Sh}}$ simply distributes the secret (or parts of it) in shares in accordance to the strategy $\mathcal{T}$.

3.1 Definitions

Let $\Pi = (\mathsf{Sh}, \mathsf{Rec})$ be a secret-sharing scheme and let $\mathcal{K}$ be a probabilistic key generation algorithm that outputs a public-private key pair $(\mathsf{PK}, \mathsf{SK})$. A subversion of Π is a pair $\widetilde{\Pi} = (\widetilde{\mathsf{Sh}}, \widetilde{\mathsf{Rec}})$, with the following features: the subverted sharing algorithm $\widetilde{\mathsf{Sh}}$ is a randomized algorithm that maps $(s, \mathsf{PK}, \mathsf{ID}, \mathcal{T})$ to a share vector $\mathbf{S}$. The input ID identifies the dealer that runs the sharing algorithm; this information is in general available in the system (e.g. the IP address or any authentication information of the client application for storage systems). $\mathcal{T}$ is a strategy that outputs the subset $T \subset \{P_1, \ldots, P_n\}$ used to leak information. The subverted reconstruction algorithm $\widetilde{\mathsf{Rec}}$ is an algorithm that maps $(\mathbf{S}_T, \mathsf{ID}, \mathsf{SK})$ to the shared secret s, where $\mathbf{S}_T$ is the subset of shares that belongs to the unqualified set T.

We give next the definitions for detection and surveillance games. In contrast to the traditional unbounded adversarial power in secret sharing, our model is defined in the computational settings [13,14]. In the following, we say that a function ϵ is *negligible* in N if for every polynomial function $p(N)$ there exists a constant c such that $\epsilon(N) < \frac{1}{p(N)}$ when $N > c$. With the notation $\mathcal{A}^{\mathtt{ALG}}(z)$ we mean that the entity $\mathcal{A}$ has oracle access to the algorithm $\mathtt{ALG}$ with knowledge of z.

Detection Advantage. Let $\Pi = (\mathsf{Sh}, \mathsf{Rec})$ be a secret sharing scheme and $\widetilde{\Pi} = (\widetilde{\mathsf{Sh}}, \widetilde{\mathsf{Rec}})$ a subversion of it. Let $\mathcal{U}$ be a detection algorithm that is not given SK. The advantage of $\mathcal{U}$ to detect the ASA is defined as:

$$\mathsf{Adv}^{\mathsf{det}}_{\Pi, \widetilde{\Pi}}(\mathcal{U}) = 2\Pr[\mathsf{DETECT}^{\mathcal{U}}_{\Pi, \widetilde{\Pi}} \Rightarrow \mathtt{true}] - 1$$

A subversion $\widetilde{\Pi}$ is *undetectable* if $\mathsf{Adv}^{\mathsf{det}}_{\Pi, \widetilde{\Pi}}(\mathcal{U})$ is negligible for any efficient $\mathcal{U}$.

Detectability measures the ability of $\mathcal{U}$ to detect an ASA. In the DETECT game, $\mathcal{U}$ must detect if it receives shares produced by the real algorithm Sh or by its subversion $\widetilde{\mathsf{Sh}}$. To capture the case of reverse engineering, we allow $\mathcal{U}$ to use the encryption key PK and the strategy $\mathcal{T}$ that are embedded in the code; of course, the detection algorithm does not have access to the decryption key SK.

Clearly, $\mathcal{B}$ wants a subversion to be undetectable. By allowing $\mathcal{U}$ full control over the secret, the shares and the embedded PK, our definition captures the strongest form of detectability.

Game DETECT$_{\Pi,\widetilde{\Pi}}^{\mathcal{U}}$
    $b \twoheadleftarrow \{0,1\}$
    $(\text{PK}, \text{SK}) \twoheadleftarrow \mathcal{K}$
    $b' \twoheadleftarrow \mathcal{U}^{\text{SHARE}}(\text{PK}, \mathcal{T})$
    return $(b = b')$

SHARE(s)
    if $b=1$ **then**
        $S \leftarrow \text{Sh}(s)$
    else
        $S \leftarrow \widetilde{\text{Sh}}(s, \text{ID}, \text{PK}, \mathcal{T})$
    return S

Game 1: DETECT (Detection Game)

Surveillance Advantage. Let $\Pi = (\text{Sh}, \text{Rec})$ be a secret sharing scheme and $\widetilde{\Pi} = (\widetilde{\text{Sh}}, \widetilde{\text{Rec}})$ a subversion of it. Let $\mathcal{B}$ (big brother) be an adversary that knows SK. The advantage of $\mathcal{B}$ to detect the ASA is defined as:

$$\text{Adv}_{\Pi,\widetilde{\Pi}}^{\text{srv}}(\mathcal{B}) = 2Pr[\text{SURV}_{\Pi,\widetilde{\Pi}}^{\mathcal{B}} \Rightarrow \textbf{true}] - 1$$

A scheme Π is *secure against surveillance* if $\text{Adv}_{\Pi,\widetilde{\Pi}}^{\text{srv}}(\mathcal{B})$ is negligible for any efficient $\mathcal{B}$ and for any $\widetilde{\Pi}$.

Surveillance advantage measures the ability of a scheme to be secure against ASAs. Clearly, $\mathcal{B}$ wants to break privacy. Our definition models the stronger property that $\mathcal{B}$ cannot even distinguish between the real algorithm Sh and its subversion $\widetilde{\text{Sh}}$; in particular, the subversion gives $\mathcal{B}$ no advantage to restore the secret by corrupting an unqualified set of parties. SURV game is similar to the DETECT game, except that the adversary $\mathcal{B}$ is given the secret key SK and cannot select the secret to be shared, but interrogates a SECRET oracle to obtain it.

Game SURV$_{\Pi,\widetilde{\Pi}}^{\mathcal{B}}$
    $b \twoheadleftarrow \{0,1\}$
    $(\text{PK}, \text{SK}) \twoheadleftarrow \mathcal{K}$
    $b' \twoheadleftarrow \mathcal{B}^{\text{SHARE}}(\text{PK}, \text{SK}, \mathcal{T})$
    return $(b = b')$

SECRET()
    $s \twoheadleftarrow \mathbb{F}^l$
    return s

SHARE()
    $s \leftarrow \text{SECRET}()$
    if $b=1$ **then**
        $S \leftarrow \text{Sh}(s)$
    else
        $S \leftarrow \widetilde{\text{Sh}}(s, \text{ID}, \text{PK}, \mathcal{T})$
    return s, S

Game 2: SURV (Surveillance Game)

We can now model a *negative result*: a scheme Π is susceptible to ASAs if there exists an undetectable subversion $\widetilde{\Pi}$ of Π that allows an efficient adversary $\mathcal{B}$ to have a non-negligible surveillance advantage (e.g. to break privacy). We call $\widetilde{\Pi}$ a *successful subversion* of Π. We show that this is the case for any LSSS in Sect. 3.3.

3.2 Share-Fixing

Inspired by the existing work on bit-fixing [15,16], we introduce share-fixing notions that we will later use to construct undetectable subversion of LSSS.

Let $\Pi = (\mathsf{Sh}, \mathsf{Rec})$ be a secret sharing scheme and $T \subset \{P_1, \ldots, P_n\}$. $\boldsymbol{S}_T$ is called a *share-fixing vector* for a secret $\boldsymbol{s}$ if there exists $\boldsymbol{S}$ a valid sharing of $\boldsymbol{s}$ such that $\boldsymbol{S}[i] = \boldsymbol{S}_T[i]$, for all $P_i \in T$. Intuitively, a share-fixing vector is a subset of ordered shares that can be expanded to a complete set of valid shares. A randomized algorithm $\mathcal{F}_\Pi$ that generates $\boldsymbol{S}_T$ for a given T and any secret $\boldsymbol{s}$ is called a *share-fixing source*. We will use $\mathcal{F}_\Pi(\boldsymbol{s}, T)$ to denote that $\mathcal{F}$ runs on input $(\boldsymbol{s}, T)$. Note that it is always possible to construct a share-fixing source by simply running $\mathsf{Sh}(\boldsymbol{s})$ and restrict its output to T.

For a share-fixing source $\mathcal{F}_\Pi$ and any secret $\boldsymbol{s}$, a randomized algorithm $\widehat{\mathsf{Sh}}$ that maps $(\boldsymbol{s}, \mathcal{F}_\Pi(\boldsymbol{s}, T))$ to a valid set of shares $\boldsymbol{S}$ such that $\boldsymbol{S}[i] = \boldsymbol{S}_T[i]$, for all $P_i \in T$ is called a *share-fixing extractor*. Intuitively, a share-fixing extractor expands the output $\boldsymbol{S}_T$ of the share-fixing source to a complete set of valid shares $\boldsymbol{S}$. Note that it is always possible to construct a share-fixing extractor by simply running $\mathsf{Sh}(\boldsymbol{s})$ repeatedly until $\boldsymbol{S}$ expands $\boldsymbol{S}_T$ (obviously, the construction is inefficient).

Extractor Detection Advantage. Let $\Pi = (\mathsf{Sh}, \mathsf{Rec})$ be a secret sharing scheme and $T \subseteq \{P_1, \ldots, P_n\}$. Let $\mathcal{F}_\Pi$ be a share-fixing source for (Π, T) and $\widehat{\mathsf{Sh}}$ a share-fixing extractor for $(\Pi, \mathcal{F}_\Pi)$. Let $\widehat{\Pi} = (\widehat{\mathsf{Sh}}, \mathsf{Rec})$ be the secret sharing scheme obtained from Π by replacing the sharing algorithm Sh with the share-fixing extractor $\widehat{\mathsf{Sh}}$. The advantage of an algorithm $\mathcal{U}$ to detect the share-fixing extractor is defined as:

$$\mathsf{Adv}_{\Pi, \widehat{\Pi}}^{\mathsf{e\text{-}det}}(\mathcal{U}) = 2Pr[\mathsf{E\text{-}DETECT}_{\Pi, \widehat{\Pi}}^{\mathcal{U}} \Rightarrow \mathsf{true}] - 1$$

A share-fixing extractor $\widehat{\mathsf{Sh}}$ is *undetectable* if $\mathsf{Adv}_{\Pi, \widehat{\Pi}}^{\mathsf{e\text{-}det}}(\mathcal{U})$ is negligible for any efficient $\mathcal{U}$.

Extraction detectability measures the ability of $\mathcal{U}$ to distinguish a share-fixing extractor $\widehat{\mathsf{Sh}}$ from the real Sh. In the E-DETECT game, $\mathcal{U}$ must detect if it receives shares produced by the real algorithm Sh or by a share-fixing extractor $\widehat{\mathsf{Sh}}$, given a share-fixing source $\mathcal{F}_\Pi$. Clearly, undetectability is impossible if the share-fixing source $\mathcal{F}_\Pi$ samples $\boldsymbol{S}_T$ from a distribution which can be efficiently distinguished from the distribution of the shares produced by the original sharing algorithm. But that is not always the case: in the proof of Theorem 1 we show that for any LSSS it is always possible to find a nonempty set T such that the distribution of the shares held by players in T is easy to simulate (i.e. it is the uniform one).

Game E-DETECT$_{\Pi,\widehat{\Pi}}^{\mathcal{U}}$
$b \leftarrow \{0,1\}$
$b' \leftarrow \mathcal{U}^{\text{SHARE}}$
return $b = b'$

SHARE$(s, \mathcal{F}_\Pi, T)$
if $b=1$ then
$\quad S \leftarrow \text{Sh}(s)$
else
$\quad S_T \leftarrow \mathcal{F}_\Pi(s, T)$
$\quad S \leftarrow \widehat{\text{Sh}}(s, S_T)$
return S

Game 3: E-DETECT (Extraction Detection Game)

Theorem 1. *Let $\Pi = (\text{Sh}, \text{Rec})$ be a LSSS. Then, there exists a nonempty unqualified set of players T of cardinality t such that if $\mathcal{F}_\Pi$ is an algorithm that maps $s \in \mathbb{F}^l$ to a uniformly random $S_T \in \mathbb{F}^t$, it holds that $\mathcal{F}_\Pi$ is a share-fixing source for (Π, T).*

Proof. Let $B \in \Gamma_{min}$ with $|B| = b$. By definition, we have that $rank(M_B) = b$ and $rank(\pi^d(M_B)) \geq b - l > 0$ with $\pi^d(M_B)$ denoting the last d columns of M_B. Let $t = rank(\pi^d(M_B))$, then there exists $T \subset B$ of cardinality t such that $rank(\pi^d(M_T)) = t$ (take as T a set of players that corresponds to nonempty proper subset of the indices of the rows that are linear independent in $\pi^d(M_B)$). Notice that T is trivially unqualified. The proof reduces to the existence of r such that $\pi^d(f) = r$ and $M_T \cdot f = S_T$, where both S_T and $\pi_l(f) = s$ are fixed. Let $M_T = (\pi_l(M_T) \mid \pi^d(M_T))$. Under this notation, $M_T \cdot f = S_T$ becomes $\pi_l(M_T) \cdot s + \pi^d(M_T) \cdot r = S_T$ or equivalently $\pi^d(M_T) \cdot r = S_T - \pi_l(M_T) \cdot s$, which always has a solution because the matrix $\pi^d(M_T)$ has full row-rank by construction.

Then, it follows that for any LSSS there exists a share-fixing extractor. More precisely:

Theorem 2. *Let $\Pi = (\text{Sh}, \text{Rec})$ be a LSSS and $\mathcal{F}_\Pi$ be a sharing-fixing source as defined in Theorem 1. Then, the algorithm $\widehat{\text{Sh}}$ in Construction 2 is an undetectable share-fixing extractor $\widehat{\text{Sh}}$ for $(\Pi, \mathcal{F}_\Pi)$.*

Proof. Let $\widehat{\text{Sh}}$ be defined as in Construction 2, where T is as in Theorem 1. $\widehat{\text{Sh}}$ computes r as a solution of $\pi^d(M_T) \cdot r = S_T - \pi_l(M_T) \cdot s$ (see Theorem 1). From the hypothesis, $\mathcal{F}_\Pi$ outputs S_T uniformly at random and hence $S_T - \pi_l(M_T) \cdot s$ is uniformly at random. Since $\pi^d(M_T)$ has full rank t, r is uniformly random in $\mathbb{F}^d$. Note that from the definition of LSSS, Sh also chooses r uniformly at random in $\mathbb{F}^d$. Once r is fixed, $\widehat{\text{Sh}}$ follows Sh exactly: forms the column vector f and computes $S = M \cdot f$. To conclude, the output distribution of $\widehat{\text{Sh}}$ equals the output distribution of Sh and the share-fixing extractor $\widehat{\text{Sh}}$ is undetectable with $\text{Adv}_{\Pi,\widehat{\Pi}}^{\text{e-det}}(\mathcal{U}) = 0$.

$\widehat{\mathsf{Sh}}(s, \mathcal{F}_\Pi, T)$

$\pi_l(\boldsymbol{f}) \leftarrow \boldsymbol{s}$

$\boldsymbol{S}_T \leftarrow \mathcal{F}_\Pi(\boldsymbol{s}, T)$ (T and $\mathcal{F}_\Pi$ as in Theorem 1)

solve $\pi^d(\boldsymbol{M}_T) \cdot \boldsymbol{r} = \boldsymbol{S}_T - \pi_l(\boldsymbol{M}_T) \cdot \boldsymbol{s}$ for $\boldsymbol{r}$, where $\pi^d(\boldsymbol{M}_T)$ and $\pi_l(\boldsymbol{M}_T)$
denote the last d columns, respectively the first l columns of $\boldsymbol{M}_T$
(if $t < d$, fix $\boldsymbol{r}$ uniformly at random from the set of possible solutions)

$\boldsymbol{f} \leftarrow (\boldsymbol{s}, \boldsymbol{r})^T$

$\boldsymbol{S} \leftarrow \boldsymbol{M} \cdot \boldsymbol{f}$

return $\boldsymbol{S}$

Construction 2: Share-fixing extractor $\widehat{\mathsf{Sh}}$ for $(\Pi, \mathcal{F}_\Pi)$

In the full version of the paper, the reader can find explicit examples of share-fixing extraction for $(\Pi, \mathcal{F}_\Pi)$ [12].

3.3 Shares Replacement Attack

We show that for any LSSS there exists an undetectable subverted version that efficiently allows surveillance. Let $\Pi = (\mathsf{Sh}, \mathsf{Rec})$ be a LSSS. Then, we construct a successful subversion $\widetilde{\Pi} = (\widetilde{\mathsf{Sh}}, \widetilde{\mathsf{Rec}})$ of Π such that an efficient adversary $\mathcal{B}$ learns the secret $\boldsymbol{s}$ or parts of it with probability 1.

Let $T = \{P_{i_1}, \ldots, P_{i_t}\}$, as defined in Theorem 1. The subverted sharing algorithm $\widetilde{\mathsf{Sh}}$ implements a share fixing source $\mathcal{F}_\Pi$ to generate a subset of shares $\boldsymbol{S}_T$ that allows $\mathcal{B}$ to compute the secret $\boldsymbol{s}$ (or a part of it), then expands $\boldsymbol{S}_T$ to a full set of shares $\boldsymbol{S}$ using the share-fixing extractor $\widehat{\mathsf{Sh}}$ from Theorem 2. To hide information about $\boldsymbol{s}$ into $\boldsymbol{S}_T$, $\widetilde{\mathsf{Sh}}$ uses a deterministic public key encryption scheme $(\mathcal{K}, \mathcal{E}, \mathcal{D})$ such that if m is sampled uniformly at random from $\mathbb{F}$ then $\mathcal{E}(m)$ is uniformly distributed in $\mathbb{F}$ and a pseudo-random generator PRG that maps a seed in $\mathbb{F}$ to an element in $\mathbb{F}^t$. It is natural to assume such constructions exist [17–22][2].

If $t \geq 2$, a random seed x is encrypted under the public key PK of $\mathcal{B}$ to obtain $\boldsymbol{S}_T[i_1]$, the first share in $\boldsymbol{S}_T$. Then, $\widetilde{\mathsf{Sh}}$ simply hides in the remaining components of $\boldsymbol{S}_T$ some of the components of $\boldsymbol{s}$ by adding them (using the addition operation from $\mathbb{F}$) to the pseudo-random values given by the output of the pseudo-random generator.

The subverted scheme is correct. Since $\boldsymbol{S}$ is a valid vector of shares, reconstruction and privacy hold by construction.

Theorem 3. *Let $\Pi = (\mathsf{Sh}, \mathsf{Rec})$ be a LSSS with $\gamma - l \geq 2$ (this assures $t \geq 2$). Then, its subversion $\widetilde{\Pi} = (\widetilde{\mathsf{Sh}}, \mathsf{Rec})$ defined in Construction 3 is successful and $\mathcal{B}$ learns the first $t - 1$ components of $\boldsymbol{s}$ with probability 1.*

---

[2] For [17] see Sect. X. *Avoiding Reblocking when Encrypting a Signed Message*.

$\widetilde{\mathsf{Sh}}(s, \mathrm{ID}, \mathrm{PK}, \mathcal{T})$
  $T \leftarrow \mathcal{T}$
  $\boldsymbol{S}_T \leftarrow \mathcal{F}_\Pi(s, T)$
  $\boldsymbol{S} \leftarrow \widehat{\mathsf{Sh}}(s, \boldsymbol{S}_T)$
  return $\boldsymbol{S}$

$\mathcal{F}_\Pi(s, T)$
  $x \twoheadleftarrow \mathbb{F}$
  $\boldsymbol{S}_T[i_1] \leftarrow \mathcal{E}(\mathrm{PK}, x)$
  $\boldsymbol{S}' \leftarrow \mathsf{PRG}(x)$
  for $j = 2 \ldots t$ do
    $\boldsymbol{S}_T[i_j] \leftarrow s[j-1] + \boldsymbol{S}'[j-1]$
  return $\boldsymbol{S}_T$

$\widetilde{\mathsf{Rec}}(\boldsymbol{S}_T, \mathrm{ID}, \mathrm{SK})$
  $x \leftarrow \mathcal{D}(\mathrm{SK}, \boldsymbol{S}[i_1])$
  $\boldsymbol{S}' \leftarrow \mathsf{PRG}(x)$
  for $j = 2 \ldots t$ do
    $s[j-1] \leftarrow \boldsymbol{S}_T[i_j] - \boldsymbol{S}'[j-1]$
  return $(s[1], \ldots, s[t-1])$

Construction 3: Subverted scheme $\widetilde{\Pi} = (\widetilde{\mathsf{Sh}}, \widetilde{\mathsf{Rec}})$ $(t \geq 2)$

Proof. In the subversion game, $\mathcal{B}$ extracts $\boldsymbol{S}_T$ from $\boldsymbol{S}$ accordingly to the embedded strategy $\mathcal{T}$ and then runs $\widetilde{\mathsf{Rec}}(\boldsymbol{S}'_T, \mathrm{ID}, \mathrm{SK})$ to get $(s'[1], \ldots, s'[t-1])$. If $s'[i] = s[i]$ for all $i = 1, \ldots, t-1$, then $\mathcal{B}$ outputs 0, otherwise $\mathcal{B}$ outputs 1. The surveillance advantage $\mathsf{Adv}^{\mathsf{srv}}_{\Pi, \widetilde{\Pi}}(\mathcal{B}) = 2|1 - 1/|\mathbb{F}|^t| - 1$ is clearly non-negligible.

In the detection game, $\boldsymbol{S}_T$ is indistinguishable from random in $\mathbb{F}^t$ by exploiting encryption and PRG security. Thus, by Theorem 2, $\mathcal{F}_\Pi$ is a share-fixing source and $\widehat{\mathsf{Sh}}$ is undetectable with $\mathsf{Adv}^{\mathsf{e\text{-}det}}_{\Pi, \widetilde{\Pi}}(\mathcal{U}) = 0$. Then, the detection advantage is $\mathsf{Adv}^{\mathsf{det}}_{\Pi, \widetilde{\Pi}}(\mathcal{U}) \leq \mathsf{Adv}_\mathcal{E}(\mathcal{U}) + \mathsf{Adv}_{\mathsf{PRG}}(\mathcal{U})$, which is negligible because of the security of the PRG and the assumption on the encryption scheme. We can therefore conclude that $\widetilde{\Pi}$ is a successful subversion.

The condition $\gamma - l \geq 2$ is satisfied by many commonly used sharing schemes. For example, it is satisfied by the additive scheme with more than 2 players and by Shamir's scheme with at least 2 privacy . See the full paper for a construction of an undetectable subversion that works when $t = 1$ [12].

4   Subversion Resilient Secret Sharing

4.1   Multi-input Secret Sharing

We aim to define (linear) secret-sharing schemes that stands against ASAs. To achieve this, we allow the parties to give input to the sharing algorithm: each player in $\mathcal{P}$ inputs a random element $u[i]$ to Sh, while the dealer inputs, as always, the secret s.

Let $\Pi = (\mathsf{Sh}, \mathsf{Rec})$ be a multi-input secret sharing scheme that consists of two algorithms such that:

- the *sharing algorithm* Sh receives as input from the dealer a secret **s** and as input from $\mathcal{P}$ a vector $\mathbf{u} = (\boldsymbol{u}[1], \ldots, \boldsymbol{u}[n])$, where $\boldsymbol{u}[i]$ is given by P_i and outputs a set of shares $\mathbf{S} = (\boldsymbol{S}[1], \ldots, \boldsymbol{S}[n])$; note that since we assume the existence of authenticated, private and subversion resilient channels between the sharing algorithm and the players, $\boldsymbol{u}[i]$ remains unknown to all parties, except P_i;
- the reconstruction algorithm Rec remains unchanged; it receives as input a set of shares **S** and outputs the secret **s** if the set of shares corresponds to a qualified set.

4.2 Definitions

Similar to Sect. 3, we introduce the definitions for detection and surveillance advantages. Notice that this section models the users' goal, so what we want is strong resilience: $\mathcal{B}$ can embed in the code the secret key SK, while $\mathcal{U}$ is not given access to the strategy and the public key. Even more, we disallow $\mathcal{U}$ to select the secret or the inputs of the players and give it access to a SECRET oracle, reflecting that $\mathcal{U}$ should detect surveillance for any input. To differentiate the games from the ones in Sect. 3 defined for strong subversion, we prefix them by R (which stands for *resilience*).

Detection Advantage. Let $\Pi = (\mathsf{Sh}, \mathsf{Rec})$ be a (multi-input) secret sharing scheme and $\widetilde{\Pi} = (\widetilde{\mathsf{Sh}}, \widetilde{\mathsf{Rec}})$ a subversion of it. Let $\mathcal{U}$ be a detection algorithm that is not given PK and $\mathcal{T}$. The advantage of $\mathcal{U}$ to detect an ASA is defined as:

$$\mathsf{Adv}^{\mathsf{r\text{-}det}}_{\Pi,\widetilde{\Pi}}(\mathcal{U}) = 2\Pr[\text{R-DETECT}^{\mathcal{U}}_{\Pi,\widetilde{\Pi}} \Rightarrow \mathbf{true}] - 1$$

A subversion $\widetilde{\Pi}$ is *undetectable* if $\mathsf{Adv}^{r-\mathsf{det}}_{\Pi,\widetilde{\Pi}}(\mathcal{U})$ is negligible for any efficient $\mathcal{U}$.

Clearly, honest players want all subversions to be easily detectable (even when they cannot perform reverse engineering). By restricting $\mathcal{U}$ from accessing anything except the interface of the sharing algorithm and allowing $\mathcal{B}$ to embed in the code the secret key SK, our definition captures a strong notion of detectability.

Surveillance Advantage. Let $\Pi = (\mathsf{Sh}, \mathsf{Rec})$ be a (multi-input) secret sharing scheme and $\widetilde{\Pi} = (\widetilde{\mathsf{Sh}}, \widetilde{\mathsf{Rec}})$ a subversion of it. Let $\mathcal{B}$ (big brother) be an adversary that knows SK. The advantage of $\mathcal{B}$ to detect an ASA is defined as:

$$\mathsf{Adv}^{\mathsf{r\text{-}srv}}_{\Pi,\widetilde{\Pi}}(\mathcal{B}) = 2\Pr[\text{R-SURV}^{\mathcal{B}}_{\Pi,\widetilde{\Pi}} \Rightarrow \mathbf{true}] - 1$$

A scheme Π is *secure against surveillance* if $\mathsf{Adv}^{r-\mathsf{srv}}_{\Pi,\widetilde{\Pi}}(\mathcal{B})$ is negligible for any efficient $\mathcal{B}$ and for any $\widetilde{\Pi}$.

SURV game is similar to the DETECT game, except that the adversary $\mathcal{B}$ is given the keys PK, SK and the strategy $\mathcal{T}$.

Game R-DETECT$_{\Pi,\widetilde{\Pi}}^{\mathcal{U}}$
   $b \twoheadleftarrow \{0,1\}$
   $(\mathrm{PK},\mathrm{SK}) \twoheadleftarrow \mathcal{K}$
   $b' \twoheadleftarrow \mathcal{U}^{\mathrm{SHARE}}$
   return $(b = b')$

SECRET()
   $s \twoheadleftarrow \mathbb{F}^l$
   $u \twoheadleftarrow \mathbb{F}^n$
   return s, u

SHARE()
   $s, u \leftarrow$ SECRET()
   if $b{=}1$ **then**
     $S \leftarrow \mathsf{Sh}(s, u)$
   else
     $S \leftarrow$
     $\widetilde{\mathsf{Sh}}(s, u, \mathrm{ID}, \mathrm{PK}, \mathrm{SK}, \mathcal{T})$
   return s, u, S

Game 4: R-DETECT (Detection Game)

Game R-SURV$_{\Pi,\widetilde{\Pi}}^{\mathcal{B}}$
   $b \twoheadleftarrow \{0,1\}$
   $(\mathrm{PK},\mathrm{SK}) \twoheadleftarrow \mathcal{K}$
   $b' \twoheadleftarrow \mathcal{B}^{\mathrm{SHARE}}(\mathrm{PK}, \mathrm{SK}, \mathcal{T})$
   return $(b = b')$

SECRET()
   $s \twoheadleftarrow \mathbb{F}^l$
   $u \twoheadleftarrow \mathbb{F}^n$
   return s, u

SHARE()
   $s, u \leftarrow$ SECRET()
   if $b{=}1$ **then**
     $S \leftarrow \mathsf{Sh}(s, u)$
   else
     $S \leftarrow$
     $\widetilde{\mathsf{Sh}}(s, u, \mathrm{ID}, \mathrm{PK}, \mathrm{SK}, \mathcal{T})$
   return S

Game 5: R-SURV (Surveillance Game)

We can now model a *positive result*: a scheme Π is resilient to ASAs if all possible subversions $\widetilde{\Pi}$ of Π are detectable. We call Π *subversion resilient*. We give a secure construction in this sense in Sect. 4.3.

4.3 Subversion Resilient Multi-input LSSS

Let $\Pi = (\mathsf{Sh}, \mathsf{Rec})$ be a LSSS. We construct $\Pi^* = (\mathsf{Sh}^*, \mathsf{Rec}^*)$ multi-input LSSS that cannot be subverted without violating detectability. Let PRG be a pseudo-random generator that maps a seed in $\mathbb{F}$ to an element in $\mathbb{F}^d$.

Theorem 4. *The multi-input LSSS $\Pi^* = (\mathsf{Sh}^*, \mathsf{Rec}^*)$ defined in Construction 4 is subversion resilient.*

Proof. First, we note that the shares by Sh^* are a deterministic function of $\boldsymbol{u}$ and $\boldsymbol{s}$. The detection algorithm simply takes the values $\boldsymbol{u}[i]$ produced by each player and verifies that the shares sent are the ones that would be produced by Sh^*. Any subversion with advantage δ must produce a different set of shares with probability greater or equal to δ (if at least one player is honest, $\boldsymbol{u}[1] \oplus \ldots \oplus \boldsymbol{u}[n]$ is uniformly random and hence $\boldsymbol{r}$ is uniformly random from the security of PRG). We can therefore conclude that $\mathsf{Adv}^{\mathsf{r\text{-}det}}_{\Pi^*, \widetilde{\Pi^*}}(\mathcal{U}) \geq \delta$ for any possible subversion $\widetilde{\Pi^*}$. $\quad\square$

$\mathsf{Sh}(\boldsymbol{s}, \boldsymbol{u})$ $\mathsf{Rec}(\boldsymbol{S}_B)$

$\quad \boldsymbol{r} \leftarrow \mathsf{PRG}(\boldsymbol{u}[1] \oplus \cdots \oplus \boldsymbol{u}[n])$ if B *is qualified* then

$\quad \boldsymbol{f}^T \leftarrow (\boldsymbol{s}, \boldsymbol{r})^T$ $\boldsymbol{s} \leftarrow \boldsymbol{N}_B \cdot \boldsymbol{S}_B$

$\quad \boldsymbol{S} \leftarrow \boldsymbol{M} \cdot \boldsymbol{f}$ else

$\quad$ return $\boldsymbol{S}$ $\boldsymbol{s} \leftarrow \perp$

                                  return s

Construction 4: Subversion Resilient Multi-Input LSSS $\Pi^* = (\mathsf{Sh}^*, \mathsf{Rec}^*)$

Discussion. Our modeling does not allow big brother to select the secret. Otherwise, if detection and surveillance games run independently, it is trivial for big brother to generate an undetectable subversion. Namely, it subverts the algorithm as follows: if the secret queried is a fixed element (e.g. an element deterministically computed from the key), then the subverted algorithm outputs specific shares, otherwise it generates proper shares. Note that this subversion is undetectable since the key is randomly sampled. This reflects the fact that in practice big brother can always embed hidden pattern which will allow surveillance when this pattern is matched by a secret. This could be used to notice unauthorized storage of sensitive documents by embedding a secret pattern within the documents and then subverting the algorithm to misbehave under this hidden pattern. The best that a user can therefore hope to do is to be able to detect whether or not the sharing could have allowed surveillance. Hence, we could allow big brother to input the secret in the surveillance game, but require that detection is continuously performed at runtime. In terms of games, this can be easily modeled by giving the subverted algorithm permission to select the secret, while detection algorithm runs on all this secrets and the corresponding outputs. It is immediate that our construction remains secure under this settings, since any subversion would require different shares than the ones that would have been produced by Sh with very high probability.

Acknowledgements. Samuel Ranellucci and Irene Giacomelli acknowledge support from the Danish National Research Foundation and The National Science Foundation of China (under the grant 61361136003) for the Sino-Danish Center for the Theory of Interactive Computation and from the Center for Research in Foundations of Electronic Markets (CFEM), supported by the Danish Strategic Research Council within which part of this work was performed. Partially supported by Danish Council for Independent Research via DFF Starting Grant 10-081612. Partially supported by the European Research Commission Starting Grant 279447.

Ruxandra F. Olimid was supported by the strategic grant POSDRU/159/1.5/ S/137750, "Project Doctoral and Postdoctoral programs support for increased competitiveness in Exact Sciences research" cofinanced by the European Social Found within the Sectorial Operational Program Human Resources Development 2007–2013.

References

1. Bellare, M., Paterson, K.G., Rogaway, P.: Security of symmetric encryption against mass surveillance. In: Garay, J.A., Gennaro, R. (eds.) CRYPTO 2014, Part I. LNCS, vol. 8616, pp. 1–19. Springer, Heidelberg (2014)
2. Subbiah, A., Blough, D.M.: An approach for fault tolerant and secure data storage in collaborative work environments. In: StorageSS, pp. 84–93 (2005)
3. Storer, M.W., Greenan, K.M., Miller, E.L., Voruganti, K.: Potshards - a secure, recoverable, long-term archival storage system. TOS 5(2), 5 (2009)
4. Wylie, J.J., Bigrigg, M.W., Strunk, J.D., Ganger, G.R., Kiliççöte, H., Khosla, P.K.: Survivable information storage systems. Computer 33(8), 61–68 (2000)
5. Cleversafe. http://www.cleversafe.com/ Accessed September 2015
6. Dyadic. https://www.dyadicsec.com/ Accessed September 2015
7. Young, A., Yung, M.: The dark side of "black-box" cryptography, or: should we trust capstone? In: Koblitz, N. (ed.) CRYPTO 1996. LNCS, vol. 1109, pp. 89–103. Springer, Heidelberg (1996)
8. Young, A., Yung, M.: Kleptography: using cryptography against cryptography. In: Fumy, W. (ed.) EUROCRYPT 1997. LNCS, vol. 1233, pp. 62–74. Springer, Heidelberg (1997)
9. Lampson, B.W.: A note on the confinement problem. Commun. ACM 16(10), 613–615 (1973)
10. Simmons, G.J.: The prisoners' problem and the subliminal channel. In: Advances in Cryptology, Proceedings of CRYPTO 1983, Santa Barbara, California, USA, pp. 51–67, 21–24 August 1983
11. Ateniese, G., Magri, B., Venturi, D.: Subversion-resilient signature schemes. In: Cryptology ePrint Archive, Report 2015/517 (2015). http://eprint.iacr.org/. (to apper in Proceedings of the 2015 ACM SIGSAC Conference on Computer and Communications Security)
12. Giacomelli, I., Olimid, R.F., Ranellucci, S.: Security of linear secret-sharing schemes against mass surveillance. In: Cryptology ePrint Archive, Report 2015/683 (2015). http://eprint.iacr.org/
13. Beimel, A.: Secret-sharing schemes: a survey. In: Chee, Y.M., Guo, Z., Ling, S., Shao, F., Tang, Y., Wang, H., Xing, C. (eds.) IWCC 2011. LNCS, vol. 6639, pp. 11–46. Springer, Heidelberg (2011)
14. Rogaway, P., Bellare, M.: Robust computational secret sharing and a unified account of classical secret-sharing goals. In: Proceedings of the 2007 ACM Conference on Computer and Communications Security, CCS 2007, Alexandria, Virginia, USA, pp. 172–184, 28–31 October 2007

15. Gabizon, A., Raz, R., Shaltiel, R.: Deterministic extractors for bit-fixing sources by obtaining an independent seed. SIAM J. Comput. **36**(4), 1072–1094 (2006)
16. Kamp, J., Zuckerman, D.: Deterministic extractors for bit-fixing sources and exposure-resilient cryptography. SIAM J. Comput. **36**(5), 1231–1247 (2007)
17. Rivest, R.L., Shamir, A., Adleman, L.M.: A method for obtaining digital signatures and public-key cryptosystems. Commun. ACM **21**(2), 120–126 (1978)
18. Naccache, D., Stern, J.: A new public-key cryptosystem. In: Fumy, W. (ed.) EURO-CRYPT 1997. LNCS, vol. 1233, pp. 27–36. Springer, Heidelberg (1997)
19. Chevallier-Mames, B., Naccache, D., Stern, J.: Linear bandwidth naccache-stern encryption. In: Ostrovsky, R., De Prisco, R., Visconti, I. (eds.) SCN 2008. LNCS, vol. 5229, pp. 327–339. Springer, Heidelberg (2008)
20. Bogdanov, A., Viola, E.: Pseudorandom bits for polynomials. SIAM J. Comput. **39**(6), 2464–2486 (2010)
21. Viola, E.: The sum of D small-bias generators fools polynomials of degree D. Comput. Complex. **18**(2), 209–217 (2009)
22. Wang, L., Hu, Z.: New sequences of period p^n and p^{n+1} via projective linear groups. In: Information Security and Cryptology - 8th International Conference, Inscrypt 2012, Beijing, China, Revised Selected Papers, pp. 311–330, 28–30 November 2012

Secure Set-Based Policy Checking and Its Application to Password Registration

Changyu Dong[1] and Franziskus Kiefer[2]([⊠])

[1] Department of Computer and Information Sciences, University of Strathclyde, Glasgow, UK
changyu.dong@strath.ac.uk
[2] Surrey Centre for Cyber Security, Department of Computer Science, University of Surrey, Guildford, UK
mail@franziskuskiefer.de

Abstract. Policies are the corner stones of today's computer systems. They define secure states and safe operations. A common problem with policies is that their enforcement is often in conflict with user privacy. In order to check the satisfiability of a policy, a server usually needs to collect from a client some information which may be private. In this work we introduce the notion of secure set-based policy checking (SPC) that allows the server to verify policies while preserving the client's privacy. SPC is a generic protocol that can be applied in many policy-based systems. As an example, we show how to use SPC to build a password registration protocol so that a server can check whether a client's password is compliant with its password policy without seeing the password. We also analyse SPC and the password registration protocol and provide security proofs. To demonstrate the practicality of the proposed primitives, we report performance evaluation results based on a prototype implementation of the password registration protocol.

1 Introduction

Policies are widely used in the context of computer systems and security. A policy defines a set of rules, over elements such as resources and participants in a system. It governs the system's behaviour with the goal of keeping the system safe. This allows organisations to ensure that the system is always in a well defined and secure state. Policies can be used in, for example, access control, authentication, trust management, firewalls and many other places.

While policies offer security protection, they sometimes raise privacy concerns [9]. This is especially true in large distributed systems such as the Internet where there is no pre-established trust relationship between parties interacting with each other. One typical scenario is that a server wants to restrict access to certain resources and defines a policy so that only those who satisfy this policy can access those resources. Often to evaluate this policy, the server needs to collect some information from a client and check the information against the policy. This information can be sensitive, e.g. credentials that should be kept

© Springer International Publishing Switzerland 2015
M. Reiter and D. Naccache (Eds.): CANS 2015, LNCS 9476, pp. 59–74, 2015.
DOI: 10.1007/978-3-319-26823-1_5

private or other personal information, thus the client may not want to release
it to the server. This privacy problem motivates the notion of secure set-based
policy checks (SPC) we are exploring in this work.

In an SPC protocol, a server holds a public policy based on some set-
theoretical semantics and the client holds a set that represents required information. After running the protocol, the server gets only a single bit information, i.e.
whether the client's set satisfies the policy, but nothing else about the client's
set. Thus SPC allows the server to securely check the policy while protecting
the client's privacy. SPC is a general building block that can be applied in many
scenarios to allow privacy preserving policy checking. One particular example
we will show in this paper is how to enforce password policies using SPC in
password registration. We will discuss more applications such as policy checks
for access control, friendship analysis and genome testing in Sect. 7.

Contributions and Organisation. In this paper, we propose secure set-based policy checking (SPC), a new privacy preserving protocol. SPC uses a generic and
expressive representation of policies based on the notion of sets, thus can be
applied in many policy based systems. We then show an efficient instantiation of
SPC based on linear secret sharing schemes and the Oblivious Bloom Intersection protocol. These two building blocks rely mostly on arithmetic operations in
small fields and symmetric cryptography. As a consequence, our SPC construction is very efficient. We believe the high efficiency will make SPC an attractive
choice for applications that require privacy preserving policy checking. While
SPC is interesting on its own, we further show how it can be used to solve real
world problems. We develop a new password registration protocol that uses SPC
so that the server can verify that a password chosen by a client is compliant with
a password policy without seeing the password. We analyse the security and provide proofs of both the SPC protocol and the password registration protocol. We
have implemented a prototype of the password registration protocol and evaluated the performance based on the implementation. The performance figure
shows that our protocol is much more efficient than the password registration
protocol (ZKPPC) from [16]. Furthermore, we sketch a few other application
scenarios in which SPC can be used.

The paper is organised as follows: in Sect. 2, we briefly review related work; in
Sect. 3, we introduce necessary preliminaries and cryptographic building blocks;
in Sect. 4, we show the SPC protocol; in Sect. 5, we show the password registration protocol; performance evaluation results are given in Sect. 6; in Sect. 7,
further applications of SPC are discussed; in Sect. 8, we conclude the paper and
discuss possible future work. In the appendix we sketch security proofs for the
protocols.

2   Related Work

Policy evaluation involving sensitive information has been a long established
problem. Duma et al. [9] argued that uncontrolled exposure of private information is a major risk for Internet users and showed that policy evaluation can

lead to undesirable information leakage. To counter the risk, one way is to define additional policies on the client side [25]. Those policies allow the release of sensitive information only if the server can convince the client that it is trustworthy. This approach does not prevent information from flowing out of the client's control, but rather provides some assurance that only trusted servers can see the information. Another approach is to use cryptographic protocols to allow privacy preserving policy checking. In this approach, information is not revealed and the server learns only the evaluation result. It is always possible to implement a protocol for policy checking using generic two party secure computation techniques such as garbled circuits [26] but the cost would be prohibitive. Some custom protocols have been built but they either work only for a certain policy language (e.g. [17]), or they are based on cryptographic primitives such as Ciphertext Policy Attribute-based Encryption (CP-ABE) that must have a trusted third party to generate keys for users based on their private information (e.g. [19]). In contrast, SPC can support a large class of policy languages and can work without a trusted party.

Password Registration. To ensure high password entropy, servers often have policies on password complexity, e.g. a valid passwords must be a mixture of lower case, upper case, numeric characters and at least of a certain minimum length. Usually the server has to see the client's password in plaintext in order to check whether the password is compliant with the policy. However, revealing its password to the server may not be a desirable option for the client (see Sect. 5 for a further discussion). Recent work by Kiefer and Manulis [16] proposed the first protocol that allows blind registration of client passwords at remote servers. In the protocol the client sends only a cryptographic password verifier during the registration procedure. Although the server never sees the actual password, it can still enforce password policies. This protocol provides a feasible solution that solves the aforementioned problems. However, password policy checking in [16] relies heavily on zero-knowledge proofs, which is a costly cryptographic primitive and thus renders the protocol impractical.

3   Preliminaries

3.1   Policies and Linear Secret Sharing

In this paper, we consider a set-theoretical representation of policies, i.e. *monotone access structures* [14]. A policy P defines a pair $(\mathcal{S}, \Gamma_{\mathcal{S}})$ where $\mathcal{S}$ is a set and $\Gamma_{\mathcal{S}}$ is an access structure over $\mathcal{S}$. The access structure is a subset of the powerset $2^{\mathcal{S}}$, i.e. the access structure contains zero to many subsets of $\mathcal{S}$. We say an access structure $\Gamma_{\mathcal{S}}$ is monotonic if for each element in $\Gamma_{\mathcal{S}}$, all its supersets are also in $\Gamma_{\mathcal{S}}$. We say a set $\mathcal{C}$ satisfies a policy P, written as $P(\mathcal{C}) = \texttt{true}$, if $\mathcal{C} \in \Gamma_{\mathcal{S}}$. A set $\mathcal{C}$ that satisfies P is called an authorised set. Access structures capture many complex access control and authorisation policies. For example, $\mathcal{S}$ can be a set of credentials and $\Gamma_{\mathcal{S}}$ defines a monotone boolean formula of subsets of credentials that are required for authorisation.

It has long been known that an access structure can be mapped to a linear secret sharing scheme (LSSS) [2,14] by choosing a secret and split it into a set of shares according to a given access structure Γ_S defined over S. Each share is then associated with an element in S. For convenience, we will use $\widetilde{s}_i \in S$ to denote that $\widetilde{s}_i$ is a share associated with some element s_i in a set S. The following holds for a LSSS: (1) any set of shares can reconstruct the secret if the elements associated with the shares form an authorised set, and (2) any set of shares does not reveal any information about the secret if the elements associated with the shares do not form an authorised set. There are generic mechanisms to generate shares from access structures and reconstruct secrets from shares, e.g. see [2,14]. Using a LSSS, checking whether a set satisfies a policy is equivalent to checking whether a set of shares can reconstruct the secret.

3.2 Oblivious Bloom Intersection

The Oblivious Bloom Intersection (OBI) protocol by Dong et al. [8] is executed between a client and a server on the respective sets C and S. Originally, the OBI protocol was designed for Private Set Intersection (PSI) such that at the end of the protocol, the client learns the intersection $C \cap S$ and the server learns nothing. As observed in [24], OBI can be extended to a Private Set Intersection with Data Transfer protocol. In this case, the server can associate each element $s_i \in S$ with a data item d_i. At the end of the protocol, for each element in the intersection the client also receives the corresponding data item from the server. The protocol can be described at a high level as follows: let the server hold a set $S = \{s_i\}$ and a data set $S_d = \{d_i\}$. The two sets are of equal cardinality and each (s_i, d_i) can be viewed as a key-value pair. The server generates a garbled Bloom filter G_S on S and S_d using [24, Algorithm 1]. The garbled Bloom filter encodes both S and S_d in a way such that querying the key $s_i \in S$ against G_S returns the data item d_i and querying $s_j \notin S$ returns a random string. Let the client hold a set C. The client encodes the set into a conventional Bloom filter [5] B_C. The client and the server run an oblivious transfer protocol using the Bloom filter and the garbled Bloom filter as inputs. As the result, the client receives a garbled Bloom filter $G_{C \cap S}$ that encodes the intersection $C \cap S$ and the data items associated with the elements in $C \cap S$. Then the client can query $G_{C \cap S}$ with each element $c_i \in C$. If c_i is in the intersection then there must be some $s_j \in S$ such that $c_i = s_j$ and the query result is d_j, the data item associated with s_j, otherwise the client gets a random string.

In this paper we use OBI so that the server can send a set of secret shares to the client based on the client's set C without knowing anything about C. Although in general we can use any PSI with Data Transfer protocol (e.g. [12]), we choose OBI here because of its efficiency. OBI is very efficient due to the fact that it relies mostly on hash operations. The performance can be further improved by the modifications proposed by Pinkas et al. [21]. Note that although Pinkas et al. also proposed a new PSI protocol based on hashtable + oblivious transfer in [21] that is more efficient than OBI, the new PSI protocol cannot be used in our case because it does not support data transfer.

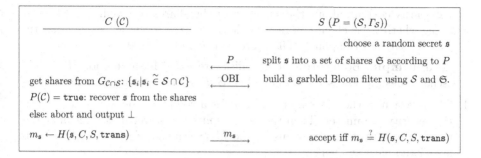

Fig. 1. Secure set-based policy checking

4   Secure Set-Based Policy Checking (SPC)

In this section we introduce a new protocol called secure set-based policy checking (SPC). In SPC, a server holds a public policy P as defined in Sect. 3 and a client holds a private set C. The goal is to allow the server to check whether C satisfies P without learning anything else about C.

Definition 1 (Secure Set-based Policy Checking, SPC). *Set-based policy checking is executed between client C with a private set C and server S with a public policy $P = (\mathcal{S}, \Gamma_S)$. Server and client retrieve $P(C)$ as result. We call a set-based policy checking protocol secure iff it fulfils the following three notions.*

1. *Correctness: Honest execution of the protocol with $P(C) = \mathtt{true}$ is accepted by the server with overwhelming probability.*
2. *Client Privacy: Server S learns nothing about the client set C other than $P(C)$.*
3. *Soundness: A client C holding C with $P(C) \neq \mathtt{true}$ has negligible probability in getting S to accept the SPC execution.*

Definition 1 says in particular that an SPC protocol provides both participants with the result of $P(C)$ while the server learns nothing about C more than it can infer from the result and public information.

4.1   SPC Instantiation

An overview of the proposed protocol is depicted in Fig. 1, using LSSS and OBI. Let $P = (\mathcal{S}, \Gamma_S)$ be the server's policy defined over its set $\mathcal{S}$ and C be the client's set. The two parties want to check $P(C)$, i.e. whether C satisfies P. In the protocol, the server first chooses a random secret and splits it according to the policy. Then the server builds a garbled Bloom filter and runs the OBI protocol with the client. At the end of the protocol, the client receives a set of shares $\{\mathfrak{s}_i | \mathfrak{s}_i \overset{\sim}{\in} \mathcal{S} \cap C\}$, i.e. each $\mathfrak{s}_i$ received is associated with an element in $C \cap \mathcal{S}$. If $P(C) = \mathtt{true}$, then the client can recover the secret from the shares it has received, because $C \cap \mathcal{S}$ must be an authorised set. If $P(C) \neq \mathtt{true}$ then the client will not receive enough shares that enable it to reconstruct the secret, and it learns nothing about the secret from the shares received. Therefore by checking whether the client can recover the secret, the server learns whether the client's set satisfies the policy. The protocol is defined as follows:

Public input: Both parties get a collision resistant hash function H, a LSSS scheme description, server policy $P = (\mathcal{S}, \Gamma_{\mathcal{S}})$, and security parameter λ.

1. The server first chooses a secret $\mathfrak{s}$ which is a random λ-bit string where λ is the security parameter. Then the server splits the secret into a set of shares $\mathfrak{S}$ according to its policy P using the LSSS scheme. Each share $\mathfrak{s}_i \in \mathfrak{S}$ is associated with an element in $\mathcal{S}$.
2. The server builds a garbled Bloom filter using $\mathcal{S}$ and $\mathfrak{S}$ as input such that each $s_i \in \mathcal{S}$ is a key and its associated secret share $\mathfrak{s}_i$ is the data value that is encoded in the garbled Bloom filter. The two parties then run the OBI protocol and the client using $\mathcal{C}$ as its input.
3. At the end of the OBI protocol the client gets a set of shares $\{\mathfrak{s}_i | \mathfrak{s}_i \overset{\sim}{\in} \mathcal{S} \cap \mathcal{C}\}$. If $\mathcal{C}$ satisfies policy P, then the shares obtained from the OBI protocol will allow the client to reconstruct the secret $\mathfrak{s}$, otherwise the client learns nothing about $\mathfrak{s}$ and aborts.
4. The client proves to the server that it knows $\mathfrak{s}$ by sending $m_{\mathfrak{s}} \leftarrow H(\mathfrak{s}, C, S,$ trans$)$ where $\mathfrak{s}$ is the secret, C and S are the identities of the two parties, and trans is the transcript of this execution. The sever checks whether $m_{\mathfrak{s}}$ is the same as it computed from its own state, if so then the client convinced the server that its set is compliant with policy P.

4.2   Security

Due to space limitations we only give lemmata and refer to the full version of this work for their proofs.

Lemma 1 (Correctness). *Let $\mathcal{C}$ and $\mathcal{S}$ denote sets from some universe and $P = (\mathcal{S}, \Gamma_{\mathcal{S}})$. Assuming the used OBI and LSSS algorithms are correct, then the SPC protocol from Fig. 1 is correct, i.e. honest execution of the protocol with $P(\mathcal{C}) = $ true is accepted by the server with overwhelming probability.*

Lemma 2 (Privacy). *Let $\mathcal{C}$ and $\mathcal{S}$ denote sets from some universe, $P = (\mathcal{S}, \Gamma_{\mathcal{S}})$ a policy and $f_{\mathsf{SPC}}(\mathcal{C}, \mathcal{S}) = (P(\mathcal{C}), P(\mathcal{C}))$. If the OBI protocol is secure and the LSSS is correct, the SPC protocol from Fig. 1 securely realises f_{SPC} in the presence of a malicious server or client.*

Lemma 2 proves that our SPC protocol ensures client privacy, i.e. does not leak any information about the client's set. We now give a lemma to show soundness of our SPC protocol that concludes the security analysis of the proposed SPC protocol.

Lemma 3 (Soundness). *Let $\mathcal{C}$ and $\mathcal{S}$ denote sets from some universe and $P = (\mathcal{S}, \Gamma_{\mathcal{S}})$ a policy. Assuming the used OBI and LSSS algorithms are secure and H is collision resistant, then the SPC protocol from Fig. 1 is sound in the presence of a malicious client, i.e. the server accepts the protocol with negligible probability if $P(\mathcal{C}) \neq $ true.*

5   A New Password Registration Protocol

Password-based authentication is the most common authentication mechanism for humans. Despite increasing attempts of replacing it from https://fidoalliance. org/ and others, something has yet to be proposed to fully replace password-based authentication. There are many reasons why it is so difficult to transition away from passwords, e.g., low-cost, user-experience and scalability. For those reasons, passwords are likely to remain as a major authentication method in the foreseeable future. The current approach for remote registration of client passwords requires the client to send its password in plaintext to the server, which stores a value derived from the password (e.g., a hash value or a verifier) in a password database. The problem with this approach is that the server sees the plaintext password and the client has no control over what the server will do with it. At first glance, revealing the password to the server seems to be harmless, but a closer look shows the opposite. Research shows that people tend to reuse the same password across different websites [7,11,13]. In this case, a compromised or malicious server can easily break into other accounts belonging to the same client after seeing the plaintext password. Even if the server is honest, the client still has to worry about whether its password is protected properly by the server. Ideally passwords should be stored in a secure form that is hard to invert such that an attacker gaining access to the password database still has difficulties to recover the passwords. Currently, password-based authentication mechanisms in literature assume the server does this, i.e. the server is trusted to store and protect the password properly and securely. However, increasing number of successful password leaks [6,20,22] suggests that many servers fail to do so. It is desirable if the server does not see the plaintext password during registration. However, this will make it difficult for the server to check whether the password chosen by the client is complex enough or long enough.

In this section, we present a new password registration protocol as an application of SPC. The protocol allows a client to register its password *blindly* on a server while still allowing the server to check whether the password is compliant with a password policy. In the protocol, rather than sending the password in plaintext to the server, the client sends blinded characters of the password. The blinded characters enable the server to check policy compliance using an SPC protocol. If a password is valid, the blinded characters are aggregated into a verifier that is stored on the server and used in future authentication protocols. Since the blinded characters are generated with proper randomness, the client can be assured that the password is secure even if the password database is compromised (modulo unavoidable offline dictionary attacks).

5.1   Passwords and Password Policies

In this paper, we consider a password to be in the basic format of a finite length string of printable characters (ASCII, UTF-8, etc.). We do not consider other forms of passwords such as graphical passwords [23]. It is a common practice to partition the password alphabet into character classes, e.g., upper case, lower case, symbols and digits. These character classes can be seen as disjoint subsets of the alphabet. A password policy is then defined to impose requirements for password complexity in terms of the minimum number of characters, minimal number of classes, and minimal number of characters in each class. For example, every valid password must have at least one character from each class and eight characters overall.

The connection between set-based policies from Sect. 3 and password policies is easy to see. Since password policies are defined in terms of thresholds and subsets over an alphabet that is a set of characters, they can be easily captured as access structures. It is also not difficult to see how SPC can be applied in the password policy checking setting, since a password can be seen as a set of characters. There is only a small gap: passwords are arbitrary strings and as such can have repeated characters. So the collection of characters in a password forms a multiset, not a set. The problem is that some policies might not be evaluated correctly using a multiset. For example, if a policy says "a valid password must have at least two symbols" and the client chooses "pa$\$w0rd", using SPC directly the password will be considered invalid, even though it does contain two symbols. This can be solved by pre-processing the characters in the alphabet and passwords.

The idea of password pre-processing is to convert each character in the password into a unique symbol by appending an "index" to the character. So if the character '\$' appears twice in a password, the first one becomes "\$1" and the second one becomes "\$2". Since \$1 and \$2 are two different strings, they are different elements when putting into a set. Therefore we can always convert a password into a set rather than into a multiset. The password pre-processing is performed by the client in the protocol. We define a function ψ for the client to convert a password (character string) into a set as follows. Let $\mathtt{pwd} = c_1, \ldots, c_x$ denote a password of x characters. Function ψ repeats the following procedure for $i = 1$ to x: first create a substring of the password from the first character to the ith character (inclusive), then count how many times the ith character appears in this substring, then append the counter to the ith character and put the result into a set. For example, "pa$\$w0rd" will be converted by ψ into $\{p1, a1, \$1, \$2, w1, 01, r1, d1\}$.

The alphabet pre-processing step is necessary because we use SPC to check whether a password satisfies a policy. The SPC protocol in Sect. 4.1 is based on set intersection. So we need to intersect the password set and the alphabet set in order to check the password policy. The password set now contains indexed characters like "p1", "\$2" rather than the original characters. The alphabet needs to be converted into a set with indexed characters as well, otherwise the intersection of the password set and alphabet set will always be empty. This step is done by the server as follows. Let $A = A_1 \cup \cdots \cup A_m$ be the alphabet where A_i is a character class (digits, lower case, etc.). The server transforms it into $\mathcal{S}$ based on the password policy P. For each A_i, in the policy there is a threshold t_i that says at least t_i characters from A_i need to appear in the password. If $t_i = 0$, then the server just skips all characters in this class A_i because they do not have to be checked. Otherwise, the server creates an empty set $\mathcal{S}_i$ and appends an index (from 1 to t_i) to each character in A_i, and puts the t_i copies of indexed characters into S_i. For example, if A_i contains lower case characters and $t_i = 2$, then $\mathcal{S}_i = \{a1, a2, b1, b2, \ldots, z1, z2\}$. The server only needs to put t_i copies of indexed characters to the set, regardless how many times the character may appears in clients' passwords. The union of $\mathcal{S}_i$ is the set S to be used later in password registration. This step only needs to be done once as long as the policy does not change.

5.2   The Password Registration Protocol

An overview of the proposed password registration protocol is given in Fig. 2. To simplify the presentation, we assume the protocol is run over a secure channel, e.g., implemented as a server authenticated TLS channel. The secure channel will address common network-based attacks such as replay, eavesdropping and man-in-the-middle. We also assume there is a session mechanism to prevent the server from learning more information about the client's password by aborting the protocol in the last step and reruning the protocol using other policies. The protocol has two phases, a setup phase and a policy checking phase. In the setup phase the client commits to its password, and each party blinds its set. The blinded sets are later used in the policy checking phase where the server checks the password policy with a secure SPC protocol (cf. Sect. 4) using the blinded sets. If the password satisfies the policy, the server stores a password verifier for future authentication purposes.

Public Input. The server publishes a password policy $P = (\mathcal{S}, \Gamma_{\mathcal{S}})$ where $\mathcal{S}$ is a set of size w transformed from alphabet A according to Sect. 5.1 and $\Gamma_{\mathcal{S}}$ is a threshold access structure defined over $\mathcal{S}$. Other public parameters consist of a security parameter λ, a pseudorandom function family f_k, and three hash functions $H_1, H_2,$ and H_3.

– **Setup Phase**
  1. The server runs KeyGen(λ): pick two large equal length prime numbers p and q according to λ, compute $N = p \cdot q$, choose at uniformly random $e \in Z_N$ such that there is an integer d that satisfies $e \cdot d = 1 \bmod \phi(N)$, and output (e, d, N). Then the server sends (e, N) to the client.
  2. The client computes a key $k = H_1(\text{pwd})$ where pwd is its password. The client uses the password pre-processing function ψ to generate $C \leftarrow \psi(\text{pwd})$. The client computes $r_i = f_k(i)$ using the pseudorandom function f on key k as well as $u_i = H_2(c_i) \cdot r_i^e$ for each $c_i \in C$. The result $(u_1, \ldots, u_v)$ is sent to the server, where v is the cardinality of C.
  3. For each $i \in [1, v]$ the server computes $u'_i = u_i^d$ and returns $(u'_1, \ldots, u'_v)$ back to the client.
  4. Upon receiving $(u'_1, \ldots, u'_v)$, the client creates an empty set $\hat{C}$ and for $i \in [1, v]$ puts $u'_i \cdot r_i^{-1} = (H_2(c_i))^d$ into $\hat{C}$. The server creates an empty set $\hat{S}$ and for $i \in [1, w]$ puts $(H_2(s_i))^d$ into $\hat{S}$, where $s_i \in S$ and w is the cardinality of S. The set $\hat{S}$ is partitioned into m subsets according to the character classes. The server also generates $\hat{P}$ from P by replacing S with $\hat{S}$.

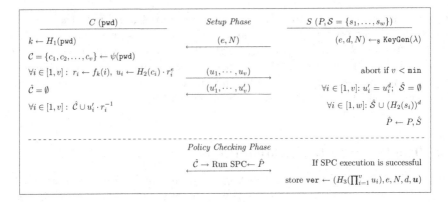

Fig. 2. Password registration using secure SPC

- **Policy Checking Phase.** This phase is essentially an execution of the SPC protocol using $\hat{C}$ and $\hat{P}$ as inputs. At the end of the SPC protocol the server learns whether the client's password satisfies the policy or not. If the SPC execution is successful, the server computes the hash of the product of the client's u_i values $h \leftarrow H_3(\prod_{i=1}^{v} u_i)$, and stores the password verifier $\mathtt{ver} = (h, e, N, d, \boldsymbol{u})$, where (e, N, d) is generated in the first step of the setup phase and $\boldsymbol{u} = \{u_1, \ldots, u_v\}$ is the vector of client "commitments".

Note that in the first step of the setup phase, $\mathtt{KeyGen}$ is essentially the RSA key generation algorithm with e chosen randomly rather than being a fixed small integer. In the protocol we use e as a salt so the verifiers will be different even if two users chooses the same password. Salting is also necessary in order to avoid rainbow table attacks where the attacker uses pre-computed values to speed up dictionary attacks.

Password Length Hiding (Enhanced Protocol). The protocol in Fig. 2 leaks the password length to the server. By counting the number of blinded characters u_i, the server learns the password length v. This is intentional because this peripheral information leakage allows the server to efficiently enforce the minimal password length in the policy. However, in cases where the password length is considered sensitive, it can be hidden from the server at small additional cost.

The client generates a set $C' \subseteq C$ and uses it in the setup phase to generate $\hat{C}$. C' contains only necessary characters to fulfil P. That is, the client first takes characters from C according to character class A_i and threshold t_i, and puts them in C'. If the size of C' is smaller than the minimal password length $\mathtt{min}$, the client pads it with other characters in C that are not in C' yet. In the setup phase, the client only uses characters in C' and obtains the corresponding $\hat{C}$. In this process, the server learns the size of C' and can check whether this is equal to the minimal password length required by the policy. The client then uses this $\hat{C}$ in the policy checking phase to convince the server about the password complexity. If the server accepts, all characters in $C \setminus C'$ that have not been sent to the server are put into an additional $u^* = r_{v+1}^{e} \cdot \prod u_i$ with $r_i \leftarrow f_k(i)$, $u_i \leftarrow H_2(c_i) \cdot r_i^{e}$ for

$c_i \in C \setminus C'$. This value u^* is then sent to the server and is multiplied with the other u_i values the server received in the setup phase. This product is then used to generate the verifier ver, i.e. ver $\leftarrow (H_3(r^e_{v+1} \prod^v_{i=1} u_i), e, N, d, \boldsymbol{u})$. Note that we require r^e_{v+1} as a multiplicand when computing u^*. Without this, the server could learn the client's password length when $C \setminus C' = \emptyset$ because the client would have nothing to send in this case.

5.3 Security Analysis

We now analyse the security of the password registration protocol. Note that in the password registration protocol, the two parties have different security requirements. For the server, privacy is not a concern since its input, the policy, is public. On the other hand, the server cares about the soundness of the protocol because an unsound protocol would allow a user to register an invalid password. For the client, privacy is the main concern. Soundness is trivial from the client's point of view. Since the policy is public, the client can check the policy by itself and can detect if the server cheats. We therefore refrain from using an over-complicated security definition and use the following comprehensible security model that is simpler. Let ver $\leftarrow \phi(\mathtt{pwd}, r)$ denote a password verifier, computed from a password $\mathtt{pwd}$ and some randomness r, and $\psi(\mathtt{pwd})$ a function to generate set C from password $\mathtt{pwd}$.

1. Privacy: A malicious server must not be able to retrieve more information from the protocol than the password verifier and the result of the policy verification. Furthermore, the verifier must not give a malicious server advantage in terms of password guessing.
2. Soundness: The server accepts a password verifier ver $\leftarrow \phi(\mathtt{pwd}, r)$ if and only if (i) the password is compliant with the server's policy, i.e. $P(C) = \mathtt{true}$ for $C \leftarrow \psi(\mathtt{pwd})$, and (ii) the verifier is uniquely defined by the password and some server known randomness, i.e. there exists no password $\mathtt{pwd}' \neq \mathtt{pwd}$ such that $\phi(\mathtt{pwd}', r) = \mathtt{ver}$ and it is not possible to find randomness $r' \neq r$ in polynomial time such that $\phi(\mathtt{pwd}, r') = \mathtt{ver}$.

Note that the strength of the privacy definition is in terms of dictionary attack resistance. This is an inherent problem of password-based protocols. All password-based protocols are susceptible to dictionary attacks if the server is considered as a potential adversary [18]. The reason is simple: for authentication purpose, the server holds a verifier derived from the client's password. An authentication protocol essentially takes the user's password as an input and compares it securely with the verifier. A malicious server can always run the protocol locally with itself playing the client's role using passwords enumerated from a dictionary. Since it is not realistic to assume any particular distribution of passwords, e.g. uniformly at random chosen passwords, the worst case security always depends on the hardness of dictionary attack and this is the strongest privacy notion possible. We will discuss what can be used to counter dictionary attack later in Sect. 5.4.

In the following we show that the enhanced version of the previously defined protocol satisfies those properties. Note that the simple version satisfies the same properties but in a weaker version, i.e. we would have to replace dictionary $\mathcal{D}_P$ in Lemma 4 with $\mathcal{D}_{P,|\mathtt{pwd}|}$, where $\mathcal{D}_{P,|\mathtt{pwd}|}$ denotes the dictionary that contains all passwords of size $|\mathtt{pwd}|$ that are policy compliant with respect to P. Note that H_2 has to be modelled as random oracle here in order to use the one-more RSA assumption [3]. For the other two hash functions H_1 and H_3 it is sufficient to assume collision resistance. Due to space limitations we refer to the full version for proofs.

Lemma 4 (Privacy). *If f_k is a secure pseudorandom function family, H_1 is collision resistant, and H_2 a random oracle, the enhanced password registration protocol offers privacy with respect to a malicious server and dictionary $\mathcal{D}_P$, which contains all valid passwords with regard to the server policy.*

Lemma 5 (Soundness). *The enhanced password registration protocol is sound with respect to a malicious client under the one-more RSA assumption if H_1 and H_3 are collision resistant hash functions, and H_2 a random oracle.*

5.4   Password-Authenticated Key Exchange for Our Protocol

In order to use a password registered with our protocol for authentication, we require an appropriate password-based authentication or authenticated key exchange (PAKE) protocol. In this section we show how to use the verifier **ver** in a common PAKE protocol. The approach we describe here is general and can be used with any PAKE protocol.

At the beginning of the authentication process, for a given client identifier the server retrieves the corresponding verifier $\mathtt{ver} = (h, e, N)$ from the database and returns (e, N) to the client. Using (e, N) and the password **pwd**, the client can recompute all u_i values and thus $h' \leftarrow H_3(u_{v+1}^e \cdot \prod_{i=1}^{v} u_i)$ as described earlier. Note that depending on the used PAKE protocol we have to ensure that H_3 maps into an algebraic structure, suitable for use with the PAKE protocol. Now client and server run any PAKE protocol on password hash h. The password hash h retains information about individual characters as well as the order of characters in the password. The first is easy to see since h is computed from the product of blinded characters in the password. To see the second, recall that each $u_i = H_2(c_i) \cdot r_i^e$ where $r_i = f_k(i)$, which is a pseudorandom number generated under a key k. The key k is derived from the password string $k \leftarrow H_1(\mathtt{pwd})$. To counter offline dictionary attack, we can use a standard key derivation functions such as PBKDF2 [15] to compute H_1 such that the key k is derived by repeatedly applying a pseudorandom function with a salt. The verifier generation algorithm also provides additional protection to offline dictionary attack. The computation involves a large random e as a salt and requires slow public key operations. The additional salt and work load make offline dictionary attack even more difficult.

Because of the way the verifier is structured, in the authentication the server needs to send an additional message, the RSA public key (e, N), to the client.

Table 1. Protocol performance (Running time in milliseconds)

	$(P1, 20)$		$(P2, 20)$		$(P3, 20)$		$(P2, 10)$		$(P2, 40)$	
	Total	Pol-ck	Total	Pol-ck	Total	Pol-ck	Total	Pol-ck	Total	Pol-ck
ZKPPC [16]	81,287	81,268	66,944	66,925	38,496	38,477	7,710	7,699	453,574	453,529
Our protocol	140	4	243	8	454	17	223	7	275	8
Improvement	580×		275×		80×		35×		1649×	

Often we can piggyback the messages in the PAKE protocol to avoid increasing communication round. For example, if we use the UC-secure PAKE protocol from Benhamouda et al. [4], the RSA public key (e, N) can be piggybacked on the server's message sent in the PAKE protocol. Thus we do not increase the round complexity and the protocol remains a one-round protocol.

6   Implementation and Evaluation

We implemented a prototype of our password registration protocol and measured the performance. To compare, we also implemented the password registration protocol (ZKPPC) proposed in [16]. Both implementations are in C and use OpenSSL 1.0.0 (https://www.openssl.org) for the underlying cryptographic operations. In the experiments, we set the security parameter to 80-bit. We used 1024-bit RSA keys and the SHA-1 hash function in our protocol. In the ZKPPC protocol we use the NIST P-192 elliptic curve. All experiments were run on a MacPro desktop with 2 Intel E5645 2.4 GHz CPUs and 32 GB RAM. Note in the experiments our implemenation only uses one CPU core and less than 1 GB RAM.

The running time of the protocols are shown in Table 1. We measured the running time with different policies and password lengths. The passwords are printable ASCII strings. The alphabet is partitioned into 4 classes: digits, lower case, upper case and symbols. We used three policies $P1, P2$ and $P3$ in the experiments, which require at least one, two and four characters in all character classes respectively. In the first row of the table, the pairs indicate the policy and the password length that were used in the experiment, e.g. $(P1, 20)$ means policy $P1$ is used and the password was 20 characters long. The table shows the total running time as well as the time spent on checking the policies (Pol-ck) in the protocol. As we can see, the performance of our protocol is much better than the ZKPPC protocol. The main difference comes from policy checking time. Policy checking in ZKPPC is done by using a zero-knowledge proof of set membership protocol. The cost of the zero-knowledge proof protocol is $6 \cdot n \cdot \sum_{i=1}^{n} \omega_i$ exponentiations, where n is the password length in the experiments, and ω_i is the size of character class to which the ith character in the password belongs. In our protocol, policy checking is done by using the SPC protocol and the cost is mainly the OBI protocol which is based on symmetric cryptography. The cost of the OBI protocol is $4.32 \cdot |\hat{S}| \cdot \lambda$ hash operations, where λ is the security parameter. More concretely, in setting $(P1, 20)$, the zero-knowledge proof based

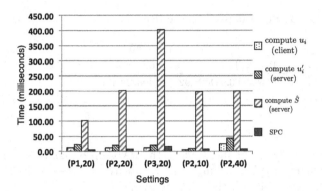

Fig. 3. Time breakdown. $(P1, 20)$ means policy $P1$ is used and the password was 20 characters long. Policies $P1, P2$, and $P3$ require at least one, two and four characters in all classes

policy checking requires around 200,000 exponentiations while our OBI based SPC requires only less than 33,000 hash operations.

We also show the running time for each step in our protocol (see Fig. 3). As we can see in the figure, the time for computing u_i and u'_i is linear in the password length, and the time for computing $\hat{S}$ and executing SPC is linear in the size of $\hat{S}$. The most costly step is in the setup phase when the server computes the encrypted version of the alphabet $\hat{S}$. A possible optimisation is to take this step offline. Since the computation of $\hat{S}$ does not depends on the client's password, the server can generate a random RSA key pair and pre-compute $\hat{S}$ before engaging with the client. The keys and pre-computed values can be stored together. Later when a client sends a registration request, the server can retrieve them and run the protocol. If this step is taken offline, then the online computation cost is small, usually no more than 100 ms in a typical setting.

7   SPC Applications

SPC can be used in many different scenarios. In the previous section we gave a detailed example of using SPC for password-policy checking on password registration. In this section we describe other use-cases of the primitive.

Policy checks for Access Control. In a role-based access control scenario [10] a user has to have a certain role in order to access a resource. In complex organisational structures it may be necessary to have a certain *combination* of roles in order to access a resource rather than just a single role. SPC can be used in this case to verify whether a client has necessary roles that allow it to access the resource. The server set $\mathcal{S}$ in this case contains secrets associated with each role S_i and the user's set $\mathcal{C}$ contains the client's secrets c_i. Access should be granted if and only if the SPC protocol is successful, i.e. the user can convince the server that he has all necessary roles.

Policies for Friendship Analysis. One popular application of set based protocols is friendship analysis. This test should determine whether two parties become friends or not depending on the number of mutual friends. SPC can be used in this scenario as a very efficient alternative while increasing privacy. Using SPC further allows to build subsets in friend sets, such as colleagues, family etc., which in turn makes the friendship-test more "accurate" while leaking as little information about the friendship relations as possible.

Genome Testing. Baldi et al. [1] propose protocols to perform privacy preserving genome testing, such as paternity tests. The tests can often be reduced to check a set of SNPs (Single Nucleotide Polymorphism) that are present in a patient's genome against some predefined sets of SNPs. Although it is not exactly policy checking, our SPC protocol can be used in this setting too.

8 Conclusion and Future Work

In this work we introduced a new notion called set-based policy checking (SPC), a new privacy preserving protocol. SPC allows a server to check whether a set held by a client is compliant with its policy, which is defined as a monotone access structure. At the end of the protocol, the server learns only a single bit of information, i.e. whether the client's set complies with the policy or not, and nothing else. We showcase the use of SPC in a new, highly efficient protocol for password registration that allows the server to impose a password policy on the client's password. To underline practicality and facilitate adoption we gave an efficient implementation of the password registration protocol together with an analysis. We further sketched other application scenarios of SPC.

Currently SPC is designed for public policies where the server makes its policy public to the client. Although in most real world policy-based systems, the policies are not considered private information, there are some scenarios in which the server may want to keep its policy private. As future work, we will investigate policy checking with hidden policies.

References

1. Baldi, P., Baronio, R., Cristofaro, E.D., Gasti, P., Tsudik, G.: Countering GAT-TACA: efficient and secure testing of fully-sequenced human genomes. In: CCS 2011, pp. 691–702. ACM (2011)
2. Beimel, A.: Secure schemes for secret sharing and key distribution. PhD thesis, Technion-Israel Institute of technology, Faculty of computer science (1996)
3. Bellare, M., Namprempre, C., Pointcheval, D., Semanko, M.: The one-more-rsa-inversion problems and the security of chaum's blind signature scheme. J. Cryptology **16**(3), 185–215 (2003)
4. Benhamouda, F., Blazy, O., Chevalier, C., Pointcheval, D., Vergnaud, D.: New techniques for SPHFs and efficient one-round PAKE protocols. In: Canetti, R., Garay, J.A. (eds.) CRYPTO 2013, Part I. LNCS, vol. 8042, pp. 449–475. Springer, Heidelberg (2013)
5. Bloom, B.H.: Space/time trade-offs in hash coding with allowable errors. Commun. ACM **13**(7), 422–426 (1970)

6. Dan Goodin. Hack of Cupid Media dating website exposes 42 million plaintext passwords (2014). http://goo.gl/sLcx4Y. Accessed 1 April 2015
7. Das, A., Bonneau, J., Caesar, M., Borisov, N., Wang, X.: The Tangled Web of Password Reuse. In: NDSS, The Internet Society (2014)
8. Dong, C., Chen, L., Wen, Z.: When private set intersection meets big data: an efficient and scalable protocol. In: ACM Conference on Computer and Communications Security, pp. 789–800 (2013)
9. Duma, C., Herzog, A., Shahmehri, N.: Privacy in the semantic web: what policy languages have to offer. In: 8th IEEE International Workshop on Policies for Distributed Systems and Networks (POLIC) 2007, pp. 109–118 (2007)
10. Ferraiolo, D.F., Kuhn, D.R.: Role-based access controls. CoRR, abs/0903.2171 (2009)
11. Florêncio, D.A.F., Herley, C.: A large-scale study of web password habits. In: 16th International Conference on World Wide Web, WWW 2007, pp. 657–666. ACM (2007)
12. Freedman, M.J., Nissim, K., Pinkas, B.: Efficient private matching and set intersection. In: Cachin, C., Camenisch, J.L. (eds.) EUROCRYPT 2004. LNCS, vol. 3027, pp. 1–19. Springer, Heidelberg (2004)
13. Gaw, S., Felten, E.W.: Password management strategies for online accounts. In: SOUPS 2006, vol. 149, ACM International Conference Proceeding Series, pp. 44–55. ACM (2006)
14. Ito, M., Saito, A., Nishizeki, T.: Secret sharing scheme realizing general access structure. Electronics and Communications in Japan (Part III: Fundamental Electronic Science) 72(9), 56–64 (1989)
15. Kaliski, B.: PKCS #5: Password-Based Cryptography Specification Version 2.0. RFC 2898 (Informational), September 2000
16. Kiefer, F., Manulis, M.: Zero-knowledge password policy checks and verifier-based PAKE. In: Kutyłowski, M., Vaidya, J. (eds.) ICAIS 2014, Part II. LNCS, vol. 8713, pp. 295–312. Springer, Heidelberg (2014)
17. Li, J., Li, N., Winsborough, W.H.: Automated trust negotiation using cryptographic credentials. In: CCS 2005, pp. 46–57. ACM (2005)
18. Menezes, A., van Oorschot, P.C., Vanstone, S.A.: Handbook of Applied Cryptography. CRC Press, Boca Raton (1996)
19. Nabeel, M., Bertino, E.: Privacy-preserving fine-grained access control in public clouds. IEEE Data Eng. Bull. 35(4), 21–30 (2012)
20. Cubrilovic, N.: RockYou hack: from bad to worse (2014). http://goo.gl/u91YHV. Accessed on 1 April 2015
21. Pinkas, B., Schneider, T., Zohner, M.: Faster private set intersection based on OT extension. In: USENIX 2014, pp. 797–812 (2014)
22. Reuters. Trove of Adobe user data found on Web after breach: security firm (2014). http://goo.gl/cpZn6B. Accessed 1 April 2015
23. Suo, X., Zhu, Y., Owen, G.S.: Graphical passwords: a survey. In: ACSAC 2005, pp. 463–472 (2005)
24. Wen, Z., Dong, C.: Efficient protocols for private record linkage. In: SAC 2014, pp. 1688–1694. ACM (2014)
25. Winsborough, W.H., Li, N.: Towards practical automated trust negotiation. In: 3rd International Workshop on Policies for Distributed Systems and Networks (POLICY 2002), Monterey, CA, USA, pp. 92–103 (June 5–7, 2002)
26. Yao, A.C.: Protocols for secure computations (extended abstract). In: 23rd Annual Symposium on Foundations of Computer Science, pp. 160–164 (1982)

SEPM: Efficient Partial Keyword Search on Encrypted Data

Yutaka Kawai[1]([✉]), Takato Hirano[1], Yoshihiro Koseki[1], and Tatsuji Munaka[2]

[1] Mitsubishi Electric Corporation, Kamakura, Japan
Kawai.Yutaka@da.MitsubishiElectric.co.jp,
Hirano.Takato@ay.MitsubishiElectric.co.jp,
Koseki.Yoshihiro@ak.MitsubishiElectric.co.jp
[2] Tokai University, Tokyo, Japan

Abstract. Searchable encryption (SE) in the public key setting is that anyone can encrypt data by using a public key and store this ciphertext on a server, and a client who has the corresponding secret key can generate search queries (say, trapdoor) in order to search for the encrypted data on the server. In this paper, we focus on *partial matching* in the public key setting in order to enhance usability. We call this "Searchable Encryption with Partial Matching (SEPM)". Few previous works of SEPM employed a strategy that a client generates ciphertexts or trapdoors on all similar words closely related to a keyword in order to realize the partial matching functionality. This means that the client has to generate trapdoors for all partial matching varieties. Therefore, this approach is inefficient due to its trapdoor size. In order to overcome this disadvantage, we introduce a new concept of *trapdoor conversion*. When a client searches for ciphertexts on the server, he generates only *one* trapdoor tk and sends it to the server. Then, the server generates trapdoors related to tk by using a conversion secret key which is generated in the setup phase and stored in the server, and searches ciphertexts from them. Intuitively, this trapdoor generation process is achieved by moving locations of characters included in a searching keyword. In order to realize this situation, we introduce a new cryptographic primitive, inner-product encryption with trapdoor conversion (IPE-TC). We propose a specific construction of IPE-TC based on *generalized inner-product encryption* and *basis conversion technique* on a dual pairing vector spaces approach.

1 Introduction

1.1 Background

Searchable Encryption in the Public Key Setting. Recently, it is expected that cloud services such as storing data on a remote third-party provider give high data availability and reduce IT infrastructure costs for a company. From a security point of view, company's sensitive data should be encrypted. On the other hand, keyword searching for storing data on the cloud is indispensable

© Springer International Publishing Switzerland 2015
M. Reiter and D. Naccache (Eds.): CANS 2015, LNCS 9476, pp. 75–91, 2015.
DOI: 10.1007/978-3-319-26823-1_6

from an availability point of view. However, data encrypting and keyword searching are incompatible in general, since keyword searching for encrypted data is intractable. A naive approach of "decrypt-and-search" is insufficient because of disclosure of decryption keys to malicious administrators or softwares on the cloud. As a solution for these problems, *searchable encryption (SE)* has been proposed.

There are two types of searchable encryption, symmetric-key type [7,8,11,21] and public-key type [1,4,6,19]. In this paper, we discuss and describe searchable encryption schemes in the public key setting. In the enrollment phase, a registrant encrypts a keyword and generates a ciphertext ct by using the public key. The ciphertext ct is stored in the server (or database). In the search phase, a client generates a *trapdoor* tk by using the secret key in order to retrieve ciphertexts which contain specific keywords. The server can search ciphertexts from the trapdoor tk without any loss of keyword confidentiality.

There are many previous works in this research field. Boneh et al. in [4] formalized searchable encryption in the public key setting and constructed a specific scheme. Abdalla et al. in [1] pointed out that searchable encryption in the public key setting is related to anonymous identity based encryption, and showed a generic construction from it. SE with conjunctive equality matching has been proposed (e.g. in [6]).

Partial Matching: Naive Methods and These Problems. Many previous works of SE mainly focus on *equality* matching functionality. However, in some practical situation, *partial* matching functionality is required. For example, we consider a situation that some client would like to search a family name for a database whose record contains a ciphertext of all names (i.e. first, middle, and family names are encrypted simultaneously). Then, the client cannot search for the database from only family names. In order to overcome this problem, the following two naive methods have been studied in previous SE.

The first method is to encrypt separately every one character (or word) included in a keyword. In this paper, we call this naive method Split-then-Enc. In the enrollment phase, a keyword is divided into a character one by one, and each character is encrypted and stored in the server. In the search phase, a keyword is divided as same as the enrollment phase and trapdoors are generated for each character. The trapdoors are sent to the server, and the server checks whether the stored ciphertexts and the trapdoors are partially matched by using equality checking.

However, in this method, the server can obtain some information from the search process. For example, we consider a situation that the keyword string "ABC" is encrypted and stored in the server. In Split-then-Enc method, the server stores ciphertexts of "A", "B", and "C", respectively. If the client search "BD" for the ciphertexts, he generates trapdoors of "B" and "D", respectively. Then, the server does equality checking for each ciphertext and each trapdoor, and learn that one of two trapdoors is matched (i.e. the ciphertext of "B" and the trapdoor of "B" are matched). On the other hand, this approach has a security issue: in addition to "BD", the server can also search "DB" for the ciphertexts.

We call this kind of keyword permutation attacks. This functionality is not desirable property in SE. Therefore, the first method has a problem of security.

The second method is to use hidden vector encryption (HVE) or inner-product encryption (IPE). Since HVE and IPE are known as an extension of (anonymous) identity based encryption, HVE and IPE can be applied to searchable encryption from the result of [1]. As a nice functionality, SE schemes constructed from HVE or IPE can use wild-card "*" which is a special symbol and matches any character. Although the wild-card searching supports for securely generating trapdoors for partial matching, the trapdoor size linearly depends on the number of partial matching patterns. For example, when the client search "AB" for ciphertexts of four characters, he has to generate trapdoors of "AB**", "*AB*", and "**AB". Therefore, the second method has an efficiency problem on trapdoor size.

On the other hand, SE schemes with partial matching in the symmetric-key setting have been proposed [7,11]. Li et al. focused on the same approach as the second method, and proposed a simple SE scheme with fuzzy matching including partial matching by enumerating and encrypting all similar words to a keyword [11]. Chase and Shen proposed an SE scheme with partial matching from another approach that employs a data structure obtained from a suffix tree to reduce the ciphertext size [7]. However, the same efficiency problem as the second method is met in these schemes, that is, the trapdoor sizes of [7,11] are not small while they are based on very efficient symmetric-key primitives.

Motivation: Secure Trapdoor Conversion by the Server. Our main motivation is to reduce the trapdoor size in the case of partial matching. For that purpose, we introduce a new concept, trapdoor conversion for searchable encryption, and formalize searchable encryption with partial matching (SEPM). We show the framework of SEPM in Fig. 1. In our SEPM, trapdoors can be transformed by the server, in contrast to the previous works. From a security point of view, the SE system is **not** secure if the server can transform freely. In our SEPM, we study a limited transformation that the server can change only the search position of trapdoors. That is to say, when partial matching is executed, the client generates only one trapdoor and the server generates valid trapdoors by shifting (converting) the trapdoor. While this approach increases server-side computing cost, this approach is reasonable since the server has huge computational resource in general and client-side computing cost can be reduced dramatically.

On the other hand, this transformation is a powerful operation, and therefore should not be execute publicly. Thus, we naturally suppose that the server has a secret key to convert trapdoors. We call this secret key "conversion secret key csk". As a security requirement, the server cannot obtain any information on keyword from ciphertexts and trapdoors but a partial matching search by converting valid trapdoors. We note that off-line keyword attacks is still possible like previous public-key SE schemes, especially when the server can do more than one guessing with the help of the trapdoor conversion. Yet, being a public-key scheme, our security definition does not treat off-line keywords guessing attack. SE with registered off-line keyword guessing attack is proposed in [22].

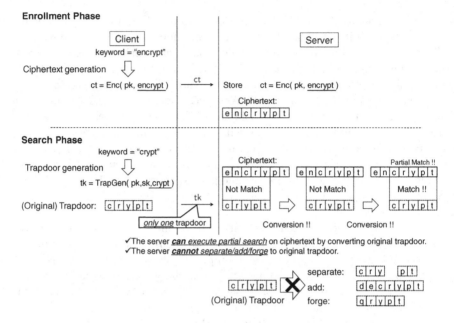

Fig. 1. Overview of our searchable encryption with partial matching

1.2 Key Techniques

In order to construct a specific SEPM scheme, we propose a new inner-product encryption scheme by combining unbounded generalized IPE [16] and basis conversion technique.

Unbounded Generalized Inner-Product Encryption [16]: The notions of inner-product encryption (IPE) introduced by Katz, Sahai and Waters [10] constitute an advanced class of encryption, and provide more flexible and fine-grained functionalities in sharing and distributing sensitive data than traditional encryption as well as identity-based encryption (IBE) [2,5,6,9,17,18,20,23]. The parameters for IPE are expressed as vectors $\vec{x}$ and $\vec{v}$, where the relation between $\vec{v}$ and $\vec{x}$ holds, i.e., a secret key with $\vec{v}$ can decrypt a ciphertext with $\vec{x}$, iff $\vec{v} \cdot \vec{x} = 0$. (Here, $\vec{v} \cdot \vec{x}$ denotes the standard inner-product.)

In some applications of IPE, the parameters for encryption are required to be hidden from ciphertexts. To capture the security requirement, Katz, Sahai and Waters [10] introduced *attribute-hiding* (based on the same notion for hidden vector encryption by Boneh and Waters [6]), which is a requirement for IPE stronger than the basic payload-hiding security requirement. Roughly speaking, attribute-hiding requires that a ciphertext conceals, in addition to its plaintext, an associated parameter, while payload-hiding only requires that a ciphertext conceals only its plaintext. Since a keyword can be set as an attribute in IPE, the attribute-hiding security is an important requirement to construct searchable encryption.

In [16], unbounded generalized IPE was proposed. A predicate vector and an attribute vector in unbounded generalized IPE are defined as $\vec{x} := \{(t, x_t) \mid t \in I_{\vec{x}}, \ x_t \in \mathbb{F}_q, \#I_{\vec{x}} = n\}$ and $\vec{v} := \{(t, v_t) \mid t \in I_{\vec{v}}, \ v_t \in \mathbb{F}_q, \#I_{\vec{v}} = n'\}$, respectively. In the case of $I_{\vec{v}} \subseteq I_{\vec{x}}$, a ciphertext of an attribute vector $\vec{x}$ can be decrypt by using a decryption key of a predicate vector $\vec{v}$ iff $\Sigma_{t \in I_{\vec{v}}} v_t x_t = 0$. That is to say, the size of decryption (trapdoor) key does not depend on $|I_{\vec{x}}|$. In order to realize the above properties, *indexing* method is developed on dual system encryption and dual pairing vector spaces (DPVS, see Sect. 2.2).

Basis Conversion Technique on DPVS. An unbounded generalized IPE is very useful for SEPM, since the client generates parameters for only $t \in I_{\vec{v}}$ that he wants to search. However, the trapdoor size still depends on the number of partial matching varieties as same as HVE, since indexes t is embedded to $\boldsymbol{k}_t$ and cannot be changed. In order to transform only indexes t of a predicate vector $\vec{v} = \{(t, v_t)\}$, we use a trick based on the DPVS framework introduced in [14], where a ciphertext $\boldsymbol{c}_{\vec{x}}$ and a decryption key $\boldsymbol{k}_{\vec{v}}$ are encoded on a random basis $\mathbb{B} := (\boldsymbol{b}_i)$ and its dual basis $\mathbb{B}^* := (\boldsymbol{b}_i^*)$.

From the property of DPVS, we can set a new basis $\mathbb{B}_{i+1} := \mathbb{B}_i \cdot W_i$ where $\mathbb{B}_i$ is a basis of DPVS and W_i is a random matrix. By flexibly using random matrices W_i, a (original) trapdoor generated from a keyword can be transformed into its related trapdoors that the positions of characters included in the keyword are different from those of the original trapdoor. In our SEPM, $W_1, \ldots, W_n$ are chosen randomly and set $\{W_i\}_{i=1,\ldots,n}$ to a conversion secret key, csk, in setup algorithm.

1.3 Our Contributions

In order to present efficient SEPM, this paper introduces a new notion of IPE, *inner-product encryption with trapdoor conversion* (IPE-TC), which is ordinary IPE with trapdoor conversion mechanism, TrapConv algorithm. TrapConv takes a trapdoor, a conversion secret key, and an additional conversion information as input, and outputs a new trapdoor. In more detail, TrapConv can change only index t of a predicate vector $\vec{v} = \{(t, v_t) \mid t \in I_{\vec{v}}\}$. We formulate such a syntax and a security definition of IPE-TC, and present a specific construction based on the unbounded generalized IPE and the basis conversion technique on DPVS mentioned in the subsection.

We give a comparison among our scheme and the previous SEPM schemes (Split-then-Enc, HVE in [19] and IPE in [16]) in Table 1. In HVE and IPE, the trapdoor size linearly depends on the number of partial matching patterns. On the other hand, the trapdoor size of the proposed scheme depends on only the size of keywords. However, since in our scheme, a trapdoor should be converted by using csk in order execute partially search. In our specific scheme, this conversion is a natural multiplication of a row vector and a matrix in the finite filed (see Sect. 4.2). Then, the conversion efficiency is sufficiently efficient compared to the matching efficiency.

Table 1. Comparison among our SEPM scheme and previous SEPM scheme, where n, m, l represent the maximum number of characters (or words) for enrolled keywords, the number of characters (or words) for searched keywords, and the number of partial matching varieties for keywords, respectively. Usually, $l > n > m$.

	Trapdoor size	Security against permutation	Search efficiency
Split-then-Enc	$O(m)$	no (see Sect. 1.1)	$O(m)$
HVE in [19]	$O(ml)$	yes	$O(n)$
IPE in [16]	$O(ml)$	yes	$O(m)$
Our SE	$O(m)$	yes	$O(ml)$

2 Preliminaries

2.1 Notations

When A is a random variable or distribution, $y \xleftarrow{\mathsf{R}} A$ denotes that y is randomly selected from A according to its distribution. When A is a set, $y \xleftarrow{\mathsf{U}} A$ denotes that y is uniformly selected from A. We denote the finite field of order q by $\mathbb{F}_q$, and $\mathbb{F}_q \setminus \{0\}$ by $\mathbb{F}_q^\times$. A vector symbol denotes a vector representation over $\mathbb{F}_q$, e.g., $\vec{x}$ denotes $(x_1, \ldots, x_n) \in \mathbb{F}_q^n$. For two vectors $\vec{x} = (x_1, \ldots, x_n)$ and $\vec{v} = (v_1, \ldots, v_n)$, $\vec{x} \cdot \vec{v}$ denotes the inner-product $\sum_{i=1}^n x_i v_i$. The vector $\vec{0}$ is abused as the zero vector in $\mathbb{F}_q^n$ for any n. X^{T} denotes the transpose of matrix X. A bold face letter denotes an element of vector space $\mathbb{V}$, e.g., $\boldsymbol{x} \in \mathbb{V}$. When $\boldsymbol{b}_i \in \mathbb{V}$ ($i = 1, \ldots, n$), $\mathrm{span}\langle \boldsymbol{b}_1, \ldots, \boldsymbol{b}_n \rangle \subseteq \mathbb{V}$ (resp. $\mathrm{span}\langle \vec{x}_1, \ldots, \vec{x}_n \rangle$) denotes the subspace generated by $\boldsymbol{b}_1, \ldots, \boldsymbol{b}_n$ (resp. $\vec{x}_1, \ldots, \vec{x}_n$). For bases $\mathbb{B} := (\boldsymbol{b}_1, \ldots, \boldsymbol{b}_N)$ and $\mathbb{B}^* := (\boldsymbol{b}_1^*, \ldots, \boldsymbol{b}_N^*)$, $(x_1, \ldots, x_N)_\mathbb{B} := \sum_{i=1}^N x_i \boldsymbol{b}_i$ and $(y_1, \ldots, y_N)_{\mathbb{B}^*} := \sum_{i=1}^N y_i \boldsymbol{b}_i^*$. $\vec{e}_j$ denotes the canonical basis vector $(\overbrace{0 \cdots 0}^{j-1}, 1, \overbrace{0 \cdots 0}^{n-j}) \in \mathbb{F}_q^n$. $GL(n, \mathbb{F}_q)$ denotes the general linear group of degree n over $\mathbb{F}_q$.

2.2 Dual Pairing Vector Spaces (DPVS)

Definition 1. *"Symmetric bilinear pairing groups"* $(q, \mathbb{G}, \mathbb{G}_T, G, e)$ *are a tuple of a prime* q, *cyclic additive group* $\mathbb{G}$ *and multiplicative group* $\mathbb{G}_T$ *of order* q, $G \neq 0 \in \mathbb{G}$, *and a polynomial-time computable non-degenerate bilinear pairing* $e : \mathbb{G} \times \mathbb{G} \to \mathbb{G}_T$ *i.e.,* $e(sG, tG) = e(G, G)^{st}$ *and* $e(G, G) \neq 1$. *Let* $\mathcal{G}_{\mathsf{bpg}}$ *be an algorithm that takes input* 1^λ *and outputs a description of bilinear pairing groups* $(q, \mathbb{G}, \mathbb{G}_T, G, e)$ *with security parameter* λ.

In this paper, we concentrate on the symmetric version of dual pairing vector spaces [12,13], constructed by using symmetric bilinear pairing groups.

Definition 2. *"Dual pairing vector spaces (DPVS)"* $(q, \mathbb{V}, \mathbb{G}_T, \mathbb{A}, e)$ *by a direct product of symmetric pairing groups* $(q, \mathbb{G}, \mathbb{G}_T, G, e)$ *are a tuple of prime* q,

N-dimensional vector space $\mathbb{V} := \overbrace{\mathbb{G} \times \cdots \times \mathbb{G}}^{N}$ over $\mathbb{F}_q$, cyclic group $\mathbb{G}_T$ of order q, canonical basis $\mathbb{A} := (\boldsymbol{a}_1, \ldots, \boldsymbol{a}_N)$ of $\mathbb{V}$, where $\boldsymbol{a}_i := (\overbrace{0, \ldots, 0}^{i-1}, G, \overbrace{0, \ldots, 0}^{N-i})$, and pairing $e : \mathbb{V} \times \mathbb{V} \to \mathbb{G}_T$. The pairing is defined by $e(\boldsymbol{x}, \boldsymbol{y}) := \prod_{i=1}^{N} e(G_i, H_i) \in \mathbb{G}_T$ where $\boldsymbol{x} := (G_1, \ldots, G_N) \in \mathbb{V}$ and $\boldsymbol{y} := (H_1, \ldots, H_N) \in \mathbb{V}$. This is non-degenerate bilinear i.e., $e(s\boldsymbol{x}, t\boldsymbol{y}) = e(\boldsymbol{x}, \boldsymbol{y})^{st}$ and if $e(\boldsymbol{x}, \boldsymbol{y}) = 1$ for all $\boldsymbol{y} \in \mathbb{V}$, then $\boldsymbol{x} = \vec{0}$. For all i and j, $e(\boldsymbol{a}_i, \boldsymbol{a}_j) = e(G, G)^{\delta_{i,j}}$ where $\delta_{i,j} = 1$ if $i = j$, and 0 otherwise, and $e(G, G) \neq 1 \in \mathbb{G}_T$. DPVS generation algorithm $\mathcal{G}_{\mathsf{dpvs}}$ takes input 1^λ ($\lambda \in \mathbb{N}$) and $N \in \mathbb{N}$, and outputs a description of $\mathsf{param}'_{\mathbb{V}} := (q, \mathbb{V}, \mathbb{G}_T, \mathbb{A}, e)$ with security parameter $\mathbb{V}$. It can be constructed by using $\mathcal{G}_{\mathsf{bpg}}$.

For a matrix $W := (w_{i,j})_{i,j=1,\ldots,N} \in \mathbb{F}_q^{N \times N}$ and element $\boldsymbol{g} := (G_1, \ldots, G_N)$ in N-dimensional $\mathbb{V}$, $\boldsymbol{g}W$ denotes $(\sum_{i=1}^{N} G_i w_{i,1}, \ldots, \sum_{i=1}^{N} G_i w_{i,N}) = (\sum_{i=1}^{N} w_{i,1} G_i, \ldots, \sum_{i=1}^{N} w_{i,N} G_i)$ by a natural multiplication of a N-dim. row vector and a $N \times N$ matrix. Thus it holds an associative law like $(\boldsymbol{g}W)W^{-1} = \boldsymbol{g}(WW^{-1}) = \boldsymbol{g}$.

We describe a random dual orthonormal basis generator $\mathcal{G}_{\mathsf{ob}}$, which is used as subroutine in our IPE scheme.

$\mathcal{G}_{\mathsf{ob}}(1^\lambda, N_0, N_1)$: $\mathsf{param}_{\mathbb{G}} := (q, \mathbb{G}, \mathbb{G}_T, G, e) \xleftarrow{\mathsf{R}} \mathcal{G}_{\mathsf{bpg}}(1^\lambda), \psi \xleftarrow{\mathsf{U}} \mathbb{F}_q^\times, g_T := e(G, G)^\psi,$

for $t = 0, 1$ $\mathsf{param}_{\mathbb{V}_t} := (q, \mathbb{V}_t, \mathbb{G}_T, \mathbb{A}_t, e) \xleftarrow{\mathsf{R}} \mathcal{G}_{\mathsf{dpvs}}(1^\lambda, N_t),$

$X_t := (\chi_{t,i,j})_{i,j} \xleftarrow{\mathsf{U}} GL(N_t, \mathbb{F}_q), (\vartheta_{t,i,j})_{i,j} := \psi \cdot (X_t^{\mathsf{T}})^{-1},$

$\boldsymbol{b}_{t.i} := \sum_{j=1}^{N_t} \chi_{t,i,j} \boldsymbol{a}_{t,j}, \quad \mathbb{B}_t := (\boldsymbol{b}_{t.1}, \ldots, \boldsymbol{b}_{t.N_t}),$

$\boldsymbol{b}_{t.i}^* := \sum_{j=1}^{N_t} \vartheta_{t,i,j} \boldsymbol{a}_{t,j}, \quad \mathbb{B}_t^* := (\boldsymbol{b}_{t.1}^*, \ldots, \boldsymbol{b}_{t.N_t}^*),$

return $(\mathsf{param}_{\vec{n}} := (\{\mathsf{param}_{\mathbb{V}_t}\}_{t=0,1}, g_T), \{\mathbb{B}_t, \mathbb{B}_t^*\}_{t=0,1}).$

2.3   Decisional Linear (DLIN) Assumption

Definition 3 (DLIN: Decisional Linear Assumption [3]). *The DLIN problem is to guess* $\beta \in \{0, 1\}$, *given* $(\mathsf{param}_{\mathbb{G}}, G, \xi G, \kappa G, \delta\xi G, \sigma\kappa G, Y_\beta) \xleftarrow{\mathsf{R}} \mathcal{G}_\beta^{\mathsf{DLIN}}(1^\lambda)$, *where* $\mathcal{G}_\beta^{\mathsf{DLIN}}(1^\lambda)$: $\mathsf{param}_{\mathbb{G}} := (q, \mathbb{G}, \mathbb{G}_T, G, e) \xleftarrow{\mathsf{R}} \mathcal{G}_{\mathsf{bpg}}(1^\lambda), \kappa, \delta, \xi, \sigma \xleftarrow{\mathsf{U}} \mathbb{F}_q, Y_0 := (\delta + \sigma)G, Y_1 \xleftarrow{\mathsf{U}} \mathbb{G}$, return $(\mathsf{param}_{\mathbb{G}}, G, \xi G, \kappa G, \delta\xi G, \sigma\kappa G, Y_\beta)$, *for* $\beta \xleftarrow{\mathsf{U}} \{0, 1\}$. *For a probabilistic machine* $\mathcal{E}$, *we define the advantage of* $\mathcal{E}$ *for the DLIN problem as:*

$$\mathsf{Adv}_{\mathcal{E}}^{\mathsf{DLIN}}(\lambda) := \left| \Pr\left[\mathcal{E}(1^\lambda, \varrho) \to 1 \,\middle|\, \varrho \xleftarrow{\mathsf{R}} \mathcal{G}_0^{\mathsf{DLIN}}(1^\lambda) \right] - \Pr\left[\mathcal{E}(1^\lambda, \varrho) \to 1 \,\middle|\, \varrho \xleftarrow{\mathsf{R}} \mathcal{G}_1^{\mathsf{DLIN}}(1^\lambda) \right] \right|.$$

The DLIN assumption is: For any probabilistic polynomial-time adversary $\mathcal{E}$, *the advantage* $\mathsf{Adv}_{\mathcal{E}}^{\mathsf{DLIN}}(\lambda)$ *is negligible in* λ.

3   Inner-Product Encryption with Trapdoor Conversion

In this section, we define a notion of inner-product encryption with trapdoor conversion, IPE-TC, and its security. In IPE-TC, an attribute and predicate vector $\vec{x}$ and $\vec{v}$ are expressed as follows, respectively.

$$\vec{x} := \{(t, x_t) | t \in I_{\vec{x}}, x_t \in \mathbb{F}_q, \ I_{\vec{x}} \subset \mathbb{N} \} \backslash \{0\}, \ \vec{v} := \{(t, v_t) | t \in I_{\vec{v}}, v_t \in \mathbb{F}_q, \ I_{\vec{v}} \subset \mathbb{N} \} \backslash \{0\}$$

Next, we define a conversion map ρ in order to consider the trapdoor conversion. For $I_{\vec{v}} = \{t_1, \ldots, t_n\}$, ρ is an index permutation denoted by

$$\rho := \begin{pmatrix} t_1, & t_2, & t_3, & \ldots, & t_{|I_{\vec{v}}|} \\ \rho(t_1) = \hat{t}_1, & \rho(t_2) = \hat{t}_2, & \rho(t_3) = \hat{t}_3, \ldots, & \rho(t_{|I_{\vec{v}}|}) = \hat{t}_{|I_{\vec{v}}|} \end{pmatrix}$$

where $\hat{t}_i \neq \hat{t}_j$ for $1 \leq i, j \leq |I_{\vec{v}}|$. Here, we set $\hat{I}_{\vec{v}} = \{\hat{t}_1, \ldots, \hat{t}_{|I_{\vec{v}}|}\}$. Simply, we denote $\hat{I}_{\vec{v}} = \{\hat{t}_1, \ldots, \hat{t}\}$ and $\{(\rho(t), v_t)\}$ by $\rho(I_{\vec{v}})$ and $\rho(\vec{v})$. Roughly speaking, an element (t, v_t) is moved to $(\hat{t}, v_t)$ by ρ. For $\vec{x}$ and $\vec{v}$, we define two relations $R(\vec{v}, \vec{x})$ and $\hat{R}(\vec{v}, \vec{x})$ as follows

$$R(\vec{v}, \vec{x}) = 1 \Leftrightarrow I_{\vec{v}} \subseteq I_{\vec{x}} \text{ and } \sum_{t \in I_{\vec{v}}} v_t x_t = 0, \ \hat{R}(\vec{v}, \vec{x}) = 1 \Leftrightarrow {}^{\exists}\rho \text{ where } R(\rho(\vec{v}), \vec{x}) = 1.$$

Intuitively, the relation $\hat{R}$ means that, for a plaintext $\vec{x}$ and a keyword $\vec{v}, \vec{x}$ contains $\vec{v}$ as character if and only if $\hat{R}(\vec{v}, \vec{x}) = 1$.

3.1   Syntax of IPE-TC

Definition 4 (Inner-Product Encryption with Trapdoor Conversion). *An inner-product encryption with trapdoor conversion scheme consists of the following five algorithms.*

Setup: *takes as input a security parameter 1^λ. It outputs a public key* pk *a master secret key* sk, *and a conversion secret key* csk.
Enc: *takes as input the public key* pk, *an attribute vector $\vec{x}$. It outputs a ciphertext* $ct_{\vec{x}}$.
TrapGen: *takes as input the public key* pk, *the master secret key* sk, *and a predicate vector $\vec{v}$. It outputs a corresponding original trapdoor key* $tk_{\vec{v}}$.
TrapConv: *takes as input the public key* pk, *a conversion secret key* csk, *the trapdoor key* $tk_{\vec{v}}$, *and a conversion map ρ. It outputs a converted trapdoor key* $\widehat{tk}_{\vec{v}}$.
Query: *takes as input the public key* pk, *the trapdoor key* $tk_{\vec{v}}$, *and the ciphertext* $ct_{\vec{x}}$. *It outputs 1 iff $R(\vec{v}, \vec{x}) = 1$. Otherwise, outputs 0.*

The correctness for an IPE-TC scheme is defined as: (1) For any $(pk, sk, csk) \xleftarrow{R}$ Setup(1^λ), any $\vec{v}$ and $\vec{x}$, a trapdoor key $tk_{\vec{v}} \xleftarrow{R}$ TrapGen$(pk, sk, \vec{v})$, and a ciphertext $ct_x \xleftarrow{R}$ Enc$(pk, \vec{x})$, we have $1 = $ Query$(pk, tk_{\vec{v}}, ct_{\vec{x}})$ if $R(\vec{v}, \vec{x}) = 1$. Otherwise, it holds with negligible probability. (2) For any (pk, sk, csk), $\vec{v}$ and $\vec{x}$, a trapdoor key $tk_{\vec{v}} \xleftarrow{R}$ TrapGen$(pk, sk, \vec{v})$, and a ρ, we have $1 = $ Query$(pk, $TrapConv$(pk, csk, tk_{\vec{v}}, \rho), ct_{\vec{x}})$ if $R(\rho(\vec{v}), \vec{x}) = 1$. Otherwise, it holds with negligible probability.

3.2 Security Definition

In this subsection, we define the security of IPE-TC. In the public key search-able encryption setting, we discuss the basic attribute-hiding security against an adversary. In this security definiton, an attacker tries to distinguish ciphertexts $\mathsf{ct}_{\vec{x}^{(0)}}$ and $\mathsf{ct}_{\vec{x}^{(0)}}$ such that $\hat{R}(\vec{v}, \vec{x}^{(0)}) = \hat{R}(\vec{v}, \vec{x}^{(1)}) = 0$ where $\vec{v}$ is any trapdoor query. That is, challenge vectors $\vec{x}^{(0)}$ and $\vec{x}^{(1)}$ does not contain $\vec{v}$.

Definition 5 (Attribute-Hiding (AH)). *The model for defining the attribute-hiding security of IPE-TC against adversary $\mathcal{A}$ (under chosen plaintext attacks) is given by the following game. An IPE-TC scheme has attribute-hiding security if, for all PPT adversaries $\mathcal{A}$, the advantage of $\mathcal{A}$ in winning the following game is negligible in the security parameter λ. We define the advantage of $\mathcal{A}$ as* $\mathsf{Adv}_{\mathcal{A}}^{\mathsf{AH}}(\lambda) := \Pr[b = b'] - \frac{1}{2}$[1].

Setup. The challenger runs the setup algorithm $(\mathsf{pk}, \mathsf{sk}, \mathsf{csk}) \xleftarrow{\mathsf{R}} \mathsf{Setup}(1^\lambda)$, and it gives the security parameter λ, the public key pk and the conversion secret key csk to the adversary $\mathcal{A}$.

Phase 1. The adversary $\mathcal{A}$ is allowed to adaptively issue a polynomial number of queries as follows.

    Trapdoor key query. For a Trapdoor key query $\vec{v}$, the challenger gives $\mathsf{tk}_{\vec{v}} \xleftarrow{\mathsf{R}} \mathsf{TrapGen}(\mathsf{pk}, \mathsf{sk}, \vec{v})$ to $\mathcal{A}$.

    Trapdoor key conversion query. For a Trapdoor key conversion query $\mathsf{tk}_{\vec{v}}$ and a conversion information ρ, the challenger gives $\hat{\mathsf{tk}}_{\vec{v}} \xleftarrow{\mathsf{R}} \mathsf{TrapGen}(\mathsf{pk}, \mathsf{csk}, \mathsf{tk}_{\vec{v}}, \rho)$ to $\mathcal{A}$.

Challenge. For a challenge query $(\vec{x}^{(0)} := \{(t, x_t^{(0)}) | t \in I_{\vec{x}^{(0)}}\}, \vec{x}^{(1)} := \{(t, x_t^{(1)}) | t \in I_{\vec{x}^{(1)}}\})$ subjected to the following restrictions: (1) $I_{\vec{x}^{(0)}} = I_{\vec{x}^{(1)}}$. (2) Any trapdoor key query $\vec{v}$ satisfies $\hat{R}(\vec{v}, \vec{x}^{(0)}) = \hat{R}(\vec{v}, \vec{x}^{(1)}) = 0$. The challenger flips a random bit $b \xleftarrow{\mathsf{U}} \{0,1\}$ and computes $\mathsf{ct}_{\vec{x}^{(b)}} \xleftarrow{\mathsf{R}} \mathsf{Enc}(\mathsf{pk}, \vec{x}^{(b)})$. It gives the challenge original ciphertext $\mathsf{ct}_{\vec{x}^{(b)}}$ to $\mathcal{A}$.

Phase 2. The adversary $\mathcal{A}$ may continue to issue trapdoor key queries, subjected to the restriction in the challenge phase.

Guess. $\mathcal{A}$ outputs its guess $b' \in \{0,1\}$ for b and wins the game if $b = b'$.

4 Proposed IPE-TC Scheme

Construction Idea. Our proposed IPE-TC scheme is based on the unbounded generalized IPE scheme [16]. In [16] of IPE, the trapdoor key $\mathsf{tk}_{\vec{v}}$ and the ciphertext $\mathsf{ct}_{\vec{x}}$ are constructed as

$$\mathsf{tk}_{\vec{v}} := (\boldsymbol{k}_0^* := (-s_0, 0, 1, \mu_0, 0)_{\mathbb{B}_0^*}, \ \boldsymbol{k}_t^* := (\mu_t(t, -1), \delta v_t, s_t, 0^7, \eta_t, 0^2)_{\mathbb{B}^*}\mathsf{for}t \in I_{\vec{v}}),$$

$$\mathsf{ct}_{\vec{x}} := (\boldsymbol{c}_0 := (\tilde{\omega}, 0, \zeta, 0, \varphi)_{\mathbb{B}_0}, \ \boldsymbol{c}_t := (\sigma_t(1, t), \omega x_t, \tilde{\omega}, 0^7, 0^2, \varphi_{t.1}, \varphi_{t.2})_{\mathbb{B}}\mathsf{for}t \in I_{\vec{x}})$$

---

[1] Also, our attribute-hiding security is known as *weak* AH [6,10,14]. On the other hand, in *fully* AH security [15], the adversary is allowed the challenge query $\vec{x}^{(0)}, \vec{x}^{(1)}$ such that $\hat{R}(\vec{v}, \vec{x}^{(0)}) = \hat{R}(\vec{v}, \vec{x}^{(1)}) = 0$ or 1.

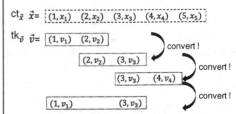

Fig. 2. Difference between generalized IPE [16] and our IPE-TC

where $(\mathbb{B}_0, \mathbb{B}_0^*)$ and $(\mathbb{B}, \mathbb{B}^*)$ are pairs of dual basis on DPVS, $s_t, \mu_0, \mu_t, \delta, \eta_t,$ $\tilde{\omega}, \zeta, \varphi, \sigma_t, \omega, \varphi_{t.1}, \varphi_{t.2} \overset{U}{\leftarrow} \mathbb{F}_q$ and $s_0 = \Sigma s_t$. In the above construction, in order to meet the decryption condition, this scheme is adopted indexing technique and n-out-of-n secret sharing trick. Since the first 2-dimension of $\boldsymbol{k}_t$ and $\boldsymbol{c}_t$ is used for indexes, all $\boldsymbol{k}_t$ and $\boldsymbol{c}_t$ can be computed on same dual basis $(\mathbb{B}, \mathbb{B}^*)$. So, in this scheme, the dimension of attribute/predicate vector is unbounded.

Our IPE-TC scheme is obtained by modifying the above structures below.

- The first 2-dimensions of $\boldsymbol{k}_t$ and $\boldsymbol{c}_t$, $\mu_t(t, -1)$ and $\sigma_t(1, t)$, are omitted. Additionally, Setup generates different dual basis pairs $(\mathbb{B}_t, \mathbb{B}_t^*)$ for $t = 1, \ldots, d$, and $\boldsymbol{k}_t$ and $\boldsymbol{c}_t$ are generated based on $\mathbb{B}_t$ and $\mathbb{B}_t^*$ where d is the maximum number of index.
- For $i = 1, \ldots, d$, Setup generates a basis $\mathbb{B}_i$ with $\mathbb{B}_i := \mathbb{B}_1 \prod_{j=1}^{i-1} W_j$ where $W_1, \ldots, W_{d-1}$ are random (conversion) matrices. By the definition of DPVS, $\mathbb{B}_i^*$ is equivalent to $\mathbb{B}_1^* \prod_{j=1}^{i-1} (W_j^{\mathrm{T}})^{-1}$.
- A conversion secret key csk is set to conversion matrices $\{W_i^{\mathrm{T}} = W_i^*\}_{i=1,\ldots,d-1}$.

An entity who has csk can convert $\boldsymbol{k}_t$ into $\boldsymbol{k}_{t+1}$ with the random matrix W_i. We show the difference between generalized IPE [16] and our IPE-TC in Fig. 2.

Construction. We describe a specific construction of our IPE-TC scheme based on DPVS. The random dual basis generator $\mathcal{G}_{\mathrm{ob}}$ is defined in Sect. 2.2 and we refer to Sect. 2.1 for notations on DPVS.

Setup$(1^\lambda, d)$: $(\mathrm{param}, (\mathbb{B}_0, \mathbb{B}_0^*), (\mathbb{B}_1, \mathbb{B}_1^*)) \overset{R}{\leftarrow} \mathcal{G}_{\mathrm{ob}}(1^\lambda, N_0 = 5, N_1 = 12)$
  For $i = 1, \ldots, d - 1$
  $W_i \overset{U}{\leftarrow} GL(N_1, \mathbb{F}_q), \quad W_i^* := (W_i^{\mathrm{T}})^{-1}, \quad \mathbb{B}_{i+1} := \mathbb{B}_i W_i, \quad \mathbb{B}_{i+1}^* := \mathbb{B}_i^* W_i^*$
  $\widehat{\mathbb{B}}_0 := (\boldsymbol{b}_{0,1}, \boldsymbol{b}_{0,3}, \boldsymbol{b}_{0,5}), \quad \widehat{\mathbb{B}}_i := (\boldsymbol{b}_{i,1}, \boldsymbol{b}_{i,2}, \boldsymbol{b}_{i,11}, \boldsymbol{b}_{0,12}),$
  $\widehat{\mathbb{B}}_0^* := (\boldsymbol{b}_{0,1}^*, \boldsymbol{b}_{0,3}^*, \boldsymbol{b}_{0,4}^*), \quad \widehat{\mathbb{B}}_i^* := (\boldsymbol{b}_{i,1}^*, \boldsymbol{b}_{i,2}^*, \boldsymbol{b}_{i,9}^*, \boldsymbol{b}_{i,10}^*)$
  return pk $:= (\mathrm{param}, \{\widehat{\mathbb{B}}_i\}_{i=0,\ldots,d}), \quad$ sk $:= (\{\widehat{\mathbb{B}}_i^*\}_{i=0,\ldots,d}), \quad$ csk $:= (\{W_i^*\}_{i=1,\ldots,d-1}).$

$\mathsf{Enc}(\mathsf{pk}, \vec{x} = \{(t, x_t) | t \in I_{\vec{x}} \subseteq \{1, \ldots, d\}\})$:

$\quad \omega, \tilde{\omega}, \zeta, \varphi_0 \xleftarrow{\mathsf{U}} \mathbb{F}_q, \quad c_0 := (\ \tilde{\omega},\ 0,\ \zeta,\ 0,\ \varphi\ )_{\mathbb{B}_0}, \quad c_T := g_T^{\zeta}$

$\quad$ For $t \in I_{\vec{x}}$, $\varphi_{t,1}, \varphi_{t,2} \xleftarrow{\mathsf{U}} \mathbb{F}_q, \quad c_t := (\ \omega x_t,\ \tilde{\omega},\ 0^6,\ 0^2,\ \varphi_{t,1}, \varphi_{t,2}\ )_{\mathbb{B}_t}$

$\quad$ return $\mathsf{ct}_{\vec{x}} = (I_{\vec{x}}, c_0, \{c_t\}_{t \in I_{\vec{x}}}, c_T)$.

$\mathsf{TrapGen}(\mathsf{pk}, \mathsf{sk}, \vec{v} = \{(t, v_t) | t \in I_{\vec{v}} \subseteq \{1, \ldots, d\}\})$: $s_t, r, \delta, \eta_0, \eta_{\mathsf{r}.0} \xleftarrow{\mathsf{U}} \mathbb{F}_q^n$,

$\quad s_0 := \Sigma_{t \in I_{\vec{v}}} s_t, \quad k_0^* := (\ -s_0,\ 0,\ 1,\ \eta_0,\ 0\ )_{\mathbb{B}_0^*}$

$\quad s_{\mathsf{r}.0} := \Sigma_{t \in I_{\vec{v}}} s_{\mathsf{r}.t} \quad k_{\mathsf{r}.0}^* := (\ -s_{\mathsf{r}.0},\ 0,\ 0,\ \eta_{\mathsf{r}.0},\ 0\ )_{\mathbb{B}_0^*}$

$\quad$ For $t \in I_{\vec{v}}$, $\eta_{t,1}, \eta_{t,2}, \eta_{t,1}', \eta_{t,2}' \xleftarrow{\mathsf{U}} \mathbb{F}_q$,

$\quad k_t^* := (\ \delta v_t,\ s_t,\ 0^6,\ \eta_{t,1}, \eta_{t,2},\ 0^2\ )_{\mathbb{B}_t^*}, k_{\mathsf{r}.t}^* := (\ 0,\ s_{\mathsf{r}.t},\ 0^6,\ \eta_{t,1}', \eta_{t,2}',\ 0^2\ )_{\mathbb{B}_t^*}$,

$\quad$ return $\mathsf{tk}_{\vec{v}} = (I_{\vec{v}}, k_0^*, k_{\mathsf{r}.0}^*, \{k_t^*, k_{\mathsf{r}.t}^*\}_{t \in I_{\vec{v}}})$.

$\mathsf{TrapConv}(\mathsf{tk}_{\vec{v}}, \rho, \mathsf{csk} = \{W_i^*\}_{i=1,\ldots,d-1})$: If $|I_{\vec{v}}| \neq |\hat{I}_{\vec{v}}|$, return $\perp$.

$\quad$ For $r, r' \xleftarrow{\mathsf{U}} \mathbb{F}_q$, $i = 1, \ldots, t_{I_{\vec{v}}}$ $(t_i \in I_{\vec{v}}, \hat{t}_i \in \hat{I}_{\vec{v}},$ by using ρ, t_i is move to $\hat{t}_i$.)

$\quad$ If $t_i = \hat{t}_i$, $k_{\hat{t}_i}^* := k_{t_i}^* + r k_{\mathsf{r}.t_i}^*$

$\quad$ If $t_i < \hat{t}_i$, $k_{\hat{t}_i}^* := k_{t_i}^* W_{t_i}^* W_{t_i+1}^* \cdots W_{\hat{t}_i-1}^* + r k_{\mathsf{r}.\hat{t}_i}$

$\quad$ If $t_i > \hat{t}_i$, $k_{\hat{t}_i}^* := k_{t_i}^* (W_{t_i-1}^*)^{-1} (W_{t_i-2}^*)^{-1} \cdots (W_{\hat{t}_i}^*)^{-1} + r k_{\mathsf{r}.\hat{t}_i}$

$\quad k_0^* = k_0^* + r k_{\mathsf{r}.0}^*$, $k_{\mathsf{r}.t}^* = r' k_{\mathsf{r}.t}^*$, return $\mathsf{tk}_{\vec{v}'} = (\hat{I}_{\vec{v}}, k_0^*, k_{\mathsf{r}.0}^*, \{k_{\hat{t}}^*, k_{\mathsf{r}.\hat{t}}^*\}_{\hat{t} \in \hat{I}_{\vec{v}}})$.

$\mathsf{Query}(\mathsf{pk}, \mathsf{ct}_{\vec{x}} = (I_{\vec{x}}, c_0, \{c_t\}_{t \in I_{\vec{x}}}, c_T), \mathsf{tk}_{\vec{v}}$

$\quad$ If $I_{\vec{x}} \subseteq I_{\vec{v}}$, return $\perp$. Otherwise $K := e(c_0, k_0^*) \cdot \prod_{t \in I_{\vec{x}}} e(c_t, k_t^*)$.

$\quad$ If $c_T = K$ return 1. Otherwise, return 0.

Security and Overview of Proof. We describe the overview of security proof for our proposed IPE-TC scheme. We will show the full proof in the full version of this paper. The security proofs of our IPE-TC scheme are similar to the security proofs of [16].

Theorem 1. *The proposed IPE-TC scheme is attribute-hiding against chosen plaintext attacks under the DLIN assumption.*

Proof Outline of Theorem 1: To prove Theorem 1, we employ Game 0 through Game 4. In Game 0, all the replies to $\mathcal{A}$'s queries are in normal forms. In Game 1, c_0 and c_t of the challenge ciphertext is changed to semi-functional form in Eq. (3). Let ν_1 be the maximum number of $\mathcal{A}$'s trapdoor key queries and trapdoor key conversion queies. In Game 2-ℓ-1 $(\ell = 1, \ldots, \nu_1)$, the reply to the ℓ-th trapdoor key query (or trapdoor key conversion query) is change to pre-semi-functional form in Eq. (4). In Game 2-ℓ-2 $(\ell = 1, \ldots, \nu_1)$, the reply to the ℓ-th trapdoor key query (or trapdoor key conversion query) is change to semi-functional form in Eq. (5). In Game 3, c_0 and c_t of the challenge ciphertext is changed to semi-randomized form in Eq. (6). Finally, in Game 4, c_t of the challenge ciphertext is changed to randomized form in Eq. (7). In final Game 4, the advantage of the adversary is zero. As usual, we prove that the advantage gaps between neighboring games are negligible by using Problem 1, 2, and 3 which are defined in Appendix A. In Game 0, a part framed by a box indicates coefficients to be changed in a subsequent game. In other games, a part framed by a box indicates coefficients which were changed in a game from the previous game.

Game 0: k_0^* and k_t^* of the reply to a trapdoor key query (or trapdoor key conversion query) for $\vec{v}$ are

$$k_0^* := (\,-s_0,\ \boxed{0}, 1\ ,\eta_0,\ 0\,)_{\mathbb{B}_0^*}, \ k_t^* := (\,\delta v_t,\ s_t,\ 0^4,\ \boxed{0^2},\ \vec{\eta}_t,\ 0^2\,)_{\mathbb{B}_t^*} \quad (1)$$

where $t \in I_{\vec{v}}, \eta_0, \delta, s_t \xleftarrow{\mathsf{U}} \mathbb{F}_q,\ \vec{\eta}_t \xleftarrow{\mathsf{U}} \mathbb{F}_q^2$, and $s_0 := \Sigma_{t \in I_{\vec{v}}} s_t$.
c_0 and c_t of the reply to a challenge query for $(\vec{x}^{(0)}, \vec{x}^{(1)})$ such that $I_{\vec{x}} := I_{\vec{x}^{(0)}} = I_{\vec{x}^{(1)}}$, and

$$c_0 := (\,\tilde{\omega},\ \boxed{0},\ \boxed{\zeta},\ 0,\ \varphi\,)_{\mathbb{B}_0}, \ c_t := (\,\boxed{\omega x_t^{(b)}},\ \tilde{\omega},\ \boxed{0^2},\ 0^2,\ \boxed{0^2},\ \vec{\varphi}_t\,)_{\mathbb{B}_t} \quad (2)$$

where $b \xleftarrow{\mathsf{U}} \{0,1\}$, $t \in I_{\vec{x}}$, $\tilde{\omega}, \zeta, \varphi, \omega \xleftarrow{\mathsf{U}} \mathbb{F}_{q,,}$ and $\vec{\varphi}_t \xleftarrow{\mathsf{U}} \mathbb{F}_q^2$.

Game 1: Game 1 is the same as Game 0 except that the reply to the challenge query for $(\vec{x}^{(0)}, \vec{x}^{(1)})$ is

$$c_0 := (\tilde{\omega}, \boxed{\tilde{\tau}}, \zeta, 0, \varphi)_{\mathbb{B}_0}, c_t := (\omega x_t^{(b)},\ \tilde{\omega},\ \boxed{\tau x_t^{(b)}, \tilde{\tau}}, 0^2, \boxed{(\tau x_t^{(b)}, \tilde{\tau}) Z_t}, \vec{\varphi}_t)_{\mathbb{B}_t} \quad (3)$$

where $t \in I_{\vec{x}}, \tau, \tilde{\tau} \xleftarrow{\mathsf{U}} \mathbb{F}_q$, $Z_t \xleftarrow{\mathsf{U}} GL(\mathbb{F}_q, 2)$.

Game 2-ℓ-1 $(\ell = 1, \ldots, \nu_1)$: Game 2-0-1 is equivalent to Game 1. Game 2-ℓ-1 is the same as Game 2-$(\ell - 1)$-1 except that the reply to the ℓ-th trapdoor query for $\vec{v}$ is

$$k_0^* := (-s_0, \boxed{-a_0}, 1, \eta_0, 0)_{\mathbb{B}_0^*}, k_t^* := (\delta v_t, s_t, 0^4, \boxed{(\pi v_t^{(b)}, a_t) U_t}, \vec{\eta}_t, 0^2)_{\mathbb{B}_t^*} \quad (4)$$

where $t \in I_{\vec{v}}, \pi, a_t \xleftarrow{\mathsf{U}} \mathbb{F}_q, a_0 := \sum_{t \in I_{\vec{v}}} a_t, U_t := (Z_t^{-1})^{\mathrm{T}}$.

Game 2-ℓ-2 $(\ell = 1, \ldots, \nu_1)$: Game 2-0-2 is equivalent to Game 2-ν_1-1. Game 2-ℓ-2 is the same as Game 2-$(\ell - 1)$-2 except that the reply to the ℓ-th trapdoor query for $\vec{v}$ is

$$k_0^* := (-s_0, \boxed{r_0}, 1, \eta_0, 0)_{\mathbb{B}_0^*}, k_t^* := (\delta v_t, s_t, 0^2, 0^2, \boxed{\vec{r}_t}, \vec{\eta}_t, 0^2)_{\mathbb{B}_t^*} \quad (5)$$

where $t \in I_{\vec{v}}, r_0 \xleftarrow{\mathsf{U}} \mathbb{F}_q, \vec{r}_t \xleftarrow{\mathsf{U}} \mathbb{F}_q^2$.

Game 3: Game 3 is the same as Game 2-ν_1-2 except that the reply to the challenge query for $(\vec{x}^{(0)}, \vec{x}^{(1)})$ is

$$c_0 := (\tilde{\omega}, \tilde{\tau}, \boxed{\zeta'}, 0, \varphi)_{\mathbb{B}_0}, c_t := (\omega x_t^{(b)}, \tilde{\omega}, \tau x_t^{(b)}, \tilde{\tau}, 0^2, \boxed{\vec{z}_t}, \vec{\varphi}_t)_{\mathbb{B}_t} \quad (6)$$

where $t \in I_{\vec{x}}, \zeta' \xleftarrow{\mathsf{U}} \mathbb{F}_q$, and $\vec{z}_t \xleftarrow{\mathsf{U}} \mathbb{F}_q^2$.

Game 4: Game 4 is the same as Game 3 except that the reply to the challenge query for $(\vec{x}^{(0)}, \vec{x}^{(1)})$ is

$$c_t := (\boxed{0}, \tilde{\omega}, \boxed{0}, \tilde{\tau}, 0^2, \vec{z}_t, \vec{\varphi}_t)_{\mathbb{B}_t} \quad (7)$$

where $t \in I_{\vec{x}}$.

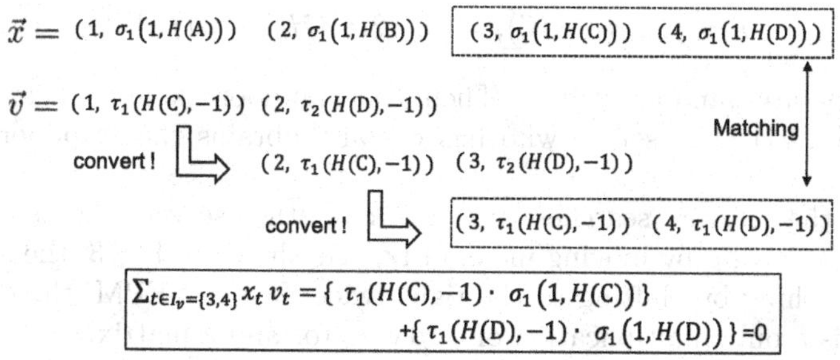

Fig. 3. Example of SEPM using IPE-TC

Let $\mathsf{Adv}_{\mathcal{A}}^{(0)}(\lambda)$, $\mathsf{Adv}_{\mathcal{A}}^{(1)}(\lambda)$, $\mathsf{Adv}_{\mathcal{A}}^{(2-\ell-1)}(\lambda)$, $\mathsf{Adv}_{\mathcal{A}}^{(2-\ell-2)}(\lambda)$, $\mathsf{Adv}_{\mathcal{A}}^{(3)}(\lambda)$, $\mathsf{Adv}_{\mathcal{A}}^{(4)}(\lambda)$, be the advantage of $\mathcal{A}$ in Game 0, 1, 2-ℓ-1, 2-ℓ-2, 3 and 4, respectively.

We will show eight lemmas (Lemmas 1–6) that evaluate the gaps between pairs of $\mathsf{Adv}_{\mathcal{A}}^{(0)}(\lambda)$, $\mathsf{Adv}_{\mathcal{A}}^{(1)}(\lambda)$, $\mathsf{Adv}_{\mathcal{A}}^{(2-\ell-1)}(\lambda)$, $\mathsf{Adv}_{\mathcal{A}}^{(2-\ell-2)}(\lambda)$, $\mathsf{Adv}_{\mathcal{A}}^{(3)}(\lambda)$, $\mathsf{Adv}_{\mathcal{A}}^{(4)}(\lambda)$.

Lemma 1. *For any adversary $\mathcal{A}$, there exists a probabilistic machine $\mathcal{B}_1$ such that for any security parameter λ, $|\mathsf{Adv}_{\mathcal{A}}^{(0)}(\lambda) - \mathsf{Adv}_{\mathcal{A}}^{(1)}(\lambda)| \leq \mathsf{Adv}_{\mathcal{B}_1}^{P1}(\lambda)$.*

Lemma 2. *For any adversary $\mathcal{A}$, there exists a probabilistic machine $\mathcal{B}_2$ such that for any security parameter λ, $|\mathsf{Adv}_{\mathcal{A}}^{(2-(\ell-1)-1)}(\lambda) - \mathsf{Adv}_{\mathcal{A}}^{(2-\ell-1)}(\lambda)| \leq \mathsf{Adv}_{\mathcal{B}_{2-\ell-1}}^{P2}(\lambda) + 2/q$ where $\mathcal{B}_{2-\ell-1}(\cdot) := \mathcal{B}_2(\ell, \cdot)$.*

Lemma 3. *For any adversary $\mathcal{A}$ and security parameter λ, $|\mathsf{Adv}_{\mathcal{A}}^{(2-\ell-1)}(\lambda) = \mathsf{Adv}_{\mathcal{A}}^{(2-\ell-2)}(\lambda)|$.*

Lemma 4. *For any adversary $\mathcal{A}$ and security parameter λ, $|\mathsf{Adv}_{\mathcal{A}}^{(3)}(\lambda) - \mathsf{Adv}_{\mathcal{A}}^{(2-\nu_1-2)}(\lambda)| \leq 1/q$.*

Lemma 5. *For any adversary $\mathcal{A}$, there exists a probabilistic machine $\mathcal{B}_4$ such that for any security parameter λ, $|\mathsf{Adv}_{\mathcal{A}}^{(4)}(\lambda) - \mathsf{Adv}_{\mathcal{A}}^{(3)}(\lambda)| \leq \mathsf{Adv}_{\mathcal{B}_4}^{P3}(\lambda) + 3/q,.$*

Lemma 6. *For any adversary $\mathcal{A}$ and security parameter λ, $\mathsf{Adv}_{\mathcal{A}}^{(5)}(\lambda) = 0$.*

5   Overview of SEPM Using IPE-TC

In this section, we explain SEPM using our IPE-TC scheme. In SEPM, a keyword corresponds to a predicate/attribute vector. We consider an example that a ciphertext contains a keyword "ABCD". In this case, an attribute vector $\vec{x}$ is

$$\vec{x} = \{\ (1, \sigma_1(1, \mathcal{H}(A))),\ (2, \sigma_2(1, \mathcal{H}(B))),\ (3, \sigma_3(1, \mathcal{H}(C))),\ (4, \sigma_4(1, \mathcal{H}(D)))\ \}$$

where $\sigma_1, \ldots, \sigma_4$ are random values in $\mathbb{F}_q$ and $\mathcal{H} : \{0,1\}^* \rightarrow F_q$ is a cryptographic hash function. Then the ciphertext on $\vec{x}$ is $\mathsf{ct}_{\vec{x}} := (I_{\vec{x}} = \{1, \ldots, 4\}, c_0, c_1, \ldots, c_4, c_T)$. If a client search "CD", a predicate vector $\vec{v}$ is encoded as

$$\vec{v} = \{ \ (1, \tau_1(\mathcal{H}(\mathsf{C}), -1)), \ (2, \tau_2(\mathcal{H}(\mathsf{D}), -1)) \ \}$$

where τ_1, τ_2 are random values. Then the trapdoor $\mathsf{tk}_{\vec{v}}$ under $\vec{v}$ is ($I_{\vec{v}} = \{1, 2\}, \boldsymbol{k}_0^*, \boldsymbol{k}_1^*, \boldsymbol{k}_2^*$). The server who has csk and obtains the trapdoor $\mathsf{tk}_{\vec{v}}$ into ciphertexts.

When the server searches $\mathsf{tk}_{\vec{v}}$ on $\mathsf{ct}_{\vec{x}}$, the server checks $e(\boldsymbol{c}_0, \boldsymbol{k}_0^*)$. $\prod_{t \in I_{\vec{v}}} e(\boldsymbol{c}_t, \boldsymbol{k}_t^*) = c_T$ by moving index of $\mathsf{tk}_{\vec{v}}$. As shown in Fig. 3, the server can confirm matching by shifting to the right twice. In this SEPM, the conversion procedure is a only multiplication of a row vector and a matrix.

From the above explanation, IPE-TC is very useful tool to achieve SEPM.

A   Preliminaries Lemmas

Definition 6 (Problem 1). Problem 1 *is to guess* β, *given* (param, $\widehat{\mathbb{B}}_0, \widehat{\mathbb{B}}_0^*$, $\{\widehat{\mathbb{B}}_t, \widehat{\mathbb{B}}_t^*\}_{t=1,\ldots,d}, \boldsymbol{e}_{\beta,0}, \{\boldsymbol{e}_{\beta,t,i}\}_{t=1,\ldots,d,i=1,2}) \xleftarrow{\mathsf{R}} \mathcal{G}_{\beta}^{\mathsf{P1}}(1^{\lambda}, d)$ *where*

$\mathcal{G}_{\beta}^{\mathsf{P1}}(1^{\lambda}, d):$ (param, $(\mathbb{B}_0, \mathbb{B}_0^*), (\mathbb{B}_1, \mathbb{B}_1^*)) \xleftarrow{\mathsf{R}} \mathcal{G}_{\mathsf{ob}}(1^{\lambda}, N_0 := 5, N_1 := 12)$,

for $i = 1, \ldots, d-1$,

$$W_i \xleftarrow{\mathsf{U}} GL(N_1, \mathbb{F}_q), \quad W_i^* := (W_i^{\mathrm{T}})^{-1}, \quad \mathbb{B}_{i+1} := \mathbb{B}_i W_i, \quad \mathbb{B}_{i+1}^* := \mathbb{B}_i^* W_i^*$$
$$\widehat{\mathbb{B}}_0 := (\boldsymbol{b}_{0,1}, \boldsymbol{b}_{0,3}, \boldsymbol{b}_{0,5}), \quad \widehat{\mathbb{B}}_i := (\boldsymbol{b}_{i,1}, \boldsymbol{b}_{i,2}, \boldsymbol{b}_{i,11}, \boldsymbol{b}_{i,12})$$
$$\widehat{\mathbb{B}}_0^* := (\boldsymbol{b}_{0,1}^*, \boldsymbol{b}_{0,3}^*, \boldsymbol{b}_{0,4}^*), \quad \widehat{\mathbb{B}}_i^* := (\boldsymbol{b}_{i,1}^*, \boldsymbol{b}_{i,2}^*, \boldsymbol{b}_{i,9}^*, \boldsymbol{b}_{i,10})$$

$\varphi_0, \omega \xleftarrow{\mathsf{U}} \mathbb{F}_q, \tau \xleftarrow{\mathsf{U}} \mathbb{F}_q^{\times}, \ \boldsymbol{e}_{0,0} := (\omega, 0, 0, 0, \varphi_0)_{\mathbb{B}_0}, \ \boldsymbol{e}_{1,0} := (\omega, \tau, 0, 0, \varphi_0)_{\mathbb{B}_0}$, for $t = 1, \ldots, d, i = 1, 2; \ Z_t \xleftarrow{\mathsf{U}} GL(2, \mathbb{F}_q), \ \vec{e}_1 := (1, 0), \ \vec{e}_2 := (0, 1), \ \vec{\varphi}_{t,i} \xleftarrow{\mathsf{U}} \mathbb{F}_q^2$ $\boldsymbol{e}_{0,t,i} := (\omega \vec{e}_i, \ 0^6, \ 0^2, \ \vec{\varphi}_{t,i})_{\mathbb{B}_t}, \ \boldsymbol{e}_{0,t,i} := (\omega \vec{e}_i, \ \tau \vec{e}_i, \ 0^2, \ \tau \vec{e}_i Z_t, \ 0^2, \ \vec{\varphi}_{t,i})_{\mathbb{B}_t}$, return (param, $\widehat{\mathbb{B}}_0, \widehat{\mathbb{B}}_0^*, \{\widehat{\mathbb{B}}_t, \widehat{\mathbb{B}}_t^*\}_{t=1,\ldots,d}, \boldsymbol{e}_{\beta,0}, \{\boldsymbol{e}_{\beta,t,i}\}_{t=1,\ldots,d,i=1,2})$.

for $\beta \xleftarrow{\mathsf{U}} \{0, 1\}$. *For a probabilistic adversary* $\mathcal{B}$, *the advantage of* $\mathcal{B}$ *for Problem 1 is defined as* $\mathsf{Adv}_{\mathcal{B}}^{\mathsf{P1}}(\lambda) := |\Pr[1 \leftarrow \mathcal{B}(1^{\lambda}, \varrho)| \varrho \xleftarrow{\mathsf{R}} \mathcal{G}_0^{\mathsf{P1}}(1^{\lambda}, \vec{n})] - \Pr[1 \leftarrow \mathcal{B}(1^{\lambda}, \varrho)| \varrho \xleftarrow{\mathsf{R}} \mathcal{G}_1^{\mathsf{P1}}(1^{\lambda}, \vec{n})]|$

Lemma 7. *Problem 1 is computationally intractable under the DLIN assumption.*

The proof of Lemma 7 is similar to the proof of Lemma 3 in [16].

Definition 7 (Problem 2). Problem 2 *is to guess* β, *given* (param, $\widehat{\mathbb{B}}_0, \widehat{\mathbb{B}}_0^*$, $\{\widehat{\mathbb{B}}_t, \widehat{\mathbb{B}}_t^*\}_{t=1,\ldots,d}, \{\boldsymbol{h}_{\beta,t,i}^*, \boldsymbol{e}_{t,i}\}_{t=1,\ldots,d,i=1,2}) \xleftarrow{\mathsf{R}} \mathcal{G}_{\beta}^{\mathsf{P2}}(1^{\lambda}, d)$ *where*

$\mathcal{G}_{\beta}^{\mathsf{P2}}(1^{\lambda}, d):$ (param, $(\mathbb{B}_0, \mathbb{B}_0^*), (\mathbb{B}_1, \mathbb{B}_1^*)) \xleftarrow{\mathsf{R}} \mathcal{G}_{\mathsf{ob}}(1^{\lambda}, N_0 := 5, N_1 := 12)$

for $t = 1, \ldots, d-1, \quad W_i \xleftarrow{\mathsf{U}} GL(N_1, \mathbb{F}_q), \quad W_i^* := (W_i^{\mathrm{T}})^{-1}$,

$$\mathbb{B}_{i+1} := \mathbb{B}_i W_i, \ \widehat{\mathbb{B}}_0 := (\boldsymbol{b}_{0,1}, \boldsymbol{b}_{0,3}, \boldsymbol{b}_{0,5}), \ \widehat{\mathbb{B}}_i := (\boldsymbol{b}_{i,1}, \boldsymbol{b}_{i,2}, \boldsymbol{b}_{i,11}, \boldsymbol{b}_{i,12})$$
$$\mathbb{B}_{i+1}^* := \mathbb{B}_i^* W_i^* \ \widehat{\mathbb{B}}_0^* := (\boldsymbol{b}_{0,1}^*, \boldsymbol{b}_{0,3}^*, \boldsymbol{b}_{0,4}^*), \widehat{\mathbb{B}}_i^* := (\boldsymbol{b}_{i,1}^*, \boldsymbol{b}_{i,2}^*, \boldsymbol{b}_{i,9}^*, \boldsymbol{b}_{i,10}^*)$$

$$\boldsymbol{h}^*_{0,0} := (\delta, 0, 0, \eta_0, 0)_{\mathbb{B}^*_0} \quad \boldsymbol{h}^*_{1,0} := (\delta, \rho, 0, \eta_0, 0)_{\mathbb{B}^*_0}$$

$$\boldsymbol{e}_0 := (\omega, \tau, 0, 0, \varphi_0)_{\mathbb{B}_0}, \quad \vec{e}_1 := (1, 0), \ \vec{e}_2 := (0, 1) \in \mathbb{F}^2_q,$$

for $t = 1, \ldots, d, i = 1, 2;$ $Z_t \xleftarrow{\mathsf{U}} GL(2, \mathbb{F}_q),$ $U_t \xleftarrow{\mathsf{U}} (Z_t^{-1})^{\mathsf{T}},$ $\vec{\eta}_{t,i}, \vec{\varphi}_{t,i} \xleftarrow{\mathsf{U}} \mathbb{F}^2_q$

$$\boldsymbol{h}^*_{0,t,i} := (\ \delta\vec{e}_i, \ 0^6, \ \vec{\eta}_t, \ 0^2 \ )_{\mathbb{B}^*_t}, \quad \boldsymbol{h}^*_{1,t,i} := (\ \delta\vec{e}_i, \ 0^4, \ \rho\vec{e}_i U_t \ \vec{\eta}_t, \ 0^2 \ )_{\mathbb{B}^*_t}$$

$$\boldsymbol{e}_{t,i} := (\ \omega\vec{e}_i, \ \tau\vec{e}_i, \ 0^2, \ \tau\vec{e}_i Z_t, \ 0^2, \ \vec{\varphi}_t \ )_{\mathbb{B}_t}$$

return $(\mathrm{param}, \widehat{\mathbb{B}}_0, \widehat{\mathbb{B}}^*_0, \{\widehat{\mathbb{B}}_t, \widehat{\mathbb{B}}^*_t\}_{t=1,\ldots,d}, \{\boldsymbol{h}^*_{\beta,t,i}, \boldsymbol{e}_{t,i}\}_{t=1,\ldots,d,i=1,2})$

for $\beta \xleftarrow{\mathsf{U}} \{0, 1\}$. For a probabilistic adversary $\mathcal{B}$, the advantage of $\mathcal{B}$ for Problem 2 is defined as same as Definition 6.

Lemma 8. *Problem 2 is computationally intractable under the DLIN assumption.*

The proof of Lemma 8 is similar to the proof of Lemma 4 in [16].

Definition 8 (Problem 3). Problem 3 *is to guess* β, *given* $(\mathrm{param}, \mathbb{B}_0, \mathbb{B}^*_0, \{\mathbb{B}_i, \widehat{\mathbb{B}}^*_i\}_{i=1,\ldots,d}, \{\boldsymbol{h}^*_t, \boldsymbol{e}_{\beta,t}\}_{t=1,\ldots,d}) \xleftarrow{\mathsf{R}} \mathcal{G}^{P3}_\beta(1^\lambda, d)$ *where*

$\mathcal{G}^{P3}_\beta(1^\lambda, d) : (\mathrm{param}, (\mathbb{B}_0, \mathbb{B}^*_0), (\mathbb{B}_1, \mathbb{B}^*_1)) \xleftarrow{\mathsf{R}} \mathcal{G}_{\mathrm{ob}}(1^\lambda, N_0 := 5, N_1 := 12)$

for $i = 1, \ldots, d - 1$

$W_i \xleftarrow{\mathsf{U}} GL(N_1, \mathbb{F}_q), \ W^*_i := (W^{\mathsf{T}}_i)^{-1}, \ \mathbb{B}_{i+1} := \mathbb{B}_i W_i \ \mathbb{B}^*_{i+1} := \mathbb{B}^*_i W^*_i$

for $t = 1, \ldots, d$ $\widehat{\mathbb{B}}^*_t := (\boldsymbol{b}^*_{t,2}, \boldsymbol{b}^*_{t,4}, \ldots, \boldsymbol{b}^*_{t,12}), \ u, \omega, \tau, \xleftarrow{\mathsf{U}} \mathbb{F}_q, \ \vec{r}_t, \vec{z}_t, \vec{\eta}_t, \vec{\varphi}_t \xleftarrow{\mathsf{U}} \mathbb{F}^2_q$

$\boldsymbol{h}^*_t := (u, \ 0, \ 0^4, \ \vec{r}_t, \ \vec{\eta}_t, \ 0^2)_{\mathbb{B}^*_t}$

$\boldsymbol{e}_{0,t} := (0, \ 0, \ 0^4, \ \vec{z}_t, \ 0^2, \ \vec{\varphi}_t)_{\mathbb{B}_t}, \ \boldsymbol{e}_{1,t} := (\omega, \ 0, \ \tau, \ 0^3, \ \vec{z}_t, \ 0^2, \ \vec{\varphi}_t)_{\mathbb{B}_t}$

return $(\mathrm{param}, \mathbb{B}_0, \mathbb{B}^*_0, \{\mathbb{B}_i, \widehat{\mathbb{B}}^*_i\}_{i=1,\ldots,d}, \{\boldsymbol{h}^*_t, \boldsymbol{e}_{\beta,t}\}_{t=1,\ldots,d})$

for $\beta \xleftarrow{\mathsf{U}} \{0, 1\}$. For a probabilistic adversary $\mathcal{B}$, the advantage of $\mathcal{B}$ for Problem 3 is defined as same as Definition 6.

Lemma 9. *Problem 3 is computationally intractable under the DLIN assumption.*

The proof of Lemma 9 is similar to the proof of Lemma 5 in [16].
The full proofs of Lemmas 7, 8 and 9 are shown in the full version of this paper.

References

1. Abdalla, M., Bellare, M., Catalano, D., Kiltz, E., Kohno, T., Lange, T., Malone-Lee, J., Neven, G., Paillier, P., Shi, H.: Searchable encryption revisited: consistency properties, relation to anonymous IBE, and extensions. In: Shoup, V. (ed.) CRYPTO 2005. LNCS, vol. 3621, pp. 205–222. Springer, Heidelberg (2005)
2. Bethencourt, J., Sahai, A., Waters, B.: Ciphertext-policy attribute-based encryption. In: IEEE Symposium on Security and Privacy, pp. 321–334 (2007)
3. Boneh, D., Boyen, X., Shacham, H.: Short group signatures. In: Franklin, M. (ed.) CRYPTO 2004. LNCS, vol. 3152, pp. 41–55. Springer, Heidelberg (2004)

4. Boneh, D., Di Crescenzo, G., Ostrovsky, R., Persiano, G.: Public key encryption with keyword search. In: Cachin, C., Camenisch, J.L. (eds.) EUROCRYPT 2004. LNCS, vol. 3027, pp. 506–522. Springer, Heidelberg (2004)

5. Boneh, D., Hamburg, M.: Generalized identity based and broadcast encryption schemes. In: Pieprzyk, J. (ed.) ASIACRYPT 2008. LNCS, vol. 5350, pp. 455–470. Springer, Heidelberg (2008)

6. Boneh, D., Waters, B.: Conjunctive, subset, and range queries on encrypted data. In: Vadhan, S.P. (ed.) TCC 2007. LNCS, vol. 4392, pp. 535–554. Springer, Heidelberg (2007)

7. Chase, M., Shen, E.: Substring-searchable symmetric encryption. PETS 2015 **2015**(2), 263–281 (2015)

8. Curtmola, R., Garay, J.A., Kamara, S., Ostrovsky, R.: Searchable symmetric encryption: improved definitions and efficient constructions. In: 13th ACMCCS, pp. 79–88 (2006)

9. Goyal, V., Pandey, O., Sahai, A., Waters, B.: Attribute-based encryption for fine-grained access control of encrypted data. In: Proceedings of the 13th ACM conference on Computer and Communications Security - ACM CCS 2006, pp. 89–98 (2006)

10. Katz, J., Sahai, A., Waters, B.: Predicate encryption supporting disjunctions, polynomial equations, and inner products. In: Smart, N.P. (ed.) EUROCRYPT 2008. LNCS, vol. 4965, pp. 146–162. Springer, Heidelberg (2008)

11. Li, J., Wang, Q., Wang, C., Cao, N., Ren, K., Lou, W.: Fuzzy keyword search over encrypted data in cloud computing. In: IEEE INFOCOM 2010 (Mini-Conference), pp. 1–5 (2010)

12. Okamoto, T., Takashima, K.: Homomorphic encryption and signatures from vector decomposition. In: Galbraith, S.D., Paterson, K.G. (eds.) Pairing 2008. LNCS, vol. 5209, pp. 57–74. Springer, Heidelberg (2008)

13. Okamoto, T., Takashima, K.: Hierarchical predicate encryption for inner-products. In: Matsui, M. (ed.) ASIACRYPT 2009. LNCS, vol. 5912, pp. 214–231. Springer, Heidelberg (2009)

14. Okamoto, T., Takashima, K.: Fully secure functional encryption with general relations from the decisional linear assumption. In: Rabin, T. (ed.) CRYPTO 2010. LNCS, vol. 6223, pp. 191–208. Springer, Heidelberg (2010)

15. Okamoto, T., Takashima, K.: Adaptively attribute-hiding (hierarchical) inner product encryption. In: Pointcheval, D., Johansson, T. (eds.) EUROCRYPT 2012. LNCS, vol. 7237, pp. 591–608. Springer, Heidelberg (2012)

16. Okamoto, T., Takashima, K.: Fully secure unbounded inner-product and attribute-based encryption. In: Wang, X., Sako, K. (eds.) ASIACRYPT 2012. LNCS, vol. 7658, pp. 349–366. Springer, Heidelberg (2012)

17. Ostrovsky, R., Sahai, A., Waters, B.: Attribute-based encryption with non-monotonic access structures. In: ACM CCS 2007, pp. 195–203 (2007)

18. Pirretti, M., Traynor, P., McDaniel, P., Waters, B.: Secure attribute-based systems. In: ACM CCS 2006, pp. 99–112 (2006)

19. Sedghi, S., van Liesdonk, P., Nikova, S., Hartel, P., Jonker, W.: Searching keywords with wildcards on encrypted data. In: Garay, J.A., De Prisco, R. (eds.) SCN 2010. LNCS, vol. 6280, pp. 138–153. Springer, Heidelberg (2010)

20. Shi, E., Waters, B.: Delegating capabilities in predicate encryption systems. In: Aceto, L., Damgård, I., Goldberg, L.A., Halldórsson, M.M., Ingólfsdóttir, A., Walukiewicz, I. (eds.) ICALP 2008, Part II. LNCS, vol. 5126, pp. 560–578. Springer, Heidelberg (2008)

21. Song, D.X., Wagner, D., Perrig, A.: Practical techniques for searches on encrypted data. In: Security and Privacy 2000, pp. 44–55. IEEE (2000)
22. Tang, Q., Chen, L.: Public-key encryption with registered keyword search. In: Martinelli, F., Preneel, B. (eds.) EuroPKI 2009. LNCS, vol. 6391, pp. 163–178. Springer, Heidelberg (2010)
23. Waters, B.: Ciphertext-policy attribute-based encryption: an expressive, efficient, and provably secure realization. In: Catalano, D., Fazio, N., Gennaro, R., Nicolosi, A. (eds.) PKC 2011. LNCS, vol. 6571, pp. 53–70. Springer, Heidelberg (2011)

Attacks and Malicious Code

Bad Sounds Good Sounds: Attacking and Defending Tap-Based Rhythmic Passwords Using Acoustic Signals

S. Abhishek Anand[✉], Prakash Shrestha, and Nitesh Saxena

University of Alabama at Birmingham, Birmingham, AL 35294, USA
{anandab,prakashs,saxena}@cis.uab.edu

Abstract. Tapping-based rhythmic passwords have recently been proposed for the purpose of user authentication and device pairing. They offer a usability advantage over traditional passwords in that memorizing and recalling rhythms is believed to be an easier task for human users. Such passwords might also be harder to guess, thus possibly providing higher security.

Given these potentially unique advantages, we set out to closely investigate the security of tapping-based rhythmic passwords. Specifically, we show that rhythmic passwords are susceptible to observation attacks based on acoustic side channels – an attacker in close physical proximity of the user can eavesdrop and extract the password being entered based on the tapping sounds. We develop and evaluate our attacks employing human users (human attack) as well as off-the-shelf signal processing techniques (automated attack), and demonstrate their feasibility. Further, we propose a defense based on sound masking aimed to cloak the acoustic side channels. We evaluate our proposed defense system against both human attacks and automated attacks, and show that it can be effective depending upon the type of masking sounds.

1 Introduction

Many online and offline services rely upon user authentication to protect users' data, credentials and other sensitive information, such as when used to logging into websites or devices, or to "pair" the devices [11]. Passwords and PINs represent the most dominant means of authentication deployed today. However, traditional passwords suffer from a number of well-known security and usability problems [1,14,18]. Specifically, passwords are often only weak, low-entropy secrets due to the user-memorability requirement. As such they can be easy to guess, enabling online brute-forcing attacks and offline dictionary attacks. Moreover, authentication and pairing mechanisms on constrained devices (e.g., headsets or access points) can be a challenging task due to lack of a proper input interface. Typing passwords or PINs requires a keyboard (physical or virtual) to enter the text. However, most of the constrained devices have either only a button or a microphone for input.

© Springer International Publishing Switzerland 2015
M. Reiter and D. Naccache (Eds.): CANS 2015, LNCS 9476, pp. 95–110, 2015.
DOI: 10.1007/978-3-319-26823-1_7

Tap-based rhythmic passwords [12,16] have been proposed as an alternative to traditional text based passwords as they can be unique to an individual and are much harder to replicate. Wobbrock's TapSongs [16] is a tapping-based authentication mechanism for devices having a single binary sensor. In this method, the user is required to tap a rhythm, for example a song, using the binary sensor, which can be a button or a switch. Matching the tapping pattern entered by the user with a previously stored pattern achieves the authentication. The key idea behind this mechanism is the assumption that every individual has a unique tapping pattern for a given rhythm that can serve the same purpose as other authentication modalities like signatures, fingerprints or retinal patterns. They also offer a usability advantage over traditional passwords in that perceiving, memorizing and performing rhythms is an easier task for human users, as demonstrated by music psychologists [6,7,17].

Lin et al.'s RhythmLink [12] extends the TapSongs work by using tap intervals extracted from the tapping pattern for "pairing" two devices. The peripheral device that is to be paired sends the tapping model to the user's phone that stores the timing model for authentication. Euclidean distance is used for as a heuristic for matching the received pattern with the stored pattern. Similar to TapSongs [16], if the two patterns are within a certain threshold, a successful match is determined.

Our Contributions: Given the unique security and usability advantages of tap-based rhythmic passwords, we set out to closely investigate their security. Specifically, we show that these passwords are susceptible to observation attacks based on *acoustic side channels* – an attacker in close physical proximity of the user can eavesdrop and extract the password being entered based on the tapping sounds. We develop and evaluate our attacks employing human users (*human attack*) as well as off-the-shelf signal processing techniques (*automated attack*), and demonstrate their feasibility in realistic scenarios. Our results show that the automated attack is highly successful with an average accuracy of more than 85 %. The human attack is less successful, but still succeeds with an accuracy of 66 % for short passwords (less than 10 taps) and about 21 % for long passwords (greater than 10 taps).

Going further, we propose a simple defense mechanism based on *sound masking* aimed to cloak the acoustic side channels. The idea is that the authentication terminal itself inserts acoustic noise while the user inputs the tap-based rhythmic password. We evaluate the proposed defense system against both the human attack and the automated attack. The results show that, depending upon the type of noise inserted, both automated and human attacks could be undermined effectively.

Our work highlights a practical vulnerability of a potentially attractive form of authentication and proposes a viable defense that may help mitigate this vulnerability.

Related Work: Acoustic Side Channel Attacks: Acoustic eavesdropping was first studied as a side channel attack, applicable to traditional passwords, by Asonov and Agrawal [2], where they showed that it was possible to distinguish between different keys pressed on a keyboard by the sound emanated by them. They used Fast Fourier Transform (FFT) features of press segments of keystrokes to train a neural network for identification of individual keys. Zhuang et al. [19]

improved upon the work of Asonov and Agrawal by using Mel Frequency Cepstrum Coefficient (MFCC) for feature extraction from keystroke emanations that would yield better accuracy results. Halevi and Saxena [9] further improved upon the accuracy of such class of attacks using time-frequency decoding of the acoustic signal.

In another work, Halevi and Saxena [10] extended the acoustic side channel attacks to device pairing. They demonstrated that it is possible to recover the exchanged secret during device pairing using acoustic emanations. Recent work by Shamir and Tromer [8] has shown that it is possible to extract an RSA decryption key using the sound emitted by the CPU during the decryption phase of some chosen ciphertexts. Acoustic side channel attacks have also been used against dot matrix printers by Backes et al. [4] to recognize the text being printed.

Compared to the above prior research, our work investigates the feasibility of acoustic emanations attacks against tap-based rhythmic passwords unlike traditional passwords, typed input or cryptographic secrets. In addition to automated attacks, we investigate and demonstrate the feasibility of human-based acoustic eavesdropping attacks against rhythmic passwords. It is noteworthy that the traditional passwords do not seem vulnerable to such human attacks given that it may be impossible for a human attacker to infer the key pressed based on the key-press sound (all keys may sound alike).

2   Background

2.1   System Model

The authentication system proposed by TapSongs [16] defines the following conditions to be satisfied for successful authentication of an input tap pattern. Our implementation of TapSongs, as our target system, therefore uses the exact same conditions.

- The number of taps should be same in the input pattern and the user's tap pattern stored in the system for authentication.
- The total time duration of the input pattern should be within a third of the time duration of the stored pattern for the user.
- Every time interval between consecutive tap events in the input pattern should be within three standard deviations from the corresponding time intervals in the stored tap pattern for the user.

2.2   Threat Model and Attack Phases

The threat model of our attack consists of three distinct phases: *Snooping and Recording, Processing* and *Password Reconstruction,* as described below.

Phase I: Snooping and Recording: This is the initial phase, where the adversary attempts to listen to the users' tapping. In the user study reported in the TapSongs work [16], it was found that, for a human attacker eavesdropping from a distance of 3 ft, while the victim user inputs the tap pattern, the mean login success rate is very low (10.7 %). The reason attributed to the low success rate is the unfamiliarity of the human attacker with the tap rhythm being used. Hence, while the attacker could infer the correct number of taps with a high probability (77.4 %), unfamiliarity with the rhythm made it almost impossible to imitate the tapping pattern in *real-time* during eavesdropping.

We modify the attack model used by Wobbrock [16] to increase the capability of the adversary. Our attack model is very similar to the one considered by prior research on keyboard acoustic emanations [2,19]. We assume that the adversary has installed a hidden audio listening device very close to the input device or interface being used for the tap input. A covert wireless "bug", a PC microphone (perhaps a compromised microphone belonging to the host device itself) or a mobile phone microphone are examples of such a listening device. The listening device can be programmed to record the acoustic emanations as the user taps in the rhythm, and transmit the recordings to another computer controlled by the attacker.

Thus, unlike [16], the attacker does not need to reconstruct the tap-based password in real-time, but rather the attacker can record the typed password for later *offline* processing (possibly involving training) and reconstruction. Moreover, given the recording capability, we extend the threat model of [16] to incorporate automated attacks besides human attacks.

Phase II: Processing: This phase uses the recorded audio from the earlier phase to extract the desired spectral features of the tapping pattern. The naive way to extract this information is to familiarize the attacker with the tap rhythm (human attack). The attacker can accurately know the number of taps in the pattern and to some extent, an approximation to the time interval between the taps. A potentially more accurate method is to use signal processing techniques in order to extract the relevant features from the recordings (automated attack).

Phase III: Password Reconstruction: Once the adversary has learned the tapping patterns' characteristics, it can imitate the tapping pattern to try to break the authentication functionality provided by tap-based password. If the adversary has physical access to the machine (e.g., lunch-time access to the authentication terminal or when working with a stolen terminal), the tap patterns can be entered directly to the input interface either manually or using a mechanical/robotic finger pre-programmed with the tapping pattern. In contrast, if the tap-based password is being used for remote authentication (e.g., web site login), the attacker can simply reconstruct the password using its own machine. In this case, the attacker can install an automated program (e.g., a Java robot) on its machine that will simply input the reconstructed password to the web site so as to impersonate the victim user.

3   Attack Overview and Scenarios

We classify our attack into two categories: *automated attacks* and *human attacks*.

(a) Tap performed using a key or a button, and the recording device is placed on the same surface as the input device

(b) Tap performed using a key or a button, and the recording device is hand-held

Fig. 1. Attack scenarios against rhythmic passwords (the circled device represents the audio recording device used by the attacker)

3.1 Automated Attacks

The automated attack deploys a recording device to eavesdrop upon the taps entered by the user. The tapping-based schemes require the user to tap a rhythm on a binary sensor like a button or any sensor which can be binarized to serve the purpose, like microphones or touchscreens. An attacker, who is in vicinity of the victim, records the sound generated from the tapping action and uses the recorded tapping pattern to reconstruct an approximation to the tapping pattern of the victim. As discussed in Sect. 2.2, the attack consists of three phases, each of which can be automated. We begin with the *Snooping and Recording* phase, where the attacker is recording the tapping pattern using a recorder. There can be three most likely cases, described below, based on the positioning of the input sensor used by the victim to enter the taps, the device used by the attacker and the environment in which the attack takes place.

S1: Key Tapping; Recording Device on Surface: In this scenario (Fig. 1a), the user uses a button or a key on her device for tapping a rhythm. This tapping pattern is matched against the stored pattern and success or failure is determined during authentication. When a key or button is pressed by the user, it produces a sound corresponding to key press followed by a softer sound produced due to key/button release that can be recorded by an adversary during the input. Later, the adversary can extract relevant features from the victim's tapping pattern stored in the recording. The recording itself can be done inconspicuously. Any device with a microphone, for example a smartphone or a USB recorder, can be used for recording that makes it hard to distinguish the adversary from non-malicious entity.

In order for an accurate recording of the clicks, the recording device should be as near to the victim as possible while the adversary need not be physically present during the attack. A possible setup could be hiding a microphone under the table or placing the smartphone or the USB recorder on the table, which are tuned for recording while giving no clue about their malicious intent.

S2: Key Tapping; Recording Device Hand-Held: In this scenario (Fig. 1b), the tapping pattern is being input via a button or a key on the device while the adversary records the clicks, standing close to the victim. This scenario is analogous to shoulder surfing where the adversary is recording the sound clicks while standing behind the victim, who is unaware of her input being recorded. Since, the adversary is standing behind the victim, the input device and the recording device are not in proximity of each other. Hence, the recording will be fainter than the previous scenario, if the recording device remains unchanged. Also, the air gap between the two devices dampens the audio signal, unlike in previous scenario, where the table surface allowed the sound to travel unimpeded.

3.2 Human Attacks

In the human attacks against tap-based passwords, unlike the automated attacks, the adversary himself manually tries to replicate the tapping pattern based on the recorded audio. Adversary listens to the tapping rhythm and tries to reproduce it. There are two possible human attack scenarios. In the first scenario, the adversary aurally eavesdrops while the victim is tapping the rhythmic password in real time, memorizes the tapping and tries to replicate it. As mentioned previously, this is the scenario proposed and studied by Wobbrock [16]. However, in this scenario, the adversary can not perfectly reproduce the tapping by just listening it once in real-time, but it may be possible to estimate the tapping rhythm to a certain degree of accuracy.

In the second human attack scenario, which is what we propose and investigate in this paper, we assume that an adversary installs an audio listening device near the victim device and records, while the victim is tapping. This enables the adversary to obtain a recording of tapping and listen to it multiple times. The adversary can make an estimate of the tap counts more accurately. Moreover, adversary can now train himself and can possibly replicate the tapping with better accuracy. The recording scenarios are similar to the scenarios S1 and S2 applicable to the automated attacks.

4 Attack Design and Implementation

4.1 Automated Attack

To extract the relevant features from the eavesdropped signal, we apply signal processing algorithms using MATLAB software. We begin by detecting the number of taps in the eavesdropped signal. Previous works [2,5,9,19] each have used different features to detect keystrokes from acoustic emanations. The commonly used features in these works have been Fast Fourier Transformation (FFT), Mel Frequency Cepstrum Coefficients (MFCC), Cross Correlation and Time-Frequency classifications. Since, there is no need to classify the taps, we can just use the FFT features to estimate the energy levels in the signal. A significant peak in the energy level in the frequency spectrum would indicate a possible tap.

Signal Processing Algorithm: We record the signal with a sampling frequency of 44.1 kHz, which is sufficient for reconstruction of our original signal. The processing of the recorded signal begins by converting the digital signal from time domain to frequency domain for identifying the frequency range of the tapping sound. This is achieved by calculating the Fast Fourier transformation (FFT) of the signal. We use a window of size 440 which provides a frequency resolution of roughly 100 Hz. A brief glance at the spectrogram (Fig. 2) of the signal reveals the taps, which are characterized by the sharp horizontal power peaks covering the spectrum.

We use the sum of FFT coefficients to identify the beginning of a tap. For minimizing the noise interference, we only use the samples in the frequency range of 2.5–7.5 kHz. The *sumFFT* (sum of FFT coefficients for the frequency range) graph and *sumPower* (sum of Power for the frequency range) graph are depicted in Appendix Fig. 3).

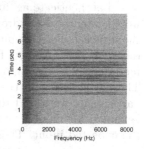

Fig. 2. Spectrogram of a sample tapping pattern

A threshold is used for discovering the start of a tap event. Initially, the threshold is set as the maximum value of the sum of FFT coefficients and decremented by 10 % after every failed authentication for each such iteration till the signal is authenticated successfully (Sect. 2.1) or the threshold reaches the minimum FFT coefficient sum. Here we assume that the time interval between two consecutive taps will not be less than 100 ms. Next, we compared the key press as a tap event and the mean of press and release as a tap event and found out that authentication accuracy was similar so we proceeded with key press. However, if the tap duration is also made a part of authentication, the mean of key press and release would be a better indicator of the tap event.

Once we obtained the number of taps and time interval between each tap event, we need to authenticate it against the model proposed by Wobbrock's TapSongs [16] for verification. In this *Password Reconstruction* phase, the attack can occur locally by tapping on the input sensor (local terminal authentication) or remotely by launching an application that emulates the tap event (remote authentication).

For an automated attack to be launched locally, we would need a mechanical device to be programmed such that it taps on the input sensor according to the features extracted during the *Processing* phase. Simple "Lego" robots can be used for this purpose (more sophisticated Lego robots against various touchscreen gestures have already been developed in prior research [15]). To launch our attack remotely, we designed a Java code using the Robot class, which simulates key press events at intervals specified by the extracted features.

4.2 Human Attack

Processing and *Password Reconstruction* in the human attack are rather straightforward. This attack requires no external processing as the attacker trains on the eavesdropped tap signal by repeatedly listening to it so as to discern the number of taps and the time interval between each taps. However, *Password Reconstruction* has to be executed soon after training is performed, otherwise the attacker may forget the tapping pattern and may have to train again.

5   Attack Experiments and Evaluation

5.1   Automated Attack

For evaluating our automated attack, we have to create a user base, who would authenticate against the tapping based authentication mechanism. They would later be eavesdropped and have their authentication compromised by the attacker. For this purpose, we conducted a user study with ten individuals (ages 24–35, 7 males; 3 females) studying Computer Science at our University, recruited by word of mouth. The study was approved by our University's IRB. The participation in the study was consent-based and strictly voluntary. The participants were told to tap out a rhythm of their choice on a MacBook Air keyboard for number of taps not exceeding 20, for creating a timing model of the expected input. Then, they were asked to authenticate against the system for a few times so as to get comfortable with the design.

The experiment was performed under two scenarios. In the first scenario (Fig. 1a), the participants were asked to make an authentication attempt by tapping out their rhythm on a single key of the keyboard, while a smartphone (Nokia Lumia 800) placed beside the keyboard, was setup for recording. The whole setup was placed at an office desk in a quiet lab environment. The recordings were taken at different distances not exceeding 1 meter. For the second setup (Fig. 1b), the smartphone was handheld by an attacker, who was standing behind the subject while they were tapping. The recording was done using a free voice recorder application.

Out of the ten participants, six chose a rhythm of less than 10 taps (short taps) and four chose a rhythm of tap length between 10–20 (long taps). We observed that the participants preferred to tap short tunes but it also made easier to discern the tapping pattern. As the tap length increases, the degree of error in the recording may increase. This may happen due to noise interference or due to soft taps by the user, which is natural while attempting to tap a long rhythm. On the other hand, for a longer tapping pattern, the user is more prone to missing out a few taps at random. Once the recordings were done, we processed the eavesdropped samples according to our algorithm described in Sect. 4.1. Once we got the time duration between each tap event and the number of tap events in the eavesdropped sample, we fed this information to a simple java application that used the *java.awt.Robot* class to recreate the tapping pattern by simulating keypress events at the given time intervals.

The results corresponding to our different testing set-ups are provided in Table 1. The detection rate for the tapping pattern is quite high, ranging from 87.5–96.3 %, highlighting the vulnerability of tap-based rhythmic passwords. As conjectured before, the attack accuracy decreases with increase in the number of taps. Another observation is that shoulder surfing is slightly less accurate than placing the recording bug on the same surface as the input device.

Table 1. Performance of the automated attack

Attack scenarios	Length of the tap pattern	Accuracy
S1	Short	96.3 %
S2	Short	92.8 %
S1	Long	87.5 %
S2	Long	87.5 %

Table 2. Performance of the human attack

Length of the tap pattern	Correct tap count	Accuracy	Avg. number of attempts for the first success (out of 5 attempts)
Short	94.4 %	66.0 %	1.9
Long	95.3 %	21.3 %	3.4

5.2 Human Attack

In our human attack user study, we recruited 10 users who served the role of the attackers. Participants were mostly Computer Science students (ages 25–35, 7 males; 3 females) recruited by word of mouth. Four users could play a musical instrument. The study was approved by our University's IRB. The participation in the study was consent-based and strictly voluntary.

As in the automated attack, we considered two types of tap rhythms – short tap rhythm and long tap rhythm. We used 5 short taps and 3 long taps. They were collected during the automated attack experiment by placing an audio listening device approximately 2 ft from the tapping device.

In the study, the participants' goal was to replicate the victim's tap-based password based on audio clips. Prior to the study, we told the participants that the purpose of the study was to collect information on how well they can replicate the tapping rhythm based on audio recordings. We purposefully did not disclose the true (security) purpose of the study so as not to bias the participants' behavior in the experiment. We explicitly informed the participants that the tapping rhythm has to be matched in its entirety for a successful replication. In real world scenario, most authentication terminals or online services block the user after 3–5 unsuccessful attempts. To simulate this, the participants in the study were instructed to replicate each of the rhythm 5 times, and as in a real world scenario, the participants would be notified of a successful or a failed attempt immediately. If they failed, they could practice more and retry in the next trials.

The human attack experiment comprised of two phases: (1) *training*, and (2) *testing*. In the training phase, each participant was asked to listen to each of the clips through a headset carefully up to a maximum of 15 times, and practice as per their comfort level by tapping either on a table nearby or keyboard without using our authentication system. In the testing phase, they were asked to replicate the tapping rhythm of the original audio clip (challenge) using our authentication system. After each unsuccessful attempt, they were instructed to listen to the audio clip carefully and practice again.

We collected 80 samples over 10 sessions with our participants. Each session involved a participant performing the attack (testing) against 5 short and 3 long tapping patterns. The experimental results are depicted in Table 2. We can see that about 94 % of the short tap entries had the correct tap count, and the average login success rate was 66 %. In contrast, even if 95 % of the long tap entries had the correct tap count, the average login success rate for long tap was only 21.3 %. The average number of attempts to achieve the first successful login was nearly 2 for short taps and 4 for long taps.

The results show that the login success rate was greater for short taps than long taps. This is intuitive as greater the length of taps, the harder it is to replicate the pattern. Although the success rate of our human attack is lower compared to that of our automated attack, it is still quite high, especially for short taps, and much higher compared to the success rate of the human attack reported in [16]. The ability to record and train on previously eavesdropped samples seems to have significantly improved the human capability to replicate the tapping pattern in our attack, rather than attempting to replicate the pattern in real-time as done in [16].

6   Defense: Masking the Audio Channel

6.1   Background

Various defense mechanisms have been proposed to safeguard against acoustic eavesdropping. Asonov et al. [2] proposed the use of silent keyboards to hide the acoustic emanations. Acoustic shielding, another defense mechanism, involves sound proofing the system by reducing the signal to noise ratio. Another approach is to deliberately insert noise within the audio signal that makes identifying the desired features, a hard task. This general idea represents an active defense mechanism and is the focus of this work in order to defeat the acoustic eavesdropping attacks explicitly against tap-based passwords. Zhuang et al. [19] briefly suggested a similar approach, but no practical mechanism was discussed.

There are many challenges that need to be met in realizing the above active defense based on masking sounds. The main criterion for this defense to be effective is that the noise spectrum should be similar to the signal spectrum with sufficient energy so as to completely blanket the acoustic signal being eavesdropped.

Another important criterion is the timing of the masking signal when it is played in parallel with the original acoustic signal. If the masking signal is continuous in nature having uniform features then the timing is of no concern. However, if the masking signal consists of discrete sounds, we need to ensure that these sounds occur at the same time as the actual sounds events in the signal we are trying to mask so that they overlap thereby hiding the features of the original sound spectrum. The last criterion is the usability of the masking signal. It should not be distracting to the user otherwise users may be hesitant to use it in real-life.

6.2   Our Defense Model

We now present an active sound masking defense mechanism to defeat the acoustic eavesdropping attacks described in previous sections of this paper. There is no extra hardware cost associated with this approach as it only requires an audio transmitter, which most devices are already equipped with.

The choice of an appropriate masking signal plays a vital role in the efficiency of the defense system. We experimented with four classes of sounds that could be used as the masking signal. The first class of masking sounds is the *white noise*. White noise has often been used as a soothing sound, hence it would pose no distraction to the user. The second class of masking sound is *music*, which again is user-friendly and pleasing.

The third class of masking sound would be random samples of the tap sound itself (*fake taps*). This sound is the natural candidate for being as similar to the actual audio signal we are trying to hide. In the context of human voices, we can use human chatter from a busy coffee shop or other public places to hide the actual conversation. In case of keystrokes, we can use random keystrokes different from the actual keystrokes for masking. For our purpose, we use the tapping sounds from the same input interface used for tapping. If the tapping device is a keyboard, we make use of random keystrokes, and if it is a button, we use button clicks (fake clicks) as the masking signal. The last class of masking sound is created by *summing up* all the above three classes into one signal. This layered approach combines the different masking capabilities from the three classes of masking signals discussed above.

In the attacks we have presented in this paper, a valid tap event is detected by having energy above a certain threshold. If we want our masking signal to be similar to the taps, we need the energy of the masking signal to be almost equal or higher than that of the taps.

6.3   Defense Experiments

For our experiment to evaluate our defense mechanism, we chose the tapping sound from a keyboard as the input device emanations, and audio recordings of the above-mentioned four classes of noises as the sound masking signals. We selected few samples of white noise and music from the Internet. To create the fake taps, we asked one of the users from our study group to randomly generate keystrokes while we recorded the produced sound that would be used as fake taps.

Next, we performed the authentication step (password entry) repeatedly with each type of masking signal playing in the background, while the attacker is eavesdropping. The control condition for this experiment was a similar setting with *no* masking sounds, simulating the original tap-based password entry without our defense mechanism.

Evaluation Against Automated Attacks: We evaluated our defense model against the automated attacks that use signal processing algorithms to detect tap events by extracting FFT features. We chose one of the users from our user study, who tapped his tap pattern in presence of each of the above described masking signals playing in the background. The number of taps present in the users' tapping pattern was 5.

Our experiments indicate that while the white noise affects the spectrum as a whole (Appendix Fig. 4(a)), it does not offer much resistance against the automated attacks, as depicted by the FFT plot of the eavesdropped signal shown in Appendix Fig. 5(a). Similarly, music is also insufficient against the automated attacks because it is unable to shield the tap sounds completely, as shown in the spectrogram in Fig. 4(b). The FFT plot in Fig. 5(b) also indicates that music can be easily excluded from taps based on its frequency distribution. Since, we summed up the frequencies between 2.5kHz–7.5kHz, any musical notes that have frequencies outside this range are filtered out.

We next tested the feasibility of sound masking with fake taps, and with a combination of white noise, music and fake taps. While both fake taps and the combined signal alone were able to mask the signal, the combined signal emerged as the preferred choice as it covered a larger area of the spectrum (Fig. 4(d)), and we believe that it would be less distracting to the users than the fake tap sounds alone due to music and white noise accompanying the signal. Figure 5(c) and (d) show the FFT vs Time plot for the user's taps when the masking signal is fake taps and the combined signal, respectively. As observed from the figures, it is hard to chose a threshold value that could accurately detect the tap events without including any fake taps.

Evaluation Against Human Attacks: For the evaluation of our defense against human attacks, we chose the same four different types of masking sounds as in our automated attack experiment: (1) white noise, (2) music, (3) fake taps, and (4) white noise, music and fake taps combined. We then conducted our human attack experiment against all the above "noisy" rhythms with one of the researcher of our team playing the role of a well-trained adversary (thus representing a potentially powerful attacker). We tested all the

Table 3. Performance of the human attack with and without our defense

Masking signal	Correct tap count	Accuracy	Avg. number of attempts for the first success (out of 5 attempts)
Short Taps			
none	96.0 %	84.0 %	1.4
white noise	100.0 %	80.0 %	1.0
music	96.0 %	80.0 %	1.4
fake taps	52.0 %	16.0 %	3.4
combined	4.0 %	0.0 %	Failed in all attempts
Long Taps			
none	100.0 %	26.7 %	1.3
white noise	100.0 %	26.7 %	3.0
music	93.3 %	33.4 %	3.7
fake taps	46.7 %	0.0 %	Failed in all attempts
combined	6.7 %	0.0 %	Failed in all attempts

samples that we used in our original human attack experiment (discussed in previous section) but in the presence of each of the four class of noises. As in our original human attack experiment, adversary went through training and testing phases against each of the 8 tapping samples (5 short and 3 long tapping patterns).

Table 3 summarizes the attacker's performance replicating the tap rhythms with and without noises. It shows that the tap rhythm with white noise or music as the masking signal did not affect the performance by much across both long and short rhythms. However, the addition of fake taps and combined signals greatly reduced the attacker's performance. With addition of fake taps, the attacker was somehow able to estimate the tap length (around 50 %) in both short and long rhythms but was not able to replicate them successfully. Addition of fake taps on short rhythm greatly reduced the attacker's accuracy of replicating the rhythm down to 16 %, while addition of combined signals completely reduced the accuracy to 0 %. In case of long tap rhythm, addition of both fake taps and combined signal completely also reduced the accuracy to 0 %.

These results show that the masking sounds consisting of fake taps and combined noises may effectively defeat a human attacker's capability to replicate a tapping pattern. Such sounds, especially the combined signal, earlier also proved effective against the automated attacks, and could therefore be a viable means to cloak the acoustic side channels underlying rhythmic passwords.

7 Discussion and Future Work

Other Rhythmic Passwords Schemes and Input Mechanisms: Several other authentication schemes have been proposed, which are based on TapSongs [16]. Marqueus et al. [13] built upon TapSongs to develop a scheme that provides inconspicuous authentication to smartphone users. Tap-based rhythmic passwords also provide an alternative to traditional authentication methods for the visually impaired mobile device users. Azenkot et al. [3] presented Passchords, a scheme that uses multiple finger taps as an authentication mechanism. They concluded that using multiple fingers in place of a single finger tap or a single button increases the entropy of the system.

Both the above schemes may also be vulnerable to acoustic eavesdropping attacks. Eavesdropping the taps on smartphone touch screen might be harder due to the low intensity of tapping sounds. The impact of observing taps against visually-impaired users may be higher given these users may not be able to detect the presence of should-surfing around them. Further work is necessary to evaluate these contexts.

In our experiments, we used a keyboard but the attack can be extended to a button using the same attack principle. Halevi and Saxena [10] have already showed that button press is also susceptible to similar acoustic eavesdropping attack though the amplitude of the signal would be considerably lower and some attack parameters need to be adjusted accordingly.

Comparing with Traditional Passwords: In light of the attacks presented in our paper, it appears that rhythmic passwords are more vulnerable to acoustic emanations compared to traditional passwords. This is natural given that eavesdropping over traditional passwords requires the attacker to infer "what keys are being pressed" (a harder task), whereas eavesdropping over rhythmic passwords only requires the attacker to learn "when the taps are being made" (an easier task). The accuracies of detecting traditional passwords based on acoustic emanations reported in previous work [9] seem lower than the accuracies of our automated attacks against rhythmic passwords. Traditional passwords do not seem vulnerable to human attacks as it may be impossible for human users to distinguish between the sounds of different keys, while rhythmic passwords are prone to such attacks too as our work demonstrated.

Usability of Our Defense: Adding the masking signal, which is comparable to the acoustic leakage in its frequency band, helps hiding the acoustic leakage in case of rhythmic passwords. We chose our masking signals based on the intuition that the usability of rhythmic password entry would not be degraded by much. However, it might not always be the most practical solution and may confuse the user possibly leading to increase in failure rate of authentication. A future user study to determine the level of distraction and confidence of the user with the masking signal may be able to determine a good choice of the masking signal.

8   Conclusion

In this paper, we evaluated the security of tap-based rhythmic authentication schemes against acoustic side channel attacks. We demonstrated that these schemes are vulnerable to such attacks and can be effectively compromised especially using automated off-the-shelf techniques. The automated attack requires minimal computational power and can be performed inconspicuously. The length of the rhythmic passwords also constitutes a security vulnerability as shorter taps are easier to perform and memorize, but are more susceptible to attacks, even those relying solely on human processing. Since rhythmic passwords provide a potentially attractive alternative to traditional authentication mechanisms, we studied how to enhance the security of these passwords against acoustic side channel attacks. Our proposed defense attempts to cloak the acoustic channel by deliberately inducing noise, and seems effective against both automated and human attacks, especially when a combination of multiple noises are used including previously recorded tap sounds.

Acknowledgment. This works has been supported in part by an NSF grant (#1209280).

Appendix: Additional Figures

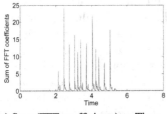
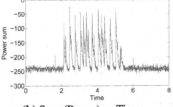

(a) Sum (FFT coefficients) vs Time   (b) Sum (Power) vs Time

Fig. 3. Signal characeristics based on FFT

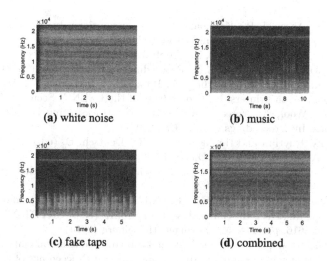

Fig. 4. Spectrographs (Time vs. Frequency plots) of tapping in presence of each type of masking sound

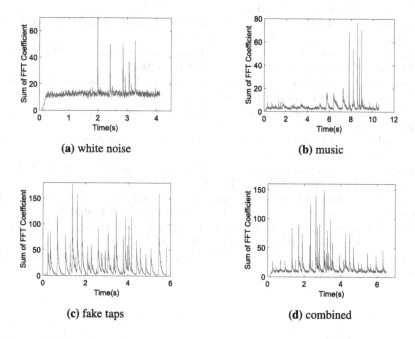

Fig. 5. FFT vs Time plot of tapping in presence of each type of masking sound

References

1. Adams, A., Sasse, M.A.: Users are not the enemy. Commun. ACM **42**(12), 41–46 (1999)

2. Asonov, D., Agrawal, R.: Keyboard acoustic emanations. In: Proceedings of the IEEE Symposium on Security and Privacy (2004)

3. Azenkot, S., Rector, K., Ladner, R., Wobbrock, J.: PassChords: secure multi-touch authentication for blind people. In: Proceedings of the ASSETS (2012)

4. Backes, M., Durmuth, M., Gerling, S., Pinkal, M., Sporleder, C.: Acoustic side-channel attacks on printers. In: Proceedings of the USENIX Security (2005)

5. Berger, Y., Wool, A., Yeredor, A.: Dictionary attacks using keyboard acoustic emanations. In: Proceedings of the CCS (2006)

6. Clarkeh, E.: Rhythm and timing in music. In: Deutsch, D. (ed.) The Psychology of Music. Academic Press, San Diego (1999)

7. Fraisse, P.: Rhythm and tempo. In: Deutsch, D. (ed.) The Psychology of Music. Academic Press, New York (1982)

8. Genkin, D., Shamir, A., Tromer, E.: RSA key extraction via low-bandwidth acoustic cryptanalysis. In: Garay, J.A., Gennaro, R. (eds.) CRYPTO 2014, Part I. LNCS, vol. 8616, pp. 444–461. Springer, Heidelberg (2014)

9. Halevi, T., Saxena, N.: A closer look at keyboard acoustic emanations: random passwords, typing styles and decoding techniques. In: Proceedings of the AsiaCCS (2012)

10. Halevi, T., Saxena, N.: Acoustic eavesdropping attacks on constrained wireless device pairing. TIFS 8(3), 563 (2013)

11. Kumar, A., et al.: Caveat emptor: a comparative study of secure device pairing methods. In: Proceedings of the PerCom (2009)

12. Lin, F.X., Ashbrook, D., White, S.: RhythmLink: securely pairing I/O-constrained devices by tapping. In: Proceedings of the UIST (2011)

13. Marques, D., Guerreiro, T., Duarte, L., Carrico, L.: Under the table: tap authentication for smartphones. In: Proceedings of the HCI (2013)

14. Morris, R., Thompson, K.: Password security: a case history. Commun. ACM 22(11), 594–597 (1979)

15. Serwadda, A., Phoha, V.V.: When kids' toys breach mobile phone security. In: Proceedings of the CCS 2013 (2013)

16. Wobbrock, J.O.: TapSongs: tapping rhythm-based passwords on a single binary sensor. In: Proceedings of the UIST (2009)

17. Yalch, R.F.: Memory in a jingle jungle: music as a mnemonic device in communicating advertising slogans. J. Appl. Psychol. 76(2), 268–275 (1991)

18. Yan, J., Blackwell, A., Anderson, R., Grant, A.: Password memorability and security: empirical results. IEEE Secur. Priv. 2(5), 25–31 (2004)

19. Zhuang, L., Zhou, F., Tygar, J.D.: Keyboard acoustic emanations revisited. TISSEC 13(1), 1–26 (2009)

iDeFEND: Intrusion Detection Framework for Encrypted Network Data

Fatih Kilic[(⊠)] and Claudia Eckert

Technische Universität München, Munich, Germany
{kilic,eckert}@sec.in.tum.de

Abstract. Network Intrusion Detection Systems have been used for many years to inspect network data and to detect intruders. Nowadays, more and more often encryption is used to protect the confidentiality of network data. When end-to-end encryption is applied, Network Intrusion Detection Systems are blind and can not protect against attacks. In this paper we present iDeFEND, a framework for inspecting encrypted network data without breaking the security model of end-to-end encryption. Our approach does not require any source code of the involved applications and thereby also protects closed source applications. Our framework works independently of the utilized encryption key. We present two use cases how our framework can detect intruders by analysing the network data and how we can test remote applications with enabled network data encryption. To achieve this iDeFEND detects the relevant functions in the target application, extracts and subsequently inspects the data. To test remote applications iDeFEND intercepts and injects user controlled data into the application to test remote applications. Finally we have implemented our framework to show the feasibility of our approach.

Keywords: Network security · Reverse engineering · Intrusion detection

1 Introduction

There is a vast amount of applications communicating over the network, whose data is confidential and therefore encrypted. Some applications do not transmit sensitive data, but even in this case a vulnerability in the application makes it prone to code execution on the system. From the view of an attacker, every communication channel to the server exposes an attack surface for intrusion. Network Intrusion Detection System (NIDSs) are used to detect such attacks. However, today's systems only protect the application on the server, but not the communication channel. To protect the transmitted data's confidentiality, applications encrypt data. When end-to-end encryption is applied, the NIDS acts blind and can not protect against attacks, such as Blind Format String Attacks [5]. Beside this, the encryption layer makes it harder for the security analyst to test the remote application. Additionally, considering widely used closed source applications in today's networks, modifications as applied by other solutions are not

© Springer International Publishing Switzerland 2015
M. Reiter and D. Naccache (Eds.): CANS 2015, LNCS 9476, pp. 111–118, 2015.
DOI: 10.1007/978-3-319-26823-1_8

applicable without reverse engineering. By terminating the encryption at another node (e.g. a proxy server), the NIDS can inspect network data, but this makes communication more insecure. End-to-end encryption is designed to terminate at the destination application to fulfil the required security. In general this does not suffice to inspect data without reverse engineering the encryption algorithm and the key. Reverse engineering of closed source applications is very time-consuming and labour-intensive. In this paper, we present iDeFEND, a generic framework to keep up the end-to-end encryption while still being capable to inspect plaintext data. We show the features of iDeFEND by describing two use cases for applications using encrypted network communication. As a first use case we present how we inspect plaintext network data and how we identify intruders. As a second use case we present a method to support analysts in testing network applications and to look for vulnerabilities. Our approach does not require any source code of the involved applications, nor the encryption key, nor information about the algorithm. iDeFEND is using a different approach to solve the problem of encrypted network traffic. Instead of rebuilding the communication channel, we use the same channel of the application. We extract the information directly from the memory of the target application. This makes the whole encryption transparent from our view and we do not need to care about the encryption at all. We work a layer above the encryption and monitor every traffic in plaintext. In summary, our contributions are the following. Our framework allows to

- identify network security related functions in applications.
- extract unencrypted network data out of the application without breaking the security of the encryption.
- remote test applications using encrypted traffic without the need for reverse engineering of the encryption algorithm and key.

The rest of the paper is structured as follows. First we describe the overall design of iDeFEND in Sect. 2. We show how we reverse engineer the relevant functions of the application in Sect. 3. In Sect. 4 we show how we extract the plaintext network data and use a *Monitor* module to inspect the data for malicious content. Furthermore, in Sect. 5 we show how we intercept and modify the network communication before the plaintext data is processed for send or receive. We describe how we implemented the framework in Sect. 6. Section 7 presents related work. We summarize the paper in Sect. 8.

2   Framework Design

In this section we present the concept and the design of our framework for inspecting plaintext network data. If the whole network communication is encrypted, the application usually contains two wrapper functions. One is responsible for encrypting the plaintext and sending the data afterwards over the network. In our paper we label this function EnCrypt & Send (CaS). The other function is responsible for receiving the network data and decrypting it afterwards to process the plaintext data. We label this function as Receive & DeCrypt (RaD). These functions contain the plaintext data that is sent/received over the network. Both functions represent the core functionality for our framework. These functions are used in our use cases for extraction, interception and injection.

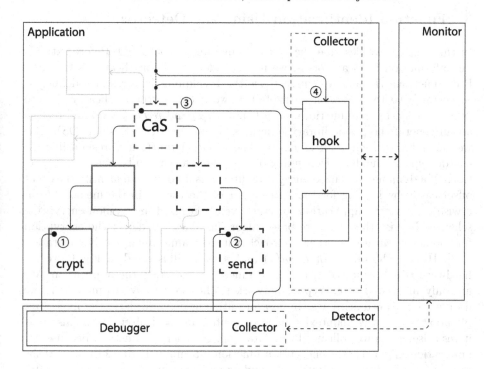

Fig. 1. iDeFEND design

Figure 1 depicts the design of iDeFEND using the function CaS as an example. The case with RaD is analogous. Our framework consists of three parts: the *Detector*, the *Collector* and the *Monitor* modules. The *Detector* module is responsible for reverse engineering the offsets for the functions CaS and RaD. The application on the left side in Fig. 1 contains the Control Flow Graph (CFG) with the CaS function in the center. Tracking back the functions *crypt*(1) and *send*(2) using the underlying *Debugger* inside the *Detector* module, we have an intersection at CaS. The detection of the functions is described in detail in Sect. 3. The *Collector* module is responsible for gathering the plaintext data used for network communication from the application. This module requires the already identified offsets of CaS and RaD. iDeFEND supports two types of the *Collector*. One method is using the *Debugger* in the *Detector* module to directly extract or intercept/modify the plaintext data on CaS(3) or RaD before it is processed by the target application. The other method is placing the *Collector* directly into the process space of the application. This is setting a hook(4) on the function CaS and RaD to capture the information passed to these functions. Each time the application sends or receives encrypted network data, the *Collector* will gather the plaintext data. We pass the collected data to the the *Monitor* module. This module is responsible for handling the plaintext data and for providing an interface to NIDSs.

3   Function Identification Using the Detector

In this section, we describe the *Detector* module of iDeFEND. Before extracting information from a process, we need to identify the application's CaS and RaD functions. To achieve this, we use the breakpoint features of a debugger. Since we have to deal with encrypted network traffic, the application has to provide at least three functions: *crypt*(1), *send*(2) and *receive*. Send and receive are in general the public library functions of the Operating System (OS), thus we can retrieve their address easily. The *crypt*(1) function is responsible for en-/decrypting the data. Depending on the algorithm it can be one or two functions. If a dynamically linked encryption library is used, we can identify the crypt offset easily by looking for the API export of the library in the memory. Otherwise we scan the application for static values utilized in common encryption schemes. In case the signature based algorithm does not detect the encryption functionality, we use another approach with dynamic binary instrumentation [1,3]. Having the offsets of *crypt*(1) and *send*(2) illustrated in Fig. 1, we set hardware Breakpoint (BPs) on these functions and start the application. We are only interested in encrypted network traffic, so we have to make sure we do not catch too much data. In case of outgoing network data, the important plaintext is only the plaintext that is encrypted and sent afterwards. False positives arise, when we collect all the data from the encrypt function, because the application might use the encryption function internally. Figure 2 illustrates the possible states of the application depending on the occurrence of the BPs. After starting the application we wait until the first encryption BP occurs otherwise we stay in the same state (Wait). At this point, we are in the state *C*. We save the application state including all relevant data, such as registers, the memory content and the application stack. After resuming the application the next BP is either on *crypt*(1) or on *send*(2). At *crypt* the application is encrypting some data for sending or internal use. At *send*(2) the application is going to send some data and we change to the final state *CaS*. At this final state, there are only two possibilities. Either some plaintext data is transmitted over the network and the encryption was for internal use, or the encrypted data is transmitted over the network. We evaluate this by comparing the data modified by the encrypt function with the data accessed by the send function in state *C*. If we have a match, we look for the CaS function by comparing the partly reconstructed CFG of both states with each other and look for an intersection. We retrieve the execution flow by backtracing the caller functions. We aim for the intersection of both execution flows. This is most likely the CaS function. In the case of incoming network data, we have to detect the RaD functionality. This works analogous to the identification of CaS.

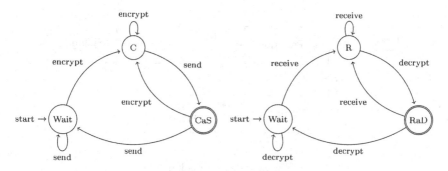

Fig. 2. *Debugger* states

4   Information Extraction Using the Collector

In this section, we describe the methods to extract the necessary information from the detected CaS and RaD functions to pass it to the *Monitor* module. This feature is supporting the use case of inspecting plaintext network data to identify intruders. The method is describing the module *Collector* in iDeFEND. Our framework supports two ways for extraction. First we describe the *Collector* module using the *Debugger* illustrated at the bottom in Fig. 1. We place one BP at the entry of CaS(3) and another one inside the RaD. The plaintext of the encrypted messages is passed to the function CaSa as function parameter. When the application halts at CaS(3), we retrieve the data from the parameters. In the case of RaD the encrypted message is decrypted and parsed afterwards. To extract this data we set the BP immediately after the decryption is done. When the application halts at RaD, we extract the plaintext either from the return value or the modified input parameters. The location of the decrypted data is already identified by the *Detector* module. The next step is to pass it to the *Monitor* module to analyse it. Our second method uses the *Collector* module inside the target application, illustrated on the right side of the application in Fig. 1. Instead of exits to the debugger we run our own code inside the target process. For this purpose, we inject our own module into the target application. Figure 3 shows how we use a trampoline to redirect the detected functions to a place inside our module. To achieve this, we replace the initial prologue of the detected functions with a *jmp* instruction. This redirects the program to our code. In our additional code we save the input parameters to the original function. We restore the original prologue of the hooked function, call it with the original parameters and save the return value. Another thread collects the extracted data and delivers it to the *Monitor* module. Our function returns during this information exchange and the applications resumes as intended.

5   Packet Injection and Interception

In this section we consider the second use case and describe the method for sending user controlled arbitrary data using the application's CaS function.

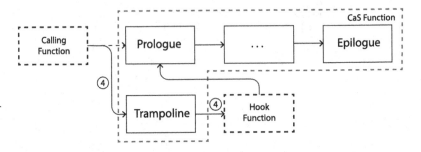

Fig. 3. Function hooking

To achieve this, we use an equal technique as described for the *Collector* module in Sect. 4 to load our own module *Injector* into the target application. Having our module inside the target application, we build an Inter Process Communication (IPC) to exchange data with the module. To send arbitrary data to the server, we use this channel to pass our plaintext network data to the Injector. As being part of the application, we call the CaS function directly with our input as parameter and let the application do all the necessary data modification, like splitting, encrypting and sending. As IPC channel for communicating with CaS, we use code injection to place our precompiled calling stub into the application. This stub will get the objects for sending directly from the new allocated memory inside the application and call the CaS. The benefit here is, that we do not have to care about any algorithm or the encryption key. We also do not have to care about the states the encryption algorithm proposes as in stream ciphers. iDeFEND is also able to intercept and modify the plaintext data transmitted over the network. We use the same hooking technique as described for the *Collector* module in Sect. 4. Each time a packet is sent or received our hooked function retrieves the data. We use the IPC to interact with the security analyst using an external graphical user interface. At this point, the application is halted and the tester inspects or alters the data for testing purposes.

6   Implementation

We have implemented a prototype of our framework. Our implementation was running on a machine with an Intel Core i7-4600U CPU 2.10GHz CPU and 8GB RAM. We used two virtual machines with Windows 7 Professional with Service Pack 1 and Ubuntu 14.04 LTS as OS. The *Detector* module uses a self-written debugger to place and handle hardware BPs inside the target application. We set two hardware BPs on *crypt* and *send* to detect CaS, RaD is detected analogously. The *Collector* inside the *Detector* module places a BP at the entry of CaS(3) to extract the parameters given to the function and another one inside the RaD to have access to the already decrypted data. When the application halts at one BP, we gather the memory pointer directly from the stack and registers. After dereferencing the pointer we extract the plaintext data out of the memory.

Since this technique stops the application for all incoming and outgoing network packets, the application slows down. To avoid this, we implemented another method to extract the data without incurring performance. We execute our code directly inside the target process space. The benefit in doing so is, that we sustain effectiveness and do not delay the target application during the information extraction. Executing additional code in another process is easily achieved using module injection. This allows us to provide code fragments or even functions in the target application. Our framework supports two methods to inject additional code into the target process. On Windows OS we use the default debugging API calls to load our Dynamic Link Library (DLL) into the application. The second method can be used for Windows and Linux OSs. We scan for unused memory inside the binary, which is called code cave. We use the code cave to insert the code snippet for loading the module and execute it by manually setting the instruction pointer (IP) of the application [8]. After the injection of our module, the hooks to the CaS and RaD functions are placed. Our *Collector* logs the parameters and return values of the hooked functions and passes them to the *Monitor* module. By default iDeFEND performs this by using a IPC with the *Monitor* module running on the same system. The modules do not have to run together on the same machine. The *Collector* module of iDeFEND can also be used separately. We set up a clean test system to use the *Detector* module and to generate the relevant offsets for CaS and RaD. This data is written into a config file and the *Collector* module loads the offsets to attach to the productive system and start extracting the plaintext data. iDeFEND also allows to send the gathered data from the *Collector* module over the network to run the *Monitor* module and a NIDS on a different machine.

7 Related Work

Many NIDSs exist to analyse the network traffic in order to detect exploits. Li et al. [7] present different concepts for NIDSs, common standards and trends of development, stating that network-based NIDS do not detect anomalies within encrypted traffic. Kenkre et al. [4] present a real time NIDS and the applied techniques. The paper states how to combine logging, network based NIDS and prevention system. Koch et al. [6] describe the problems of knowledge-based NIDSs with encrypted networks and propose a behaviour-based detection architecture measuring similarities in network traffic to detect intruders. Knowledge-based NIDSs are only able to inspect the encrypted network data by having the appropriate key. Further, the NIDS performs a man-in-the-middle attack by breaking the confidentiality of the message. Yamada et al. [9] and Goh et al. [2] use a shared secret between the end-host in private networks and the NIDS to circumvent this problem. Currently, there is no good solution to inspect encrypted network data to detect possible attacks. The approach of iDeFEND is different. We provide an interface to make the encryption transparent for current methods, reducing the problem of detecting intruders on encrypted network data is reduced to the problem of detecting intruders on plaintext network data.

8   Conclusion

We proposed iDeFEND, a framework for intrusion detection in encrypted network communication. We have shown how we inspect the encrypted network data of closed source applications in a use case. We have also shown how we test network applications using encrypted network traffic. In this paper, we demonstrated a method to automatically identify the related functions for encrypted network communication inside applications. We made use of the identified functions to extract plaintext network data from the application using the *Collector* module. We used the collected data for further analysis in our *Monitor* module to detect exploits. We also presented a way how closed sourced network based applications transmitting encrypted data are tested for vulnerabilities without reverse engineering of the encryption algorithm and key. We used the identified functions to intercept and modify the current plaintext network data to change the parameters sent to the target application. We also used the identified function to inject arbitrary data and enforced a unintended data transmission. We used the collected data to build a bunch of valid data packets for sending to the destination application. iDeFEND also acts as an interface for techniques and tools available for security analysis and intrusion detection.

References

1. Calvet, J., Fernandez, J.M., Marion, J.-Y.: Aligot: cryptographic function identification in obfuscated binary programs. In: ACM Conference on Computer and Communications Security, pp. 2–4 (2012)
2. Goh, V.T., Zimmermann, J., Looi, M.: Intrusion detection system for encrypted networks using secret-sharing schemes. In: 2nd International Cryptology Conference (Cryptology 2010), Malaysian Society for Cryptology Research, July 2010
3. Gröbert, F., Willems, C., Holz, T.: Automated identification of cryptographic primitives in binary programs. In: Sommer, R., Balzarotti, D., Maier, G. (eds.) RAID 2011. LNCS, vol. 6961, pp. 41–60. Springer, Heidelberg (2011)
4. Kenkre, P.S., Pai, A., Colaco, L.: Real time intrusion detection and prevention system. In: Satapathy, S.C., Biswal, B.N., Udgata, S.K., Mandal, J.K. (eds.) Proc. of the 3rd Int. Conf. on Front. of Intell. Comput. (FICTA) 2014- Vol. 1. AISC, vol. 327, pp. 405–411. Springer, Heidelberg (2015)
5. Kilic, F., Kittel, T., Eckert, C.: Blind format string attacks. In: International Workshop on Data Protection in Mobile and Pervasive Computing (2014)
6. Koch, R., Golling, M., Rodosek, G.D.: Behavior-based intrusion detection in encrypted environments. IEEE Commun. Mag. **52**(7), 124–131 (2014)
7. Li, X., Meng, J., Zhao, H., Zhao, J.: Overview of intrusion detection systems. J. Appl. Sci. Eng. Innovation **2**(6), 230–232 (2015)
8. Runtime process infection. http://phrack.org/issues/59/8.html. Accessed 09 June 2015
9. Radu, V.: Application. In: Radu, V. (ed.) Stochastic Modeling of Thermal Fatigue Crack Growth. ACM, vol. 1, pp. 63–70. Springer, Heidelberg (2015)

On the Weaknesses of PBKDF2

Andrea Visconti[✉], Simone Bossi, Hany Ragab, and Alexandro Calò

Department of Computer Science, Università degli Studi di Milano, Milan, Italy
andrea.visconti@unimi.it,
{simone.bossi2,hany.ragab,alexandro.calo}@studenti.unimi.it

Abstract. Password-based key derivation functions are of particular interest in cryptography because they (a) input a password/passphrase (which usually is short and lacks enough entropy) and derive a cryptographic key; (b) slow down brute force and dictionary attacks as much as possible. In PKCS#5 [17], RSA Laboratories described a password based key derivation function called PBKDF2 that has been widely adopted in many security related applications [6,7,11]. In order to slow down brute force attacks, PBKDF2 introduce CPU-intensive operations based on an iterated pseudorandom function. Such a pseudorandom function is HMAC-SHA-1 by default. In this paper we show that, if HMAC-SHA-1 is computed in a standard mode without following the performance improvements described in the implementation note of RFC 2104 [13] and FIPS 198-1 [14], an attacker is able to avoid 50 % of PBKDF2's CPU intensive operations, by replacing them with precomputed values. We note that a number of well-known and widely-used crypto libraries are subject to this vulnerability.In addition to such a vulnerability, we describe some other minor optimizations that an attacker can exploit to reduce even more the key derivation time.

Keywords: Key derivation function · CPU-intensive operations · Passwords · PKCS#5 · Optimizations

1 Introduction

Passwords are widely used to protect secret data or to gain access to specific resources. For sake of security, they should be strong enough to prevent well-know attacks such as dictionary and brute force attacks. Unfortunately, user-chosen passwords are generally short and lack enough entropy [9,16,18]. For these reasons, they cannot be directly used as a key to implement secure cryptographic systems. A possible solution to this issue is to adopt a key derivation function (KDF), that is a function which takes a source of initial keying material and derives from it one or more pseudorandom keys. Such a key material can be the output of a pseudo-random number generator, a bit sequence obtained by a statistical sampler, a shared Diffie-Hellman value, a user-chosen password, or any bit sequence from a source of more or less entropy [12]. KDF that input user passwords are known as password-based KDF. Such functions are of particular

© Springer International Publishing Switzerland 2015
M. Reiter and D. Naccache (Eds.): CANS 2015, LNCS 9476, pp. 119–126, 2015.
DOI: 10.1007/978-3-319-26823-1_9

interest in cryptography because they introduce CPU-intensive operations on the attacker side, increasing the cost of an exhaustive search. By applying a KDF to a user password, we allow legitimate users to spend a moderate amount of time on key derivation, while increase the time an attacker takes to test each possible password. The approach based on KDF not only slows down a brute force attack as much as possible but also allows to increase the size of a cryptographic key.

In PKCS#5 [17], RSA Laboratories provides a number of recommendations for the implementation of password-based cryptography. In particular, they described Password-Based Key Derivation Function version 2 (PBKDF2), a function widely used to derive keys and implemented in many security-related systems. For example, PBKDF2 is involved in Android's full disk encryption (since version 3.0 Honeycomb to 4.3 Jelly Bean)[1], in WPA/WPA2 encryption process [11], in LUKS [7,10], EncFS [2], FileVault Mac OS X [6,8], GRUB2 [3], Winrar [5], and many others.

In order to slow down the attackers, PBKDF2 uses a salt to prevent building universal dictionaries, and an iteration count which specifies the number of times the underlying pseudorandom function is called to generate a block of keying material. The number of iterations is a crucial point of the KDF. The choice of a reasonable value for the iteration count depends on the environment and can vary from an application to another. In SP 800-132 [15], Turan et al. suggests that it is a good practice to select the iteration count as large as possible, as long the time required to generate the key is acceptable for the user. Moreover, they specify that for very critical keys on very powerful system an iteration count of 10,000,000 may be appropriate, while a minimum of 1,000 iterations is recommended for general purpose.

PBKDF2 introduce CPU-intensive operations based on an iterated pseudorandom function. Such a pseudorandom function is HMAC-SHA-1 by default.

In this paper we show that, if HMAC-SHA-1 is computed in a standard mode without following the performance improvements described in the implementation note of RFC 2104 [13] and FIPS 198-1 [14], an attacker is able avoid 50 % of PBKDF2's CPU intensive operations, by replacing them with precomputed values. Readers note that a number of well-known and widely-used crypto libraries e.g., [1,4], are subject to this vulnerability, therefore an attacker is able to derive keys significantly faster than a regular user can do. Moreover, we present some other minor optimizations (based on the hash function used) that can be exploited by an attacker to reduce even more the key derivation time.

The remainder of the paper is organized as follows. In Sect. 2, we present Password Based Key Derivation Function version 2 (PBKDF2). In Sect. 3 we briefly describe HMAC, that is the pseudorandom function adopted in PBKDF2. In Sect. 4 we present the weaknesses of PBKDF2. Finally, discussion and conclusions are drawn in Sect. 5.

---

[1] At the time of writing this represents 58 % of the Android devices market share (see developer.android.com).

2   PBKDF 2

Password Based Key Derivation Function version 2, PBKDF2 for short, is a key derivation function published by RSA Laboratories in PKCS #5 [17]. In order to face brute force attacks based on weak user passwords, PBKDF2 introduce CPU-intensive operations. Such operations are based on an iterated pseudorandom function (PRF) — e.g. a hash function, cipher, or HMAC — which maps input values to a derived key. One of the most important properties to assure is that PBKDF2 is cycle free. If this is not so, a malicious user can avoid the CPU-intensive operations and get the derived key by executing a set of equivalent, but less onerous, instructions. Unlike its predecessor (PBKDF version 1) in which the length of the derived key is bounded by the length of the underlying PRF output, PBKDF2 can derive keys of arbitrary length. More precisely, PBKDF2 generates as many blocks T_i as needed to cover the desired key length. Each block T_i is computed iterating the PRF many times as specified by an iteration count. The length of such blocks is bounded by $hLen$, which is the length of the underlying PRF output. In the sequel by PRF we will refer to HMAC with the SHA-1 hash function, that is the default as per [17]. Note that HMAC can be used with any other iterated hash functions such as RIPEMD, SHA-256 or SHA-512.

PBKDF2 inputs a user password/passphrase p, a random salt s, an iteration counter c, and derived key length $dkLen$. It outputs a derived key DK.

$$DK = PBKDF2(p, s, c, dkLen) \tag{1}$$

The derived key is defined as the concatenation of $\lceil dkLen/hLen \rceil$-blocks:

$$DK = T_1 || T_2 || \ldots || T_{\lceil dkLen/hLen \rceil} \tag{2}$$

where

$$T_1 = Function(p, s, c, 1)$$
$$T_2 = Function(p, s, c, 2)$$
$$\ldots$$
$$T_{\lceil dkLen/hLen \rceil} = Function(p, s, c, \lceil dkLen/hLen \rceil).$$

Each single block T_i is computed as

$$T_i = U_1 \oplus U_2 \oplus \ldots \oplus U_c \tag{3}$$

where

$$U_1 = PRF(p, s||i)$$
$$U_2 = PRF(p, U_1)$$
$$\ldots$$
$$U_c = PRF(p, U_{c-1})$$

3   HMAC

Hash-based Message Authentication Code (HMAC) is an algorithm for computing a message authentication code based on a cryptographic hash function. The
definition of HMAC [13] requires (a) H : any cryptographic hash function, (b)
K : the secret key, and (c) $text$: the message to be authenticated. As described
in RFC 2104 [13], HMAC can be defined as follows:

$$HMAC = H(K \oplus opad, H(K \oplus ipad, text)) \qquad (4)$$

where H is the chosen hash function, K is the secret key, and $ipad$, $opad$ are the
constant values (respectively, the byte 0x36 and 0x5C repeated 64 times) XORed
with the password. Equation 4 can be graphically represented as in Fig. 1.

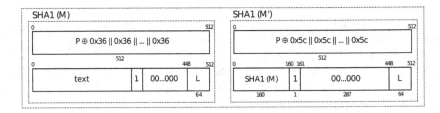

Fig. 1. HMAC-SHA-1

4   Weaknesses

In this section we present some weaknesses of PBKDF2. The major one concerns
the precomputation of specific values that can be reused during the key derivation process. The others aim to avoid useless operations during the computation
of the hash function. We will describe these weaknesses using as an example the
parameters defined by LUKS format [9,10] — i.e., a salt length of 256 bits, and
HMAC-SHA-1 as PRF.

4.1   Precomputing a Message Block

Looking closely at Fig. 2, note the following: (a) first message block of a keyed
hash function is repeated c times (the dark gray rectangles in Fig. 2), (b) first
message block of a second keyed hash function is repeated c times (the light gray
rectangles in Fig. 2), (c) all dark gray rectangles have the same content and they
can assume only the values SHA1$(P \oplus ipad)$, and (d) all light gray rectangles have
the same content and they can assume only the values SHA1$(P \oplus opad)$. Thus,
it is possible to compute these two blocks in advance — i.e., SHA1$(P \oplus ipad)$
and SHA-1$(P \oplus opad)^2$ — and then use such values for c times. In so doing, an

---

^{2} Readers note that the weakness is independent of the hash functions used and
remains valid with any others.

PBKDF2 SCHEMA

$DK = T_1 \| T_2 \| \ldots \| T_{i = \lceil dkLen/hLen \rceil}$

$T_i = F(P, S, c, i)$

$F(P, S, c, i) = U_1 \oplus U_2 \oplus \ldots \oplus U_c$

$U_1 = HMAC\text{-}SHA1(P, S \| i)$

$U_2 = HMAC\text{-}SHA1(P, U_1)$

$\vdots$

$U_c = HMAC\text{-}SHA1(P, U_{c-1})$

$U_1 = HMAC\text{-}SHA1(P, S \| i)$

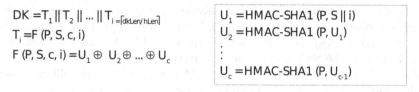

$U_2 = HMAC\text{-}SHA1(P, U_1)$

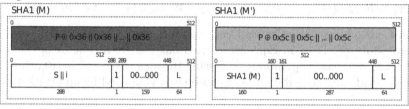

$U_c = HMAC\text{-}SHA1(P, U_{c-1})$

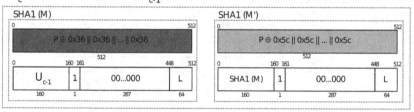

Fig. 2. PBKDF2 schema (HMAC computed in a standard mode)

attacker is able to avoid 50 % of the operations involved in the key derivation process (although the user can benefit from this optimization as well). Moreover, in real applications the counter c can be computed by benchmarking the user's system [7,9]. If this optimization is not implemented in crypto libraries, the benchmark fails to deliver the appropriate value for the counter, reducing the security level of the application.

4.2 Useless XOR Operations

It is easy to observe that each SHA1 message block, performed on a 512-bits string and formatted as shown in Fig. 3, has a run of several consecutive zeros (light gray rectangles). More precisely, in the second SHA1 message block there are 287 zeros in the padding scheme and other 54 zeros in L (i.e., 64-bits message length). Readers note that each SHA1 message block is split in sixteen 32-bits words, called $W_0 \ldots W_{15}$, and then expanded into eighty words, called $W_0 \ldots W_{79}$, using the following equation:

$$W_t = ROTL((W_{t-3} \oplus W_{t-8} \oplus W_{t-14} \oplus W_{t-16}), 1) \qquad t \in [16 \ldots 79] \qquad (5)$$

Because we have a run of several consecutive zeros, a number of W_t are set to zero. More precisely, in Eq. 5 are carried out 192 XOR, but 27 of them are involved in zero based operations. Following the idea suggested in [19], these W_t do not provide any contribution and can be easily omitted by an attacker.

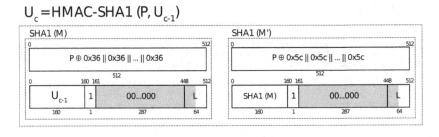

Fig. 3. Zero-padding scheme

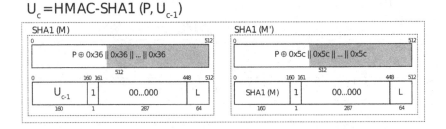

Fig. 4. Constant-padding scheme

In addition, an attacker is able to avoid some other useless operations in the word-expansion. As shown in Fig. 4, the constant 0x36 and 0x5C are used to pad the first message block up to the hash block size (dark and light gray rectangles). Since passwords are generally short, a number of W_t in Eq. 5 are set to the same value. If we XOR the same value twice, we get back the initial value. Again, these operations do not provide any additional contribution and can be omitted.

4.3   Precomputing a Word-Expansion

The last weakness described is a minor weakness. This provides the possibility to precompute the word-expansion part of the second message block of a keyed hash function (light gray rectangle in Fig. 5). Indeed, such a block is password-independent, and given a salt s (recall that s is a public information) an attacker is able to compute the expansion $W_0 \ldots W_{79}$ in advance. A malicious user can reused the values precomputed with a dictionary of potential passwords to speed up a brute force attack.

$U_1 = \text{HMAC-SHA1 } (P, S \parallel i)$

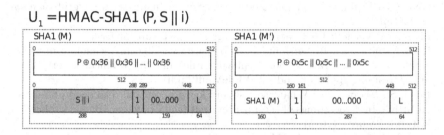

Fig. 5. Precomputing a specific word-expansion

5   Discussion and Conclusions

Passwords are generally short and lack enough entropy, therefore they cannot be directly used as a key to implement secure cryptographic systems. A possible solution to this issue is to adopt password-based key derivation functions.

This paper addressed the security of PBKDF2, one of the most commonly used function to derive cryptographic keys. We provided a detailed analysis of PBKDF2 schema and described some weaknesses that affect a number of well-known and widely-used crypto libraries such as [1, 4].

The first one concerns the possibility to precompute the first message block of a keyed hash function and reuse such a value in all the subsequent HMAC invocations. This weakness allows an attacker to avoid 50 % of PBKDF2's CPU intensive operations, replacing them with constant values. Crypto libreries are subjected to this vulnerability if they do not implement the performance improvements described in RFC 2104 [13] and FIPS 198-1 [14].

The second one concerns the possibility to avoid useless XOR operations. Indeed, introducing zero-based operations and XORing the same value twice do not provide any additional contribution to the word expansion of SHA-1. Note that the same approach can be also applied to the word expansion of SHA-2 family hash functions.

The third one concerns the possibility to precompute the word-expansion of a specific 512-bits message block.

Readers note that the weaknesses of PBKDF2 described in this paper can be easily mitigated by selecting an iteration count c as large as possible and implementing the performance improvements that save the computation of several message blocks of a keyed hash function.

References

1. ARM mbed TLS, Version: 1.3.11. https://tls.mbed.org/
2. EncFS Encrypted Filesystem. https://sites.google.com/a/arg0.net/www/encfs
3. GNU GRUB Manual, Version: 2.00. http://www.gnu.org/software/grub/manual/grub.html
4. Libgcrypt, Version: 1.6.3. https://www.gnu.org/software/libgcrypt/
5. RAR Archive Format, Version: 5.0. http://www.rarlab.com/technote.htm
6. Apple Inc.: Best Practices for Deploying FileVault 2. Technical report (2012). http://training.apple.com/pdf/WP_FileVault2.pdf
7. Bossi, S., Visconti, A.: What users should know about full disk encryption based on LUKS. In: Proceedings of the 14th International Conference on Cryptology and Network Security (2015)
8. Choudary, O., Grobert, F., Metz, J.: Infiltrate the Vault: Security Analysis and Decryption of Lion Full Disk Encryption. Cryptology ePrint Archive, Report 2012/374 (2012). https://eprint.iacr.org/2012/374.pdf
9. Fruhwirth, C.: New methods in hard disk encryption (2005). http://clemens.endorphin.org/nmihde/nmihde-A4-ds.pdf
10. Fruhwirth, C.: LUKS On-Disk Format Specification Version 1.2.1 (2011). http://wiki.cryptsetup.googlecode.com/git/LUKS-standard/on-disk-format.pdf
11. IEEE 802.11 WG: Part 11: wireless LAN medium access control (MAC) and physical layer (PHY) specifications. IEEE Std 802.11 i-2004 (2004)
12. Krawczyk, H.: Cryptographic Extraction and Key Derivation: The HKDF Scheme. Cryptology ePrint Archive, Report 2010/264 (2010)
13. Krawczyk, H., Bellare, M., Canetti, R.: RFC 2104: HMAC: Keyed-hashing for message authentication (1997)
14. NIST: FIPS PUB 198: The Keyed-Hash Message Authentication Code (HMAC) (2002)
15. NIST: SP 800–132: Recommendation for password-based key derivation (2010)
16. NIST: SP 800–63-2 Version 2: Electronic authentication guideline (2013)
17. RSA Laboratories: PKCS #5 V2.1: Password Based Cryptography Standard (2012)
18. Shannon, C.E.: Prediction and entropy of printed English. Bell Syst. Tech. J. **30**(1), 50–64 (1951)
19. Steube, J.: Optimizing computation of Hash-Algorithms as an attacker (2013). http://hashcat.net/events/p13/js-ocohaaaa.pdf

Security Modeling and Verification

Verifiable Random Functions from (Leveled) Multilinear Maps

Bei Liang[1,2,3]([✉]), Hongda Li[1,2,3], and Jinyong Chang[1,3]

[1] State Key Laboratory of Information Security, Institute of Information Engineering
of Chinese Academy of Sciences, Beijing, China
{liangbei,lihongda,changjinyong}@iie.ac.cn
[2] Data Assurance and Communication Security Research Center
of Chinese Academy of Sciences, Beijing, China
[3] University of Chinese Academy of Sciences, Beijing, China

Abstract. Verifiable random functions (VRFs), firstly proposed by
Micali, Rabin, and Vadhan (FOCS 99), are pseudorandom functions
with the additional property that the party holding the seed sk can
generate a non-interactive, publicly verifiable proof π for the statements
"$F_{sk}(x) = y$", for any input x. To date only a few VRF schemes are
known and most known constructions either allow only a small input
space, or don't achieve full adaptive security under a non-interactive complexity
assumption. The only known adaptively secure VRF scheme with
exponentially-large input space is based on ℓ-Decisional Diffie-Hellman
Exponent assumption (Hohenberger and Waters, Eurocrypt 2010).

In this work, we present a VRF scheme which is proved adaptively
secure for exponentially-large input spaces under (n, k)-Modified Multilinear
Decisional Diffie-Hellman Exponent assumption. Our construction
is directly derived from the construction of constrained VRFs given
by Fuchsbauer (SCN 14) based on (leveled) multilinear-maps. Since in
Fuchsbauer's scheme the adaptive security is obtained via complexity
leveraging, which leads to a security loss that is exponential in the input
length. Our core idea is to apply a simulation technique similar to the
VRF analysis of Hohenberger (Eurocrypt 2010), where we partition the
input space into those for which we can provide a proof and those for
which we cannot. We then show that with non-negligible probability, the
adversary will only query us on inputs for which we can provide proofs,
except for the challenge query, for which the proof is unknown.

Keywords: Verifiable Random Functions (VRFs) · Constrained VRFs ·
Multilinear maps

1 Introduction

Verifiable Random Functions (VRFs) were proposed by Micali, Rabin and
Vadhan [15]. Informally, a VRF behaves similar to a pseudorandom function

This research is supported by the Strategy Pilot Project of Chinese Academy of
Sciences (Grant No. Y2W0012203).

© Springer International Publishing Switzerland 2015
M. Reiter and D. Naccache (Eds.): CANS 2015, LNCS 9476, pp. 129–143, 2015.
DOI: 10.1007/978-3-319-26823-1_10

(see Goldreich, Goldwasser and Micali [8]) and also enables a verifier to verify, given an input x, an output y and a proof π, that the function has been correctly computed on x. More precisely, a VRF is associated with a secret key sk and a corresponding public verification key pk. As usual, sk allows the evaluation of function $y = F_{sk}(x)$ on any input x and the generation of a proof $\pi = P_{sk}(x)$. This proof can be used in conjunction with pk to convince a verifier that y is the correct output on input x. For security, VRFs must satisfy the provability (or correctness), uniqueness and pseudorandomness properties. *Uniqueness* guarantees that the verifier cannot accept two different values for an input x, even if pk is generated dishonestly; *Pseudorandomness* states that having only pk and oracle access to $F_{sk}(\cdot)$ and $P_{sk}(\cdot)$, the value $y = F_{sk}(x)$ looks random to any polynomially bounded adversary who did not query $F_{sk}(x)$ explicitly.

Due to their strong properties, VRFs are a fascinating primitive that have several theoretical and practical applications. Abdalla et al. [1] provided a nice summary of applications, including resettable zero-knowledge proofs [14] and verifiable transaction escrow schemes [12], to name a few.

Current State of the Art. However, in spite of their popularity, constructing VRFs seems to be challenging, because only a few schemes are known so far, e.g., [1,4,5,11,13,15]. Micali, Rabin and Vadhan proposed a construction (in the plain model) in [15], which is built in two steps. Firstly they constructed a verifiable unpredictable function (VUF) based on the RSA problem and then they showed a generic transformation to convert a VUF into a VRF using the Goldreich-Levin theorem [9] (that extracts one random bit from polynomially-many unpredictable bits). Lysyanskaya [13] provided a VRF scheme relying on a strong version of the Diffie-Hellman assumption, which was also constructed as a transformation from a VUF. Unfortunately, because of several inefficient steps involved in the transformation, the VRF resulting from this transformation is very inefficient and, furthermore, it loses a quite large factor in its exact security reduction.

The subsequent works suggest direct and (more) efficient constructions of VRFs without relying on the Goldreich-Levin transformation. Dodis [4] presented a VRF scheme based on a "DDH-like" interactive assumption that is called sum-free decisional Diffie-Hellman assumption. In [5], Dodis and Yampolskiy gave a very efficient VRF under a non-interactive, bilinear Diffie-Hellman inversion assumption by applying the Boneh-Boyen signatures scheme [2]. Abdalla, Catalano and Fiore [1] gave two VRF constructions and showed the relationship between VRFs and Identity-Based Encryption. In particular, they showed that any IBE scheme with certain properties (e.g., deterministic key generation) implies VRFs. All the schemes mentioned so far share the limitation of supporting only a small domain. Hohenberger and Waters [11] first provided a VRF for an input space of exponential size with full adaptive security without applying complexity leveraging or interactive assumption.

Recently, Fuchsbauer [6] defined an extended notion of VRFs which was called constrained VRFs. Informally, a constrained VRF is a special kind of VRF that allows one to derive a constrained key sk_S with respect to some set

$S \subseteq \mathcal{X}$ from the master secret key sk. The constrained key sk_S allows the computation of $F_{sk}(x)$ and $P_{sk}(x)$ only for $x \in S$. By adding a level in the group hierarchy based on the constructions of constrained PRFs given by Boneh and Waters [3], Fuchsbauer [6] also provided two multilinear-maps-based instantiations of constrained VRFs for "bit-fixing" sets and sets that can be decided by a polynomial-size circuit. However, they proved that the selective pseudorandomness of their VRFs can be reduced to the multilinear DDH assumption without any security loss. In the proof a reduction algorithm will firstly guess the attacker's challenge input. Thus, to obtain adaptive pseudorandomness needs complexity leveraging, which leads to a security loss that is exponential in the input length.

The main motivating question of our work is whether we can obtain a multilinear-maps-based VRF of adaptive pseudorandomness based on standard complexity assumption without any exponential loss.

Our Contribution. In this work, we aim to realize multilinear-maps-based VRFs without applying complexity leveraging. We show how to achieve this result using the artificial abort technique introduced by Waters [16]. More precisely, we apply a reduction technique where the input space is compressed in the reduction algorithm's view to a much smaller space. We can parameterize this compression such that the reduction algorithm knows the VRF value for all but a set S of size $\approx 1/Q(\lambda)$ of the input, where $Q(\lambda)$ is the (polynomial) number of queries made by an attacker and λ is a security parameter. We then show that with non-negligible probability, the adversary will only query us on inputs for which we can provide proofs, except for the challenge query landed in S, for which the proof is unknown.

The VRF scheme is directly derived from the construction of constrained VRFs given by Fuchsbauer [6]. Let the length of input be ℓ. It is defined over a leveled multilinear group, which is a sequence of groups $\boldsymbol{G} = (\mathbb{G}_1, \ldots, \mathbb{G}_\ell)$, each $\mathbb{G}_i$ of large prime order $p > 2^\lambda$ and of generator g_i, associated with a set of bilinear maps $\{e_{i,j} : \mathbb{G}_i \times \mathbb{G}_j \to \mathbb{G}_{i+j} | i, j \geq 1; i+j \leq \ell\}$. The setup algorithm will choose random $\alpha \in \mathbb{Z}_p$ and 2ℓ random elements $(d_{1,0}, d_{1,1}), \ldots, (d_{\ell,0}, d_{\ell,1}) \in \mathbb{Z}_p^2$. Let $g = g_1$. The secret key is $sk = (\alpha, \{d_{i,b}\}_{i \in [1,\ell], b \in \{0,1\}})$ and public key is $pk = (A = g^\alpha, \{D_{i,b} = g^{d_{i,b}}\}_{i \in [1,\ell], b \in \{0,1\}})$. The evaluation of the VRF on input $x = x_1 \| \ldots \| x_\ell$ is $y = F_{sk}(x) = (g_\ell)^{\alpha \Pi_{i=1}^\ell d_{i,x_i}}$, and proof of the VRF is defined as $\pi = P_{sk}(x) = (g_{\ell-1})^{\Pi_{i=1}^\ell d_{i,x_i}}$. The value π can be used to check whether some $y \in \mathbb{G}_\ell$ equals $F_{sk}(x)$: we compute $D(x) = (g_\ell)^{\Pi_{i=1}^\ell d_{i,x_i}}$ by applying the bilinear maps to $D_{1,x_1}, D_{2,x_2}, \ldots, D_{\ell,x_\ell}$, and then check whether $e(g, \pi) = D(x) \wedge e(A, \pi) = y$.

By using the artificial abort technique, the adaptive pseudorandomness will hold under a slightly different assumption. We prove the adaptive pseudorandomness of VRF scheme under the (n, k)-Modified Multilinear Decisional Diffie-Hellman Exponent $((n, k)$-MMDDHE) assumption for $n = O(Q(\lambda) \cdot \ell)$, which is a decisional version of the (n, k)-Modified Multilinear Computational Diffie-Hellman Exponent $((n, k)$-MMCDHE) assumption introduced by Hohenberger et al. [10]. This assumption gives the reduction algorithm $g_1^{a^i c}$ for $i = 1$ to n and

$g_{\ell-1}^{a^i c^\ell}$ for $i = 1$ to $2n$ except for a "hole" at $i = n$. In our reduction, we associate each $D_{i,b}$ value with a value $g^{a^{\hat{r}_{i,b}} c}$ for some $\hat{r}_{i,b}$. The terms are further randomized so as to information-theoretically hide $\hat{r}_{i,b}$ from the outside. We ignore the randomization terms for this discussion. For any input x, the reduction can evaluate the function and give a proof if $\sum_{i=1}^{\ell} \hat{r}_{i,x_i} \neq n$. For all other inputs $x \in S$ such that $\sum_{i=1}^{\ell} \hat{r}_{i,x_i} = n$, the reduction algorithm can successfully use an answer to defeat the (n, k)-MMDDHE assumption.

To achieve a polynomial (in ℓ) reduction we must find a way to put a proper fraction of the inputs in S and to make the distribution of inputs in S close to random across the coins of the reduction. For this final goal, we parameterize and analyze our scheme in a manner similar to the VRF analysis of Hohenberger et al. [11] and Waters's Identity-Based Encryption system [16]. In Waters framework, he gave a technique for partitioning approximately a (hidden) $\approx 1/Q(\lambda)$ of the inputs into what he called a challenge set S and the other $1 - 1/Q(\lambda)$ to be inputs that a reduction algorithm could evaluate the function and proof. We will apply a similar partitioning approach, except we must adapt it to the multilinear-maps-based structure of our VRF.

We finally remark that once we achieve a VRF for large enough input size ℓ, we can apply collision resistant hash function to get a VRF for the input domain of $\{0,1\}^*$. Firstly, we could simply let the setup algorithm choose a collision resistant hash function $H : \{0,1\}^* \to \{0,1\}^\ell$. The VRF would hash the input down to ℓ bits and then apply the core VRF. It is fairly straightforward to show that an successful attack would imply either finding a collision or attacking the core VRF.

Organization. The rest of this paper is organized as follows. In Sect. 2 we give the definition of verifiable random functions and describe the basic tools—leveled multilinear groups which will be used in our construction. In Sect. 3 we provide our instantiation of VRF. In Sect. 4 we prove the security of the VRF scheme. In Sect. 5 we make a conclusion.

2   Preliminaries

2.1   Verifiable Random Function

In this section, we review verifiable random functions (VRFs). Such functions are similar to pseudorandom functions, but differ in two main aspects: Firstly, the output of the function is publicly verifiable, i.e., there exists an algorithm that returns a proof π which shows that y is the output of the function on input x. Secondly, the output of the function is unique, i.e., there cannot exist two images (and proofs) that verify under the same preimage. The formal definitions below is due to Micali et al. [15].

Definition 1 (Verifiable Random Function). *A family of functions $\mathcal{F} = \{f_s : \{0,1\}^{in(\lambda)} \to \{0,1\}^{out(\lambda)}\}_{s \in \{0,1\}^{seed(\lambda)}}$, where in, out, seed are all polynomials in the security parameter 1^λ, is a family of verifiable random functions if there exists a tuple of algorithms (Setup, Eval, Prove, Verify) such that:*

- *Setup(1^λ) is a probabilistic polynomial-time algorithm that on inputs the security parameter λ, outputs a pair of keys (pk, sk), and the description of VRF $F(sk, \cdot)$ and $P(sk, \cdot)$.*
- *Eval(sk, x) is a deterministic polynomial-time algorithm that takes as input a secret key $sk \in \{0,1\}^{seed}$ and $x \in \{0,1\}^{in}$, and outputs a function value $y \in \{0,1\}^{out}$ that evaluates $f_{sk}(x)$.*
- *Prove(sk, x) is a deterministic polynomial-time algorithm that takes as input a secret key $sk \in \{0,1\}^{seed}$ and $x \in \{0,1\}^{in}$, and outputs a proof π related to x.*
- *Verify(pk, x, y, π) is a (possibly) probabilistic polynomial-time algorithm that takes as input public key pk, x, y, and proof π, and outputs 1 if π is a valid proof for the statement "$f_{sk}(x) = y$". Otherwise it outputs 0.*

Formally, we require the tuple (Setup, Eval, Prove, Verify) satisfying the following properties:

Provability. *For all $\lambda \in \mathbb{N}$, all $(pk, sk) \leftarrow$ Setup(1^λ) and all $x \in \{0,1\}^{in}$, if $y =$ Eval(sk, x) and $\pi =$ Prove(sk, x), then Verify(pk, x, y, π) = 1.*

Uniqueness. *For all $\lambda \in \mathbb{N}$, all $(pk, sk) \leftarrow$ Setup(1^λ), all $x \in \{0,1\}^{in}$, there does not exist a tuple (y_0, π_0, y_1, π_1) such that*

(1) $y_0 \neq y_1$, (2) Verify(pk, x, y_0, π_0) = 1, and (3) Verify(pk, x, y_1, π_1) = 1.

Pseudorandomness. *For all PPT adversaries $\mathcal{A} = (\mathcal{A}_1, \mathcal{A}_2)$, we require that the probability $\mathcal{A}$ succeeds in the experiment $\mathbf{Exp}_{\mathcal{A}}^{Pse}(\lambda)$ is at most $\frac{1}{2} + negl(\lambda)$, where the experiment is defined below.*

Experiment $\mathbf{Exp}_{\mathcal{A}}^{Pse}(\lambda)$

1. *$(pk, sk) \leftarrow$ Setup(1^λ);*
2. *$(x^*, state) \leftarrow \mathcal{A}_1^{Func(sk, \cdot)}(pk)$;   //Oracle Func($sk, \cdot$) returns Eval($sk, \cdot$) and Prove($sk, \cdot$).*
3. *$b \xleftarrow{\$} \{0,1\}$;*
4. *$y_0 \leftarrow$ Eval(sk, x^*); $y_1 \xleftarrow{\$} \{0,1\}^{out(\lambda)}$;*
5. *$b' \leftarrow \mathcal{A}_2^{Func(sk, \cdot)}(state, y_b)$;*
6. *Output 1 iff $b' = b$ and x^* was not asked to the Func($sk, \cdot$) oracle.*

2.2   Assumption

Recently, Garg, Gentry, and Halevi [7] proposed candidate constructions for leveled multilinear forms. We will present some of our constructions using the abstraction of leveled multilinear groups. The candidate constructions of [7] implement an abstraction called graded encodings which is similar, but slightly different from multilinear groups.

Leveled Multilinear Groups. We assume the existence of a group generator $\mathcal{G}$, which takes as input a security parameter 1^λ and a positive integer k to indicate the number of levels. $\mathcal{G}(1^\lambda, k)$ outputs a sequence of groups $\boldsymbol{G} = (\mathbb{G}_1, \dots, \mathbb{G}_k)$ each of large prime order $p > 2^\lambda$. In addition, we let g_i be a canonical generator of $\mathbb{G}_i$ (and is known from the group's description). We let $g = g_1$.

We assume the existence of a set of bilinear maps $\{e_{i,j} : \mathbb{G}_i \times \mathbb{G}_j \to \mathbb{G}_{i+j} | i, j \geq 1; i + j \leq k\}$. The map $e_{i,j}$ satisfies the following relation:

$$e_{i,j}(g_i^a, g_j^b) = g_{i+j}^{ab} : \quad \forall a, b \in \mathbb{Z}_p.$$

When the context is obvious, we will sometimes drop the subscripts i, j, For example, we may simply write:

$$e(g_i^a, g_j^b) = g_{i+j}^{ab}.$$

We now give the modified multilinear computational Diffie-Hellman exponent assumption which is introduced by Hohenberger et al. [10].

Assumption 1 ((n, k)-Modified Multilinear Computational Diffie-Hellman Exponent [10]). *The (n, k)-Modified Multilinear Computational Diffie-Hellman Exponent ((n, k)-MMCDHE) problem is as follows: A challenger runs $\mathcal{G}(1^\lambda, k - 1)$ to generate groups and generators of order p. Then it picks random $a, b, c \in \mathbb{Z}_p$.*

The assumption then states that given

$$g = g_1, \ g^b, \ \forall i \in [1, n] \ g^{a^i c}, \ \forall i \neq n \in [1, 2n] \ (g_{k-2})^{a^i c^{k-1}},$$

it is hard to compute $(g_{k-1})^{a^n c^{k-1} b} \in \mathbb{G}_{k-1}$ with better than negligible advantage (in security parameter λ).

The decisional version of modified multilinear computational Diffie-Hellman assumption [10] is the following:

Assumption 2 ((n, k)-Modified Multilinear Decisional Diffie-Hellman Exponent). *The (n, k)-Modified Multilinear Decisional Diffie-Hellman Exponent ((n, k)-MMDDHE) problem is as follows: A challenger runs $\mathcal{G}(1^\lambda, k - 1)$ to generate groups and generators of order p. Then it picks random $a, b, c \in \mathbb{Z}_p$.*

The assumption then states that given

$$g = g_1, \ g^b, \ \forall i \in [1, n] \ g^{a^i c}, \ \forall i \neq n \in [1, 2n] \ (g_{k-2})^{a^i c^{k-1}},$$

it is hard to distinguish the element $T = (g_{k-1})^{a^n c^{k-1} b} \in \mathbb{G}_{k-1}$ from a random group element in $\mathbb{G}_{k-1}$, with better than negligible advantage (in security parameter λ).

3   VRF Construction from the (n, K)-MMDDHE Assumption

Let VRF=(Setup, Eval, Prove, Verify) be the following construction.

Setup$(1^\lambda, 1^\ell)$. The setup algorithm takes as input the security parameter λ as well as the input length ℓ. It firstly runs $\mathcal{G}(1^\lambda; \ell)$ and outputs a sequence of groups $\boldsymbol{G} = (\mathbb{G}_1, \ldots, \mathbb{G}_\ell)$ of prime order p, with canonical generators $g_1, \ldots, g_\ell$, where we let $g = g_1$. It chooses random $\alpha \in \mathbb{Z}_p$ and 2ℓ random elements $(d_{1,0}, d_{1,1}), \ldots, (d_{\ell,0}, d_{\ell,1}) \in \mathbb{Z}_p^2$, and sets $A = g^\alpha$ and $D_{i,b} = g^{d_{i,b}}$ for $i \in [1, \ell]$ and $b \in \{0, 1\}$.

The VRF public key pk consists of the group sequence $(\mathbb{G}_1, \ldots, \mathbb{G}_\ell)$ along with A and $D_{i,b}$ for $i \in [1, \ell]$ and $b \in \{0, 1\}$. The VRF secret key sk consists of the group sequence $(\mathbb{G}_1, \ldots, \mathbb{G}_\ell)$ along with α and $d_{i,b}$ for $i \in [1, \ell]$ and $b \in \{0, 1\}$.

Eval(sk, x). For $x \in \{0, 1\}^\ell$, the function $F_{sk}(x)$ evaluates $x = x_1 \| x_2 \| \ldots \| x_\ell$ as:

$$y = F_{sk}(x) = (g_\ell)^{\alpha \Pi_{i=1}^\ell d_{i, x_i}}.$$

Prove(sk, x). This algorithm outputs a proof π defined as

$$\pi = (g_{\ell-1})^{\Pi_{i=1}^\ell d_{i, x_i}}.$$

Verify(pk, x, y, π). The first step is to verify that all parts of the input are properly encoded group elements; in particular, that the value y and proof π contain legal encodings of elements in $\mathbb{G}_\ell$ and $\mathbb{G}_{\ell-1}$ respectively. Next, compute $D(x) = e(D_{1,x_1}, D_{2,x_2}, \ldots, D_{\ell,x_\ell}) = (g_\ell)^{\Pi_{i=1}^\ell d_{i,x_i}}$ and check if the following equations are satisfied:

$$e(g, \pi) = D(x) \quad \text{and} \quad e(A, \pi) = y.$$

Output 1 if and only if all checks verify.

4   Proof of Security

Theorem 1. *The VRF construction in Sect. 3 is secure with respect to Definition 1 under the (n, k)-MMDDHE assumption.*

Proof. The *provability* property is verifiable in a straightforward manner from the construction.

The *uniqueness* property also follows easily from the group structure. In particular, consider a public key $pk = \big(\boldsymbol{G}, A = g^\alpha, \{D_{i,b} = g^{d_{i,b}}\}_{i \in [n], b \in \{0,1\}}\big)$, with $C \in \mathbb{G}_1$ and $D_{i,b} \in \mathbb{G}_1$, a value $x \in \{0, 1\}^\ell$ and values $(y_0, \pi_0), (y_1, \pi_1) \in \mathbb{G}_\ell \times \mathbb{G}_{\ell-1}$ that satisfy

$$e(g, \pi_\beta) = (g_\ell)^{\Pi_{i=1}^\ell d_{i, x_i}} \quad \text{and} \quad e(A, \pi_\beta) = y_\beta,$$

for $\beta \in \{0, 1\}$. It suffices to show that $y_0 = y_1$. By the properties of the bilinear map e the first verification equation yields $\pi_\beta = (g_{\ell-1})^{\Pi_{i=1}^\ell d_{i, x_i}}$, which implies $\pi_0 = \pi_1$. The second equation yields $y_0 = e(C, \pi_0) = e(C, \pi_1) = y_1$.

Showing *pseudorandomness* will require more work. Intuitively, to show pseudorandomness we will employ a proof framework introduced by Hohenberger [10] that allows us to partition the inputs into two sets: those the simulator can properly answer and those we hope the adversary chooses as a challenge.

We show that if there exists a PPT adversary $\mathcal{A}$ which makes Q Fun queries in the pseudorandomness game and succeeds with probability $\frac{1}{2} + \epsilon$. Then we show how to use $\mathcal{A}$ to create an adversary $\mathcal{B}$ which breaks the (n, k)-MMDDHE assumption with probability $\frac{1}{2} + \frac{3\epsilon}{64Q(\ell+1)}$, where $n = 4Q(\ell + 1)$ and $k = \ell + 1$ and ℓ is the bit length of the VRF input.

The simulator $\mathcal{B}$ takes as input an MMCDHE instance

$$\left(g, g^b, \forall \in [1, n] \; g^{a^i c}, \forall i \neq n \in [1, 2n] \; (g_{k-2})^{a^i c^{k-1}}, T\right)$$

together with the group descriptions where $n = 4Q(\ell + 1)$ and $k = \ell + 1$. The simulator's challenge is to distinguish the element T is $(g_{k-1})^{a^n c^{k-1} b} = (g_\ell)^{a^n c^\ell b} \in \mathbb{G}_{k-1}$ or a random group element in $\mathbb{G}_{k-1}$. The simulator $\mathcal{B}$ plays the role of the challenger in the game as follows.

Setup. The simulator firstly sets an integer $z = 4Q$ and chooses an integer, t, uniformly at random between 0 and ℓ. Recall that Q is the number of Fun queries made by the adversary $\mathcal{A}$ and ℓ is the bit length of the VRF input. It then chooses random integers $r_{1,0}, r_{1,1}, \ldots, r_{\ell,0}, r_{\ell,1}, r'$ between 0 and $z - 1$. Additionally, the simulator chooses random values $s_{1,0}, s_{1,1}, \ldots, s_{\ell,0}, s_{\ell,1} \in \mathbb{Z}_p^*$. These values are all kept internal to the simulator.

Let x_i denote the ith bit of x. For $x \in \{0, 1\}^\ell$, define the functions:

$$C(x) = zt + r' + \sum_{i=1}^{\ell} r_{i, x_i}, \qquad J(x) = \prod_{i=1}^{\ell} s_{i, x_i}.$$

For $x \in \{0, 1\}^\ell$, define the binary function:

$$K(x) = \begin{cases} 0, & \text{if } r' + \sum_{i=1}^{\ell} r_{i, x_i} \equiv 0 \bmod z; \\ 1, & \text{otherwise.} \end{cases}$$

The simulator sets the public key as $D_{1,0} = (g^{a^{(zt+r'+r_{1,0})} c})^{s_{1,0}}$, $D_{1,1} = (g^{a^{(zt+r'+r_{1,1})} c})^{s_{1,1}}$, $D_{i,0} = (g^{a^{r_{i,0}} c})^{s_{i,0}}$ and $D_{i,1} = (g^{a^{r_{i,1}} c})^{s_{i,1}}$ for $i = 2$ to ℓ, and $A = g^b$. It outputs the public key as $\left(G, A, \{D_{i,b}\}_{i \in [1,\ell], b \in \{0,1\}}\right)$, where implicitly the secret key contains the values b, $d_{1,0} = a^{r_{1,0}} c s_{1,0}$, $d_{1,1} = a^{r_{1,1}} c s_{1,1}$, $d_{i,0} = a^{r_{i,0}} c s_{i,0}$ and $d_{i,1} = a^{r_{i,1}} c s_{i,1}$ for $i = 2$ to ℓ. It passes the public key to the adversary $\mathcal{A}$. We observe that all parameter terms are simulatable since all powers of a in the exponent are at most $zt + 2(z - 1) = 4Q\ell + 2(4Q - 1) = 4Q(\ell + 2) - 2 < n$ for any possible choice of $r', r_{i,b}, t$. Moreover, the terms $\{s_{i,b}\}_{i \in [1,\ell], b \in \{0,1\}}$ values distribute the parameters uniformly at random.

Oracle Fun$(sk, \cdot)$ Queries. The adversary $\mathcal{A}$ will ask for VRF evaluations and proofs. On query input x, the simulator firstly checks if $C(x) = n$ and aborts if this is true. Otherwise, it outputs the value

$$F(sk, x) = e\big(g^b, (g_{k-2})^{a^{C(x)}c^{k-1}}\big)^{J(x)} = (g_{k-1})^{ba^{C(x)}c^\ell J(x)}.$$

It also computes

$$\pi = \big((g_{k-2})^{a^{C(x)}c^{k-1}}\big)^{J(x)}.$$

Given the above settings, we can verify that for any value of $x \in \{0,1\}^\ell$, the maximum value of $C(x)$ is $z\ell + (\ell+1)(z-1) < 2z(\ell+2) = 2n$. Thus, if $C(x) \neq n$, then the simulator can correctly compute the function evaluations and proofs.

Response. Eventually adversary $\mathcal{A}$ will provide a challenge input x^*. If $C(x^*) = n$, $\mathcal{B}$ will return the value T. When $\mathcal{A}$ responds with a guess b', $\mathcal{B}$ will also output b' as its (n,k)-MMDDHE guess. If $C(x^*) \neq n$, $\mathcal{B}$ outputs a random bit as its (n,k)-MMDDHE guess.

This ends our description of (n,k)-MMDDHE adversary $\mathcal{B}$.

A Series of Games Analysis. We now argue that any successful adversary $\mathcal{A}$ against our scheme will have success in the game presented by $\mathcal{B}$. To do this, we firstly define a sequence of games, where the first game models the real security game and the final game is exactly the view of the adversary when interacting with $\mathcal{B}$. We then show via a series of claims that if $\mathcal{A}$ is successful against Game j, then it will also be successful against Game $j+1$.

Game 1: This game is defined to be the same as the VRF pseudorandomness game in Definition 1.

Game 2: The same as Game 1, with the exception that we keep a record of each query made by $\mathcal{A}$, which we'll denote as $\boldsymbol{x} = (x^{(1)}, \ldots, x^{(Q)}, x^*)$, where x^* is the challenge input. At the end of the game, we set $z = 4Q$ and choose a random integer t between 0 and ℓ and random integers $\boldsymbol{r} = (r_{1,0}, r_{1,1}, \ldots, r_{\ell,0}, r_{\ell,1}, r')$ between 0 and $z-1$. We define the regular abort indicator function:

$$\mathsf{regabort}(\boldsymbol{x}, \boldsymbol{r}, t) = \begin{cases} 1, & \text{if } C(x^*) \neq n \; \bigvee_{i=1}^{Q} K(x^{(i)}) = 0; \\ 0, & \text{otherwise.} \end{cases}$$

This function $\mathsf{regabort}(\boldsymbol{x}, \boldsymbol{r}, t)$ evaluates to 0 if the queries $\boldsymbol{x}$ will not cause a regular abort for the given choice of simulation values $\boldsymbol{r}, t$. Consider the probability over all simulation values for the given set of queries $\boldsymbol{x}$ as $\zeta(\boldsymbol{x}) = \Pr_{\boldsymbol{r},t}[\mathsf{regabort}(\boldsymbol{x}, \boldsymbol{r}, t) = 0]$.

As in [16], the simulator estimates $\zeta(\boldsymbol{x})$ as ζ' by evaluating $\mathsf{regabort}(\boldsymbol{x}, \boldsymbol{r}, t)$ with fresh random $\boldsymbol{r}, t$ values a total of $O(\epsilon^{-2}\ln(\epsilon^{-1})\zeta_{\min}^{-1}\ln(\zeta_{\min}^{-1}))$ times, where $\zeta_{\min} = \frac{1}{8Q(\ell+1)}$. This does not require running the adversary $\mathcal{A}$ again. $\mathcal{A}$'s success in the game is then determined as follows:

1. *Regular Abort.* If $\mathsf{regabort}(\boldsymbol{x}, \boldsymbol{r}, t) = 1$, then flip a coin $b \in \{0,1\}$ and say that $\mathcal{A}$ wins if $b = 0$ and loses otherwise.
2. *Balancing (Artificial) Abort.* Let $\zeta_{\min} = \frac{1}{8Q(\ell+1)}$ as derived from Claim. If $\zeta' \geq \zeta_{\min}$, $\mathcal{B}$ will abort with probability $\frac{\zeta' - \zeta_{\min}}{\zeta'}$ (not abort with probability $\frac{\zeta_{\min}}{\zeta'}$). If it aborts, flip a coin $b \in \{0,1\}$ and say that $\mathcal{A}$ wins if $b = 0$ and loses otherwise.

3. Otherwise, $\mathcal{A}$ wins if it correctly guessed b' as in the real security game.

Game 3: The same as Game 2, with the exception that $\mathcal{B}$ tests if any abort conditions are satisfied, with each new query, and if so, follows the abort procedure immediately (i.e., flips a coin $b \in \{0, 1\}$ and says that $\mathcal{A}$ wins if $b = 0$.)

Game 3 is exactly the view of $\mathcal{A}$ when interacting with $\mathcal{B}$. We will shortly prove that if $\mathcal{A}$ succeeds in Game 1 with probability $\frac{1}{2} + \epsilon$, then it succeeds in Game 3 with probability $\frac{1}{2} + \frac{3\epsilon}{64Q(\ell+1)}$.

Establishing Three Claims about the Probability of Aborting. Before doing so, we establish one claim which was used above and two claims which will be needed shortly. Our first claim helps us establish a minimum probability that a given set of queries do not cause a *regular* abort. We use this minimum during our balancing abort in Game 2, to "even out" the probability of an abort over all possible queries. In the next two claims, we employ Chernoff Bounds to establish upper and lower bounds for any abort (regular or balancing) for any set of queries. The latter two claims will be used in the analysis of $\mathcal{A}$'s probability of success in Game 2.

Lemma 1. *Let* $\zeta_{min} = \frac{1}{8Q(\ell+1)}$. *For any query vector* $\boldsymbol{x}$, $\zeta(\boldsymbol{x}) \geq \zeta_{min}$.

Lemma 2. *For any set of queries* $\boldsymbol{x}$, *the probability that there is an abort (i.e., regular or balancing) is* $\geq 1 - \zeta_{min} - \frac{3}{8}\zeta_{min}\epsilon$.

Lemma 3. *For any set of queries* $\boldsymbol{x}$, *the probability that there is no abort (i.e., regular or balancing) is* $\geq \zeta_{min} - \frac{1}{4}\zeta_{min}\epsilon$.

Proof of Lemmas 1, 2 and 3 are similar to a related argument in [16] and appears in Appendix A.

Analyzing $\mathcal{A}$'s Probability of Success in the Games. Define $\mathcal{A}$'s probability of success in Game x as $\Pr[\mathcal{A}$ succeed in Game $x]$. We reason about the probability of $\mathcal{A}$'s success in the series of games as follows.

Lemma 4. *If* $\Pr[\mathcal{A}$ *succeed in Game* $1] = \frac{1}{2} + \epsilon$, *then* $\Pr[\mathcal{A}$ *succeed in Game* $2] \geq \frac{1}{2} + \frac{3\epsilon}{64Q(\ell+1)}$.

Proof. We begin by observing that $\Pr[\mathcal{A}$ succeed in Game $2]$ is

$$= \Pr[\mathcal{A} \text{ succeed in Game } 2|\text{abort}] \cdot \Pr[\text{abort}]$$
$$+ \Pr[\mathcal{A} \text{ succeed in Game } 2|\overline{\text{abort}}] \cdot \Pr[\overline{\text{abort}}] \tag{1}$$

$$= \frac{1}{2}\Pr[\text{abort}] + \Pr[\mathcal{A} \text{ succeed in Game } 2|\overline{\text{abort}}] \cdot \Pr[\overline{\text{abort}}] \tag{2}$$

$$= \frac{1}{2}\Pr[\text{abort}] + \Pr[b = b'|\overline{\text{abort}}] \cdot \Pr[\overline{\text{abort}}] \tag{3}$$

$$= \frac{1}{2}\Pr[\text{abort}] + \Pr[\overline{\text{abort}}|b = b'] \cdot \Pr[b = b'] \tag{4}$$

$$= \frac{1}{2}\Pr[\text{abort}] + (\frac{1}{2} + \epsilon) \cdot \Pr[\overline{\text{abort}}|b = b'] \tag{5}$$

$$\geq \frac{1}{2}(1 - \zeta_{\min} - \frac{3}{8}\zeta_{\min}\epsilon) + (\frac{1}{2} + \epsilon)(\zeta_{\min} - \frac{1}{4}\zeta_{\min}\epsilon) \tag{6}$$

$$\geq \frac{1}{2} + \frac{3\zeta_{\min}\epsilon}{8} \tag{7}$$

$$\geq \frac{1}{2} + \frac{3\epsilon}{64Q(\ell+1)}. \tag{8}$$

Equation 2 follows from the fact that, in the case of abort, $\mathcal{A}$'s success is determined by a coin flip. Equation 3 simply states that, when there is no abort, $\mathcal{A}$ wins if and only if it guesses correctly. Equation 4 follows from Bayes' Theorem. In Eq. 5, we observe that $\Pr[b = b']$ is exactly $\mathcal{A}$'s success in Game 1. Now, the purpose of our balancing abort is to even the probability of aborting, for all queries of $\mathcal{A}$, to be roughly $\zeta_{\min}$. This will also get rid of the conditional dependence on $b = b'$. There will be a small error, which must be taken into account. We set $\zeta_{\min} = \frac{1}{8Q(\ell+1)}$ from Lemma 1. We know, for all queries/challenge, that $\Pr[\text{abort}] \geq 1 - \zeta_{\min} - \frac{3}{8}\zeta_{\min}\epsilon$ from Lemma 2 and that $\Pr[\overline{\text{abort}}] \geq \zeta_{\min} - \frac{1}{4}\zeta_{\min}\epsilon$ from Lemma 3. Plugging these values into Eqs. 5 and 8 establishes the lemma.

Lemma 5. $Adv_{\mathcal{A}}[\text{Game } 3] = Adv_{\mathcal{A}}[\text{Game } 2]$.

Proof. We make the explicit observation that these games are equivalent by observing that their only difference is the time at which the regular aborts occur. The artificial abort stage is identical. All public parameters, evaluations and proofs have the same distribution up to the point of a possible abortion. In Game 2, the simulator receives all the queries x, then checks if $\text{regabort}(x, r, t) = 1$ and aborts, taking a random guess, if so. In Game 3, the simulator checks with each new query x if $K(x) = 0$, which implies that the ending regabort evaluation will be 1, and aborts, taking a random guess, if so. Therefore, the output distributions will be the same.

5   Conclusions

Verifiable random functions (VRF) are an interesting and useful cryptographic primitive. But constructing a VRF with large input space and full adaptive security from a non-interactive complexity assumption has proven to be a challenging task. In this work, we presented a construction which can handle arbitrarily-large inputs (by firstly applying a collision-resistant hash function) based on the (n, k)-Modified Multilinear Decisional Diffie-Hellman Exponent assumption. The proof of adaptive pseurandomness used a partitioning approach similar to the VRF analysis of Hohenberger [11] and Waters's Identity-Based Encryption system [16], which is adapted to the multilinear-maps-based structure of our VRF.

A   Appendix

A.1   Proof of Lemma 1

Proof. In other words, the probability of the simulation not triggering a general abort is at least ζ_{min}. This analysis follows that of [16], which we reproduce here for completeness. Without loss of generality, we can assume the adversary always makes the maximum number of queries Q (since the probability of not aborting increases with fewer queries). Fix an arbitrary $x = (x^{(1)}, \ldots, x^{(Q)}, x^*) \in \{0,1\}^{(Q+1)\times\ell}$. Then, with the probability over the choice of r, t, we have that $\Pr[\text{abort on } x]$ is

$$=\Pr\Big[C(x^*) = n \wedge \bigwedge_{i=1}^{Q} K(x^{(i)}) = 1\Big] \tag{9}$$

$$=\Pr\Big[\bigwedge_{i=1}^{Q} K(x^{(i)}) = 1\Big] \cdot \Pr\Big[C(x^*) = n \Big| \bigwedge_{i=1}^{Q} K(x^{(i)}) = 1\Big] \tag{10}$$

$$=\Big(1 - \Pr\Big[\bigwedge_{i=1}^{Q} K(x^{(i)}) = 0\Big]\Big) \cdot \Pr\Big[C(x^*) = n \Big| \bigwedge_{i=1}^{Q} K(x^{(i)}) = 1\Big] \tag{11}$$

$$\geq \Big(1 - \sum_{i=1}^{Q} \Pr[K(x^{(i)}) = 0]\Big) \cdot \Pr\Big[C(x^*) = n \Big| \bigwedge_{i=1}^{Q} K(x^{(i)}) = 1\Big] \tag{12}$$

$$=\Big(1 - \frac{Q}{z}\Big) \cdot \Pr\Big[C(x^*) = n \Big| \bigwedge_{i=1}^{Q} K(x^{(i)}) = 1\Big] \tag{13}$$

$$=\Big(1 - \frac{Q}{z}\Big) \cdot \Pr\Big[zt + r' + \sum_{i=1}^{\ell} r_{i,x_i^*} = n \Big| \bigwedge_{i=1}^{Q} K(x^{(i)}) = 1\Big] \tag{14}$$

$$=\frac{1}{\ell + 1} \cdot \Big(1 - \frac{Q}{z}\Big) \cdot \Pr\Big[K(x^*) = 0 \Big| \bigwedge_{i=1}^{Q} K(x^{(i)}) = 1\Big] \tag{15}$$

$$=\frac{1}{\ell + 1} \cdot \Big(1 - \frac{Q}{z}\Big) \cdot \frac{\Pr[K(x^*) = 0] \cdot \Pr[\bigwedge_{i=1}^{Q} K(x^{(i)}) = 1 | K(x^*) = 0]}{\Pr[\bigwedge_{i=1}^{Q} K(x^{(i)}) = 1]} \tag{16}$$

$$\geq \frac{1}{(\ell + 1)z} \cdot \Big(1 - \frac{Q}{z}\Big) \cdot \Pr\Big[\bigwedge_{i=1}^{Q} K(x^{(i)}) = 1 | K(x^*) = 0\Big] \tag{17}$$

$$=\frac{1}{(\ell + 1)z} \cdot \Big(1 - \frac{Q}{z}\Big) \cdot \Big(1 - \Pr\Big[\bigvee_{i=1}^{Q} K(x^{(i)}) = 0 | K(x^*) = 0\Big]\Big) \tag{18}$$

$$\geq \frac{1}{(\ell + 1)z} \cdot \Big(1 - \frac{Q}{z}\Big) \cdot \Big(1 - \sum_{i=1}^{Q} \Pr[K(x^{(i)}) = 0 | K(x^*) = 0]\Big) \tag{19}$$

$$=\frac{1}{(\ell + 1)z} \cdot \Big(1 - \frac{Q}{z}\Big)^2 \tag{20}$$

$$\geq \frac{1}{(\ell+1)z} \cdot \left(1 - \frac{2Q}{z}\right) \tag{21}$$

$$= \frac{1}{8Q(\ell+1)} \tag{22}$$

Equations 13 and 17 derive from $\Pr[K(x^i) = 0] = \frac{1}{z}$ for any query x^i and $\Pr[K(x^*) = 0] = \frac{1}{z}$ for any challenge x^*. Equation 15 gets a factor of $\frac{1}{\ell+1}$ from the simulator taking a guess of t. Equation 16 follows from Bayes' Theorem. Equation 20 follows from the pairwise independence of the probabilities that $K(x^i) = 0$, $K(x^*) = 0$ for any pair of queries $x^i \neq x^*$, since they will differ in at least one random r_j value. Equation 22 follows from our setting of $z = 4Q$.

A.2   Proof of Lemma 2

Proof. Let $\zeta_x = \zeta(x)$, as defined in Sect. 4, be the probability that a set of queries x do not cause a regular abort. In Game 2, $T = O(\epsilon^{-2}\ln(\epsilon^{-1})\zeta_{\min}^{-1}\ln(\zeta_{\min}^{-1}))$ samples are taken to approximate this value as ζ_x'. By Chernoff Bounds, we have that for all x

$$\Pr[T\zeta_x' < T\zeta_x(1 - \frac{\epsilon}{8})] < e^{-[128\epsilon^{-2}\ln((\epsilon/8)^{-1})\zeta_{\min}^{-1}\ln(\zeta_{\min}^{-1})(\zeta_{\min})(\epsilon/8)^2/2]},$$

which reduces to

$$\Pr[\zeta_x' < \zeta_x(1 - \frac{\epsilon}{8})] < \frac{\epsilon}{8}\zeta_{\min}.$$

The probability of not aborting is equal to the probability of not regular aborting (RA) times the probability of not artificial aborting (AA). Recall that for a measured ζ_x' an artificial abort will not happen with probability $\frac{\zeta_{\min}}{\zeta_x'}$. The probability of aborting is therefore

$$\Pr[\text{abort}] = 1 - \Pr[\overline{\text{abort}}] = 1 - \Pr[\overline{\text{RA}}]\Pr[\overline{\text{AA}}] = 1 - \zeta_x\Pr[\overline{\text{AA}}]$$

$$\geq 1 - \zeta_x\left(\frac{\epsilon}{8}\zeta_{\min} + \frac{\zeta_{\min}}{\zeta_x(1 - \epsilon/8)}\right)$$

$$\geq 1 - \left(\frac{\epsilon}{8}\zeta_{\min} + \frac{\zeta_{\min}}{1 - \epsilon/8}\right)$$

$$\geq 1 - \left(\frac{\epsilon}{8}\zeta_{\min} + \zeta_{\min}(1 + \frac{2\epsilon}{8})\right)$$

$$\geq 1 - \zeta_{\min} - \frac{2\epsilon}{8}\zeta_{\min}.$$

A.3   Proof of Lemma 3

Proof. Let $\zeta_x = \zeta(x)$, as defined in Sect. 4, be the probability that a set of queries x do not cause a regular abort. In Game 2, $T = O(\epsilon^{-2}\ln(\epsilon^{-1})\zeta_{\min}^{-1}\ln(\zeta_{\min}^{-1}))$ samples are taken to approximate this value as ζ_x'. By Chernoff Bounds, we have that for all x

$$\Pr[T\zeta_x' > T\zeta_x(1 + \frac{\epsilon}{8})] < e^{-[256\epsilon^{-2}\ln((\epsilon/8)^{-1})\zeta_{\min}^{-1}\ln(\zeta_{\min}^{-1})(\zeta_{\min})(\epsilon/8)^2/4]},$$

which reduces to

$$\Pr[\zeta_x' > \zeta_x(1 + \frac{\epsilon}{8})] < \frac{\epsilon}{8}\zeta_{\min}.$$

The probability of not aborting is equal to the probability of not regular aborting (RA) times the probability of not artificial aborting (AA). Recall that for a measured ζ_x' an artificial abort will not happen with probability $\frac{\zeta_{\min}}{\zeta_x'}$. Therefore, for any x, the $\Pr[\overline{AA}] \geq (1 - \frac{\epsilon}{8}\zeta_{\min})\frac{\zeta_{\min}}{\zeta_x(1+\epsilon/8)}$. It follows that

$$\Pr[\overline{\text{abort}}] = \Pr[\overline{RA}]\Pr[\overline{AA}] = \zeta_x\Pr[\overline{AA}]$$

$$\geq \zeta_x(1 - \frac{\epsilon}{8}\zeta_{\min})\frac{\zeta_{\min}}{\zeta_x(1 + \epsilon/8)}$$

$$\geq \zeta_{\min}(1 - \frac{\epsilon}{8})^2$$

$$\geq \zeta_{\min}(1 - \frac{\epsilon}{4}).$$

References

1. Abdalla, M., Catalano, D., Fiore, D.: Verifiable random functions from identity-based key encapsulation. In: Joux, A. (ed.) EUROCRYPT 2009. LNCS, vol. 5479, pp. 554–571. Springer, Heidelberg (2009)
2. Boneh, D., Boyen, X.: Short signatures without random oracles. In: Cachin, C., Camenisch, J.L. (eds.) EUROCRYPT 2004. LNCS, vol. 3027, pp. 56–73. Springer, Heidelberg (2004)
3. Boneh, D., Waters, B.: Constrained pseudorandom functions and their applications. In: Sako, K., Sarkar, P. (eds.) ASIACRYPT 2013, Part II. LNCS, vol. 8270, pp. 280–300. Springer, Heidelberg (2013)
4. Dodis, Y.: Efficient construction of (distributed) verifiable random functions. In: Desmedt, Y.G. (ed.) PKC 2003. LNCS, vol. 2567, pp. 1–17. Springer, Heidelberg (2002)
5. Dodis, Y., Yampolskiy, A.: A verifiable random function with short proofs and keys. In: Vaudenay, S. (ed.) PKC 2005. LNCS, vol. 3386, pp. 416–431. Springer, Heidelberg (2005)
6. Fuchsbauer, G.: Constrained verifiable random functions. In: Abdalla, M., De Prisco, R. (eds.) SCN 2014. LNCS, vol. 8642, pp. 95–114. Springer, Heidelberg (2014)
7. Garg, S., Gentry, C., Halevi, S.: Candidate multilinear maps from ideal lattices. In: Johansson, T., Nguyen, P.Q. (eds.) EUROCRYPT 2013. LNCS, vol. 7881, pp. 1–17. Springer, Heidelberg (2013)
8. Goldreich, O., Goldwasser, S., Micali, S.: How to construct random functions. J. ACM 33(4), 792–807 (1986)
9. Goldreich, O., Levin, L.A.: A hard-core predicate for all one-way functions. In: 21st Annual ACM Symposium on Theory of Computing, pp. 25–32. ACM Press, Seattle, Washington, USA, 15–17 May 1989
10. Hohenberger, S., Sahai, A., Waters, B.: Full domain hash from (leveled) multilinear maps and identity-based aggregate signatures. In: Canetti, R., Garay, J.A. (eds.) CRYPTO 2013, Part I. LNCS, vol. 8042, pp. 494–512. Springer, Heidelberg (2013)

11. Hohenberger, S., Waters, B.: Constructing verifiable random functions with large input spaces. In: Gilbert, H. (ed.) EUROCRYPT 2010. LNCS, vol. 6110, pp. 656–672. Springer, Heidelberg (2010)

12. Jarecki, S.: Handcuffing big brother: an abuse-resilient transaction escrow scheme. In: Cachin, C., Camenisch, J.L. (eds.) EUROCRYPT 2004. LNCS, vol. 3027, pp. 590–608. Springer, Heidelberg (2004)

13. Lysyanskaya, A.: Unique signatures and verifiable random functions from the DH-DDH separation. In: Yung, M. (ed.) CRYPTO 2002. LNCS, vol. 2442, p. 597. Springer, Heidelberg (2002)

14. Micali, S., Reyzin, L.: Soundness in the public-key model. In: Kilian, J. (ed.) CRYPTO 2001. LNCS, vol. 2139, pp. 542–565. Springer, Heidelberg (2001)

15. Micali, S., Rabin, M., Vadhan, S.: Verifiable random functions. In: Proceedings of 40th IEEE Symposium on Foundations of Computer Science (FOCS), pp. 120–130. IEEE Computer Society Press (1999)

16. Waters, B.: Efficient identity-based encryption without random oracles. In: Cramer, R. (ed.) EUROCRYPT 2005. LNCS, vol. 3494, pp. 114–127. Springer, Heidelberg (2005)

A Formal Environment for MANET Organization and Security

Aida Ben Chehida Douss[1], Ryma Abassi[1]([✉]), Nihel Ben Youssef[2],
and Sihem Guemara El Fatmi[1]

[1] Higher School of Communication, Sup'Com, ISI University of Carthage Tunis,
Tunis, Tunisia
{bechehida.aida,ryma.abassi,sihem.guemara}@supcom.rnu.tn
[2] Higher Institute of Computer Science, ISI University of Carthage Tunis,
Tunis, Tunisia
nihel.benyoussef@gmail.com

Abstract. A Mobile Ad-hoc Network (MANET) allows the communication of autonomous nodes without any preexistent network infrastructure. This main characteristic may introduce several vulnerabilities which can be exploited by malicious nodes. Thus, one of the basic requirements for the well behavior of such network is to detect and isolate such nodes. Recently, we proposed a reputation based trust management scheme detecting and isolating malicious nodes. This scheme was built upon a specific clustering algorithm baptized MCA (Mobility-based Clustering Approach) and based on two phases: the setting up and the maintenance. In the setting up phase, stable clusters are generated with one-hop members and elected cluster-heads (CHs). In the maintenance phase, the organization of the clusters is maintained in presence of mobility using adequate algorithms. The whole proposition was called TMCA (Trust based MCA) and was also extended with a delegation process resulting a proposition baptized DTMCA (Delegation process TMCA). Once DTMCA is defined, we have found important to validate formally each one of its components in order to avoid any conflict, lack or misbehaving situations. This process requires in a first step a formal specification. This is our main concern in this paper where we propose in a first part a formal specification using inference systems based on logical rules. Two inference systems are proposed. The first one handles the MCA maintenance phase and the second one specifies the TMCA scheme on which the delegation process is integrated. A formal validation using these inference systems is proposed in a second step in order to prove the soundness and the completeness of the various propositions.

Keywords: MANET security · Clustering · Inference system · Formal validation · Soundness · Completeness

1 Introduction

Due to the lack of centralized administration or fixed network infrastructure, Mobile Ad hoc NETworks (MANETs) [1] may be unstable and vulnerable.

© Springer International Publishing Switzerland 2015
M. Reiter and D. Naccache (Eds.): CANS 2015, LNCS 9476, pp. 144–159, 2015.
DOI: 10.1007/978-3-319-26823-1_11

Consequently, their security issue has become a prevalent research area over the last years making available different mechanisms to secure them and more precisely their routing process.

In recent works, we proposed a reputation-based trust management scheme securing routing process in MANETs by detecting malicious nodes and isolating them. This scheme is built upon a recently proposed Mobility-based Clustering Approach (MCA). MCA is based on two major phases: setting up and maintenance. The setting up phase organizes MANETs into clusters with one-hop members and elected Cluster-heads (CHs). In the MCA maintenance phase, algorithms are proposed to react to all topology changes that may occur in the network such as the displacement of a node, the failure of a member node or a CH, or the arrival of a new node.

The whole reputation-based trust management scheme is baptized TMCA (Trust management scheme for MCA). To detect malicious routing behavior, TMCA uses CHs direct observations as well as alerts exchanged between them. TMCA is based on four modules: (1) the monitoring module to detect malicious behaviors, (2) the reputation module to update reputation values, (3) the isolation module to isolate misbehaving nodes and (4) the identity recognition module to assess alerts sources.

Moreover and in order to improve network performance and to maintain its stability, TMCA scheme is extended with a Delegation process (DTMCA). DTMCA allows the CH transferring its privileges to a chosen cluster member in case of displacement or energy dissipation.

The whole proposition performances are then evaluated using simulations. The obtained results showed a significantly improvement in terms of overhead, throughput, packets loss ratio, etc.

However, regardless of DTMCA good performances, deploying such scheme is error prone and it appears necessary to validate it before its real implementation.

According to [2], validation of a model can be done by showing that this model is mathematically sound and that its specification is complete with respect to its input space. More precisely, two main properties have to be considered as proposed in [3]: (1) soundness stating that the proposed model reacts correctly and (2) completeness stating that the model is complete i.e. no other situation can be found. However, the first step towards the validation of a given model is its specification in an automated and generic method [4].

The first concern in this paper is then to propose a formal and automated method handling the MCA maintenance phase as well as the TMCA scheme and the delegation process. This method is based on necessary and sufficient conditions for the simultaneous validation of soundness and completeness. The conditions are presented using inference systems.

The validation task is for its part performed in the second part of this paper. Soundness is proved by showing that the proposed scheme reacts correctly. Completeness is proved by assessing that all potential situations are handled by the inference system.

The remaining part of this paper is organized as follows. In Sect. 2, the reputation based trust management scheme built upon the MCA approach is recalled.

Section 3 details the proposed inference system handling the MCA maintenance phase and elaborates the proposed validation procedure proving the soundness and completeness properties. Section 4 introduces the proposed inference system handling the TMCA scheme as well as the delegation process and presents validation procedures proving the soundness and completeness properties of TMCA and DTMCA schemes. Finally, Sect. 5 concludes this paper.

2   A Reputation-Based Trust Management Scheme

Recently, we proposed a reputation-based trust management scheme enhancing MANET security by detecting misbehaving behaviors and isolating them using the Watchdog mechanism as used in [5]. The scheme in question is built upon a specific clustering approach MCA (Mobility-based Clustering Approach) handling the network organization. The whole proposition is baptized TMCA (Trust MCA). TMCA is also extended with a delegation process called DTMCA (Delegation-based TMCA), allowing the CH's privileges delegation to a chosen cluster member in case of displacement or energy dissipation.

MCA organizes nodes into clusters [6] with one-hop member nodes and elected CHs and maintains also the organization of these clusters in the presence of mobility. It consists of two phases: Setting up and maintenance.

The setting up phase is based on two components: cluster identification and cluster-head election.

Cluster identification is used to generate the restricted (one-hop) neighborhood noted RN where each node i generates its RN_i: two nodes j and k belong to the same RN_i, if j and k are neighbors. The generated RN represents then the node's cluster.

Cluster-head election is used to elect CHs for each cluster: nodes with the lowest weight among their RN neighbors declare themselves CHs. All RN neighbors of an elected CH join it then as members.

After the setting up phase is performed, stable clusters are generated. A cluster is stable if it is independent of all other MANET clusters, if all its nodes only have a unique role (CH or member node) and if it is fully connected i.e. all nodes belonging to the same cluster are one-hop neighbors.

The maintenance phase maintains the organization of clusters in the presence of mobility. In this phase, algorithms are proposed to react to all topology changes that may occur in the network such as the failure of a member node or a CH, the displacement of a node or the arrival of a new node.

In fact, when a node i detects the failure of a node j belonging to its cluster, two cases are then conceivable: (1) node i is a CH and node j its cluster member, in such case, member j is simply dropped from i's cluster, (2) node i is a member node and node j its CH, then node i drops node j from its cluster. If i has the lowest weight among its cluster members, it declares itself as CH.

However, when a node i detects a new node j (node j is detached from its cluster or it joined the network for the first time), two cases can be distinguished: node i is a CH or node i is a member node. If node i is a CH and node j is neighbor with all its cluster members, node j is added as member node into the i cluster. However, if node j is not neighbor with all i's cluster members, CH i creates a new cluster with j and delegates its functionalities to one of its cluster member.

If node i is a member node, it first ensures that its CH k is not neighbor with j. In such case, node i notifies its CH k about the existence of a new node j and waits for the authorization of its CH to create a new cluster with j. If the CH k authorizes such action, node i becomes CH and creates a new cluster with node j. CH k removes then node i from its cluster.

Once the CHs are elected, the TMCA scheme is then triggered. Each CH tracks the behavior of its cluster members using the monitoring module based on the Watchdog mechanism. If a forwarding action is detected, the CH registers it as a positive event. Otherwise, if a rejection or a modification action is detected, the CH registers a negative event. As soon as a negative or positive event is detected, the reputation module is triggered to update the reputation value of the member node. If the reputation module receives a positive event, the reputation value is incremented by $+0.2$ until reaching a maximum value equal to $+3$. Whereas, if a negative event is received, the reputation value is decremented. Two different negative events can be distinguished. The first concerns the dropping of a packet by a member node. In this case, the reputation value is decremented by -1 until reaching a minimum value equal to -3. The second negative event concerns the modification of a forwarded packet. In this case, the reputation value is decremented by -2 until reaching -3. When the reputation value of a member node falls below -3, the reputation module relays the information to the isolation module, which isolates the malicious member node.

TMCA implements also a rehabilitation mechanism for malicious nodes well behaving during a given time. In fact, each CH continues monitoring the behavior of its malicious member nodes. If a malicious member node behaves well, the reputation module is triggered to increment the reputation value of this member node by $+0.1$ instead of $+0.2$. Once the reputation value of the malicious member node reaches the neutral value 0, the rehabilitation mechanism removes the rehabilitated node from the blacklist.

The DTMCA process is called when the residual energy of the CH falls below a certain threshold E_{min} or when the CH is obliged to divide its cluster (in the MCA maintenance phase). In this case, the CH delegates its functionalities to a member node having the highest reputation value and the lowest weight value.

Several simulations were conducted in order to evaluate the performances of the whole proposed DTMCA scheme and have shown satisfying performance results. However, these results may not be sufficient in order to have a complete and generic security scheme assuring the protection of a network. Therefore, we have chosen in this paper to support our simulation work by adding a formal validation environment based on the two traditional main properties: soundness and completeness. The first step towards validation process is its formal specification. Hence, in the following, we specify our proposal using inference systems. This system is based on the use of logical rules consisting of a function which takes premises, analyses their applicability and returns a conclusion. Hence, two inference systems are proposed, the first one handles the MCA maintenance phase and the second one is concerned by the TMCA scheme and the delegation process. Then, the validation task is performed to prove the soundness and the completeness of the various propositions.

3   MCA Formal Specification and Validation

In this section, we propose first an inference system handling the MCA maintenance phase and composed by several rules corresponding to the potential changes that may occur in MANET. Second, the soundness and completeness properties of the proposed inference system are proved by checking that clusters remain stable even after a topology change and by assessing that all situations are handled by the proposed inference system.

Few works using inference systems have been proposed in the literature ([7,8]). Ben Youssef et al. proposed in [7] a formal and automatic method for checking whether a firewall reacts correctly with respect to a security policy. The proposed method was presented in an inference system. A procedure for checking the consistency of a security policy was also proposed which is a necessary condition for the soundness and completeness verification. In [8], authors proposed to enrich the OrBAC model with an integrity mechanism. The proposition was called I-OrBAC (Integrity OrBAC). The idea was illustrated by a security policy example to demonstrate the expressiveness of the model. Role priority concept as well as an algorithm was also proposed to make the security policies more flexible. The authors used the inference system to describe the proposed algorithm.

In the following, we propose a formal and automated expression of the proposed MCA maintenance algorithms using an inference system.

3.1   Preliminaries

The proposed inference system is based on the following assumptions:

- The MCA setting up phase is already made i.e. MANET is organized into clusters. Each cluster is composed by one-hop members and an elected CH.
- The pre-processing phase is made periodically i.e. each node is always aware about its one-hop and two-hop neighbors as well as its neighbors' weights.
- The proposed inference system is triggered in three cases:

1. when a novel node arrives in the MANET,
2. when a node moves from its cluster to another cluster or,
3. when a member node or a CH fails.

- When a new node arrives or detaches from its cluster, it can detect CH nodes or member nodes or both. The new node always joins the neighbor node having the smallest weight.
- The inference system stops once all the new nodes and failed nodes are treated.

3.2 Formal Specification

In this section, necessary and sufficient conditions handling changes that could happen in MANET topologies are proposed. The conditions are presented by an inference system shown in Fig. 1. Used notations are defined in Table 1.

The rules of the system called inference rules apply to triples $(N, C_{old}, \emptyset)$ whose first component N is a set of couples (x, y), where x denotes a new or a failed node in MANET and y its restricted one hop neighborhood $RN(x)$. The second component C_{old} represents the "initial" set of clusters generated after the MCA setting up phase and the third component C_{new} is the set of new clusters generated by some inference rules to handle specific situations of MANET topology changes. Initially C_{new} is empty.

The inference rules CH_{full}, CH_{in} and CH_{out} address the case of the arrival of new nodes or the displacement of existing nodes.

$M_{failure}$ and $CH_{failure}$ are concerned with existing nodes failures.

In the following, the detail of each inference rule is presented.

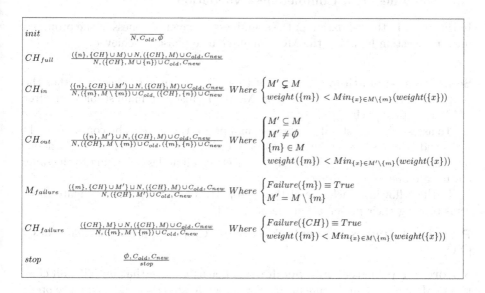

Fig. 1. MCA's inference system

CH_{full} *inference rule.* CH_{full} is triggered when a new or a moving node n detects a whole cluster in C_{old} containing a CH and all its member nodes M. In this case, CH integrates n into its cluster as a member node.

CH_{in} *inference rule.* CH_{in} deals with a new or a moving node n neighboring a CH and only a subset M' of its members M in a C_{old}'s cluster.

Using this inference rule, a node m, member of M and having the lowest weight among M, is elected to be the new CH of the C_{old}'s cluster instead of the old CH. Moreover, a new cluster in C_{new} is built with as CH the new elected CH and as member the node n.

CH_{out} *inference rule.* The inference rule CH_{out} applies when the neighborhood of a new node n includes only a subset not empty M' of member nodes in an existing cluster of C_{old}.

In this case, a node m, member of M' and having the lowest weight, is detached from C_{old}'s cluster to be the CH of a new cluster in C_{new} having as member the node n.

$M_{failure}$ *inference rule.* $M_{failure}$ is applied to remove a member node m in an existing cluster of C_{old} if it fails (*Failure (m)* $\equiv$ *True*).

$CH_{failure}$ *inference rule.* $CH_{failure}$ deals with a failure of a CH. In this case, one of its member m, having the lowest weight, is elected to recover its role.

The inference system stops when all nodes (new, moving or failed node) are handled. In the next section, the soundness and the completeness of the proposed inference system are proved.

3.3   Soundness and Completeness Validation

In this section, the validation of the soundness and completeness of the proposed inference system handling the MCA maintenance phase is achieved.

Soundness Validation. The goal of this sub section is to check whether the proposed inference system is sound i.e. MANET clusters remain stable even after MANET topology changes.

To assess clusters stability, three formal properties have to be considered: (1) Independence: each node belongs to only one cluster (2) Single role: all nodes only have a unique role and (3) Fully connection: all nodes belonging to the same cluster are one-hop neighbors.

In the following, each one of these properties is defined and adequate theorems proving their preservation are proposed.

Property 1 (Independence). Two clusters C_i and C_j are independent iff $C_i \cap C_j = \emptyset$.

Theorem 1 (Clusters independence). Let us assume that initially, all clusters in MANET are independent. If $(N, C_{old}, \emptyset)$ |-* *stop* then Independence property is preserved.

Proof. If $(N, C_{old}, \emptyset)$ |-* *stop* then only one inference rule among CH_{in}, CH_{out}, CH_{full}, $M_{failure}$ or $CH_{failure}$ applies for each element in N. Hence, we have to verify whether the application of each inference rule locally keeps this property.

- When a new node n arrives and its neighborhood matches an entire cluster of C_{old}, only CH_{full} will be applied by integrating n only in C_{old}'s cluster. Therefore, Clusters remain independent.
- When n detects only a subset of nodes in a cluster of C_{old}, two cases are possible:

Table 1. Inference systems notations

Notation	Meaning
N	A set of couples (x,y) where: - x: a new or a failed node. - y: RN (x)
C_{old}	The "initial" set of clusters generated after the MCA setting up phase
C_{new}	The set of new clusters generated by some inference rules
CH	A CH in a given cluster
M	The set of member nodes belonging to a given cluster
m	A member node belonging to the set of members M
$Weight\ (n)$	The weight of the node n belonging to N
$Failure\ (n)$	The status of a node n i.e. true if it fails otherwise false
$Energy\ (n)$	The node n's residual energy
E	The set of events detected by CHs using the TMCA monitoring module. Three types of events can be detected: - A positive event: E_{pos} - A dropping packet event: E_{drop} - A modification packet event: E_{modif}
BL	The set of blacklists maintained by CHs
RP	The set of members' reputations maintained by CHs
$rp\_value\ (m)$	The reputation value of a member node m

1. when n is close to the CH of C_{old}'s cluster and to a subset M' of its members, only the rule CH_{in} is applied by moving CH and n to a new cluster in C_{new} and keeping other nodes in the C_{old}'s cluster,
2. when n is not approaching the CH of C_{old} 's cluster but only a subset M' of its members, only CH_{out} is concerned by moving one member m and the node n in another cluster in C_{new} and keeping the other nodes in C_{old}'s cluster.

Thus, in both situations, $C_{old} \cap C_{new} = \emptyset$.

– When the set N includes failed member nodes, only $M_{failure}$ is applied by removing it from its cluster. Otherwise i.e. if a CH fails, only $CH_{failure}$ is applied by removing CH, and electing another member as a CH. Let us note that in failure situations, modifications occur within a single cluster without altering the others.

Therefore, the Independence property is preserved.

Property 2 (Single role). "A node has a single role (CH or member node): Given a cluster C (CH, M), $M \cap \{CH\} = \emptyset$.

Theorem 2 (Single node role). Assuming that initially, all nodes in MANET have a single role, if $(N, C_{old}, \emptyset)$ |-* $stop$ then single role property is preserved.

Proof. By assuming that, after MCA setting up phase, nodes have a single role, we should check whether the application of each inference rule locally maintains this property. If $(N, C_{old}, \emptyset) \vdash^* stop$ then only one inference rule among CH_{in}, CH_{out}, CH_{full}, $M_{failure}$ or $CH_{failure}$ applies for each element in N.

- When a new node n arrives and its neighborhood matches an entire cluster of C_{old}, only CH_{full} will be applied by including n in the set of members M in C_{old}'s cluster. Therefore, {CH} and M remain disjoint.
- If n detects only a subset of nodes in C_{old}, two cases are conceivable: (1) When n is close to the CH of a C_{old}'s cluster and to a subset M' of its members, only the rule CH_{in} is applied by moving CH and n to a new cluster in C_{new} where {CH} remains a cluster head and n takes the role of member and the rest of the nodes in C_{old}'s cluster preserve their roles, except an elected member node m which henceforth becomes a CH. (2) when n is not approaching the CH but only a subset M' of its members, only CH_{out} is concerned by moving one member m and the node n in another cluster in C_{new} where m becomes a CH and n its member and the other nodes in C_{old} keep their roles.

Thus, in these two situations, we have $M \cap \{CH\} = \emptyset$ in both C_{old} and C_{new}.

- For failure situations nodes, for the case of a member node, only $M_{failure}$ is applied by removing it from its cluster and all the roles are maintained. Otherwise, for the case of CH failure, only $CH_{failure}$ is applied by removing CH, and electing another member as a CH, its role as a member is disappeared.

Therefore, the single role property is preserved.

Property 3 (Fully connection). "A cluster C is fully connected iff all nodes in C are one-hop neighbors.

Theorem 3 (Fully connected clusters). Assuming that initially, all nodes in MANET are fully connected, if $(N, C_{old}, \emptyset) \vdash^* stop$ then fully connection property is preserved.

Proof. After MCA setting up phase, all clusters are fully connected. Hence, we check whether the application of each inference rule locally maintains this property. If $(N, C_{old}, \emptyset) \vdash^* stop$ then only one inference rule CH_{in}, CH_{out}, CH_{full}, $M_{failure}$ or $CH_{failure}$ applies for each element in N.

- CH_{full} is applied when a new node n arrives and its neighborhood matches an entire cluster of C_{old}. In this case, n is included in the cluster which is kept fully connected intuitively.
- When n approaches only a subset of nodes in C_{old}, two cases are possible:

1. when n is close to the CH of C_{old}'s cluster and to a subset M' of its members, only the rule CH_{in} is applied by moving CH and n to a new fully connected cluster in C_{new} and the other nodes in C_{old}'s cluster remain linked as originally.
2. when n is not approaching the CH of C_{old}'s cluster but only a subset M' of its members, in this case, only CH_{out} is concerned by moving one member m and the node n in another fully connected cluster in C_{new} and the other nodes in C_{old}'s cluster keep remain intact.

Thus, after dealing both situations, all nodes in C_{old} and C_{new} clusters are one-hop neighbors.

- For a failed member node, only $M_{failure}$ is applied by removing it from its cluster. In this case, it is kept fully connected. Besides, $CH_{failure}$ is applied when a CH fails by removing it, and electing another member m as a CH. Since the neighborhood of m is unchanged, the fully connection property is preserved.

Property 4 (Stability). A cluster is stable iff it is independent from any other clusters, if all its nodes have a unique role and if it is fully connected.

Corollary (Soundness). Assuming that initially, MANET is stable, if $(N, C_{old}, \emptyset)$ $|$-$^{*}stop$ then stability property is preserved.

Proof. Using theorems 1, 2 and 3, if $(N, C_{old}, \emptyset)$ $|$-$^{*}stop$ then independence, single role and fully connection properties are preserved. Hence, MANET remains stable.

Completeness Validation. Once the soundness of the proposed inference system is proved, we proceed to the validation of its completeness. This is achieved by assessing that all potential situa-tions are handled by the inference system.

Theorem 4 (Completeness). If MANET remains stable after arrival, displacement or failure of nodes then $(N, C_{old}, \emptyset)$ $|$-$^{*}stop$.

Proof. Assume that MANET remains stable after arrival, displacement or failure of a set k of nodes. The stability implies that all clusters are independent, fully connected and including single node roles.

Two situations can be distinguished:

1. When a node n_i arrives or an existent node moves: in this case, we assumed that it should be close to only one non empty set C_{ni} of nodes. This set C_{ni} is included or equal to an existent cluster of C_{oldi} (CH_i, M_i). If C_{ni} does not include a CH, then CH_{out} applies, n_i will join a new cluster C_{newi+1}. If C_{ni} is equal to C_{oldi}, then CH_{full} is applied by adding n_i in it. If C_{ni} includes a CH and a subset of its members, CH_{in} is concerned by integrating n_i in MANET specially in the cluster $C_{newi} + 1$.
2. When a node n_i fails, its treatment depends on its role: if n_i is a CH, $CH_{failure}$ is applied, else, $M_{failure}$ handles failed member nodes.

In both cases, n_i is removed from MANET. It follows that $(N, C_{old}, \emptyset)$ $|$-$(N_1, C_{old1}, C_{new1})|$-$...(\emptyset, C_{oldk}, C_{newk})|$-$^{*}stop$.

4 TMCA and Delegation Process Specification and Validation

TMCA and DTMCA can misbehave due to conflicts or lacks. In fact, it appears necessary to specify it with a formal and automated expression and then to validate it before its real implementation. Hence, this section is based on two-folds.

First, the various TMCA modules as well as the delegation process are specified formally using an inference system. Then the soundness and the completeness properties of the proposed inference system are validated.

4.1   Formal Specification

In this section, necessary and sufficient conditions handling changes that could happen in MANET topologies are proposed. The conditions are presented by an inference system shown in Fig. 2. Used notations in the proposed inference system are defined in Table 1.

Such as depicted in Fig. 2, the inference rules composing the proposed inference system apply to quadruple (C_{old}, E, RP, BL) whose first component C_{old} is the initial set of stable clusters generated after the MCA setting up phase. Each cluster is composed by a CH and a set of members M.

The second component E represents the set of events detected by CHs. In fact, four types of events can be detected by CHs:

- A positive event E_{pos}: a member node broadcasts the received packet without altering its content.
- A dropping packet event E_{drop}: a member node drops the received packet instead of broadcasting it.
- A modification packet event E_{modif}: a member node modifies the content of a received packet before broadcasting it.
- A delegation event E_{delg}: a CH detects that its residual energy falls below a given minimum energy E_{min}.

Initially E is empty.

The third component RP is the set of cluster members' reputation values maintained by CHs according to events received from the TMCA monitoring module. Finally, the last component BL represents the set of blacklists maintained by CHs and containing all detected malicious nodes in the network.

Six inference rules compose the proposed inference system. E_{pos} addresses the case of a positive event detection. The inference rule $Black_{event}$ represents a positive event detection by a CH concerning a blacklisted member node. $Rehab_{event}$ is concerned by the rehabilitation mechanism. The inference rule $Isola_{event}$ handles the isolation of a malicious member node. E_{drop} represents the detection of a dropping packet event and the last inference rule E_{modif} adresses the case of a modification packet event detection.

The inference system stops when all detected events are handled. In the following, each of the proposed inference rule is detailed.

E_{pos} *inference rule.* E_{pos} deals with a positive event detected by a CH concerning one of its cluster member m ($\{E_{pos}\} \bigcup E$) not belonging to the blacklist BL and having a reputation value between -3 and 3 ($\{CH\}$,-3<rp_value ($\{m\}$) <3) $\bigcup RP$).

In this case, the TMCA reputation module increments the reputation value of the corresponding member node by 0.2 ($\{CH\}$, rp_value ($\{m\}$)+0.2) $\bigcup RP$).

Black$_{event}$ inference rule. Black$_{event}$ applies when a CH detects a positive event concerning one of its blacklisted cluster member m having a reputation value between -3 and 0 ($\{m\} \cup BL$). Using this inference rule, the TMCA reputation module is triggered to increment the reputation value of this member node m by +0.1 instead of +0.2 ($\{CH\}$, rp_value ($\{m\}$)+0.1) $\cup$ RP).

Rehab$_{event}$ inference rule. Rehab$_{event}$ is applied to rehabilitate a blacklisted member node m ($\{m\} \cup BL$) having a reputation value above the neutral value 0 once a positive event is detected. In this case, the rehabilitation mechanism removes the rehabilitated node m from the blacklist (BL \ $\{m\}$).

Isola$_{event}$ inference rule. Isola$_{event}$ applies when the reputation value of a given member node m reaches the minimum value -3 (rp_value ($\{m\}$)<=-3) $\cup$ RP), this latter is considered as malicious and the isolation module is triggered to blacklist it (BL $\cup$ $\{m\}$).

E$_{drop}$ inference rule. When a CH detects the dropping of a packet by a member node m ((($\{E_{drop}\} \cup E$)), the E$_{drop}$ inference rule is applied by triggering the TMCA reputation module to decrement the node m's reputation value by -1 ($\{CH\}$, rp-value($\{m\}$) - 1) $\cup$ RP).

E$_{modif}$ inference rule. E$_{modif}$ deals with a modification packet event detection by a CH concerning a cluster member m. In this case, the node m's reputation value is decremented by 2 ($\{CH\}$,rp-value($\{m\}$) - 2) $\cup$ RP).

E$_{delg}$ inference rule. E$_{delg}$ deals with the delegation process. This rule is triggered once the residual energy of a CH falls below a given threshold. In this case, the CH delegates its functionalities to one of its cluster member having the lowest weight and the highest reputation value.

4.2   Soundness and Completeness Validation

This sub section is concerned by the validation of the soundness and the completeness of the proposed inference system.

Soundness Validation. Soundness validation checks whether the proposed inference system is sound by considering one formal property: Logical blacklist. Maintained CHs' blacklists are logical if two conditions are satisfied: (1) all blacklisted nodes have a reputation value between the neutral reputation value 0 and the minimum threshold -3 and (2) all not blacklisted nodes have a reputation value greater than -3 and lesser than 3. Hence, the soundness property is proved by showing that maintained CHs' blacklists remain logical even after members' reputation values updates.

In the following, the logical blacklist property is defined and an adequate theorem proving its preservation is proposed.

Property (Logical blacklist). A maintained blacklist is logical iff ($\{m\} \in BL$ $\wedge$ -3<= rp-value ($\{m\}$) <0) $\vee$ ($\{m\} \notin BL \wedge$ -3< rp_value ($\{m\}$) <= 3).

Theorem. Assuming that initially, maintained blacklists are logical. All member nodes are not blacklisted and have the neutral reputation value equal to 0. If $(C_{old}, \emptyset, RP, BL)|\text{-}^*stop$ then logical blacklist property is preserved.

Proof. If $(C_{old}, \emptyset, RP, BL)|\text{-}^*stop$ then only one inference rule among E_{pos}, $Black_{event}$, $Rehab_{event}$, $Isola_{event}$, E_{drop} or E_{modif} applies for each member node m in C_{old}. Hence, we have to verify whether the application of each inference rule locally keeps this property.

- When a positive event is detected by a CH concerning a not blacklisted member node m (m $\notin$ BL), only the inference rule E_{pos} is applied by incrementing m's reputation value by 0.2. Having that m is not blacklisted and its reputation value is between -3 and 3, then the property is preserved.
- When a positive event is detected concerning a blacklisted member m (m $\in$ BL), then the $Black_{event}$ inference rule is triggered by incrementing the node m's reputation value by 0.1. Having that m is blacklisted and has a reputation value between -3 and 0 then the property is preserved.
- If a CH detects that one of its blacklisted member m has a reputation value greater than 0, it applies the $Rehab_{event}$ inference rule to remove m from its blacklist ({m} \ BL). The property is preserved because m no longer belongs to the BL and its reputation value is greater than 0.
- The $Isola_{event}$ inference rule is used if a member node m's reputation value falls below -3 and it is not blacklisted. In this case, m is considered as malicious and it is blacklisted. Having that m's reputation value is greater than 0 and it is added into the blacklist, then the property is preserved.
- When a negative event is detected by a CH concerning a not blacklisted member m, two cases are conceivable: if the packet dropping event is detected, m's reputation value is decremented by 1 like depicted in E_{drop} inference rule, however if the modification packet event is detected (E_{modif} rule), its reputation is decremented by 2. In both situations, the property is preserved because m's reputation value is between -3 and 3 and it is not blacklisted.

Therefore, the logical blacklist property is preserved.

Completeness Validation. Having that the soundness property of the proposed inference system is proved; we proceed now to the verification of its completeness.

Theorem (Completeness). If maintained blacklists remain logical even after members' reputation values updating, then $(C_{old}, \emptyset, RP, BL)|\text{-}^*stop$.

Proof. Assume that maintained blacklists remains logical after updating the reputation value of a set k of member nodes. Four situations can be distinguished according to the event detected by the CH:

1. If the positive event is detected concerning a member n_i, then two cases can be distinguish. If the member n_i is not blacklisted, then the E_{pos} inference rule is applied by incrementing the node n_i's reputation by 0.2. However, if n_i

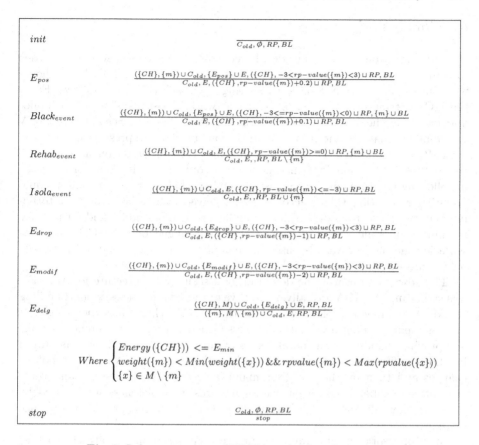

Fig. 2. Inference system of TMCA and delegation process

is blacklisted, its reputation is incremented by 0.1 according to the $Black_{event}$ inference rule.

2. If the negative event is detected concerning a member n_i, then the E_{drop} inference rule is applied if the member node n_i rejects a received packet, and the E_{modif} inference rule is triggered if n_i modifies the content of a packet.

3. When a CH detects that the reputation value of one of its cluster member n_i reaches the neutral value 0, then the $Rehab_{event}$ inference rule is triggered to remove n_i from the blacklist.

4. When a CH detects that the reputation value of one of its cluster member n_i falls below the minimum value -3, then the $Isola_{event}$ inference rule is applied to add n_i into the blacklist.

It follows that $(C_{old}, \emptyset, RP, BL)|\text{-}(C_{old1}, \emptyset, RP, BL)|\text{-}...(C_{oldk}, \emptyset, RP, BL)|\text{-}^* stop.$

5   Conclusion

Recently, we proposed a reputation-based trust management scheme in order to counter malicious routing behavior and isolate it in MANET. This scheme was built upon a Mobility-based Clustering Approach (MCA) as follows: First, the MCA setting up phase organizes the network into stable clusters with one-hop members then elects CHs with the minimum weight. Second, the MCA maintenance phase, maintains the organization of clusters in presence of mobility.

TMCA scheme detects malicious routing behavior based on a reputation value. It is built upon four modules actives only for CHs: monitoring module allowing CH to monitor the cluster members' behaviors, reputation module updating reputation values according to received events from the monitoring module, an isolation module isolating malicious member nodes and an identity recognition module assessing alerts sources exchanged between CHs. A rehabilitation mechanism was also used to rehabilitate malicious nodes if they well behave after a given timer.

The next goal towards the definition of a security architecture for MANET was validating DTMCA formally. Hence, we proposed inference systems handling the MCA maintenance phase as well as the TMCA scheme and the delegation process. Next, we built a validation process using the proposed inference systems and proving soundness and completeness of our proposal. Soundness was proved by showing first that the clusters remain stable even after MANET topology changes and then by showing that maintained CHs' blacklists remain logical even after members' reputation values updates. Completeness was proved by assessing that all potential situations are handled by the proposed inference systems.

In future work, we aim validate our proposal based on real attacks such as collusion or DDOS (Distributed Denial of Service) attacks.

References

1. Sharma, S.K., Kumar, R., Gangwar, A., Pakhre, K.: Routing protocols and security issues in MANET: a survey. Int. J. Emerg. Technol. Adv. Eng. (IJETAE) 4(4), April 2014
2. Lindsay, P.A.: "Specification and validation of a network security policy model", Technical report. 97–05, Software Verification Research Centre, the University of Queensland, April 1997
3. IEEE Guide to Software Requirements Specification. ANSI / IEEE Std 830 (1998)
4. Abassi, R., Guemara El Fatmi, S.: A novel validation method for firewall security policy. J. Inf. Assur. Secur. 4, 329–337 (2009)
5. Kumar, B.P., Sekhar, P.C., Papanna, N., Bhushan, B.B.: A survey on MANET security challenges and routing protocol. Int. J. Comput. Technol. Appl. (IJCTA) 4, 248–256 (2013)
6. Nassuora, A.B., Hussein, A.R.H.: CBPMD: a new weighted distributed clustering algorithm for mobile Ad hoc networks (MANETs). Am. J. Sci. Res. 22, 43–56 (2011). ISSN, 1450–223X

7. Youssef, N.B., Bouhoula, A., Jasquemard, F.: Automatic verification of conformance of firewall configurations to security policies. In: Proceedings of the IEEE Symposium on Computers and Communications, ISCC 2009, Sousse, Tunisia (2009)
8. El Hassani, A.A., El Kalam, A.A., Bouhoula, A., Abassi, R., Ouahman, A.A.: Integrity-OrBAC: a new model to preserve critical infrastructures integrity. Int. J. Inf. Secur. (2014)

Analysis and Implementation of an Efficient Ring-LPN Based Commitment Scheme

Helger Lipmaa$^{(\boxtimes)}$ and Kateryna Pavlyk

University of Tartu, Tartu, Estonia
helger.lipmaa@gmail.com

Abstract. We analyze an efficient parallelizable commitment scheme that is statistically binding and computationally hiding under a variant of the decisional Ring-LPN assumption, conjectured to be secure against quantum computers. It works over medium-size binary finite fields, with both commitment and verification being dominated by 38 finite field multiplications. Such efficiency is achieved due to a precise analysis (that takes into account recent attacks against LPN) of underlying parameters. We report an initial parallel implementation by using the standard OpenCL library on three different platforms. On the AMD Radeon HD 7950 GPU, one can commit to 1024-bit messages in 1 bit per 104.7 cycles. We consider the analysis (which results in concrete parameters that subsequent work can try to falsify) together with the implementation the two most important aspects of the current work.

Keywords: Commitment schemes · GPU implementation · Learning parity with noise · Postquantum

1 Introduction

A commitment scheme allows Alice to send a hidden value to Bob, so that she can later open the commitment only to the original value (the binding property), while before the opening the committed value stays hidden from Bob (the hiding property). Being one of the most basic public-key primitives, commitment schemes play an important role in the design of various cryptographic protocols. E.g., to achieve security against malicious participants, a participant can first commit to his inputs, and then present a zero-knowledge proof of correct behavior on the committed data. To not hinder real-life use, apart from being secure, a commitment scheme should also be highly efficient.

Probably the best known commitment scheme is the Pedersen scheme [15], computationally binding under the discrete logarithm assumption. However, the discrete logarithm assumption can be broken by using quantum computers. It is desirable to design postquantum commitment schemes, i.e., commitment schemes, secure against quantum computers. Such schemes can be used to design postquantum cryptographic protocols.

Moreover, one is interested in the design of *lightweight* postquantum commitment schemes. Here, by lightweight we mean real efficiency on (readily)

© Springer International Publishing Switzerland 2015
M. Reiter and D. Naccache (Eds.): CANS 2015, LNCS 9476, pp. 160–175, 2015.
DOI: 10.1007/978-3-319-26823-1_12

available laptop or desktop computers. Existing commitment schemes are usually not lightweight. For example, the Pedersen commitment scheme requires a committer to execute two exponentiations, and is thus not very efficient. Moreover, to achieve reasonable efficiency, Pedersen commitment scheme has to be implemented over well-chosen elliptic curves, by using far from mundane implementation techniques. (See, e.g., [7].) This makes implementation (and its verification) itself a burdensome process.

Currently, more and more computationally intensive tasks are done by GPU-s (graphics processors) that can solve many parallelizable computational problems much faster than the CPU-s. Most of the conventional (public-key) cryptographic primitives have not been designed with such architectures in mind. Thus, it is becoming necessary to design cryptographic primitives that are fast on SIMD (Single Instruction Multiple Data) architectures, implemented by modern GPU-s. At the current moment, even relatively cheap laptops have GPU-s that offer computational power vastly superior to the CPU-s. We expect this trend to continue in the future. Given quick advances in technology, in a few years such GPU-s will become available on tablets and smartphones.

Two most promising directions to achieve security against quantum computers seem to be (closely intertwined) lattice-based and code-based cryptography. Based on lattices, it is known how to implement very many functionalities (including, say, fully-homomorphic encryption), though often not efficiently enough for practice. Using code-based cryptography, it is known how to implement a somewhat smaller number of functionalities, but often very efficiently.

One of the most interesting code-based assumptions is *learning parity with noise* (LPN, [2]). Based on LPN and its variants, it is known how to design efficiently various symmetric primitives and protocols. Especially promising are ring-based variants of such protocols, first considered in [10]. However, design of similarly efficient public-key primitives is seriously lagging, and even recent approaches, like public-key cryptosystems based on the decisional transposed ring-LPN (TRLPN) assumption [8], are not yet sufficiently efficient.

We propose a new lightweight statistically binding and quantum-secure computationally hiding commitment scheme. While the new commitment scheme is a variant of some previous commitment schemes [11], we provide a much more precise analysis of the security parameters than given in previous work. In particular, we take into account recent attacks [9]. We also provide a partially optimized implementation on contemporary GPU-s.

Let $\mathfrak{R} = \mathbb{Z}_2[X]/(f(X))$ be binary finite field, where $f(X)$ is a degree-n irreducible polynomial. We commit to $m \in \mathfrak{R}$, by using a randomizer $(r, e) \in \mathfrak{R}^2$ and a public key $(M, R) \in \mathfrak{R}^{19 \times 2}$. The commitment is equal to $Mm \oplus Rr \oplus e$, where the noise e comes from a capped Bernoulli distribution (see Sect. 2) with parameter $\tau \approx 0.128118$. (See the analysis in Sect. 4.)

We show that the new commitment scheme is binding if and only if the additive noise e is sufficiently small (in the sense of the ℓ_1-norm). This follows from a generalization and a careful analysis of the Gilbert-Varshamov bound to the finite field, where one of the steps in the generalization crucially depends on the fact that $\mathfrak{R}$ is a field. On the other hand, if the added noise is too small, then the decisional TRLPN problem of Damgård and Park [8] becomes easy and thus the commitment scheme is not hiding. (This follows from the existing attacks against the LPN problem, see [9] and the references therein.) Hence, we have to choose the underlying parameters carefully, so that the commitment scheme be both binding and hiding yet efficient.

We recommend parameters (e.g., $n = 1024$ and $\tau = 0.128118$, that offers 140-bit security against known attacks, see Sect. 4) under which the new commitment scheme is statistically binding and computationally hiding. The proposed value of τ depends on several factors, including the loss of security due to the use of capped Bernoulli lemma, the preciseness of the Gilbert-Varshamov bound, and intricate details on the best known attacks against LPN [9].

Interestingly, the new commitment scheme is significantly more efficient than the most efficient known public-key cryptosystems [8] based on the same assumption. In the case of known public-key cryptosystems [8] the degree n (at least 10 000 bits[1] compared to 1 024 bits at the same security level) of the polynomial f is significantly higher than in our case. This can be compared to the case of discrete logarithm-based schemes, where there is only minimal difference in the efficiency between commitment schemes (e.g., Pedersen) and public-key cryptosystems (e.g., Elgamal). We leave it as an open question whether there is some intrinsic reason behind this.

The new commitment scheme is a ring-LPN based variant of previous LPN-based commitment schemes [11,13]. However, using a different assumption (ring-LPN) requires establishing concrete security parameters. As we will see in this paper, the choice of parameters under which this scheme is both secure under existing attacks yet efficient is far from being trivial. In comparison, [11] does not analyze concrete parameters at all and thus can be seen as being rather theoretical in its approach. Some of their choices (e.g., $N = K$ where N and K are the two main parameters of the LPN assumption) are applicable also in our case but they would make the new scheme unnecessarily inefficient. Finally, in the case where the best known attacks will be improved, one can use our methodology to increase some of the parameters of the new commitment scheme.

Given our security analysis, both commitment and verification are dominated by 38 binary finite field multiplications in a medium-size field, with $n = 1024$. This can be compared to say Pedersen commitment, where one has to execute exponentiations in an elliptic curve group defined over a smaller finite field group (e.g., over $\mathbb{F}_p$, with $\log_2 p \approx 256$). Apart from the obvious efficiency benefits, implementing of the new scheme from scratch is also much easier, partially since one can avoid learning the intricacies of elliptic curves.

To emphasize both on the parallelizability and the conceptual simplicity of the new commitment scheme, we finish the paper with a description of an initial, very simple, implementation. This implementation is not of industrial strength, but is mostly just provided to give a rough idea of achievable speed. More precisely, we implemented both a matrix-to-vector multiplication and a finite field

---

[1] This estimate, given in [8], does not account for the recent attacks [4,9]. According to [4], the key length of the public-key cryptosystem of [8] should be even larger.

multiplication over the finite field $\mathbb{F}_{2^{1024}}$. In addition, one can reuse extensive literature on the fast implementations of finite field multiplications: while we focused on the simplicity of the implementation, we are sure that up-to-date algorithms achieve better efficiency. The timings, reported in Table 1, should then be multiplied by 38 (plus a small epsilon to account for finite field additions) to obtain the timings of both commitment and verification.

Our implementation uses the OpenCL standard for parallel programming. We tested this implementation on a rather mediocre[2] NVIDIA Quadro 2000M GPU (available in medium-class laptops), on a modern AMD Radeon HD 7950 GPU, and on the Intel i7-2860QM CPU, the results are summarized in Table 1.

As shown in Sect. 5, since the HD 7950 implementation only utilizes 272 cores out of 1792, one can implement on average $1792/272 \approx 6.59$ binary finite field multiplications in parallel. Since one commitment requires 38 multiplications, in average one can schedule $1792/272/38 \approx 0.173$ commitments of 1024-bit messages per execution. Thus, one can commit to 1 bit per $18,488.6/(0.173 \cdot 1024) \approx 104.7$ cycles on the AMD GPU. (See Table 1 for the origin of the number $18,488.6$.) We emphasize that this is the peak throughput number, given full pipelines and optimal scheduling and that at this moment, this is only an estimation. We provide an efficiency comparison with the Pedersen commitment scheme in Sect. 5.

2 Preliminaries

By default, all vectors are column vectors. For $\boldsymbol{a} \in \mathbb{Z}_2^n$, let $\boldsymbol{a}[i]$ be its ith coordinate. Thus, $\boldsymbol{a} = (\boldsymbol{a}[1], \ldots, \boldsymbol{a}[n])$. For a vector $\boldsymbol{a} \in \mathbb{Z}_2^n$, let $||\boldsymbol{a}||_1 = \sum \boldsymbol{a}[i] = \sharp\{i : \boldsymbol{a}[i] \neq 0\}$ be its Hamming weight. For a set A, $a \xleftarrow{r} A$ means that a is uniformly picked from A, and for a randomized algorithm $\mathcal{A}$, $a \xleftarrow{r} \mathcal{A}$ means that a is uniformly picked by $\mathcal{A}$. Let κ be the computational security parameter, and let λ be the information-theoretical security parameter. In practice, one can assume that $\kappa = 128$ and $\lambda = 40$. We give κ and λ as unary inputs (denoted by 1^κ and 1^λ) to some of the algorithms.

A *commitment scheme* enables a party to commit to a message, and open it later to the same value. On the one hand, the commitment must hide the message. On the other hand, the committer should not be able to open the commitment to anything else but the original message. More formally, a commitment scheme (in the public parameters model) is a tuple of three efficient algorithms, gen, com and ver. The algorithm $\mathsf{gen}(1^\kappa, 1^\lambda)$ generates public parameters gk for the commitment scheme. After that, the randomized algorithm $\mathsf{com}_{\mathsf{gk}}(m; \cdot)$ commits to a message m by picking a uniformly random randomizer $r \xleftarrow{r} \mathcal{R}$ (here, $\mathcal{R}$ is a randomizer set specified by the commitment scheme and κ) and outputting $(y, z) \leftarrow \mathsf{com}_{\mathsf{gk}}(m; r)$. Here, y is the commitment to m, while z is the decommitment value. It is usually required that one can efficiently reconstruct m from z.

---

[2] This GPU is more than 35 times slower than the fastest GPU-s in the market, according to https://en.bitcoin.it/wiki/Non-specialized_hardware_comparison (accessed in June 2015).

The verification algorithm ver verifies that z is the correct decommitment of y, i.e., $\mathsf{ver}_{\mathsf{gk}}(y, z)$ outputs either 1 or 0. It is required that $\mathsf{ver}_{\mathsf{gk}}(\mathsf{com}_{\mathsf{gk}}(m; r)) = 1$ for all valid gk, m and r.

A commitment scheme is *statistically binding* if with probability $1 - \kappa^{-\omega(1)}$ over the choice of gk, for any $m_1 \neq m_2$, r_1 and r_2, if $(y_i, z_i) = \mathsf{com}_{\mathsf{gk}}(m_i; r_i)$ then $y_1 \neq y_2$. A commitment scheme is computationally hiding if, given y, it is computationally difficult to infer any information about m. More precisely, the commitment scheme (gen, com, ver) is *computationally hiding*, if for any non-uniform probabilistic polynomial time stateful adversary $\mathcal{A}$, the following value is negligible in κ:

$$\left| \Pr \left[\begin{array}{l} \mathsf{gk} \leftarrow \mathsf{gen}(1^\kappa, 1^\lambda), (m_1, m_2) \leftarrow \mathcal{A}(\mathsf{gk}), \alpha \xleftarrow{r} \{1, 2\}, r \xleftarrow{r} \mathcal{R} : \\ \mathcal{A}(\mathsf{com}_{\mathsf{gk}}(\mathsf{gk}, m_\alpha; r)) = \alpha \end{array} \right] - \frac{1}{2} \right| .$$

An $[N, K]$ code C over a finite alphabet Σ is a subset of Σ^N. The elements of C are the codewords of C. If $|\Sigma| = q$, C is called a q-ary code. Associated with a code is an encoding map E that maps the message set Σ^K to Σ^N. The code is then the image of the encoding map, and it is said to be of length N and rank K. An $[N, K]$ code is called *linear* if any linear combination of its codewords is also a codeword. A *generator matrix* $\boldsymbol{R}$ of a linear $[N, K]$ code is a $N \times K$ matrix whose rows form a basis of the code. The (minimum) *distance* D of code C is the minimal Hamming distance between two distinct codewords of C. An $[N, K]$ code with a minimal distance D is known as an $[N, K, D]$ code. For arbitrary linear code C, its minimum distance equals the minimum Hamming weight of a nonzero codeword of C (see Proposition 2.1, [16]). According to the Singleton bound, $N - K + 1 \geq D$. According to the Gilbert-Varshamov bound, a random $[N, K]$ code has distance that matches the Singleton bound.

The code C has covering radius [6] d_C when the distance between C and any element of Σ^N is not more than d_C. An $[N, K, D] d_C$ *covering code* is a linear code with parameters $[N, K, D]$ and covering radius d_C. Denote $\varrho = d_C/N$. The best possible covering radius d_C satisfies the sphere-covering bound $\sum_{i=0}^{d_C} \binom{N}{i} \geq 2^{N-K}$ [6], or alternatively $2^K \geq 2^N/|B_N(d_C)| \geq 2^{(1-H_2(\varrho))N}$, where $H_2(p) = -p \log_2 p - (1-p) \log_2(1-p)$, $p \in [0, 1]$, is the binary entropy function.

For $N \in \mathbb{N}^+$, let χ_N be a distribution over $\mathbb{Z}_2^N$. Let $K < N$ be another positive integer. The *decisional* (χ_N, N, K)-*LPN problem* [2] is (t, ε)-hard if for every distinguisher $\mathcal{D}$ of size t:

$$\left| \Pr_{\boldsymbol{R}, \boldsymbol{s}, \boldsymbol{e}} [\mathcal{D}(\boldsymbol{R}, \boldsymbol{R}\boldsymbol{s} \oplus \boldsymbol{e}) = 1] - \Pr_{\boldsymbol{R}, \boldsymbol{r}} [\mathcal{D}(\boldsymbol{R}, \boldsymbol{r}) = 1] \right| \leq \varepsilon,$$

where $\boldsymbol{R} \xleftarrow{r} \mathbb{Z}_2^{N \times K}$, $\boldsymbol{s} \xleftarrow{r} \mathbb{Z}_2^K$, $\boldsymbol{e} \xleftarrow{r} \chi_N$, and $\boldsymbol{r} \xleftarrow{r} \mathbb{Z}_2^N$. $\mathcal{D}$ also has access to the description of χ_N.

In the standard definition of the decisional LPN problem, the error distribution χ_N is the Bernoulli distribution with a parameter $0 < \tau < 1/2$, i.e., every bit $\boldsymbol{e}[i]$ is chosen independently and identically distributed with $\Pr[\boldsymbol{e}[i] = 1] = \tau$. In this case, we write $\chi_N = \mathsf{Ber}_\tau^N$. The decisional $(\mathsf{Ber}_\tau^N, N, K)$-LPN problem is closely related to the long-standing open problem of efficiently decoding random linear codes, and — assuming $N = \Theta(K)$ like in the current paper — is believed to be hard even in the presence of quantum computers. Moreover, the search (given $\boldsymbol{Rs} \oplus \boldsymbol{e}$, compute $\boldsymbol{s}$) and the decision version of the LPN assumption are known to be polynomially equivalent [12]. The first subexponential algorithm to solve the (search) LPN was proposed in [3]. The most efficient currently known attack is by Guo, Johansson, and Löndahl [9].[3]

Consider a coin that shows heads with probability τ and tails with probability $1 - \tau$. The Hoeffding inequality states that the probability that N coin tosses yields heads at least $(\tau + \varepsilon)N$ times is at most $1 - \exp(-2\varepsilon^2 N)$. I.e., if a random variable comes from the Bernoulli distribution with parameter τ, then by the Hoeffding inequality it is larger than $\tau^* N$ with probability $2^{-\lambda}$, where

$$\tau^* := \tau + \sqrt{\frac{\lambda}{2 \log_2 e \cdot N}} . \tag{1}$$

Thus, when working with the decisional LPN assumption, one can always assume that $||\boldsymbol{e}||_1 \leq \tau^* N$. Following [11], we denote by $\overline{\mathsf{Ber}}_\tau^N$ the corresponding *capped Bernoulli distribution*, and by $(\overline{\mathsf{Ber}}_\tau^N, N, K)$-LPN the resulting assumption. I.e., $\boldsymbol{e} \xleftarrow{r} \overline{\mathsf{Ber}}_\tau^N$ means that $\boldsymbol{e}$ is first chosen according to Ber_τ^N. If $||\boldsymbol{e}||_1 > \tau^* N$, one resamples $\boldsymbol{e}$ again until its norm becomes not greater than $\tau^* N$. Clearly, $(\overline{\mathsf{Ber}}_\tau^N, N, K)$-LPN is difficult iff $(\mathsf{Ber}_\tau^N, N, K)$-LPN is difficult; see [11].

Heyse et al. [10] proposed a ring variant of the decisional LPN assumption. A variant of it, TRLPN, was defined by Damgård and Park [8]. Consider the ring $\mathfrak{R} = \mathbb{Z}_2[X]/(f(X))$, where f is some degree n irreducible polynomial over $\mathbb{Z}_2[X]$. (See [10] for a treatment in the case f is reducible.) The elements of $\mathfrak{R}$ are thus degree-n polynomials over $\mathbb{Z}_2[X]$, with their addition and multiplication defined modulo f. Define $||m||_1 := \sum_{i=0}^{n-1} m_i$, and for a vector $\boldsymbol{e} \in \mathfrak{R}^a$ for some a, let $||\boldsymbol{e}||_1 := \sum_{i=1}^a ||e_i||_1$ be its ℓ_1-norm.

For a polynomial ring $\mathfrak{R} = \mathbb{Z}_2[X]/(f(X))$, let $\mathsf{Ber}_\tau^{\mathfrak{R}}$ denote the distribution over polynomials from $\mathfrak{R}$, where each of the coefficients of the polynomial is drawn independently from Ber_τ. For N with $n \mid N$, the capped Bernoulli distribution $\overline{\mathsf{Ber}}_\tau^{\mathfrak{R},N/n}$ is defined in a natural way: one first chooses $\boldsymbol{a} \xleftarrow{r} \overline{\mathsf{Ber}}_\tau^N$, and then outputs $\boldsymbol{e}$, where $e_i \leftarrow \sum_{j=0}^{n-1} a_{(i-1)n+j+1} X^j$ for $1 \leq i \leq N/n$.

Let $N > K$, and let ψ be a distribution on $\mathbb{Z}_2^{N \times K}$. The *decisional* $(\chi_N, N, K; \psi)$-*LPN problem* [8] is defined exactly as the decisional (χ_N, N, K)-LPN problem, except that $\boldsymbol{R}$ is drawn from ψ. Now, for a ring element $r = \sum_{i=0}^{n-1} r_i X^i \in \mathfrak{R}$, let $\mathsf{vec}(r)$ be the natural isomorphic mapping of its coefficient vector to $\mathbb{Z}_2^n$, that is, $\mathsf{vec}(r)[i] = r_{i-1}$. For $r \in \mathfrak{R}$, we define $\mathsf{mat}(r) \in \mathbb{Z}_2^{n \times n}$ to be the matrix for which $\mathsf{mat}(r)^\top \cdot \mathsf{vec}(r') = \mathsf{vec}(r \cdot r')$ for all $r' \in \mathfrak{R}$. The ith column vector of $\mathsf{mat}(r)$ is equal to $\mathsf{vec}(rX^{i-1})$, $\mathsf{mat}(r)^{(i)} = \mathsf{vec}(rX^{i-1})$.

---

[3] In a recent eprint, [4] made the complexity analysis of [9] somewhat more precise. However, since it is currently only an eprint, we will ignore its analysis.

Let $K = 2n$ and $N > K$ be such that $n \mid N$. Let $\Psi^{\mathfrak{R},N,K}$ denote the distribution over $\mathbb{Z}_2^{N \times K}$, whose samples consist of $(N/n) \times 2$ square matrices from $\mathbb{Z}_2^{n \times n}$, where each square matrix is individually sampled as $\mathsf{mat}(r)$ for uniformly random $r \overset{r}{\leftarrow} \mathfrak{R}$. As in [8], we call the decisional $(\chi_N, N, K; \Psi^{\mathfrak{R},N,K})$-LPN problem the *decisional transposed ring-LPN (TRLPN) problem*. More precisely, in TRLPN, the adversary has access to $(f, \tau, \boldsymbol{R}, \boldsymbol{y})$, and has to guess whether $\boldsymbol{y} = \boldsymbol{Rx} \oplus \boldsymbol{e}$, for random $\boldsymbol{x}$ and a small-weight $\boldsymbol{e}$, or $\boldsymbol{y}$ is random.

The decisional TRLPN problem is motivated by the fact that if $\boldsymbol{A} = \mathsf{mat}(a)$ and $\boldsymbol{b} = \mathsf{vec}(b)$, then $\boldsymbol{A}^\top \boldsymbol{b} = \mathsf{mat}(a)^\top \mathsf{vec}(b) = \mathsf{vec}(a \cdot b)$ can be computed by using a single ring multiplication, that depending on the choice of f can be computationally more efficient than a general matrix-vector product. More importantly, instead of communicating $2N/n$ matrices $\boldsymbol{A} \in \mathbb{Z}_2^{n \times n}$ as the public key, it suffices to communicate $2N/n$ ring elements, and memory requirements of all relevant algorithms will be reduced by a factor of n. See [10] for more motivation.

The difficulty of the TRLPN problem is positively correlated with the parameters n and τ. Since the efficiency mainly depends on n, one should choose as small n as possible such that there still exists a $\tau > 0$ so that the constructed primitive or protocol is secure. For an efficient implementation, it is also desirable that n is a power of 2.

For a ring $\mathfrak{R} = \mathbb{Z}_2[X]/(f(X))$, let $t_\times^{\mathfrak{R}}$ denote the computational complexity of one ring multiplication (as a function of f and thus also of n).

3   Ring-LPN Based Commitment Scheme

In [11], the authors proposed an LPN-based commitment scheme. We follow a route that is common both in coding theory (in the context of cyclic codes) and cryptography (in the context of lattices but also LPN [10]), by embedding vectors from $\mathbb{Z}_2^n$ to the ring $\mathbb{Z}_2[X]/(f(X))$, where f is a well chosen (irreducible) degree-n polynomial. This enables to replace matrices with ring elements, and matrix-to-vector multiplications with ring multiplications. The most intricate part of the construction is its choice of parameters, coupled by a precise analysis of their correctness. The commitment scheme is given in Fig. 1.

We recall that the distribution $\Psi^{\mathfrak{R},N,K}$ is defined over $N \times K$ matrices. In particular, the expected value of $||\boldsymbol{e}||_1$ is equal to $\tau \cdot N$, and thus by the Hoeffding inequality, $||\boldsymbol{e}||_1 \leq D'$ with a high probability. For efficiency purposes, one should choose an irreducible $f(X)$ with a minimal number of non-zero monomials. Clearly, the commitment algorithm computes $(\boldsymbol{M}, \boldsymbol{R}) \cdot (m, r)^\top \oplus \boldsymbol{e}$.

Before stating Theorem 1 about the security of the commitment scheme, we first establish some technical lemmas. The first lemma motivates the stated lower bound $\beta \geq \lceil 2/(1 - 2\tau^*) \rceil$. Intuitively, we have an $[N, K, D]$ code for K as in the definition of the protocol, and $D = 2\tau^* N + 1$ as in Theorem 1. The Singleton bound gives us the following lower bound on N. This result is also necessary since there is a mutual dependency between τ^* (given in Eq. (1)) and N (defined in the commitment scheme). In an actual implementation, one should set N to be

Public Parameters Generation $\mathsf{gen}(1^\kappa, 1^\lambda)$: generate TRLPN parameters n and $\tau > 0$. Let τ^* be as in Eq. (1). Let $K = 2n$ and $N = \beta n$ for some integer $\beta \geq \lceil 2/(1 - 2\tau^*) \rceil$. Define $D' := \lfloor \tau^* \cdot N \rfloor$. Choose a suitable degree-n irreducible polynomial f, and let $\mathfrak{R} := \mathbb{Z}_2[X]/(f(X))$. Choose uniformly random $\boldsymbol{M} \xleftarrow{} \mathfrak{R}^{N/n}$ and $\boldsymbol{R} \xleftarrow{} \mathfrak{R}^{N/n}$. Output $\mathsf{gk} := (f, \tau, \boldsymbol{M}, \boldsymbol{R})$.

Commitment $\mathsf{com}_{\mathsf{gk}}(m; \cdot, \cdot)$: If $m \notin \mathfrak{R}$, then reject. Choose random $r \xleftarrow{} \mathfrak{R}$ and $e \xleftarrow{} \overline{\mathsf{Ber}}_\tau^{\mathfrak{R}, N/n}$. Output $\mathsf{com}_{\mathsf{gk}}(m; r, e) = (\boldsymbol{y}, z) \leftarrow (\boldsymbol{M}m \oplus \boldsymbol{R}r \oplus \boldsymbol{e}, (m, r))$ with $\boldsymbol{y} \in \mathfrak{R}^{N/n}$.

Verification $\mathsf{ver}_{\mathsf{gk}}(\boldsymbol{y}, z = (m, r))$: reject if $\boldsymbol{y} \notin \mathfrak{R}^{N/n}$, $m \notin \mathfrak{R}$, or $r \notin \mathfrak{R}$. Otherwise, compute $\boldsymbol{e} \leftarrow \boldsymbol{y} \oplus \boldsymbol{M}m \oplus \boldsymbol{R}r$, and accept iff $||\boldsymbol{e}||_1 \leq D'$.

Fig. 1. The commitment scheme

equal to the smallest multiplier of n greater or equal than the bound computed in Lemma 1, and only then compute τ^* from it according to Eq. (1).

Lemma 1. *Consider* $\tau < 1/2$, $\tau^* < 1/2$ *as in Eq.* (1), $K = 2n$, *and* $D = 2\tau^* N + 1$. *Then in any* $[N, K, D]$ *code,* $N \geq \frac{2}{1-2\tau^*} \cdot n = \frac{2}{1-2\tau} \cdot n - (\sqrt{4n(1-2\tau)\lambda \ln 2 + \lambda^2 \ln^2 2} - \lambda \ln 2)/(1-2\tau)^2$. *If* $n \mid N$, *then* $N \geq 3n$.

Proof. By the Singleton bound, $N \geq K + D - 1$. Due to the choice of K and D, this means that $N \geq 2n + 2\tau^* N$, and thus the minimum choice for N is $N = \frac{2}{1-2\tau^*} \cdot n$. Combining this value of N with τ^* as in Eq. (1), after solving a quadratic equation $(1-2\tau)N\sqrt{2\log_2 e} - 2\sqrt{\lambda N} - 2n\sqrt{2\log_2 e} = 0$, and taking the smaller of two solutions, $\sqrt{N} = (\sqrt{\lambda \ln 2} - \sqrt{\lambda \ln 2 + 4n(1-2\tau)})/(\sqrt{2}(1-2\tau))$, we get the first claim of the current lemma. The second claim (i.e., that if $n \mid N$ then $N \geq 3n$) follows, since $\tau > 0$. $\qquad\square$

One can take any value of N, $n \mid N$, that satisfies this lemma. To improve on efficiency, we recommend to choose N to be first integer larger than $K/(1-2\tau^*)$ that divides by n. In practice, since we have $\tau^* \leq 1/4$, we can always take $N = 2K$. However, when $\tau^* \leq 1/6$, we only need $N \geq \frac{3 \cdot 2n}{2} = 3n$ while $K = 2n$. Thus, in a paradoxical manner, a smaller τ^*, and thus a smaller τ, *may* help to improve the efficiency of this commitment scheme. However, as we will see later, such a small value of N would collapse the security for other reasons.

We show next that this commitment scheme is binding if the following probability $\mathsf{GV}^\mathfrak{R}$ (the *Gilbert-Varshamov bound for finite fields*; a variant of the well-known Gilbert-Varshamov bound) is (say) $1 - 2^{-\lambda}$.

Definition 1. *Let* f *be a degree-n polynomial that is irreducible over* $\mathbb{Z}_2$. *Assume that* $\mathfrak{R} = \mathbb{Z}_2[X]/(f(X))$ *and* $0 < D \leq N - K + 1$. *Let* $(\mathfrak{R}^2)^*$ *denote* $\mathfrak{R}^2 \setminus \boldsymbol{0}_2$, *where* $0 \in \mathfrak{R}$. *Define*

$$\mathsf{GV}^\mathfrak{R}(N, K, D) := \min_{x \in (\mathfrak{R}^2)^*} \Pr_{\boldsymbol{A} \xleftarrow{} \mathfrak{R}^{(N/n) \times 2}} [||\boldsymbol{A} \cdot \boldsymbol{x}||_1 \geq D].$$

We bound $\mathsf{GV}^\mathfrak{R}$ under the assumption that f is irreducible. The following lemma basically states that a random linear code with a generator matrix, distributed according to $\Psi^{\mathfrak{R}, N, K}$, meets the Singleton bound with a very high probability.

Lemma 2. Let $N = \beta n$ for an integer $\beta \geq 2$, $K = 2n$, and D be as in the commitment scheme of Sect. 3 such that $D < N/3 + 2$. Assume that $0 < D \leq N - K + 1$. Then

$$\mathsf{GV}^{\mathfrak{R}}(N, K, D) \geq 1 - 2^{-n(\beta - \beta(H_2((D-2)/(\beta n))+2))+1}.$$

Proof. For some $x \in (\mathfrak{R}^2)^*$, denote $S := \Pr_{A \leftarrow \mathfrak{R}^{\beta \times 2}}[\|A \cdot x\|_1 \leq D - 1]$. Since $\mathfrak{R}$ is a field, every non-zero element of it is irreducible. (Here we need $\mathfrak{R}$ to be a field.) Thus, for any non-zero $m \in \mathfrak{R}$ and any $y_i \in \mathfrak{R}$, $i \in \{1, \beta\}$, $j \in \{1, 2\}$, $\Pr_{A_{ij} \leftarrow \mathfrak{R}}[A_{ij} m = y_i] = \Pr_{A_{ij} \leftarrow \mathfrak{R}}[A_{ij} = m^{-1} y_i] = \frac{1}{2^n}$. Thus, since A is chosen uniformly, $x \neq \mathbf{0}_2$ and the vector consisting of uniformly chosen coordinates is uniformly chosen, then also $y = Ax$ is uniformly random.

Now, we estimate S as the number of all $y \in \mathfrak{R}^{\beta}$ with $\|y\|_1 \leq D - 1$ divided by the ring size $|\mathfrak{R}^{\beta}|$. For $y \in \mathfrak{R}^{\beta}$, let $y^* \in \mathbb{Z}_2^N$ be its canonical representation as a bit-vector, i.e., $y^*_{in+j} = y_i[j]$. Clearly, $\|y\|_1 = \|y^*\|_1$. Thus, we need to find S, the number of all $y^* \in \mathbb{Z}_2^N$ with $\|y^*\|_1 \leq D - 1$, which is equal to $\sum_{j=1}^{D-1} S_j$, where $S_j = |\{y^* : \|y^*\|_1 = j\}| = \binom{N}{j}$ is the number of vectors from $\mathbb{Z}_2^N$ that have exactly j non-zero coefficients. In other words, $S = B_N(D-2)/2^N$, where $B_N(D - 2)$ is the size of the Hamming ball of radius $D - 2$. Then using the following well-known bound for the sum of the first k binomial coefficients for fixed t, $0 \leq k \leq t/2$, $B_t(k) = \sum_{i=0}^k \binom{t}{i} \leq \binom{t}{k}(1 + k/(t - 2k + 1))$, since $D < N/2 + 2$ (this follows from $D < N/3 + 2$ that we made) we obtain $S = B_N(D - 2)/2^N \leq \frac{1}{2^N} \cdot \binom{N}{D-2} \cdot (1 + (D - 2)/(N - 2D + 5))$. Using the Stirling approximation of the factorial, it is easy to see that for every $0 \leq \alpha \leq 1$ it holds that $\lim_{t \to \infty} \frac{1}{t} \log_2 \binom{t}{\alpha t} = H_2(\alpha)$ while $\log_2 \binom{t}{\alpha t} \leq t H_2(\alpha)$, where $H_2(p) = -p \log_2 p - (1 - p) \log_2(1 - p)$, $p \in [0, 1]$, is the standard binary entropy function. Thus $\binom{t}{k} \leq 2^{t H_2(k/t)}$, and we obtain that

$$S \leq \frac{2^{N \cdot H_2((D-2)/N)}}{2^N} \cdot \left(1 + \frac{D - 2}{N - 2D + 5}\right). \tag{2}$$

Since by assumption $D < N/3 + 2$, we may replace $1 + \frac{D-2}{N-D+5}$ with 2, thus obtaining $S \leq 2^{N H_2((D-2)/N) - N + 1}$.

Now a union bound over all non-zero x implies that for all messages x, it holds that $\Pr_A[\|A \cdot x\|_1 \leq D - 1] \leq 2^{2n} 2^{N H_2((D-2)/N) - N + 1}$, and $\mathsf{GV}^{\mathfrak{R}}(N, K, D) \geq 1 - 2^{-N(1 - H_2((D-2)/N)) + 2n + 1}$. □

We comment that we made only three approximations: the first one to bound the sum of binomial coefficients, the second one to bound a binomial by using its Stirling approximation, and then bounding a fraction in Eq. (2) by 2. All three approximations are very tight in their regions.

Theorem 1. *Consider the ring $\mathfrak{R} = \mathbb{Z}_2[X]/(f(X))$ for an irreducible degree-n polynomial f. Let $D = 2D' + 1$, where D' is as in the description of the commitment scheme Γ of the current section. Γ is statistically binding with probability $\mathsf{GV}^{\mathfrak{R}}(N, K, D)$. If the decisional $(\overline{\mathsf{Ber}}_\tau^{\mathfrak{R}, N/n}, N, K; \Psi^{\mathfrak{R}, N, K})$-LPN problem (i.e., a TRLPN problem) is (t, ε)-hard, then Γ is $(t - \Theta(t_\times^{\mathfrak{R}}), 2\varepsilon)$-computationally hiding.*

Proof. STATISTICAL BINDING: Assume that for $(y_j, z_j) = \mathsf{com}_{\mathsf{gk}}(m_j; r_j, e_j)$ where $j \in \{1, 2\}$, $y_1 = y_2$. Thus, $(M, R) \cdot (m_1 \oplus m_2, r_1 \oplus r_2)^\top = e_1 \oplus e_2$. Since $(m_1, r_1) \neq (m_2, r_2)$, with probability $\mathsf{GV}^{\mathfrak{R}}(N, K, D)$, $\|e_1 \oplus e_2\|_1 \geq D$. However, $\|e_1 \oplus e_2\|_1 \leq \|e_1\|_1 + \|e_2\|_1 \leq D' + D' < D$. Contradiction with the choice of N.

COMPUTATIONAL HIDING: Assume by contradiction that $\mathcal{A} = \mathcal{A}_{\mathsf{hiding}}$ is a time $t_{\mathcal{A}}$ adversary that can break the hiding property of the new commitment scheme with probability $1/2 + \varepsilon_{\mathcal{A}}$ for some $\varepsilon_{\mathcal{A}} > 0$. We construct the following adversary $\mathcal{B} = \mathcal{B}_{\mathsf{lpn}}$ that breaks the decisional LPN assumption with the help of $\mathcal{A}$ in related time, with probability $1/2 + \varepsilon_{\mathcal{A}}/2$. From this, the claim follows.

1. The challenger first generates the parameters (f, τ). She sets $\beta \xleftarrow{r} \{1, 2\}$. If $\beta = 1$, then she sets $y \leftarrow Rr \oplus e$ for $R \xleftarrow{r} \mathfrak{R}^{N/n}$, $r \xleftarrow{r} \mathfrak{R}$ and $e \xleftarrow{r} \overline{\mathsf{Ber}}_\tau^{\mathfrak{R}, N/n}$. Otherwise, she sets $R \xleftarrow{r} \mathfrak{R}^{N/n}$ and $y \xleftarrow{r} \mathfrak{R}^{N/n}$. She sends (f, τ, R, y) to $\mathcal{B}$.
2. $\mathcal{B}$ creates $M \xleftarrow{r} \mathfrak{R}^{N/n}$. He sends $\mathsf{gk} \leftarrow (f, \tau, M, R)$ to $\mathcal{A}$.
3. Given input gk, $\mathcal{A}$ sends to $\mathcal{B}$ a challenge pair (m_1, m_2).
4. $\mathcal{B}$ picks $\alpha \xleftarrow{r} \{1, 2\}$. He sends $Mm_\alpha \oplus y$ to $\mathcal{A}$. $\mathcal{A}$ answers with α'.
5. If $\alpha = \alpha'$ ($\mathcal{A}$ guessed correctly), then $\mathcal{B}$ outputs $\beta' \leftarrow 1$ (guesses that $\beta = 1$), otherwise $\mathcal{B}$ outputs $\beta' \leftarrow 2$ (guesses that $\beta = 2$).

Clearly, the computation of $\mathcal{B}$ is dominated by $t_{\mathcal{A}} + N/n \cdot t_\times^{\mathfrak{R}}$, where $t_\times^{\mathfrak{R}}$ denotes the computational complexity of one ring multiplication. Here, $N/n \cdot t_\times^{\mathfrak{R}}$ enters from the computation of the vector-to-scalar-product $M \cdot m_\alpha$.

If $\beta = 1$, then $Mm_\alpha \oplus y = Mm_\alpha \oplus Rr \oplus e$, which is a valid output of $\mathsf{com}_{\mathsf{gk}}(m_\alpha; r, e)$, and by assumption on $\mathcal{A}$, $\mathcal{A}$ can guess α from this with probability $\frac{1}{2} + \varepsilon_{\mathcal{A}}$. If $\beta = 2$, then $M \cdot m_\alpha \oplus y$ is uniformly random (and thus does not depend on α), and thus $\mathcal{A}$ can guess α from this with probability $\frac{1}{2}$. By a standard argument, $\Pr[\beta' = \beta] = \Pr[\beta' = \beta | \beta = 1] \Pr[\beta = 1] + \Pr[\beta' = \beta | \beta = 2] \Pr[\beta = 2] = \Pr[\beta' = 1 | \beta = 1] \cdot \frac{1}{2} + \Pr[\beta' = 2 | \beta = 2] \cdot \frac{1}{2} = \Pr[\alpha = \alpha' | \beta = 1] \cdot \frac{1}{2} + \Pr[\alpha \neq \alpha' | \beta = 2] \cdot \frac{1}{2} = (\frac{1}{2} + \varepsilon_{\mathcal{A}}) \cdot \frac{1}{2} + \frac{1}{2} \cdot \frac{1}{2} = \frac{1}{2} + \frac{\varepsilon_{\mathcal{A}}}{2}$. Thus, $\mathcal{B}$ breaks the decisional LPN assumption with probability $1/2 + \varepsilon_{\mathcal{A}}/2$ in time that is dominated by $t_{\mathcal{A}} + N/n \cdot t_\times^{\mathfrak{R}}$ operations. $\square$

4   Recommended Parameter Choices

To achieve binding, we must assume that the parameters n and τ (and thus also D) are chosen so that $\mathsf{GV}^{\mathfrak{R}}(N, K, D) \geq 1 - 2^{-\lambda}$. On the other hand, to achieve computational hiding, n and τ are such that the decisional TRLPN problem is $(\kappa^{\omega(1)}, \kappa^{-\omega(1)})$-hard. Since the complexity of the best known attacks [4,9] depends intimately on the choice of several internal variables, we used the following strategy. We computed for every β from 10 to 25 (where $N = \beta n$ as before), the value of D such that Lemma 2 returns an upper bound $2^{-\lambda} \leq 2^{-40}$. We then found, for this D, the minimum value of β for which the attack of [9] has computational complexity of at least 2^{130} bit operations; this fixes also the maximum value of $\tau^* = D/(2\beta n)$ and thus of τ.

We now give more details. The most efficient known attack against LPN was recently published in [9]. This attack uses covering codes. Assume that we have an $[n'', \ell]d_C$ covering code, for certain parameters n'' and ℓ. As in [9], assume that d_C is the smallest integer, such that $\sum_{i=0}^{d_C} \binom{n''}{i} > 2^{n''-\ell}$. The latter optimistic estimate comes from the sphere-covering bound (i.e., assuming that there is a perfect $[n'', \ell]$ code with covering radius d_C). In reality, for most of the values n'' it is not known how to construct such codes; thus, in practice, the attack from [9] has worse complexity than we estimate in what follows.

In bit operations, the computational complexity of the attack from [9] is $2^{f_{n,\tau}(q,a,t,b,w_0,w_1,\ell,n'')}$, where

$$f_{n,\tau}(q,a,t,b,w_0,w_1,\ell,n'') := T_{pre} +$$

$$\frac{aqn + (n+1)tq + m\sum_{i=0}^{w_0}\binom{n'-n''}{i}i + (n''-\ell)(2m+2^\ell) + \ell 2^\ell \sum_{i=0}^{w_0}\binom{n'-n''}{i}}{\Pr(w_0, n'-n'') \cdot \Pr(w_1, n'')}. \quad (3)$$

Here T_{pre} is the precomputation time of the Four Russian Matrix Inversion algorithm [1], the rest is the complexity of five-step LPN solving algorithm using covering codes [9]. Here (n, τ) are parameters of the LPN instance, q is the number of queries, $m = q - n - t2^b$, and q satisfies $q - t2^b > 1/(\varepsilon^{2^{t+1}} \cdot (\varepsilon')^{2w_1})$, where $\varepsilon = 1 - 2\tau$, $\varepsilon' = 1 - \frac{2d_C}{n''}$. The lower bound for q is due to the fast Walsh-Hadamard transform used in the solving phase of the algorithm from [9]. The probability $\Pr(w,j) = \sum_{i=0}^{w}(1-\tau)^{j-i}\tau^i\binom{j}{i}$ expresses the possibility of having at most w errors in j positions, therefore the denominator of Eq. (3) is the success probability in one iteration. See [4,9] for detailed explanation of the parameters. The only value that directly depends on d_C is ε', and the latter only gives a lower bound on $q - t2^b$.

We note that [4,9] did not add the term T_{pre} to the computational complexity. According to [1] (page 145), $T_{pre} = \sum_{i=0}^{a-1}(3\cdot 2^s - 4)(n-is-s) = -\frac{1}{2}a(3\cdot 2^s - 4)(as - 2n + s)$ in the case of a $n \times n$ matrix, where s is a parameter such that $a = \lceil n/s \rceil$. Assuming $a = n/s$, $T_{pre} \approx 1.5 \cdot 2^{n/a}(a-1)n$, and thus for any given n we can find numerically a value a that results in $T_{pre} \approx 2^{128}$.

In particular, in the most interesting case when $n = 1024$ (choosing n to be a power of 2 makes it possible to use a number of optimizations), we are forced to take $\beta = 19$, resulting in $\tau = 0.128118$. In this case, the best parameters for the attack from [9] that we found are (here we use the notation from [9]; see [9] for a definition of each parameter) $q \approx 2^{104.9}$, $a = 9$, $t = 6$, $b = 101$, $w_0 = 2$, $c = 30$, $\ell = 101$, and $n'' = 390$. With those parameters, the attack from [9] (when using Eq. (3) for computational complexity) takes approximate time $2^{131.1}$. However, the given complexity formula of this attack assumes the existence of a perfect $[390, 101]$ covering code. Since there is no such perfect code, the actual attack will be presumably less efficient.

Since the number of multiplications the new commitment scheme uses is 2β, and each multiplications takes $\Theta(n^2)$ bit-operations, we can estimate the computational complexity by measuring the parameter $2\beta n^2$. We emphasize that the actual computational complexity can only be measured by an optimized implementation, see Sect. 5.

5   Efficiency Issues and Implementation

Recall that the length of the public key is $\Theta(n)$ bits (with the recommended parameters, $N/n = 38$ ring elements, and up to n bits to describe f.) The commitment and the verification time are both dominated by $38t_\times^\mathfrak{R}$ bit-operations. In the case where $\mathfrak{R}$ supports Fast Fourier Transform (e.g., when $f(X) = X^n - 1$), then $t_\times^\mathfrak{R} = \Theta(n \log n)$. Then, both time complexities are $\Theta(n \log n)$. In the case $f(X)$ is irreducible, one cannot implement the usual Fast Fourier Transform. While Cyclotomic Fast Fourier Transform [17] has additive complexity $O(n^2/(\log n)^{\log_2(8/3)})$, we leave implementing that algorithm as a further work and — for the sake of simplicity — concentrate instead on quadratic-time algorithms. One reason for that is to emphasize that this commitment scheme is extremely competitive even in the case of suboptimal implementations.

Importantly, the new commitment scheme is parallelizable. First, all 38 field multiplications, needed in one commitment or verification, can be performed in parallel. On top of it, every field multiplication can be parallelized by itself. In particular, in the field multiplication $a(X) = b(X)c(X)$ every coefficient a_i can be computed in parallel. Since all values a_i are independent, this means that parallelization of factor of n can be achieved. In practice, however it may be faster to compute some w coefficients at once, where w is either the machine word length or some other related constant.

Based on such considerations, we implemented a single finite field $\mathbb{F}_{2^{1024}}$ multiplication on several modern data-parallel computational architectures. More precisely, we used the OpenCL environment that is an open standard for the general-purpose computation for GPU-s. In addition to GPU-s, one can use OpenCL to develop parallel implementations on modern multicore CPU-s.

We report implementation results on three different platforms. First, NVIDIA's rather old mobile GPU Quadro 2000M[4]. Second, on AMD's gaming GPU RADEON HD 7950, and third, on Intel's Core i7-2860QM CPU. (See Table 1). We remark that the used CPU supports 256-bit integer operations via AVX (Advanced Vector Extensions). According to information on Bitcoin mining (see footnote 2), some of the cutting edge GPU-s perform 35 times faster than the Quadro 2000M (not even talking about CPU-s).

In what follows, we describe a partial implementation of the LPN-based commitment scheme and of the ring-LPN based commitment scheme.

LPN-Based Commitment Scheme. First, we implemented a partial version of the ring-LPN based commitment scheme, by first precomputing (once) the matrices $\mathsf{mat}(\boldsymbol{M}_i)$ and $\mathsf{mat}(\boldsymbol{R}_i)$, and then implementing only the matrix-to-vector multiplication. This means that the CPU has to store the whole matrix $\mathsf{mat}(x)$ ($n^2/8$ bytes, i.e., 128 KiB when $n = 1024$). (In the ring-based implementation, described later, memory consumption will be obviously smaller.) Here, we used L-bit (for a parameter L that depends on the concrete GPU/CPU)

---

[4] http://www.nvidia.com/content/PDF/product-comparison/Product-Comparison-Quadro-mobile-series.pdf, accessed in June 2015.

operations, this means that an L-bit entry-wise product can be implemented as a single word-wide AND operation.

Moreover, we implemented both uncoalesced and coalesced field multiplication. In the coalesced implementation, we parallelized the work so that every byte of y in the multiplication $y = Ax$ is computed by a different GPU core. This means that we utilize $n/8$ cores. (I.e., 128 cores, when $n = 1024$. If there are less — say c — cores available, then every core has to execute $n/(8c)$ threads.) Since each core computes 8 coefficients of $a(X)$, its computation is dominated asymptotically by $8n/L$ (word-wide) AND and XOR operations, on top of which one has to add $8\log_2 L$ bit-operations that are required to compute Hamming weight, together with some additional operations.

In the uncoalesced implementation, every core computes a single coefficient of y. This is followed by a short epilogue where the outputs of eight consequent cores are combined into one output byte. Here, we need n cores (i.e., given c cores, every core has to execute n/c threads). Every core's computation is dominated asymptotically by n/L (word-wide) AND and XOR operations, followed by $\log_2 L$ bit-operations to compute Hamming weight. However, our uncoalesced implementation requires 3 synchronized rounds to combine the results of consequent cores into one output byte. Every such round has to start with a synchronization (**barrier** in OpenCL). Since synchronization is somewhat costly (and we also need more cores), in some of the cases an coalesced implementation (that theoretically requires 8 times more computation) is actually faster.

To optimize the throughput, we had to include some hand optimizations. First, we had to find out the optimal unroll count: if the loops are not unrolled at all, then the computation time is dominated by the costly branch instructions. However, if there are too many unrolls, then due to the way OpenCL operates, there is going to be a large usage of hardware registers, which makes computation lower. The latter specifically affects the GPU-s of NVIDIA due to the worse optimization by the compiler. To take this into account, in the case of the Quadro 2000M, we also used the NVIDIA's extension (via compiler flag `-cl-nv-maxrregcount`) to OpenCL that allows to limit the number of used registers to some value reg. We again chose the value reg carefully so as to increase the throughput. (No such extension exists for AMD's GPU or Intel's CPU.)

To summarize, in the case $n = 1024$ we obtain the results given in Table 1. We expect that a carefully parallelized implementation of the new commitment scheme will be much faster on HD 7950 and other top-of-the-line GPU-s. Moreover, we used the OpenCL library for the compatibility with both NVIDIA's and AMD's GPU-s (and with multicore CPU-s). If one is interested in the top performance on the NVIDIA's GPU-s only, one could use the CUDA library (or even program in the PTX virtual assembly language). Due to the larger dependency on the hardware, a well-optimized CUDA program is usually significantly faster than an OpenCL program on the same hardware platform. The same comments hold also for the implementation ring-LPN based commitment scheme that we describe in the next subsubsection.

Table 1. Some values about the used GPU-s and CPU-s as returned by the OpenCL's `clGetDeviceInfo` command, together with our implementation data

	GPU 1	GPU 2	CPU 1
clGetDeviceInfo string	Return value	Return value	Return value
DEVICE_NAME	Tahiti	Quadro 2000M	Intel(R) Core(TM) i7-2860QM CPU @ 2.50GHz
DEVICE_VENDOR	Advanced Micro Devices, Inc.	NVIDIA Corporation	Intel(R) Corporation
DEVICE_VERSION	OpenCL 1.2 AMD-APP (1642.5)	OpenCL 1.1 CUDA	OpenCL 1.2 (Build 57)
DRIVER_VERSION	1642.5 (VM)	347.52	5.0.0.57
DEVICE_MAX_COMPUTE_UNITS	28	4	8
DEVICE_MAX_CLOCK_FREQUENCY	960	1100	2500
DEVICE_GLOBAL_MEM_SIZE	3221225472	2147483648	2147352576
Cores	1792	192	8
Optimal parameters and timing (matrix-to-vector)			
Implementation	Uncoalesced	Uncoalesced	Coalesced
L	ulong2 (128 bits)	ulong (64 bits)	ulong2 (128 bits)
max reg count	N/A	180	N/A
unroll	4	5	11
mult per second (per core)	70 313.60	30 547.41	46 019.33
cycles per core	13 653.1	36 009.6	54 325.0
threads	128	128	1024
cycles × ♯threads / ♯cores	975.2	24006.4	6953600
Timing (finite field multiplication)			
mult per second (per core)	51923.78	70861.68	35348.18
cycles per core	18488.640	15523.20	70725
Threads	272	272	272
cycles × ♯threads / ♯cores	2821.5	21991	2404650

Ring-LPN Based Commitment Scheme. We also implemented a binary finite field $\mathbb{F}_{2^{1024}}$ multiplication. Here, we used a version of the Brauer's exponentiation algorithm (first used in the context of finite field multiplication by Lopéz and Dahab [14]). That is, in the computation of a $\mathbb{F}_{2^{1024}}$ multiplication $c(X) = a(X)b(X)$, we first precompute $a(X)b'(X)$ for all degree-$(\leq W)$ polynomials $b'(X)$. After that, we use a parallel variant of the school book multiplication method, where each thread uses W-bit precomputed values to compute an L-bit intermediate result in an $(n/L) \times (2n/L)$ matrix. (Note that there are $(n/L) \cdot (n/L + 1)$ threads, since the rest of the entries of this matrix are equal to 0.) We then sum up in parallel the entries in every column of the intermediate matrix, obtaining a degree $2n$ polynomial $c'(X)$, and then reduce $c'(X)$ modulo $f(X)$. Since we chose $f(X)$ with a small Hamming weight (namely, 5), the reduction step is almost negligible. In our implementation, $L = 64$ and $W = 4$; those constants were chosen to minimize the execution time. This means that the maximal number of threads is 272. Similar strategy was outlined in say [5], but our implementation is independent.

Since the CPU has 8 cores and the HD 7950 GPU has 1792 cores, the 7950 GPU is approximately 850 times faster, see the last row of Table 1. Thus, on the HD 7950 GPU, one can implement $1792/272 \approx 6.59$ finite field multiplications in parallel. Since one commitment (and verification) requires 38 multiplications, one can schedule on average $1792/(272 \cdot 38) = 0.173$ commitments of 1024-bit numbers in parallel.

Interestingly, our implementation of the finite field multiplication on the HD 7950 GPU and the Intel CPU is somewhat slower than the matrix-to-vector multiplication (in cycles per core), while on the Quadro 2000M the opposite is true. The relative slow-down on the first two processing units is due to the fact that in our implementation of matrix-to-vector multiplication, we use the ulong2 data type to perform 128-bit operations in parallel, while in our implementation of finite field multiplications, we did only use the 64-bit ulong data type. The implementation of finite-field implementations also uses more threads than the the matrix-to-vector multiplication. This can mean that if the communication and storage of the public key is not a bottleneck, one might actually want to implement the (non-ring) LPN based commitment scheme.

Comparison with Pedersen Commitment. In the case of the simplest discrete logarithm-based commitment scheme, the Pedersen commitment, the committer has (m, r) and then computes $y = g^m h^r$. The verifier just recomputes y, given the same m and r. Assuming that one uses elliptic curves, the committer's and the verifier's computation is dominated by two exponentiations.

Efficiency-wise, the main difference between the described commitment scheme and the Pedersen scheme is that in the former, one has to execute a small number of multiplications (over a medium-sized finite field) while in the Pedersen scheme one has to execute a small number of *exponentiations* (in elliptic curves defined over a small finite field). Every exponentiation requires at least κ finite field multiplications in a field of the size $\approx 2^{2\kappa}$. Thus, Pedersen with $\kappa = 128$ uses at least $128/38 \approx 3.4$ times more multiplications than the new commitment scheme. Moreover, Pedersen has additional overhead due to the use of much more complicated elliptic-curve group multiplications instead of simpler finite-field multiplications. Finally, Pedersen is not as readily parallelizable as the new commitment scheme, and it only allows to commit to 256-bit strings instead of 1024-bit strings. For concrete numbers, we refer to say [7] for a recent highly optimized implementation (that uses a 254-bit base field) of an elliptic curve exponentiation with $\geq 100\,000$ cycles. Thus in their implementation of Pedersen, it takes at least 787 cycles to commit to a bit as compared with ≈ 104.7 cycles to implement the new commitment scheme on the AMD GPU.

Finally, recall that discrete logarithm is not secure against quantum computers, while LPN is assumed to be. Hence, the described commitment scheme is not only more efficient, but also presumably more (quantum-)secure. Moreover, recent attacks have indicated that discrete logarithm might not be as secure against conventional (non-quantum) computers as thought up to now.

Acknowledgments. The first author was supported by Estonian Research Council and European Union through the European Regional Development Fund. The second author was supported by institutional research funding IUT20-57 of the Estonian Ministry of Education and Research.

References

1. Bard, G.V.: Algebraic Cryptanalysis. Springer (2009)
2. Blum, A., Furst, M.L., Kearns, M., Lipton, R.J.: Cryptographic primitives based on hard learning problems. In: Stinson, D.R. (ed.) CRYPTO 1993. LNCS, vol. 773, pp. 278–291. Springer, Heidelberg (1994)
3. Blum, A., Kalai, A., Wasserman, H.: Noise-Tolerant learning, the parity problem, and the statistical query model. In: STOC 2000, pp. 435–440 (2000)
4. Bogos, S., Tramèr, F., Vaudenay, S.: On Solving LPN using BKW and Variants. Technical Report 2015/049, International Association for Cryptologic Research (2015). http://eprint.iacr.org/2015/049. Accessed 30 January 2015
5. Bose, U., Bhattacharya, A.K., Das, A.: GPU-based implementation of 128-bit secure eta pairing over a binary field. In: Youssef, A., Nitaj, A., Hassanien, A.E. (eds.) AFRICACRYPT 2013. LNCS, vol. 7918, pp. 26–42. Springer, Heidelberg (2013)
6. Cohen, G., Honkala, I., Litsyn, S., Lobstein, A.: Covering Codes. North-Holland Mathematical Library, vol. 54. North Holland (2005)
7. Costello, C., Hisil, H., Smith, B.: Faster compact diffie–hellman: endomorphisms on the x-line. In: Nguyen, P.Q., Oswald, E. (eds.) EUROCRYPT 2014. LNCS, vol. 8441, pp. 183–200. Springer, Heidelberg (2014)
8. Damgård, I., Park, S.: Is public-key encryption based on LPN practical? Technical Report 2012/699, International Association for Cryptologic Research (2012). http://eprint.iacr.org/2012/699. Accessed 8 October 2013
9. Guo, Q., Johansson, T., Löndahl, C.: Solving LPN using covering codes. In: Sarkar, P., Iwata, T. (eds.) ASIACRYPT 2014. LNCS, vol. 8873, pp. 1–20. Springer, Heidelberg (2014)
10. Heyse, S., Kiltz, E., Lyubashevsky, V., Paar, C., Pietrzak, K.: Lapin: an efficient authentication protocol based on ring-LPN. In: Canteaut, A. (ed.) FSE 2012. LNCS, vol. 7549, pp. 346–365. Springer, Heidelberg (2012)
11. Jain, A., Krenn, S., Pietrzak, K., Tentes, A.: Commitments and efficient zero-knowledge proofs from learning parity with noise. In: Wang, X., Sako, K. (eds.) ASIACRYPT 2012. LNCS, vol. 7658, pp. 663–680. Springer, Heidelberg (2012)
12. Katz, J., Shin, J.S.: Parallel and concurrent security of the HB and HB$^+$ protocols. In: Vaudenay, S. (ed.) EUROCRYPT 2006. LNCS, vol. 4004, pp. 73–87. Springer, Heidelberg (2006)
13. Kawachi, A., Tanaka, K., Xagawa, K.: Concurrently secure identification schemes based on the worst-case hardness of lattice problems. In: Pieprzyk, J. (ed.) ASIACRYPT 2008. LNCS, vol. 5350, pp. 372–389. Springer, Heidelberg (2008)
14. López, J., Dahab, R.: High-speed software multiplication in F2m. In: Roy, B., Okamoto, E. (eds.) INDOCRYPT 2000. LNCS, vol. 1977, pp. 203–212. Springer, Heidelberg (2000)
15. Pedersen, T.P.: Non-interactive and information-theoretic secure verifiable secret sharing. In: Feigenbaum, J. (ed.) CRYPTO 1991. LNCS, vol. 576, pp. 129–140. Springer, Heidelberg (1992)
16. Roth, R.: Introduction to Coding Theory. Cambridge University Press (2006)
17. Wu, X., Wang, Y., Yan, Z.: On algorithms and complexities of cyclotomic fast fourier transforms over arbitrary finite fields. IEEE Transactions on Signal Processing **60**(3), 1149–1158 (2012)

Secure Multi-party Computation

Practical Password-Based Authentication Protocol for Secret Sharing Based Multiparty Computation

Ryo Kikuchi$^{(\boxtimes)}$, Koji Chida, Dai Ikarashi, and Koki Hamada

NTT Corporation, Tokyo, Japan
{kikuchi.ryo,chida.koji,ikarashi.dai,hamada.koki}@lab.ntt.co.jp

Abstract. The speed of secret sharing (SS)-based multiparty computation (MPC) has recently increased greatly, and several efforts to implement and use it have been put into practice. Authentication of clients is one critical mechanism for implementing SS-based MPC successfully in practice. We propose a password-based authentication protocol for SS-based MPC. Our protocol is secure in the presence of secure channels, and it is optimized for practical use with SS-based MPC in the following ways.

- Threshold security: Our protocol is secure in the honest majority, which is necessary and sufficient since most practical results on SS-based MPC are secure in the same environment.
- Establishing distinct channels: After our protocol, a client has *distinct* secure and two-way authenticated channels to each server, which is necessary for SS-based MPC and different from the usual setting.
- Ease of implementation: Our protocol consists of SS and operations involving SS, which can be reused from an implementation of SS-based MPC.

Furthermore, we implemented our protocol with an optimization for the realistic network and confirm that the protocol is practical. A client received the result within 2 s even when the network delay was 200 ms, which is almost the delay that occurs between Japan and Europe.

Keywords: Password · Authentication · Secret sharing · Multiparty computation

1 Introduction

Secret sharing (SS) and SS-based multiparty computation (MPC) are very popular topics in cryptography. SS is a way to securely share data. Data is divided into *shares* by a *client* and distributed among *servers*. A qualified coalition of servers can reconstruct the data from their shares, and no one else can obtain information about that data. (k, n)-threshold secret-sharing ((k, n)-SS) is a common class of SS in which there are n servers, and any coalition that includes k or more servers is qualified. It has a certain collusion resistance such that even

© Springer International Publishing Switzerland 2015
M. Reiter and D. Naccache (Eds.): CANS 2015, LNCS 9476, pp. 179–196, 2015.
DOI: 10.1007/978-3-319-26823-1_13

if $k - 1$ servers are compromised, shared data are kept secret. SS-based MPC provides a mechanism in which one can perform a function involving secretly shared data, while no one else can obtain information about the data.

Much research has been done on SS-based MPC, and many protocols have been proposed. Constructing these protocols has been a commonly theoretical aspect of cryptographic study, and a fundamental theory was developed between the mid-1980s and mid-2000s. (k, n)-SS-based MPC with unconditional security is one of the most frequently used protocols since it is considered to be the most efficient protocol. The speed of these protocols has recently increased greatly, and several efforts to implement and use SS-based MPC have been put into practice [8,10,12,26]. Authentication of clients is one critical mechanism for implementing SS-based MPC successfully in practice. It is natural to qualify who uses SS-based MPC for some reasons, e.g., the outputs of SS-based MPC are somewhat sensitive, or a service provider wants to charge clients. Therefore, this is the issue that we address in the paper to use SS-based MPC in practice, we have to develop a practical authentication protocol for successful implementation.

One of the most popular methods of authentication is using a password. A password is easy to memorize, and password-based authentication does not require extra devices such as security tokens, so we focus on password-based authentication in the paper.

1.1 Requirements for SS-Based MPC's Authentication

What authentication protocol is required for the practical use of SS-based MPC? First, the authentication protocol should have collusion resistance. Let us consider a case of SS-based MPC that is secure against t corruptions, for example. A natural combination of SS-based MPC and ordinary password authentication should be either a client using n different passwords for each server or using a unique password for all servers. The former eliminates the benefit of password authentication since a client must choose passwords independently and remember all of them. The latter eliminates all the benefits of SS-based MPC. A single corrupted server can extract a password through an offline dictionary attack as passwords tend to have small entropy. Then, the corrupted server impersonates the other servers and breaches the security. Most practical results of SS-based MPC are secure in the honest majority (precisely, $t < n/2$ or $t < n/3$) [8,10,12,20,24,26]. To maintain the security of SS-based MPC, the authentication protocol should be secure in the honest majority.

Second, a client should establish *distinct* secure channels to each server after the authentication. The aim of the authentication itself is to check whether or not the client is legitimate. However, after the authentication, a client may send shares to the servers. For secure SS-based MPC, a share must be sent to only a legitimate server, and any other servers should not be able to obtain the share. This means that the client should establish distinct secure channels to each server. This setting differs from the usual ones considered in threshold password-based authenticated key-exchange (TPAKE) [32,34] and password protected/authenticated SS (PPSS) [2,13].

Third, constructing the authentication protocol with SS and operations involving SS is preferable. SS-based MPC consists of SS and operations involving SS. Therefore, if the authentication protocol can be implemented with these resources, it will simplify the implementation. If the authentication protocol uses an original public-key technique, one has to implement it such as by exponentiation over a large group. It is troublesome and sometimes greatly increases the cost.

1.2   Our Contribution

We formalize a password-based authentication protocol for SS-based MPC (*PASM*). PASM supports password setup/update, which is useful depending on the application. The security definition of PASM can be derived from that of TPAKE [32,34] and password-based authentication [23]. We propose a PASM protocol satisfying three conditions: secure in the honest majority, establishing distinct channels between a client and each server after the authentication, and consisting of operations involving SS.

PASM assumes two types of channels among participants. The first is secure channels [15] with two-way authentication among the servers. This means that any server can interact with another server without leaking information about a sent message, i.e., secure channel, the sender knows the receiver who can receive the message, and the receiver knows the sender who sent the message, i.e., two-way authentication. Such channels can be instantiated (but not restricted) by sharing pre-shared keys between all pairs of servers. The second is secure channels with one-way authentication between a client and each server. This means that any server can interact with the client without leaking information about the sent message, and the client knows the server who can receive the message, but the server does not know the client who sent the message, i.e., one-way authentication. Such channels can be instantiated by TLS server authentication assuming a public key infrastructure (PKI).

PASM is not key-exchange but authentication. Key-exchange is more general, but authentication is sufficient since we assume the two types of secure channels. If a client is accepted in PASM, the servers recognize that the client is a legitimate user. In other words, secure channels with one-way authentication between a client and each server become the ones with two-way authentication. Therefore, the client and servers can communicate with each other securely by using the channels.

In addition, we implemented our PASM protocol with an optimization for a realistic network model we call the *gateway* network model. In this model, there is a gateway, and all communications are relayed by the gateway. In practice, the gateway network model may be used with the two reasons. First, communication channels between a server to another server can be reduced. Second, the gateway can synchronize the servers in the mutual execution easily, and prevents the order of shares from being changed even if two clients request the authentication nearly at the same time. The optimization in the model is sending "accept" to the client as soon as possible by bringing the gateway into the authentication.

As an experimental result, a client received an authentication result within 2 s even when the network delay was 200 ms, which is almost that between Japan and Europe.

Bagherzandi et al. [2] proposed password protected SS (PPSS) [2]. In PPSS, a client obtains legitimate shares if the password is correct. The aim of PPSS is not to establish a secure channel but to reconstruct the secret. Camenisch et al. proposed another PPSS [13] that achieves universal composability [14].

1.3   Related Works

Bellovin and Merritt [6] proposed the first protocol for password-based key generation. Although the protocol of [6] can be attacked and fixed [33], there have been many following protocols [7,25,36], which have not been proven, and their security is based on heuristic arguments. Halevi and Krawczyk [23] first gave a formal definition on password-based authentication and key-exchange. There have been many studies with provable security, and the main field is in two-party setting, e.g., [11,21,22,27–30].

Ford and Kaliski [19] first considered a new model where the password is stored in $n > 1$ servers. This is called threshold password-based authenticated key-exchange (TPAKE). In the case of $n > 2$, there are two provably secure TPAKEs. MacKenzie et al. [32] proposed a TPAKE that tolerates less than $n-1$ collusions. Where only the servers use the public key. Raimondo and Gennaro [34] proposed a TPAKE that tolerates less than $n/3$ collusions.

Relation to TPAKE. TPAKE has a similar function to PASM. However, TPAKE and PASM are difficult to be compared with each other because of the following sense.

– A client has distinct channels to each server after PASM, while the client has the common key among all servers in TPAKE.
– PASM is an authentication, while TPAKE is a key-exchange.
– PASM assumes two types of channels, while TPAKE does not in general.

We can try to uniform the conditions as follows.

– We assume that the secure channels with two-way authentication are instantiated by an AE with pre-shared keys.
– We assume that the secure channels with one-way authentication are instantiated by the KEM-DEM framework with PKI.
– We regard PASM as key-exchange protocol with PKI that finally outputs the key used in DEM instead of *accept*.

If we admit the above, our protocol with Kurosawa-Desmedt [31] in fact costs fewer number exponentiations and fewer number of communication moves compared to the other provably secure TPAKEs [32,34], while our protocol requires PKI.

However, this uniforming is too forceful. It compares authentication with key-exchange in only the viewpoint of key-exchange, though a role of authentication may be different from the one of key-exchange. In addition, it is strange that "Key-exchange" was finished before the authentication ends. Therefore, we believe that it is appropriate to conclude that PASM and TPAKE are incomparable.

1.4   Protocol Overview

PASM consists of three phases consisting of password setup, authentication, and password update. The technical key is the authentication, so we describe this phase here.

We use Shamir's SS, which is a threshold SS scheme, as a building block. Let w be a valid password that has already been registered and w' be a password used by a (possibly invalid) client. The valid password is stored in the secretly shared form, i.e., the server has $[w]$, where $[\cdot]$ denotes a share of (k, n)-Shamir. In the idle state, the servers cooperate with each other to generate a random share $[r]$ and zero share $[\![0]\!]$, where $[\![\cdot]\!]$ denotes a share of $(2k - 1, n)$-Shamir. These shares can be generated by the well-known protocols.

A client sends the shares of the password, $[w']$, to every server. Then each server computes $[r]([w] - [w']) + [\![0]\!]$, reconstructs it, and checks whether or not the reconstructed value is zero. If the password is invalid, the reconstructed value is a random number thanks to r, and $[r]([w] - [w']) + [\![0]\!]$ is a uniformly distributed share thanks to $[\![0]\!]$. Therefore, the reconstruction does not leak any information about the password.

The above is an intuitive flow of the authentication. However, it is not enough to be secure. The adversary may wait until all other servers have sent their shares and change the share to bias the reconstructed value. To prevent such attack, a different $[r]$ and $[\![0]\!]$ are prepared for each server, and each server reconstruct and check $r(w - w') = 0$. If $w \neq w'$, the reconstructed values the adversary can obtain are independently random, so the adversary cannot obtain information of w. In addition, even if the adversary sends an invalid share, it is difficult to change the reconstructed value of an honest server to 0 since r is independently random.

2   Preliminaries and Models

We introduce the syntax of our password-based authentication protocol for SS-based MPC and the setting where it works. Here, $x \leftarrow y$ means that x is uniformly at random if y is a finite set; otherwise, simply substitute y into x. For probabilistic algorithm A, $y \leftarrow \mathsf{A}(x)$ means that y is the output of A with input x and uniformly picked randomness. If $\mathbb{T}$ is a set, $|\mathbb{T}|$ denotes the number of elements that belong to $\mathbb{T}$.

2.1 Communication Model

The participants of our authentication protocol consist of a client C and servers S_i for $1 \leq i \leq n$. We assume two types of communication channel among the participants in the paper.

Communication Channel Among Servers. We assume that communication channels among S_i for $1 \leq i \leq n$ are secure channels [15] with two-way authentication. This means that a channel only leaks the message length, only allows the adversary to forward or delete messages, and the sender/receiver knows who is the receiver/sender. The channel is, for example, instantiated by an authenticated[1] encryption (AE) with pre-shared keys; distinct keys are shared among S_i for $1 \leq i \leq n$ beforehand. When S_i sends a to S_j, S_i encrypts a via AE with a pre-shared key between S_i and S_j and sends the ciphertext to S_j. S_j decrypts the ciphertext with the pre-shared key and obtains a.

Communication Channel Between Client and Servers. We assume that communication channels between C and each S_i for $1 \leq i \leq n$ are secure channels with one-way authentication. This means that a channel only leaks the message length and allows the adversary to forward or delete messages. In addition, C knows which S_i is the receiver, but S_i does not. The channel is, for example, instantiated by TLS server authentication. A concrete instantiation using the KEM-DEM [17] framework and PKI is the following. We consider C and S_i establish the channel here. S_i generates keys of KEM and publishes a public key and its certificate. C verifies the certificate, obtains a symmetric key for DEM, and sends the symmetric key via KEM. S_i decrypts the ciphertext and obtains the symmetric key. After that, all messages interacted with between C and S_i are encrypted via DEM with the symmetric key.

2.2 Shamir's Secret Sharing

We introduce the definitions and security notion for Shamir's SS [35], which is a component of our PASM protocol.

Let $\mathscr{F}$ be a finite field. Let $[s]_i$ be a *share* of data $s \in \mathscr{F}$ in (k, n)-Shamir for server S_i, $\langle s \rangle_i$ be a similar share for $(2k-2, n)$-Shamir, and $[\![s]\!]_i$ be a similar share for $(2k-1, n)$-Shamir. Let $\mathbb{Q}$ be a coalition of parties and $[s]_\mathbb{Q}$ denote a set of shares $o[s]_i \mid i \in \mathbb{Q}_p$. We assume that the number of corrupted parties is t such that $t < k$ holds. We say $([s]_1, \ldots, [s]_n)$ is *uniformly random* if it is uniformly randomly chosen from the set of shares whose data is s. We say $[r]$, where $r \leftarrow \mathscr{F}$, is a random share and $[\![0]\!]$ is a zero share. (k, n)-Shamir consists of two algorithms, a share generation algorithm Share and share reconstruction algorithm Rec described below.

---

[1] This "authentication" means the capability to detect an instance of tampering.

- Share: For input $s \in \mathscr{F}$, choose a random polynomial $f(x)$ over $\mathscr{F}$ whose degree is $k - 1$ such that $f(0) = s$ holds. Then, set $[s]_i = f(i)$ and output $([s]_0, \ldots, [s]_n)$.
- Rec: For input k shares $([s]_{i_1}, \ldots, [s]_{i_k})$, compute $s = \sum_{1 \leq j \leq k} \frac{\prod_{1 \leq \ell \leq k, \ell \neq j} i_\ell}{\prod_{1 \leq \ell \leq k, \ell \neq j} i_\ell - i_j} [s]_{i_j}$.

$(2k - 2, n)$-Shamir and $(2k - 1, n)$-Shamir are the same as (k, n)-Shamir except that the degree of $f(x)$ is $2k - 3$ and $2k - 2$, respectively.

In addition, we use the following property of (k, n) and $(2k - 1, n)$-Shamir. For all $|\mathbb{V}| = 2k - 1$ and $\mathbb{V} \subseteq \{1, \ldots, n\}$, there are public $\lambda_1^{(\mathbb{V})}, \ldots, \lambda_{2k-1}^{(\mathbb{V})}$ such that $s_1 s_2 = \sum_{i \in \mathbb{V}} \lambda_i^{(\mathbb{V})} [s_1]_i [s_2]_i$ and $s = \sum_{i \in \mathbb{V}} \lambda_i^{(\mathbb{V})} [\![s]\!]_i$ hold. In other words, $\lambda^{(\mathbb{V})}$ denotes the coefficients of Lagrange interpolation in $(2k - 1, n)$-Shamir.

The security requirement of (k, n)-SS is called *privacy*. (k, n)-Shamir has perfect privacy against $k - 1$ corruptions, which means that the distribution of $k - 1$ shares is the same as that of uniformly random $k - 1$ elements in $\mathscr{F}$.

2.3 Password-Based Authentication Protocol for SS-Based MPC

PASM protocol provides not only authentication but also password setup and password update protocols.

The formal syntax of PASM is as follows. Each C has its password w, which is uniformly drawn from a dictionary $\mathbb{D}$. Each S_i has a list $\mathscr{L}_{S_i}$ that logs a (share of) password and corresponding client pair. The authentication protocol is performed by a coalition of parties S_i for $i \in \mathbb{V}$ where $\mathbb{V} \subseteq \{1, \ldots, n\}$.

PASM consists of the following three protocols.

- SETUP: The inputs are a password w for C and $\mathscr{L}_{S_i}$ for S_i, where $1 \leq i \leq n$. After the protocol, C outputs *success/fail*, and S_i for $1 \leq i \leq n$ outputs (renewal) $\mathscr{L}_{S_i}$ or *fail*.
- AUTH: The inputs are w' for C and $\mathscr{L}_{S_i}$ for S_i, where $i \in \mathbb{V}$. After the protocol, C and S_i for $i \in \mathbb{V}$ output *accept/reject*.
- UPDATE: The inputs are the current password w and new password w^* for C and $\mathscr{L}_{S_i}$ for S_i, where $1 \leq i \leq n$. After the protocol, C outputs *success/fail*, and S_i for $1 \leq i \leq n$ outputs (renewal) $\mathscr{L}_{S_i}$ or *fail*.

Security Aspects. We define the security of our protocol as an analogy of password authentication [5,23] and (threshold) PAKE [1,4,32,34]. The participants are clients and n servers. It is required that non-legitimate clients cannot be accepted even if the adversary $\mathcal{A}$ adaptively corrupts $k - 1$ servers.

Now, we give the formal definition of security. Let $\mathbb{U} = \mathbb{C} \cup \mathbb{S}$ be a set of all participants. $\mathcal{U}^{\text{SETUP}(i)}$, $\mathcal{U}^{\text{AUTH}(i)}$, and $\mathcal{U}^{\text{UPDATE}(i)}$ denote the i-th instances of SETUP, AUTH, and UPDATE for $\mathcal{U} \in \mathbb{U}$, respectively. Note that we separate the instances of SETUP, AUTH, and UPDATE to clarify which instance is an authentication.

We formulate corruptions of the adversary $\mathcal{A}$ as follows. We say that $\mathcal{U}$ is corrupted when $corrupt_{\mathcal{U}} = true$. This flag, $corrupt_{\mathcal{U}}$, is set to $true$ if one of the following queries has been sent.

- **Corrupt**(C_i): This query models corruption of C_i. The reply of this query is the password of C_i. We then set $corrupt_{C_i} \leftarrow true$. (It means that $\mathcal{A}$ gets access to the channels to each S_i).
- **Corrupt**(S_i): This query models corruption of S_i. The reply of this query is all the (share of) passwords stored in S_i. We then set $corrupt_{S_i} \leftarrow true$.

All transactions occur only through oracle queries. The queries model the capabilities of $\mathcal{A}$: corrupting some participants, sending a tampered message, etc. There are six oracles that model a passive/active attack to SETUP/UPDATE/AUTH, respectively. The oracle queries are as follows.

- **ExecSetup**($C_i^{\text{SETUP}(j_0)}, S_1^{\text{SETUP}(j_1)}, \ldots, S_n^{\text{SETUP}(j_n)}$): This query models passive attacks in which $\mathcal{A}$ eavesdrops on honest executions on SETUP. The reply of this query is the all of the exchanged messages of corrupted instances during the honest execution of SETUP among $C_i^{\text{SETUP}(j_0)}$ and $S_1^{\text{SETUP}(j_1)}, \ldots, S_n^{\text{SETUP}(j_n)}$.
- **SendSetup**($\hat{u}, \mathcal{U}^{\text{SETUP}(i)}, m$): This query models active attacks in which $\mathcal{A}$ chooses the message m and sends it to $\mathcal{U}^{\text{SETUP}(i)}$ in the name of $\hat{u}$. The oracle replies the message that $\mathcal{U}^{\text{SETUP}(i)}$ would send upon receipt of m, only if $corrupt_{\hat{u}} = true$.
- **ExecUpdate**($C_i^{\text{UPDATE}(j_0)}, S_1^{\text{UPDATE}(j_1)}, \ldots, S_n^{\text{UPDATE}(j_n)}$): This query models passive attacks on UPDATE. The reply of this query is the all of the exchanged messages of corrupted instances during the honest execution of UPDATE among $C_i^{\text{UPDATE}(j_0)}$ and $S_1^{\text{UPDATE}(j_1)}, \ldots, S_n^{\text{UPDATE}(j_n)}$.
- **SendUpdate**($\hat{u}, \mathcal{U}^{\text{UPDATE}(i)}, m$): This query models active attacks in which $\mathcal{A}$ chooses the message m and sends it to $\mathcal{U}^{\text{UPDATE}(i)}$ in the name of $\hat{u}$. The oracle replies the message that $\mathcal{U}^{\text{SETUP}(i)}$ would send upon receipt of m, only if $corrupt_{\hat{u}} = true$.
- **ExecAuth**($C_i^{\text{AUTH}(j_0)}, S_{\ell_1}^{\text{AUTH}(j_1)}, \ldots, S_{\ell_{|V|}}^{\text{AUTH}(j_{|V|})}$): This query models passive attacks on AUTH. The reply of this query is all of the exchanged messages of corrupted instances among $C_i^{\text{AUTH}(j_0)}$ and $S_{\ell_1}^{\text{AUTH}(j_1)}, \ldots, S_{\ell_{|V|}}^{\text{AUTH}(j_{|V|})}$.
- **SendAuth**($\hat{u}, \mathcal{U}^{\text{AUTH}(j)}, m$): This query models active attacks in which $\mathcal{A}$ chooses the message m and sends it to $\mathcal{U}^{\text{AUTH}(j)}$ in the name of $\hat{u}$. The oracle replies the message that $\mathcal{U}^{\text{AUTH}(i)}$ would send upon receipt of m, only if $corrupt_{\hat{u}} = true$.

The notion of *partnering* represents which participants are authenticated. We use this notion as in [1,4], which is based on session identifiers *sid* and partner identifiers *pid*. For all $C_i^{\text{AUTH}(j_0)}$ where $corrupt_{C_i} \neq true$, $C_i^{\text{AUTH}(j_0)}$ has $pid = \{j_1, \ldots, j_{|V|}\}$ and *sid*. Here, *sid* is the concatenation of all massages sent and received by $C_i^{\text{AUTH}(j_0)}$ in its communication. For all $S_{\ell_i}^{\text{AUTH}(j_i)}$ where $corrupt_{S_{\ell_i}} \neq true$, $S_{\ell_i}^{\text{AUTH}(j_i)}$ also has $pid = C_{i'}^{\text{AUTH}(j_0')}$ and *sid*. Here, *sid* is the concatenation of all massages sent and received by $S_{\ell_i}^{\text{AUTH}(j_i)}$ except the communication among servers. We say $C_i^{\text{AUTH}(j_0)}$ that has (pid, sid) and $corrupt_{C_i} \neq 0$, and $S_{\ell_{i'}}^{\text{AUTH}(j_{i'})}$ that has $(pid'_{S_{\ell_{i'}}}, sid'_{S_{\ell_{i'}}})$ for $i' \in V$ and $corrupt_{S_{\ell_{i'}}} \neq true$, are *partnered* if all $\ell_{i'} \in pid$, $pid' = C_i^{\text{AUTH}(j_0)}$, and sid and all $sid'_{S_{\ell_{i'}}}$ are the same.

We say $\mathcal{A}$ wins if there is at least one $S_i^{\text{AUTH}(j_0)}$ for $i \in V$ and $corrupt_{S_i} \neq 0$ that outputs *accept* but has no partner instances. Now, we define the security of PASM.

Definition 1. *Let $\mathbb{D}$ be a dictionary, q_{se} be the number of* **SendAuth** *queries and q_{up} be the number of* **SendUpdate** *queries. We say* PASM $=$ (SETUP, AUTH, UPDATE) *is ϵ secure against impersonation if for all $\mathcal{A}$,*

$$\text{Adv}_{\mathbb{D}}^{\text{PASM}}(\mathcal{A}) \; = \; \Pr[\mathcal{A} \; wins] \; \leq \; \frac{q_{se} + q_{up}}{|\mathbb{D}|} + \epsilon.$$

The advantage, $\text{Adv}_{\mathbb{D}}^{\text{PASM}}(\mathcal{A})$, is not negligible since a password has only low entropy. The best lower bound is that $\text{Adv}_{\mathbb{D}}^{\text{PASM}}(\mathcal{A})$ equals to $\frac{q_{se} + q_{up}}{|\mathbb{D}|}$. Note that $\text{Adv}_{\mathbb{D}}^{\text{PASM}}(\mathcal{A})$ is proportional to the number of not only q_{se} but also q_{up} since UPDATE inherently includes AUTH.

3 Our Basic Protocol

In this section, we propose our PASM protocol and discuss its security.

3.1 General Architecture

We assume that there are secure channels with two-way authentication among all S_i for $1 \leq i \leq n$ and secure channels with one-way authentication between C and each S_i for $1 \leq i \leq n$. After the protocol, the channels between C and the others become secure channels with two-way authentication. Therefore, C and S_i for $1 \leq i \leq n$ interact with each other by using the channels after the authentication.

Our basic protocol succeeds as follows.

1. A client registers its password through SETUP.
2. Before authentication, the servers performs RANDSHAREGEN and ZEROSHAREGEN.
3. The client is to be authenticated through AUTH.
4. If needed, the client updates its password through UPDATE.

3.2 Details of the Protocol

For clarity of the protocol, we assume that any $\mathcal{U}$ immediately outputs *reject/fail* and halts when $\mathcal{U}$ receives "reject"/"fail" from another $\mathcal{U}'$, and we omit this from the description of the protocol. In addition, we say "$\mathcal{U}$ broadcasts a" when $\mathcal{U}$ sends a to all participants.

Protocol 1. SETUP

Input: $w \in \mathbb{D}$ for C, $\mathscr{L}_i$ for S_i where $1 \leq i \leq n$
Output: *success/fail* for C, and a (updated) $\mathscr{L}_i$ or *fail* for S_i where $1 \leq i \leq n$
  1: C computes $([w]_1, \ldots, [w]_n) \leftarrow \mathsf{Share}(w)$ and sends $(C, [w]_i)$ to S_i for $1 \leq i \leq n$
  2: **each** S_i for $1 \leq i \leq n$ **do**
  3:    **if** $(C, *) \in \mathscr{L}_i$ **then** outputs *fail*, sends "fail" to C_i, and halts
  4:    $\mathscr{L}_i \leftarrow \mathscr{L}_i \cup \{(C, [w]_i)\}$
  5:    broadcasts "success" to C_i
  6: **if** C receives n "successes", **then** outputs *success*
  7: **each** S_i for $1 \leq i \leq n$ **do**
  8:    **if** receives n "successes", **then** outputs $\mathscr{L}_i$

Password Setup. We first describe the SETUP in Protocol 1. This simply sends Shamir's share to S_i for $1 \leq i \leq n$.

Authentication. We next describe AUTH, which consists of two steps. The first step is generating random shares and zero shares, which is performed among S_i for $1 \leq i \leq n$. The second is authenticating C by using the random shares and zero shares. The first step is independent of C and the password, so it can be performed in the idle state. There are several ways to generate random shares and zero shares, so we give an example here; other ways are shown in Appendix A.

Let $\{x_{i,j}\}_{i=1,\ldots,n-k+1}^{j=1,\ldots,n}$ be an $(n-k+1) \times n$ Vandermonde matrix. We describe (an example of) the first step in Protocols 2 and 3. The random share is generated through the technique of Damgård and Nielsen [18]. The zero share is generated by almost the same technique generating a random share whose degree is $2k-2$ and then multiplying the coordinate of Shamir's SS by the share. These protocols

---

Protocol 2. RANDSHAREGEN

Input: Nothing
Output: $[r^{(j)}]_i$ for S_i, where $1 \leq i \leq n$, $1 \leq j \leq n-k+1$, and $r^{(j)} \leftarrow \mathscr{F}$
  1: **each** S_i for $1 \leq i \leq n$ **do**
  2:    $r_i' \leftarrow \mathscr{F}$
  3:    $([r_i']_1, \ldots, [r_i']_n) \leftarrow \mathsf{Share}(r_i')$
  4:    Send $[r_i']_j$ to S_j for $1 \leq j \leq n$
  5: **each** S_i for $1 \leq i \leq n$ **do**
  6:    $[r^{(j)}]_i = \sum_{\ell=1}^n x_{j,\ell} [r_\ell']_i$ for $j \leq n-k+1$
  7: **return** $[r^{(j)}]_i$ for S_i, where $1 \leq i \leq n$ and $1 \leq j \leq n-k+1$

---

generate $n-k+1$ random/zero shares at once, so all S_i for $1 \leq i \leq n$ repeat the protocols until enough random/zero shares are prepared.

The second step is described in Protocol 4. This step requires $2k-1$ random shares and $2k-1$ zero shares per one authentication. In this step, $2k-1$ servers participate in the protocol. Let $\mathbb{V} \subseteq \{1, \ldots, n\}$ be the servers that participate in this step. Intuitively, the protocol attempts to compute $w - w'$ to check whether

Protocol 3. ZeroShareGen

Input: Nothing

Output: $[\![0^{(j)}]\!]_i$ for S_i, where $1 \leq i \leq n$, $1 \leq j \leq n-k+1$

1: **each** S_i for $1 \leq i \leq n$ **do**
2:     $r_i' \leftarrow \mathscr{F}$
3:     Generate $\langle r_i' \rangle_1, \ldots, \langle r_i' \rangle_n$ via the sharing algorithm of $(2k-2, n)$-Shamir with input r_i'
4:     Send $\langle r_i' \rangle_j$ to S_j for $1 \leq j \leq n$
5: **each** S_i for $1 \leq i \leq n$ **do**
6:     $\left\langle r^{(j)} \right\rangle_i = \sum_{\ell=1}^{n} x_{j,\ell} \langle r_\ell' \rangle_i$ for $j \leq n-k+1$
7:     $[\![0^{(j)}]\!]_i = i \left\langle r^{(j)} \right\rangle_i$
8: **return** $[\![0^{(j)}]\!]_i$ for S_i, where $1 \leq i \leq n$, $1 \leq j \leq n-k+1$

Protocol 4. Auth (after generation of $2k-1$ random shares and $2k-1$ zero shares)

Input: $w' \in \mathbb{D}$ for C, $\mathscr{L}_i$, $\left\{ [r^{(S_j)}]_i \right\}_{j \in \mathbb{V}}$ and $\left\{ [\![0^{(S_j)}]\!]_i \right\}_{j \in \mathbb{V}}$ for S_i, where $i \in \mathbb{V}$

Output: *accept*/*reject* for C and S_i, where $i \in \mathbb{V}$

1: **each** S_i for $i \in \mathbb{V}$ **do**
2:     sends $nonce_i \leftarrow \mathbb{N}_{non}$ to C
3: C computes $([w']_1, \ldots, [w']_n) \leftarrow \mathsf{Share}(w')$ and sends $([w']_i, nonce_i)$ to S_i for $i \in \mathbb{V}$
4: **each** S_i for $i \in \mathbb{V}$ **do**
5:     **if** $nonce_i \neq nonce_i'$ or $(C, [w]_i) \notin \mathscr{L}_i$, **then** broadcasts "reject", outputs *reject* and halts
6:     Send $\delta_i^{(S_j)} = [r^{(S_j)}]_i([w]_i - [w']_i) + [\![0^{(S_j)}]\!]_i$ to S_j for $j \in \mathbb{V}$
7: **each** S_i for $i \in \mathbb{V}$ **do**
8:     **if** $\sum_{j \in \mathbb{V}} \lambda_j^{(\mathbb{V})} \delta_j^{(S_i)} \neq 0$, **then** broadcasts "reject", outputs *reject* and halts
9:     broadcasts "accept"
10: **each** C and S_i for $i \in \mathbb{V}$ **do**
11:     **if** receives $2k-1$ "accepts", **then** outputs *accept*

---

w' equals w. However, $w - w'$ may leak information of the difference, so we mask it by using the random shares and the zero shares.

Password Update. We finally describe Update in Protocol 5. This simply performs Auth and substitutes the password shares if C is accepted.

Theorem 1. *Let q_{se} be the number of **SendAuth** queries and q_{up} be the number of **SendUpdate** queries. If $n \geq 2k-1$ and $\mathcal{A}$ statically corrupts at most $k-1$ of S_i, Then our protocol is $\prod_{i=1}^{q_{se}+q_{up}-1} \left(1 - \frac{i}{|\mathbb{N}_{non}|}\right) + \frac{q_{se}+q_{up}}{|\mathscr{F}|^k}$ secure against impersonation.*

Due to space limitation, we give the sketch of proof here. In Setup, C only sends the shares via secure channels so it does not compromise the security. RandShareGen is one of the protocol proposed in [18] and ZeroShareGen

---

Protocol 5. UPDATE

Input: $w', w^* \in \mathbb{D}$ for C, $\mathscr{L}_i$, $\left([r^{(S_1)}]_i, \ldots, [r^{(S_n)}]_i\right)$ and $\left([\![0^{(S_1)}]\!]_i, \ldots, [\![0^{(S_n)}]\!]_i\right)$ for each S_i

Output: *success/fail* for C, and a (updated) $\mathscr{L}_i$ or *fail* for each S_i, $1 \le i \le n$

1: C with input w' and S_i for $i \in \mathbb{V}$ perform AUTH
2: **if** one of the outputs of AUTH is *reject*, **then** halts
3: C with input w^* and S_i for $1 \le i \le n$ perform SETUP, except step 4 is changed as
$\mathscr{L}_i \leftarrow \mathscr{L}_i \backslash \{(C, [w']_i)\} \cup \{(C, [w^*]_i)\}$.

---

is the same protocol except each S_i computes a local multiplication in the final step. UPDATE is just a combination of SETUP and AUTH. Therefore, we focus on the security of AUTH (after generation of random/zero shares).

Without loss of generality, we assume that $\mathbb{V} = \{1, \ldots, 2k-1\}$ and $S_1, \ldots, S_{k-1}$ are corrupted. In addition, we assume that *nonce* is not duplicated by admitting the security loss $\prod_{i=1}^{q_{\mathrm{se}}+q_{\mathrm{up}}-1}\left(1 - \frac{i}{|\mathbb{N}_{\mathrm{non}}|}\right)$.

The goal of AUTH is generating a *uniformly random* $[\![r(w-w')^{(\mathcal{U})}]\!]$ that is revealed by $\mathcal{U}$. If $[\![r(w-w')^{(\mathcal{U})}]\!]$ is generated correctly, revealed value, $r(w-w')$, is 0 if $w = w'$ and a random value otherwise.

First, we assume that $\mathcal{A}$ follows the protocol. In this case, we confirm that $\delta_i^{(\mathcal{U})} = [r^{(\mathcal{U})}]_i([w]_i - [w']_i) + [\![0^{(\mathcal{U})}]\!]_i$ for $i \in \mathbb{V}$ plays a role of uniformly random $[\![r(w-w')^{(\mathcal{U})}]\!]$. A simple product of $[r^{(\mathcal{U})}]_i$ and $([w]_i - [w']_i)$ is $[\![r(w-w')^{(\mathcal{U})}]\!]_i$. However, this share is *not* uniformly random since $[w]_i$ and $[w']_i$ may be common. In fact, $\mathcal{A}$ can extract w from $[r_1]([w] - [w'])$ and $[r_2]([w] - [w'])$ by Chinese remainder theorem. In contrast, by adding $[\![0^{(\mathcal{U})}]\!]_i$, all a_j that satisfies $\delta_i^{(\mathcal{U})} = r(w-w') + \sum_{j=1}^{2k-1} a_j i^j$ are uniformly random. Therefore, $\delta_i^{(\mathcal{U})}$ for $i \in \mathbb{V}$ is a uniformly random $[\![r(w-w')^{(\mathcal{U})}]\!]$.

Second, we consider the case $\mathcal{A}$ deviates from the protocol and a legitimate client C is authenticated. $\mathcal{A}$ obtains $[w_1], \ldots, [w_{k-1}]$ and $\delta_j^{(S_i)}$ for $1 \le i \le k-1$ and $k-1 \le j \le 2k-1$. $[w_1], \ldots, [w_{k-1}]$ are uniformly random elements in $\mathscr{F}$ since (k, n)-Shamir is perfectly private against $k-1$ corruptions. In addition, $\delta_j^{(S_i)}$ for $1 \le i \le k-1$ are uniformly random $[\![r(w-w')^{(S_i)}]\!]$ since $\delta_j^{(S_i)}$ is independent of $\mathcal{A}$'s behavior. Therefore, the reconstructed values are independent of the password and $\mathcal{A}$ cannot obtain information about the password.

Finally, we consider the case $\mathcal{A}$ deviates from the protocol and impersonates C with a guessed password w'. $\mathcal{A}$ should make $r(w-w')^{(S_i)} = 0$ for all S_i, where $corrupt_{S_i} \ne true$. From the above discussion, $\mathcal{A}$ does not know the password w and randomness r. $\mathcal{A}$ can modify $\delta_j^{(S_i)}$ for $1 \le j \le k-1$ and $k \le i \le 2k-1$ into $\widehat{\delta}_j^{(S_i)}$. It means that $\mathcal{A}$ changes the reconstructed value from $r(w-w')^{(S_i)}$ to $r(w-w')^{(S_i)} + \lambda_i^{(\mathbb{V})}(\widehat{\delta}_j^{(S_i)} - \delta_j^{(S_i)})$. However, if $w \ne w'$, $r(w-w')^{(S_i)}$ is uniformly randomly distributed. Therefore, $\mathcal{A}$ cannot make the reconstructed value 0 except that the probability of $w = w'$ or $r' + \lambda_i^{(\mathbb{V})}(\widehat{\delta}_j^{(S_i)} - \delta_j^{(S_i)}) = 0$, where $r' \leftarrow \mathscr{F}$.

This probability is $\frac{q_{se}+q_{up}}{|\mathbb{D}|} + \frac{q_{se}+q_{up}}{|\mathcal{F}|}$, and the advantage is as the statement since $\mathcal{A}$ have to make the above thing for all S_i, where $corrupt_{S_i} \neq true$. $\square$

4 Optimization for Practical Network Model and Experiment

4.1 Network Model

SS-based MPC is implemented over certain network. Typical examples are as follows.

– Gateway network model: There is a gateway $\mathcal{G}$, and all communications are relayed by $\mathcal{G}$. It includes the case that one of S_i additionally acts as $\mathcal{G}$.
– Point-to-point network model: All participants are connected to each other.

In theory, we typically assume the point-to-point network model. However, in practice, the gateway network model may be used due to the two reasons. The first is the reduced number of connections. The model reduces the cost of laying the connections and simplifies managing the connections in parallel. The second is mutual execution of shared data. Let's consider a case where many users access an SS-based MPC system. If the inconsistency occurs, e.g., some shares are renewed by a client and the other shares are renewed by another client, any server cannot notice it by itself. Therefore, mutual execution is critical in SS-based MPC to avoid the above. In the gateway network model, mutual execution can be done by the gateway managing to write/delete shares.

4.2 Optimization for Gateway Network Model

Although our basic PASM protocol can be used in the gateway network model, we optimize the AUTH of our protocol to improve the response time to a client as follows.

– Before AUTH, the servers additionally prepares $[r^{(\mathcal{G})}]$ and $[\![0^{(\mathcal{G})}]\!]$.
– In step 6, each S_i additionally computes $\delta_i^{(\mathcal{G})} = [r^{(\mathcal{G})}]_i([w]_i - [w']_i) + [\![0^{(\mathcal{G})}]\!]_i$ and sends $\delta_i^{(\mathcal{G})}$ to $\mathcal{G}$.
– Before step 7, $\mathcal{G}$ sends "reject" to the client if $\sum_{j \in \mathbb{V}} \lambda_j^{(\mathbb{V})} \delta_j^{(\mathcal{G})} \neq 0$ or sends "accept" to the client otherwise.

The optimization does not compromise security even if $\mathcal{G}$ is additionally corrupted since the authentication step between a client and the servers is maintained.

We count the communication rounds between $\mathcal{C}$ and $\mathcal{G}$ and between $\mathcal{G}$ and S_i separately. All moves of the protocol are unchanged. However, $\mathcal{C}$ can receive the (tentative) authentication result before AUTH ends. $\mathcal{C}$ receives the authentication result after 3 $\mathcal{C}$-$\mathcal{G}$ and 5 $\mathcal{G}$-S_i moves in our basic protocol and after 3 $\mathcal{C}$-$\mathcal{G}$ and 3

G-S_i moves in our protocol with optimization. Therefore, from the viewpoint of a client, our protocol is "faster" than the above protocol.

When we in fact use the authentication protocol, if C receives "accept" from G, s/he considers that the authentication is accepted and sends a message via the channels. There is little possibility that G accepts C, but another S_i does not in real systems. If by any chance S_i does not accept, C receives, for example, "an internal error" from S_i. Even in this case, this is not a problem C has already sent a message since the message can be read by only the legitimate server. Although the number of gaps between the moves of two protocols is a few, the response time of the protocol can be large since the network delay tends to be large in SS-based MPC. Each server may be settled in different places such as different countries to assure their administration independence and ability to tolerate disaster.

4.3   Experimental Results

We implemented and evaluated the response time of our protocol with optimization. In the experiment, we assumed that $n = 5$ and $k = 3$ since they are small in most practical results of SS-based MPC [9,12]. We implemented AUTH on the gateway network model. It is future work to experiment SETUP and UPDATE, and PASM on the point-to-point network model. We measure the time of following steps that includes the time taken to establish secure channels with RSA-PKCS #5 and AES by using OpenSSL.

1. A client verifies the certificates of servers' public keys,
2. the client encrypts distinct symmetric keys with the public keys,
3. the client performs Protocol 4 with the optimization. All communications between the client and servers are encrypted with the symmetric keys.
4. the client outputs *accept*.

The steps does not include the time taken to establish secure channels among S_i and the time taken to generate random and zero shares since they can be performed before the authentication protocol performed.

All the experiments were conducted on two laptop machines. One had the role of a client. It used MAC OS X 10.8.4 with a 2.9 GHz Intel Core i7 and 8 GB of physical memory. The other's role was as a gateway and servers. It used Cent OS 6.4 with a 2.9 GHz Intel Core i7 and 1 GB of physical memory, and it executed six virtual machines (VMs), one gateway and five servers, and allocated one core per VM. We implemented the client program with C++ and the gateway and server program with C++ and Java, where the Share and Rec algorithms of SS was implemented with C++ and other operations such as modular addition/multiplication were implemented with Java.

We insisted that our protocol be fast for practical use even when the network delay is large, so we conducted the experiment under various network delays. The network delay was simulated by the tc command, which was implemented on Linux. The network delay means the round-trip delay. The results listed in Table 1 shows the average of 100 executions.

Table 1. Experimental result

Network delay (ms)	0	50	100	150	200	250	300
Response time (sec)	0.23	0.64	1.06	1.42	1.80	2.21	2.60

"ms" denotes millisecond and "sec" denotes second. Network delay means the simulated network delay, which is round trip. Response time means the time from when a client sends the request for authentication to when the client receives the authentication result

As a result, even if there was a 200 ms delay, which is almost that between Japan and Europe in the Internet, authentication was executed within 2 s.

5 Conclusion

Recently, several efforts to implement and use SS-based MPC have been put into practice. Authentication of clients is one critical mechanism for implementing SS-based MPC successfully in practice. Our observation is that the authentication protocol must have threshold security, establish distinct channels. In addition, constructing the protocol with SS and operations involving SS is preferable. We formalized such authentication protocol as PASM and proposed the PASM protocol. Our protocol is secure assuming the existence of two types of channels, which are instantiated by the popular cryptographic primitives. Furthermore, we implement our protocol with an optimization for the realistic network model. We confirmed that the protocol is practical since a client received the result within 2 s even when the network delay was 200 ms, which is almost the delay that occurs between Japan and Europe.

A Other Methods to Generate Random and Zero Shares

We give several methods to generate random shares and zero shares.

The first method is just relying on C, which generates the random and zero shares in SETUP and sends them to all S_i at the *same* time a share of a password is sent. This does not compromise security since the password, and the random and zero shares are sent by the same client. If the random or zero shares are short, S_i requests C to generate them after AUTH is correctly finished with the acceptance.

The second method is that S_i generates random and zero shares in the idle state. Damgård and Nielsen [18] and Beerliová-Trubíniová and Hirt [3] proposed a random share generation protocol called "DN-Rand" and "BH-Rand," respectively. We can prepare random shares by using these protocols straightforwardly. A zero share is generated in almost the same way to generate random shares. First, generate random shares whose degree is $2k - 2$ and then multiply S_i's "coordinate" of Shamir's SS. The zero share generation protocol is as follows.

1. Each S_i generates a $(2k - 2, n)$-random share $\langle r_i \rangle_j$.
2. Each S_i locally computes $[\![0]\!]_i = i \times \langle r_j \rangle_i$.

The third method is that S_i also generates random and zero shares in the idle state. This way is more efficient than using DN-Rand and HB-Rand instead of using pseudo-randomness. Cramer et al. [16] showed that if all S_i share seeds among themselves before the protocol, they can produce *replicated* random shares by themselves and locally convert them to Shamir's random shares. Let $\mathbb{B} = \{\beta_1, \ldots, \beta_{|\mathbb{B}|}\}$ be a set of $n - k + 1$ combinations of S_i from n servers where $|\mathbb{B}| = \binom{n}{n-k+1}$, $v_{\beta_1}, \ldots, v_{\beta_{|\mathbb{B}|}}$ be independently and uniformly chosen seeds, f_{β_j} be the function satisfying $f_{\beta_j}(0) = 1$, $f_{\beta_j}(\ell) = 0$ for $S_\ell \notin \beta_j$, and its degree be $k - 1$. In the initial setup, make each S_i have v_{β_j}, where $S_i \in \beta_j$. To generate a random share, each S_i computes pseudo-randomness Υ_{β_j} from v_{β_j} for $S_i \in \beta_j$. Then, each S_i computes $[r]_i = \sum_{S_i \in \beta_j} f_{\beta_j}(i)\Upsilon_{\beta_j}$. A zero share is generated with the same technique described in the previous paragraph. First, generate a $(2k - 2, n)$ random share $\langle r \rangle_i$ and multiply S_i's coordinate.

References

1. Abdalla, M., Fouque, P.-A., Pointcheval, D.: Password-based authenticated key exchange in the three-party setting. In: Vaudenay, S. (ed.) PKC 2005. LNCS, vol. 3386, pp. 65–84. Springer, Heidelberg (2005)
2. Bagherzandi, A., Jarecki, S., Saxena, N., Lu, Y.: Password-protected secret sharing. In: ACM Conference on Computer and Communications Security, pp. 433–444 (2011)
3. Beerliová-Trubíniová, Z., Hirt, M.: Perfectly-secure MPC with linear communication complexity. In: TCC, pp. 213–230 (2008)
4. Bellare, M., Pointcheval, D., Rogaway, P.: Authenticated key exchange secure against dictionary attacks. In: Preneel, B. (ed.) EUROCRYPT 2000. LNCS, vol. 1807, pp. 139–155. Springer, Heidelberg (2000)
5. Bellare, M., Rogaway, P.: Entity authentication and key distribution. In: Stinson, D.R. (ed.) CRYPTO 1993. LNCS, vol. 773, pp. 232–249. Springer, Heidelberg (1994)
6. Bellovin, S.M., Merritt, M.: Encrypted key exchange: password-based protocols secure against dictionary attacks. In: 1992 IEEE Computer Society Symposium on Research in Security and Privacy, pp. 72–84. Oakland, CA, USA, 4–6 May 1992
7. Bellovin, S.M., Merritt, M.: Augmented encrypted key exchange: a password-based protocol secure against dictionary attacks and password file compromise. In: Proceedings of the 1st ACM Conference on Computer and Communications Security, CCS 1993, pp. 244–250. Fairfax, Virginia, USA, 3–5 November 1993
8. Bogdanov, D., Laur, S., Willemson, J.: Sharemind: a framework for fast privacy-preserving computations. In: Jajodia, S., Lopez, J. (eds.) ESORICS 2008. LNCS, vol. 5283, pp. 192–206. Springer, Heidelberg (2008)
9. Bogdanov, D., Niitsoo, M., Toft, T., Willemson, J.: High-performance secure multi-party computation for data mining applications. Int. J. Inf. Sec. 11(6), 403–418 (2012)
10. Bogdanov, D., Talviste, R., Willemson, J.: Deploying secure multi-party computation for financial data analysis. In: Keromytis, A.D. (ed.) FC 2012. LNCS, vol. 7397, pp. 57–64. Springer, Heidelberg (2012)

11. Brainard, J.G., Juels, A., Kaliski, B., Szydlo, M.: A new two-server approach for authentication with short secrets. In: Proceedings of the 12th USENIX Security Symposium, Washington, D.C., USA, 4–8 August 2003
12. Burkhart, M., Strasser, M., Many, D., Dimitropoulos, X.A.: SEPIA: privacy-preserving aggregation of multi-domain network events and statistics. In: USENIX Security Symposium, pp. 223–240 (2010)
13. Camenisch, J., Lysyanskaya, A., Neven, G.: Practical yet universally composable two-server password-authenticated secret sharing. In: ACM Conference on Computer and Communications Security, pp. 525–536 (2012)
14. Canetti, R.: Universally composable security: a new paradigm for cryptographic protocols. In: FOCS, pp. 136–145 (2001)
15. Coretti, S., Maurer, U., Tackmann, B.: Constructing confidential channels from authenticated channels—public-key encryption revisited. In: Sako, K., Sarkar, P. (eds.) ASIACRYPT 2013, Part I. LNCS, vol. 8269, pp. 134–153. Springer, Heidelberg (2013)
16. Cramer, R., Damgård, I.B., Ishai, Y.: Share conversion, pseudorandom secret-sharing and applications to secure computation. In: Kilian, J. (ed.) TCC 2005. LNCS, vol. 3378, pp. 342–362. Springer, Heidelberg (2005)
17. Cramer, R., Shoup, V.: Design and analysis of practical public-key encryption schemes secure against adaptive chosen ciphertext attack. SIAM J. Comput. **33**(1), 167–226 (2004)
18. Damgård, I.B., Nielsen, J.B.: Scalable and unconditionally secure multiparty computation. In: Menezes, A. (ed.) CRYPTO 2007. LNCS, vol. 4622, pp. 572–590. Springer, Heidelberg (2007)
19. Ford, W., Kaliski Jr., B.S.: Server-assisted generation of a strong secret from a password. In: WETICE, pp. 176–180 (2000)
20. Genkin, D., Ishai, Y., Prabhakaran, M., Sahai, A., Tromer, E.: Circuits resilient to additive attacks with applications to secure computation. In: STOC, pp. 495–504 (2014)
21. Gennaro, R.: Faster and shorter password-authenticated key exchange. In: Canetti, R. (ed.) TCC 2008. LNCS, vol. 4948, pp. 589–606. Springer, Heidelberg (2008)
22. Gennaro, R., Lindell, Y.: A framework for password-based authenticated key exchange. ACM Trans. Inf. Syst. Secur. **9**(2), 181–234 (2006)
23. Halevi, S., Krawczyk, H.: Public-key cryptography and password protocols. ACM Trans. Inf. Syst. Secur. **2**(3), 230–268 (1999)
24. Ikarashi, D., Kikuchi, R., Hamada, K., Chida, K.: Actively private and correct MPC scheme in $t < n/2$ from passively secure schemes with small overhead. IACR Cryptology ePrintArchive, p. 304 (2014)
25. Jablon, D.P.: Strong password-only authenticated key exchange. Comput. Commun. Rev. **26**(5), 5–26 (1996)
26. Kamm, L., Bogdanov, D., Laur, S., Vilo, J.: A new way to protect privacy in large-scale genome-wide association studies. Bioinformatics **29**(7), 886–893 (2013)
27. Katz, J., MacKenzie, P.D., Taban, G., Gligor, V.D.: Two-server password-only authenticated key exchange. In: Ioannidis, J., Keromytis, A.D., Yung, M. (eds.) ACNS 2005. LNCS, vol. 3531, pp. 1–16. Springer, Heidelberg (2005)
28. Katz, J., Ostrovsky, R., Yung, M.: Efficient password-authenticated key exchange using human-memorable passwords. In: Pfitzmann, B. (ed.) EUROCRYPT 2001. LNCS, vol. 2045, pp. 475–494. Springer, Heidelberg (2001)
29. Katz, J., Vaikuntanathan, V.: Round-optimal password-based authenticated key exchange. J. Cryptol. **26**(4), 714–743 (2013)

30. Kiefer, F., Manulis, M.: Distributed smooth projective hashing and its application to two-server password authenticated key exchange. In: Boureanu, I., Owesarski, P., Vaudenay, S. (eds.) ACNS 2014. LNCS, vol. 8479, pp. 199–216. Springer, Heidelberg (2014)
31. Kurosawa, K., Desmedt, Y.G.: A new paradigm of hybrid encryption scheme. In: Franklin, M. (ed.) CRYPTO 2004. LNCS, vol. 3152, pp. 426–442. Springer, Heidelberg (2004)
32. MacKenzie, P.D., Shrimpton, T., Jakobsson, M.: Threshold password-authenticated key exchange. J. Cryptol. 19(1), 27–66 (2006)
33. Patel, S.: Number theoretic attacks on secure password schemes. In: 1997 IEEE Symposium on Security and Privacy, Oakland, CA, USA, pp. 236–247, 4–7 May 1997
34. Raimondo, M.D., Gennaro, R.: Provably secure threshold password-authenticated key exchange. J. Comput. Syst. Sci. 72(6), 978–1001 (2006)
35. Shamir, A.: How to share a secret. Commun. ACM 22(11), 612–613 (1979)
36. Steiner, M., Tsudik, G., Waidner, M.: Refinement and extension of encrypted key exchange. Oper. Syst. Rev. 29(3), 22–30 (1995)

Bandwidth-Optimized Secure Two-Party Computation of Minima

Jan Henrik Ziegeldorf[(✉)], Jens Hiller, Martin Henze, Hanno Wirtz,
and Klaus Wehrle

Communication and Distributed Systems (COMSYS),
RWTH Aachen University, Aachen, Germany
{ziegeldorf,hiller,henze,wirtz,wehrle}@comsys.rwth-aachen.de

Abstract. Secure Two-Party Computation (STC) allows two mutually
untrusting parties to securely evaluate a function on their private inputs.
While tremendous progress has been made towards reducing processing
overheads, STC still incurs significant communication overhead that is in
fact prohibitive when no high-speed network connection is available, e.g.,
when applications are run over a cellular network. In this paper, we consider the fundamental problem of securely computing a minimum and its
argument, which is a basic building block in a wide range of applications
that have been proposed as STCs, e.g., Nearest Neighbor Search, Auctions, and Biometric Matchings. We first comprehensively analyze and
compare the communication overhead of implementations of the three
major STC concepts, i.e., Yao's Garbled Circuits, the Goldreich-Micali-
Wigderson protocol, and Homomorphic Encryption. We then propose
an algorithm for securely computing minima in the semi-honest model
that, compared to current state-of-the-art, reduces communication overheads by 18 % to 98 %. Lower communication overheads result in faster
runtimes in constrained networks and lower direct costs for users.

1 Introduction

The increasing collection of sensitive user data provided by mobile devices at
cloud services, e.g., in genetic testing [9], gives rise to significant privacy concerns. However, performing all necessary computations exclusively on the mobile
device, to preserve the user's privacy, is infeasible as this could disclose business
secrets of the service provider. In this scenario, Secure Two-Party Computation
(STC) presents a generic solution to reconcile these conflicting privacy interests.

The performance of STC has been thoroughly investigated in a static setting
with a high-speed LAN connection. In this setting, processing overheads are the
main performance bottleneck and tremendous improvements, both practical and
theoretical, have been made in this regard, mainly focussing on Yao's Garbled
Circuits approach [35]. STC in more constrained environments, e.g., between
mobile devices that interact spontaneously, has only recently received interest
[4,5,7,9,10,18]. Still, these works assume a network with low latency and high
throughput [5,7,10,18], prior interaction for pre-computations [5,9,18], additional

© Springer International Publishing Switzerland 2015
M. Reiter and D. Naccache (Eds.): CANS 2015, LNCS 9476, pp. 197–213, 2015.
DOI: 10.1007/978-3-319-26823-1_14

hardware or third parties [5,10], or consider only specialized applications [4,7]. In contrast, we strive to enable STCs in a purely ad-hoc manner between mobile devices and/or a cloud service over constrained, e.g., cellular, networks. In this setting, we argue for bandwidth consumption as a primary optimization goal. First, high-bandwidth STCs may quickly deplete users' data volume, inducing capped bandwidths or significant costs for subsequent communication. Second, less available bandwidth incurs significant transmission overheads which then constitute the main performance bottleneck. We show that this bottleneck eventually dominates the processing time, as also noted in [4,7,37].

In this work, we hence set out to analyze the bandwidth usage of the three major STC concepts Yao's Garbled Circuits (GCs) [35], the Goldreich-Micali-Wigderson (GMW) Protocol [16], and Homomorphic Encryption (HE). We focus on the fundamental STC problem of computing a minimum and its argument, since this problem (i) has widely been considered in all three STC concepts and (ii) is central to many STC applications, e.g., Nearest Neighbor search [30], Auctions [22], and Biometric Matching [17]. Our contributions are the following:

Thorough Analysis. We exactly quantify the communication complexity for state-of-the-art constructions and implementations of the (arg)min problem in GC, GMW, and HE. In constrained environments, we argue that the induced communication overheads quickly render mobile STCs infeasible.

Bandwidth-Optimized (arg)min. We propose an HE-based, bandwidth-optimized (arg)min algorithm that reduces the communication overhead by 18 % to 98 % compared to state-of-the-art approaches. In constrained networks with bandwidths ranging from $\leq 1\,\mathrm{MBit/s}$ (e.g., Bluetooth, 3G) to ≤ 12–$50\,\mathrm{MBit/s}$ (e.g., LTE), this translates to lower costs for end-users and even affords faster runtimes than bandwidth-heavy algorithms. We demonstrate the feasibility and performance of our protocol along a prototype implementation.

We discuss background on STC concepts and related work in Sect. 2. In Sect. 3, we analyze the communication complexity of previous (arg)min protocols. We present our improved protocol in Sect. 4 and its evaluation in Sect. 5. Section 6 concludes this paper. Note that all results also directly apply to the symmetric (arg)max problem.

2   Background

STC allows two mutually distrusting parties, i.e., a *client* $\mathcal{C}$ with private input x and a *server* $\mathcal{S}$ with private input y, to compute a known functionality $\mathcal{F}(x,y)$ without anyone learning the private inputs. Three predominant concepts for STC exist, partly building on Oblivious Transfer: Yao's Garbled Circuits, the Goldreich-Micali-Wigderson protocol, and Homomorphic Encryption.

Oblivious Transfer (OT). In the most general form of Oblivious Transfer, i.e., 1-out-of-n-OT_l^m, $\mathcal{S}$ holds m distinct n tuples of l-bit strings and $\mathcal{C}$ chooses exactly one string from each n tuple, while $\mathcal{S}$ learns nothing about $\mathcal{C}$'s choices. Formally, $\mathcal{S}$ holds $(s_{11}, ..., s_{1n}), ..., (s_{m1}, ..., s_{mn})$ with $s_{ij} \in \{0,1\}^l$ and $\mathcal{C}$ holds m choices $r_1, ..., r_m \in \{1...n\}$ and obtains the strings $s_{ir_i, 1 \leq i \leq m}$ while $\mathcal{S}$ has no output. 1-out-of-n-OT$_l^m$ can be efficiently instantiated by first reducing it to $m \log_2(n)$ invocations of 1-out-of-2-OT [27,28] and then reducing the resulting large number of long l bit OTs to a small number of short t bit *Base OTs*, i.e., 1-out-of-2-OT$_t^t$ [1,20] (*OT Extension*). The communication overhead for 1-out-of-n-OT$_l^m$ then amounts to $mnl + 3m \log(n)t$ bit, with symmetric security parameter t (e.g., AES key length). Base OTs can be implemented at the costs of an additional $2t^2 + tT$ bit, where T is the asymmetric security level (e.g., bitlength of an RSA modulus) [27,28]. The overhead for base OTs is often neglected in related work as it amortizes over a large number of OT Extensions. To further increase the communication efficiency of OT, custom OT variants exist. For GCs, e.g., general 1-out-2-OT can be replaced by *correlated* 1-out-of-2-OT [11], where S's inputs are correlated, reducing communication overhead to $m(t + l)$ bit per OT [1]. Similarly, in GMW, *random* 1-out-2-OT [11] obtains inputs randomly from a correlation-robust one-way function, reducing communication overhead to mt bits per OT [1].

Garbled Circuits (GC). Yao's Garbled Circuits [35] require to represent (automatically with special compilers) the desired functionality $\mathcal{F}(\cdot)$ as a Boolean circuit. After compiling the Boolean circuit, S *garbles* the circuit by encrypting and permuting the truth table entries for each circuit gate. Then S sends the garbled circuit $\tilde{\mathcal{F}}(\cdot)$ and its own garbled inputs $\tilde{y}$ to C. C obtains its own garbled inputs $\tilde{x}$ via correlated OT from S, with parameter $m = |x|$, the total bitlength of C's input. Finally, C evaluates $\tilde{\mathcal{F}}(\tilde{x}, \tilde{y})$ by decrypting the garbled circuit gate by gate to obtain the result. The communication overhead of GCs is almost completely due to the transmission of the garbled circuit and of the garbled inputs (via OT). It is thus critical to construct *size-efficient* circuits and to minimize inputs. The size of a circuit is usually measured in the number of Non-XOR gates, since XOR gates cause virtually no overheads due to the "free-XOR" optimization [24].

Goldreich-Micali-Wigderson (GMW). The GMW protocol [16], similarly to Yao's protocol, securely evaluates Boolean circuits. However, instead of garbling the circuit, it is evaluated jointly by C and S using an XOR-based 2-out-of-2 secret sharing scheme, i.e., Boolean sharings. The GMW protocol allows local evaluation of XOR gates while AND gates require interaction between C and S, i.e., an exchange of 2 bit and one random OT per gate. Thus, while Yao's protocol has constant round complexity, the round complexity of GMW corresponds to the multiplicative depth of the circuit, i.e., the maximum number of AND gates on any path through the boolean circuit. Besides reducing the size of circuits to reduce the communication overhead, *depth-efficient* circuits are crucial to minimize communication rounds.

Homomorphic Encryption (HE). HE-based STC protocols allow to compute specific arithmetic operations under encryption, e.g., the Paillier cryptosystem [29] allows addition. Because Fully Homomorphic Encryption schemes currently still cause prohibitive overheads, multiplication for Paillier or addition for ElGamal is more efficiently realized using interactive protocols where C helps S to perform the respective operation. Using secure addition and multiplication, $\mathcal{C}$ and $\mathcal{S}$ can evaluate a representation of $\mathcal{F}$ as an arithmetic circuit. Then, $\mathcal{S}$ evaluates $\mathcal{F}$ on $\mathcal{C}$'s encrypted input $[x]$ and its own input y (square brackets denote encryption throughout this paper, i.e., $[x]$ is an encryption of x). $\mathcal{S}$ performs some operations locally, e.g., addition and scalar multiplication, while other operations, e.g., multiplication or comparison on ciphertexts, require interaction with $\mathcal{C}$. The overhead of HE-based STC is then due to interaction and public key operations.

2.1   Related Work

Different general purpose frameworks have been proposed, e.g., a port of the FastGC framework [19] in [18] and a port of the Fairplay framework [26] in [7], as well as protocols for specialized functionalities [4,9]. While addressing mobile devices, these mostly assume a high-bandwidth network connection and consider processing and memory requirements as the main optimization goals: [25,33] reduce the memory overhead of GC-based STC by more efficient circuit representations. To reduce processing overheads, [3,36] propose efficient garbling schemes, [5,6] outsource GC from mobile devices to the cloud, and [10] use a hardware security token. In this, communication overhead as an optimization goal has received only passive or analytical attention. Notably, [4,6] only briefly argue that bandwidth efficiency is critical to minimize direct costs for users, energy consumption, and overall protocol runtime. Similar, [7,37] observe that communication overhead can dominate the runtime of mobile STC but do not propose direct improvements. In this paper, we act on these observations by considering bandwidth consumption as the primary optimization goal.

3   Analysis of Efficient Secure Argmin Protocols

In this section, we analyze the problem of securely computing the minimum and its argument. We first introduce our problem definitions, security model, and parameters before we proceed to analyze the most efficient (arg)min protocols based on GCs Subsect. 3.1, GMW Subsect. 3.2, and HE Subsect. 3.3.

Problem Definition. Given a set of n arguments $X = (x_0, ..., x_{n-1})$ and n corresponding function values $Y = (y_0 = f(x_0), ..., y_{n-1} = f(x_{n-1}))$, the task is to find x^*, resp., $f(x^*)$ s.t. $f(x^*) \leq f(x_i)$ $\forall 1 \leq i \leq n$. We refer to x^* as *argmin* and to $y^* = f(x^*)$ as *min*. We assume that the inputs X and Y are already available in garbled (GC), secret-shared (GMW), or encrypted (HE) form and the output should be protected accordingly. This represents the usual case where the (arg)min algorithm is used as a building block within another secure computation, e.g., a nearest neighbor search which requires to derive certain distances before finding their argmin [17,30]. In Appendix A, we briefly discuss a second version where $\mathcal{C}$ and $\mathcal{S}$ each hold half of the inputs and the (arg)min should be obtained in clear and only by $\mathcal{C}$.

Adversary Model. We assume a semi-honest and computationally bounded adversary. A semi-honest adversary, other than the stronger malicious one, does not deviate from the protocol but may try to learn (private) information from the protocol transcript. The semi-honest model, though more restrictive than the malicious, is widely used as it enables efficient secure computations and often serves as a stepping stone towards security against malicious adversaries.

Parameter Definitions. We denote the symmetric security level by t and the asymmetric one by T and set $t = \{80, 112, 128\}, T = \{1024, 2048, 3072\}$ for legacy security until 2010, medium security until 2030, and long-term security beyond 2030, according to the NIST recommendations [2]. We set the statistical security parameter σ to 40 bit as, e.g., proposed in [11,14,17]. Finally, we vary the bitlength of the inputs $l \in \{32, 64, 128\}$ which represents a subset of frequent choices in the related literature [6,10–12].

Table 1. Communication complexity [bit] and rounds for the argmin problem in related work and in our improved protocol.

Protocol	Communication overhead	Rounds
* Kolesnikov'09 [22] (GC)	$2l(n-1)2t + (n+1)2t$	$\mathcal{O}(1)$
Huang'11 [17] (GC)	$2l(n-1)2t + nlt + (n-1)2t$	$\mathcal{O}(1)$
Demmler'15 [11] (GC)	$3l(n-1)2t$	$\mathcal{O}(1)$
* Schneider'13 [31] (GMW)	$(n-1)(4l - \lceil \log_2(l)\rceil - 2 + \lceil\log_2(n)\rceil)(2t+2)$	$\mathcal{O}(\log_2(n)\log_2(l))$
Demmler'15 [11] (GMW)	$(n-1)(5l - \lceil \log_2(l)\rceil - 2)(2t+2)$	$\mathcal{O}(\log_2(n)\log_2(l))$
Erkin'09 [12] (HE)	$(n-1)(2l+8+10/C)T$	$\mathcal{O}(\log_2(n))$
BOMA (HE+OT)	$(n-1)(4+6/C)T+2nT/C+n(l+\sigma)+3\log_2(n)t$	$\mathcal{O}(\log_2(n))$

Overview. In the following, we analyze the most efficient (arg)min protocols for each of the three major STC concepts. The respective communication and round complexity is summarized in Table 1. Approaches marked with an asterisk restrict the argmin to $\{0, ..., n-1\}$. This restriction allows for efficiency improvements but does not fully meet our problem definition, as it would require further computation to realize the full range of applications. E.g., in biometric access control applications, the argmin is not only the index of a user but her full profile including access rights [17]. Nevertheless, we include them in our analysis since they indicate lower bounds. The last row in Table 1 shows the complexity for our improved protocol which we present and analyze in Sect. 4.

3.1   Garbled Circuits (GC)

The communication complexity of GC-based (arg)min protocols is dominated by (i) the overhead for the input transfers (via OT), (ii) the size of the garbled circuit, and (iii) the chosen garbling scheme. We neglect all other minor communication overheads, e.g., for the establishment of a network connection. The overheads (i) for transferring inputs only occur in the second version of our problem definition (cf. Appendix A). To quantify the overheads for (ii), we analyze the most efficient circuit constructions and their respective sizes below.

Regarding (iii), we use the recent "Half Gates" garbling scheme [36] which allows to garble Non-XOR gates using only two wire keys, i.e., $2t$ bits. As proven in [36], "Half Gates" is currently optimal, i.e., its communication overhead of two keys per Non-XOR gate constitutes a lower bound. The combination of the most efficient circuit construction with an optimal garbling scheme then yields state-of-the-art lower bounds on the communication complexity for GC-based (arg)min protocols.

Kolesnikov et al. present the most widely used (arg)min circuit construction in [22]. They select the min in a pairwise tournament tree fashion and construct the argmin while traversing down the tree. The circuit has a size of $2l(M-1)$ gates for finding the min and $n+1$ gates for constructing the argmin [22], resulting in a communication overhead of $(2l(n-1)+(n+1))2t$ bit. Notably, this construction limits the argmin to $\{0, ..., n-1\}$.

Huang et al. [17] propose a different construction to overcome the limitation of the argmin value space, building on the observation that encoding complex data structures directly into the circuit is expensive. Hence, while using the same circuit of size $2l(n-1)$ for finding the min as [24], they replace the argmin functionality with a custom backtracking protocol. This protocol exchanges a fully encrypted backtracking tree from which exactly one path can be decrypted using the wire keys obtained during the evaluating of the garbled min circuit. In [17] $\mathcal{C}$ is allowed to recover the argmin in clear. However, to use their construction as a building block within another secure computation, the argmin must be garbled. This results in an overhead of nlt for encrypting n l-bit argmin values in the tree's leaves and $(n-1)2t$ bit for the two wire keys in each of the $n-1$ inner nodes of the backtracking tree.

Finally, Demmler et al. present the ABY framework for STCs [11] which implements the min circuit proposed in [22] with $2l(n-1)$ gates but does not supply the argmin. We trivially extend their implementation by adding l MUX gates per comparison which, analogous to the min, propagates the l bit argmin to obtain a second construction that fulfills our general problem definition (Sect. 3). A single 1 bit MUX gate can be realized using one Non-XOR gate, hence transmitting the complete circuit requires $3l(n-1)2t$ bit of communication.

3.2 Goldreich-Micali-Wigderson (GMW)

Schneider et al. present *depth-optimized* circuit constructions for GMW [31]. Their (arg)min circuit is based on the construction by Kolesnikov et al. [22] but replaces the size-optimized l-bit comparators with depth-optimized comparators that consists of about two times more gates but allows a logarithmic instead of linear depth in l. The circuit has $(n-1)(4l - \lceil \log_2(l) \rceil - 2 + \lceil \log_2(n) \rceil)$ gates and a depth of $\mathcal{O}(\log_2(n)\log_2(l))$ [31]. To evaluate a single gate, $\mathcal{C}$ and $\mathcal{S}$ exchange 2 bit and engage in one random OT at the costs of $2t$ bit communication overhead (Sect. 2, [11]). Since this construction directly bases on Kolesnikov's [22], it has the same limitations regarding the argmin value space.

The ABY framework presented by Demmler et al. [11] also implements GMW together with the depth-optimized minimum circuit presented in [31] but without the argmin logic. Again, we extend the implementation using MUX gates to relay the argmin along with the computation of the min. In contrast to Schneider's proposed circuit, this construction fulfills our problem definition. The circuit has $(n-1)(5l - \lceil \log_2(l) \rceil - 2)$ gates and a depth of $\mathcal{O}(\log_2(n) \log_2(l))$.

3.3 Homomorphic Encryption (HE)

Most HE-based (arg)min constructions are based on the well-known DGK comparison protocol [8], which allows to compare two Paillier-encrypted integers $[a]$ and $[b]$ and obtain the result as an encrypted bit $[a \leq b]$. It has been used in a variety of applications, e.g., face recognition [12], recommender systems [14], bioinformatics [15], and clustering [13]. The most efficient construction that fulfills our problem definition has been proposed by Erkin et al. [12]. The authors arrange comparisons of values in a pairwise tournament fashion and propagate the min and argmin by multiplying with the encrypted comparison bit, i.e., $[\min(a,b)] = [a \leq b] * [a - b] + [b]$ and $[\text{argmin}(a,b)] = [a \leq b] * [id_a - id_b] + [id_b]$. Each DGK comparison needs to exchange $2l$ DGK ciphertexts and 3 Paillier ciphertexts. To propagate the min and argmin through one comparison, two ciphertext multiplications are required, causing transmission overheads of 6 Paillier ciphertexts [23]. This amounts to a communication complexity of $(n-1)(2l + 8 + 10)T$ bit. While Erkin et al. [12] do not use ciphertext packing in their original work, applying packing to the Paillier ciphertexts exchanged from the server to the client reduces the communication complexity to $(n-1)(2l + 8 + 10/C)T$ bit. Here, $C = \lfloor T/(l + \sigma + 2)) \rfloor$ is the compression rate achieved by packing multiple ciphertexts into one, as detailed in [14].

4   Bandwidth-Optimized Min and Argmin

To address the significant problems arising from high communication overheads in mobile STC, we propose BOMA, a bandwidth-optimized protocol for the secure (arg)min computation on homomorphically encrypted inputs. We emphasize that by using efficient conversions between encrypted, shared, and garbled values [11], BOMA can also be used as a building block to improve (mobile) STC frameworks, e.g., [11,19]. Following, we first present an efficient comparison protocol and based on this propose an efficient (arg)min protocol.

Efficient Secure Comparison: As an important building block, we use Kerschbaum's multi-party comparison protocol [21]. The core idea is to compute the encrypted distance $[d] = [a - b]$ between two encrypted inputs $[a]$ and $[b]$ and let all participants multiplicatively blind $[d]$ while preserving its sign before decrypting it and deciding the comparison. We adapt this multi-party protocol to the two-party setting as follows: $\mathcal{S}$ selects two large random numbers r_1 and $r_2 \in \{0,1\}^{l+\sigma}$ with $r_1 > r_2$ and computes $[\tilde{d}] = [r_1 \cdot (a-b) - r_2]$ under encryption. Note that the multiplicative blinding preserves the sign, i.e., $\tilde{d} \leq 0 \Leftrightarrow a \leq b$. $\mathcal{S}$ then sends the blinded encrypted distance $[\tilde{d}]$ to $\mathcal{C}$ who decrypts it and sends back the encrypted comparison bit $[a \leq b]$ to $\mathcal{S}$. To prevent $\mathcal{C}$ from learning the real outcome of the comparison, $\mathcal{S}$ chooses at random to compare $a \leq b$ or

$b \leq a$ and flips the received comparison bit $[a \leq b]$ accordingly by computing $[1 - (a \leq b)]$ under encryption. Our two-party version of Kerschbaum's comparison exchanges only 2 ciphertexts, i.e., $4T$ bit, between $\mathcal{C}$ and $\mathcal{S}$.

Efficient Secure (arg)min: As a first step, we replace the DGK comparison protocol in Erkin's (arg)min algorithm [12] with our two-party version of Kerschbaum's comparison protocol. By simply using a more efficient comparison protocol, we reduce the communication complexity to $(M - 1)(6 + 10/C)T$ bit, i.e., save $(M-1)(2l+2)T$ bit (cf. Table 1). This represents a significant reduction by 90 % to 97 % depending on the chosen security level t and bitlength l.

We now improve this construction with respect to both processing and communication overhead. In the first phase, the *minimum phase*, we determine the min $[y^*] = [f(x^*)]$ in pairwise comparisons arranged in a tournament fashion as before in [12]. However, we significantly reduce processing overheads and save $2\log_2(n)$ rounds by interleaving comparison and selection steps, thereby shaving off the costly ciphertext multiplications. Our second significant improvement is due to the observation that $\mathcal{C}$ learns the position of the min as a byproduct of this phase. With this information, we construct an efficient OT-based protocol for the second phase, the *minimum argument phase*, in which $\mathcal{C}$ helps $\mathcal{S}$ to obtain an encryption of the argmin $[x^*]$. In the following, we describe the two phases of our BOMA protocol, as depicted in Protocol 1, in detail.

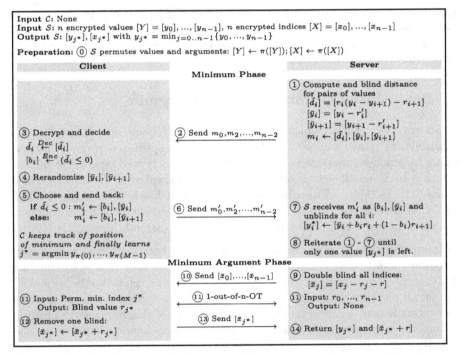

Protocol 1. Bandwidth-optimized (arg)min protocol: The min and its permuted position is calculated. Then, $\mathcal{C}$ and $\mathcal{S}$ run an OT protocol to unblind the argmin.

Minimum Phase: At the beginning, S holds the encrypted values $[y_0], ..., [y_{n-1}]$ and corresponding arguments $[x_0], ..., [x_{n-1}]$ and applies the same permutation π to both ⓪. This permutation prevents C from learning side knowledge, but has no effect on the outcome of the computation. For reasons of simplicity, we thus leave π out in the following notation. At the core of ① - ⑦ are the batched pairwise comparisons according to our two-party version of Kerschbaum's comparison protocol. In ①, S computes the distances $[d_i]$ over the $n/2$ pairs of values $[y_i]$ and $[y_{i+1}], i = 0, 2, .., n - 2$, and blinds the distances as well as the values. S then sends the blinded distances together with the blinded values $[y_i]$ and $[y_{i+1}]$ to C ②. C decrypts the distances and encrypts the binary result of the comparison ③, re-randomizes $[\bar{y}_i]$ and $[\bar{y}_{i+1}]$ ④, and chooses the smaller element ⑤. Finally, C sends back the binary result of this comparison together with only the smaller element of each comparison to S ⑥. Note that S cannot distinguish which elements were received due to the re-randomization and IND-CPA property of the cryptosystem. After unblinding the received values in ⑦, S now holds encryptions of the $n/2$ smaller values of the previous comparisons and repeats ① to ⑦ $\lceil \log_2(n) - 1 \rceil$ times until only the min $[y^*]$ remains ⑧. Our way of interleaving comparison and selection steps not only makes ciphertext packing more efficient, but significantly reduces processing costs and saves two communication rounds per level of the comparison tree, i.e., $2 \cdot \log_2(n)$ rounds in total, as compared to the construction of Erkin et al. [12] which implements selection steps via costly ciphertext multiplication.

Minimum Argument Phase: We further significantly improve the communication overhead by the observation that during the minimum phase it is easy for C to keep track of the position of the outcomes of the comparisons and thereby obtain the position j^* of the min in the *permuted* vector Y. This knowledge is not a security violation since the *permuted* position does not disclose any information to C. In the minimum argument phase, C now helps S to obtain an encryption of the argmin $[x_{j^*}]$. S first blinds all encrypted arguments $[x_j], j = 1...M$ individually by subtracting random values $r_j \in \{0,1\}^{l+\sigma}$ and a second time with a single random value $r \in \{0,1\}^{l+\sigma}$ ⑨. S packs the double blinded arguments and sends them to C ⑩. C and S subsequently engage in 1-out-of-n-$OT^1_{l+\sigma}$ after which C obtains r_{j^*}, the distinct blind of the argmin, without S learning j^* ⑪. Then, C removes this blind from $[\bar{x}_{j^*}]$ by adding r_{j^*} (which automatically re-randomizes the value) ⑫ and sends the value (still blinded by r) to S ⑬. Finally, S removes the second blind by adding r and obtains an encryption of the argmin $[x_{j^*}]$ ⑭.

Communication Complexity. The minimum phase of BOMA costs only $(n - 1)(4 + 6/C)T$ bit. By applying bandwidth-efficient OT protocols (Sect. 2), the minimum argument phase costs $n2T/C$ bit for transferring the blinded arguments and $n(l + \sigma) + 3 \log_2(n)t$ bit for the 1-out-of-n-$OT^1_{l+\sigma}$ of the blind r_{j^*}.

4.1   Security Discussion

We show that our proposed protocol is secure in the semi-honest adversary model based on the security of the employed OT and comparison primitives. In particular, we show that (i) C learns nothing and (ii) S only learns an encryption of the min and argmin but nothing else.

Security Against C. From the messages received in ②, C learns nothing about the values y_i from $\bar{y}_i$ since they are additively blinded with random numbers $r'_i \in \{0,1\}^{l+\sigma}$. Furthermore, C learns nothing from $\tilde{d}_i$ about the distance d_i between y_i and y_{i+1} due to the multiplicative and additive blinding. From the messages received in ⑩, C learns nothing since the arguments x_j are additively blinded using $r_j, r \in \{0,1\}^{l+\sigma}$. The security of ⑪ directly follows from the security proofs of the employed base OT protocol [1,20,27,28]. After the OT has finished ⑪, C learns $x_j - r$ which however is still additively blinded. Finally, C learns the position of the minimum. However, due to the random permutation π applied by S in ⓪ this knowledge is useless to C as long as S keeps π secret.

Note that we use *statistical blinding*, i.e., with low probability $\sim 1/2^{l+\sigma}$ C learns a small amount of information about the magnitude of the blinded values. We can achieve perfect security against C by choosing $\sigma = T$ and substituting Kerschbaum's statistically secure protocol [21] with a perfectly secure protocol, e.g., [34]. However, this significantly increases the communication overhead.

Security Against S. From the messages received in ⑥, S learns the encrypted comparison bit and the encrypted smaller element of the comparison. Due to the IND-CPA property of the employed Paillier cryptosystem and the applied re-randomization, S can neither decide whether $[b_i]$ is an encryption of 0 or 1 nor distinguish $[\bar{y}_i]$ from $[\bar{y}_{i+1}]$. Again, S learns nothing from the OT in ⑪ due to the security of the employed OT primitives [1,20,27,28]. Finally, S receives $[\bar{x}_{j*}]$ which it cannot distinguish from the other arguments $[\bar{x}_{i \neq j*}]$ due to the IND-CPA property of the cryptosystem. Since S can always try to break encryption to learn the inputs, we can only achieve computational security against S.

5   Evaluation

We first compare the communication overhead of existing circuit and protocol constructions against an implementation of our optimized protocol BOMA in Subsect. 5.1. Since BOMA trades increased local processing for a significant reduction in communication overhead, we evaluate processing overheads in Subsect. 5.2 and show that BOMA achieves superior performance under constrained network speeds.

5.1   Quantitative Communication Overhead Analysis

Table 2 shows the communication overhead in MiB of each algorithm over increasing input lengths of $l = 32, 64, 128$ bit in each of the three security levels. We derive the results for Koleschnikov'09 [22], Huang'11 [17], and

Table 2. Communication overhead [MiB] for varying security levels and input sizes. Gray rows denote theoretical estimates, all other values are measured. Approaches marked with an asterisk realize only a constrained argmin functionality.

n = 1000 Elements	short			medium			long		
	32	64	128	32	64	128	32	64	128
* Koles'09	1.24	2.46	4.90	1.73	3.44	6.86	1.98	3.93	7.84
(GC)	193%	370%	629%	154%	299%	554%	123%	240%	456%
Huang'11	1.54	3.07	6.12	2.16	4.30	8.56	2.47	4.91	9.79
(GC)	240%	462%	786%	192%	373%	692%	153%	299%	569%
ABY-YAO'15	1.87	3.73	7.45	2.61	5.21	10.41	2.98	5.95	11.90
(GC)	291%	562%	957%	232%	452%	840%	185%	363%	693%
* Schneider'13	2.53	4.98	9.90	3.53	6.94	13.81	4.03	7.93	15.76
(GMW)	394%	749%	1271%	314%	603%	1115%	250%	483%	917%
ABY-GMW'15	3.07	6.25	12.63	4.26	8.68	17.53	4.86	9.90	19.99
(GMW)	478%	941%	1622%	379%	754%	1416%	302%	603%	1163%
Erkin'09	9.37	17.60	34.13	18.14	34.18	66.31	26.92	50.77	98.49
(HE)	1460%	2650%	4383%	1614%	2967%	5355%	1672%	3094%	5730%
BOMA	0.64	0.66	0.78	1.12	1.15	1.24	1.61	1.64	1.72
(HE+OT)	100%	100%	100%	100%	100%	100%	100%	100%	100%

Schneider'13 [31] based on their theoretical complexities (cf. Table 1), since we could not obtain an actual implementation. Kolesnikov'09 and Schneider'13, the approaches marked with an asterisk, only realize the constrained argmin functionality and solely indicate lower bounds. For ABY-YAO'15 and ABY-GMW'15, we obtain the listed results using the C++ ABY framework [11], which we extended with the missing argmin circuits (cf. Subsect. 3.2). We implement a prototype of BOMA (our own protocol), in Python 2.7. Additionally, we re-implement the (arg)min algorithm by Erkin et al. in our framework, since the available implementation in SeComLib [32] provides neither network support nor ciphertext packing.

For all available implementations, we initially compare the measured and theoretical communication overhead to analyze (i) the accuracy of our theoretical complexity estimates and (ii) the realization of these complexities in the actual implementations. We find that the measured overhead exceeds our estimate by at most 0.5 % for ABY-YAO, 1.5 % for ABY-GMW, 2 % for BOMA (our own protocol), and by less than 6 % for our re-implementation of Erkin's protocol. This deviation stems from the fact that our theoretical complexity estimates do not consider a decrease in packing efficiency when only few ciphertexts are left at the last levels of the comparison tree. Our way of interleaving comparison and selection (Sect. 4) greatly reduces this effect compared to Erkin's protocol design.

Table 2 then shows the communication overhead comparison of existing approaches and our (arg)min protocol (BOMA). We base our evaluation of existing approaches on the best available, i.e., most efficient, constructions of circuits, garbling schemes, and oblivious transfer primitives. BOMA achieves a significant reduction in communication overhead over all settings and even in comparison to the constrained argmin circuits by Kolesnikov'09 (GC) or Schneider'13 (GMW). Specifically, BOMA achieves the largest reductions for small security levels and high bitlengths of the input. With increasing security levels, the relative improvement, in comparison to GC- and GMW-based approaches that rely on symmetric crypto, decreases while still outperforming said approaches. Conversely, larger input bitsizes benefit BOMA. While packing efficiency for communication from S to C only degrades slightly, communication from C to S, which cannot be packed, remains the same since a single l bit value always fits into one ciphertext for $l \leq T$. In contrast, the communication overhead in GC and GMW scales linearly with l. Finally, BOMA outperforms Erkin's HE-based protocol by one to two orders of magnitude in every setting.

5.2   Performance Evaluation

We measure the runtime for ABY-YAO, ABY-GMW, Erkin'09, and BOMA for varying bandwidth and latency in a local setup between a desktop client (Intel i7, $8 \times 2.93\,GHz$, 4 GB RAM) and a server (Intel Xeon, $16 \times 2.6\,GHz$, 32 GB RAM) connected through a middlebox running OpenWRT. We choose a desktop instead of a mobile client to maintain comparability as no ABY implementation for Android or iOS exists. While ABY is fully threaded and thus employs all cores on the client device, we deliberately do not parallelize the client-side functionality in our BOMA implementation to emulate processing resources comparable to those of a mobile device, e.g., a smart phone. Since all overheads scale linearly in the number of elements n, we fix $n = 1000$. This is sufficiently large to eliminate small scale effects but also maintains short runtimes allowing for a repeated, thorough evaluation, i.e., averaging all results over 30 runs.

Network Bandwidth. We first vary the bandwidth between 1 Mbit/s and 10 Mbit/s using netem on the middlebox. Table 3 gives an overview of the resulting runtimes. For short-term security and at a bandwidth of 10 Mbit/s, BOMA performs in the same order of magnitude as ABY-YAO and ABY-GMW. Reducing to 1 Mbit/s, the runtime of BOMA doubles while the runtimes of ABY-YAO and ABY-GMW increase by roughly one order of magnitude. Communication overhead clearly dominates the runtime in these approaches and BOMA hence outperforms them. As indicated by the theoretical complexity, the approach by Erkin et al. [12] is by orders of magnitude slower. For $l = 32$ and short term security, the algorithm required almost 1 min, even already without bandwidth constraints. Due to this prohibitive runtime, we waived further measurements.

Increasing the security level to medium impacts BOMA more than ABY-YAO or ABY-GMW, due to the use of asymmetric crypto. Here, BOMA roughly matches the runtime of ABY-YAO for $l = 32, 64, 128$ at bandwidths between 1 Mbit/s and 5 Mbit/s and ABY-GMW between 2 Mbit/s and 10 Mbit/s. Still, we observe that BOMA outperforms these approaches in constrained networks (1 Mbit/s to 2 Mbit/s) and/or higher input sizes $l = 64, 128$.

Increasing to long term security, we observe that processing overheads begin to dominate the performance of BOMA, i.e., the relative difference of

Table 3. Protocol runtimes [s] for varying security levels, input lengths and bandwidths for state-of-the-art GC-, GMW- and HE-based argmin protocols.

n = 1000 Elements		short			medium			long		
		32	64	128	32	64	128	32	64	128
ABY-YAO	1 Mbit/s	16.70	33.50	67.02	23.35	46.71	93.64	26.71	53.46	107.21
	2 Mbit/s	8.44	16.90	33.75	11.70	23.54	46.85	13.48	26.81	53.51
	5 Mbit/s	3.38	6.92	13.86	4.81	9.68	19.21	5.32	10.91	21.78
	10 Mbit/s	1.76	3.72	7.19	2.56	5.13	9.92	2.81	5.68	11.17
ABY-GMW	1 Mbit/s	27.61	56.15	113.45	38.28	77.95	157.46	43.54	88.79	179.21
	2 Mbit/s	13.87	28.14	56.69	19.08	38.94	78.55	21.76	44.39	89.51
	5 Mbit/s	5.74	11.56	23.10	7.86	15.84	31.79	8.95	18.03	36.21
	10 Mbit/s	3.12	6.09	11.90	4.17	8.25	16.33	4.72	9.40	18.50
BOMA	1 Mbit/s	8.96	9.41	11.00	22.74	23.88	27.20	42.86	45.59	51.57
	2 Mbit/s	6.65	7.09	8.28	18.03	19.20	22.38	36.34	38.84	44.33
	5 Mbit/s	5.33	5.72	6.74	15.34	16.54	19.39	32.46	34.92	40.23
	10 Mbit/s	4.88	5.34	6.24	14.43	15.69	18.41	31.29	33.68	38.99

the performance at speeds of 10 Mbit/s and 1 Mbit/s is much smaller than for shorter security levels. Contrarily, for ABY-GMW and ABY-YAO, which exhibit very low processing overheads, bandwidth restrictions continue to dominate the overall protocol runtime. In comparison, BOMA still outperforms ABY-YAO up to bandwidths of 2 Mbit/s and ABY-GMW up to 5 Mbit/s for $l = 128$ bit inputs. For $l = 32, 64$ and larger bandwidths, BOMA's performance is slower but in general lies within the same order of magnitude as ABY-YAO and ABY-GMW.

Network Latency. Latency has the biggest impact on GMW-based protocols which have a high round complexity of $\mathcal{O}(\log_2(n)\log_2(l))$. Assuming, e.g., a relatively high latency of 200 ms, this adds 10 s to 14 s to the overall runtime for computing the argmin over $n = 1000$ and $l = 32, 128$ bit values, respectively. Under the same assumptions, BOMA's runtime increases only by approximately 2 s due to its lower round complexity of $\mathcal{O}(\log_2(n))$. GC-based protocols experience nearly no increase in runtime due to their constant round complexity. Hence, settings with higher network latencies favor BOMA over GMW-based approaches while the overhead compared to GC-based approaches is almost negligible.

In summary, the evaluation results support our initial design goals of supporting STC in mobile environments where network bandwidths are neither constant nor comparable to fixed, high-performance settings. Specifically, the improved performance of BOMA under the reduced network speeds of 3G or LTE networks, i.e., 1 Mbit/s – 10 Mbit/s as found in typical current urban scenarios, highlights the suitability of our protocol for spontaneous interaction and applications.

6   Conclusion

In this paper, we address the important problem of securely computing the (arg)min in a mobile ad-hoc setting where protocol participants had no prior interaction. Our analysis of the most efficient GC-, GMW-, and HE-based solutions reveals significant communication overheads that can be prohibitive in constrained, e.g., cellular, networks in terms of direct costs, energy consumption, and overall protocol runtime. We hence propose BOMA, a novel (arg)min protocol based on HE and OT that reduces communication overheads by orders of magnitude compared to related work (by 18 % – 98 %). Specifically, our approach trades communication overhead for local processing. Our quantitative evaluation shows a better performance by our protocol in many settings compared to state-of-the-art GC- and GMW-based solutions, e.g., in constrained networks operating at speeds below 1 Mbit/s to 10 Mbit/s, depending on the chosen security level and bitlength of the inputs. Using efficient conversion between encrypted, shared, and garbled values [11] our protocol can be used as a valuable building block for efficient mobile STCs in GC or GMW-based frameworks [11,19].

A   Min and Argmin with Shared Inputs

In Sect. 3, we define the secure min/argmin problem as a building block within another secure computation. This definition neglects those parts of the overheads which are due to sharing inputs between client and server. We thus shortly discuss a second version of the problem where $\mathcal{C}$ and $\mathcal{S}$ each hold half of the inputs and the client obtains the output.

Table 4. Communication complexity [bit] and rounds for the second problem definition, i.e., min and argmin computation with shared inputs.

Protocol	Communication Overhead	Rounds
* Kolesnikov'09 [22] (GC)	$2l(n-1)2t + (n+1)2t + {}^3/_2 nlt$	$\mathcal{O}(1)$
Huang'11 [17] (GC)	$2l(n-1)2t + n \cdot \max\{l, t\} + (n-1)2t + {}^3/_2 nlt$	$\mathcal{O}(1)$
Demmler'15 [11] (GC)	$3l(n-1)2t + 3nlt$	$\mathcal{O}(1)$
* Schneider'13 [31] (GMW)	$(n-1)(4l - \lceil \log_2(l) \rceil - 2 + \lceil \log_2(n) \rceil)(2t+2) + nl$	$\mathcal{O}(\log_2(n)\log_2(l))$
Demmler'15 [11] (GMW)	$(n-1)(5l - \lceil \log_2(l) \rceil - 2)(2t+2) + 2nl$	$\mathcal{O}(\log_2(n)\log_2(l))$
Erkin'09 [12] (HE)	$(n-1)(2l + 8 + 10/C)T + nT$	$\mathcal{O}(\log_2(n))$
BOMA (HE+OT)	$(n-1)(4 + 6/C)T + 2nT/C + n(l+\sigma) + 3\log_2(n)t + nt$	$\mathcal{O}(\log_2(n))$

For GCs, $\mathcal{S}$ sends its garbled inputs to $\mathcal{C}$, amounting to nlt bit of communication. $\mathcal{C}$ obtains its own inputs via correlated OT from $\mathcal{S}$ at a cost of $2nlt$ bit. These overheads are halved for Kolesnikov'09 [22] where the arguments are implicit and not part of the inputs as well as for Huang'11 where the arguments are encrypted in the backtracking tree. Sharing inputs in GMW-based approaches requires only $2nl$ bit, i.e., 1 bit per input bit. Again, this overhead is halved for the restricted (arg)min circuit of Schneider'13 [31]. For both Erkin's protocol and ours, only $\mathcal{C}$'s inputs need to be sent to $\mathcal{S}$ in encrypted form, requiring $2nT$ bit of communication. We summarize the overall complexity in Table 4.

Table 5. Communication overhead [MiB] for varying security levels and input sizes. All numbers are theoretical estimates.

n = 1000 Elements	short			medium			long		
	32	64	128	32	64	128	32	64	128
* Koles'09	1.85	3.68	7.34	2.59	5.15	10.28	2.96	5.89	11.75
(GC)	225%	425%	792%	164%	320%	612%	127%	249%	483%
Huang'11	1.71	3.38	6.75	2.39	4.74	9.44	2.73	5.41	10.78
(GC)	207%	391%	727%	152%	294%	562%	117%	229%	443%
ABY-YAO'15	2.75	5.49	10.98	3.84	7.69	15.37	4.39	8.79	17.57
(GC)	334%	634%	1184%	244%	477%	915%	189%	372%	722%
* Schneider'13	2.53	4.99	9.93	3.53	6.96	13.84	4.03	7.94	15.79
(GMW)	308%	577%	1071%	224%	432%	824%	173%	336%	649%
ABY-GMW'15	2.96	6.03	12.20	4.13	8.41	17.01	4.71	9.60	19.42
(GMW)	360%	697%	1316%	262%	522%	1013%	202%	406%	798%
Erkin'09	9.12	16.97	32.64	18.14	33.79	65.08	27.16	50.62	97.52
(HE)	1108%	1960%	3520%	1152%	2096%	3875%	1167%	2141%	4008%
BOMA	0.82	0.87	0.93	1.58	1.61	1.68	2.33	2.36	2.43
(HE+OT)	100%	100%	100%	100%	100%	100%	100%	100%	100%

We implement and evaluate this second (arg)min problem. As before, we observe an implementation overhead of at most 3 % compared to the complexities in Table 4. Only the measurements for ABY-YAO significantly deviate by 14 % and 27 % coupled with a large standard deviation in the send traffic. Since this renders the measurements incomparable, we present only a comparison of the theoretical communication overhead in Table 5. The results are qualitatively very similar to the results for our initial problem definition (Table 2 in Subsect. 5.1). Furthermore, the processing required for sharing the inputs is very low in all approaches. Thus, for our second problem definition, we expect qualitatively very similar results to those presented in Subsect. 5.2.

References

1. Asharov, G., Lindell, Y., Schneider, T., Zohner, M.: More efficient oblivious transfer and extensions for faster secure computation. In: ACM CCS. ACM (2013)
2. Barker, E., Barker, W., Burr, W., Polk, W., Smid, M.: Nist special publication 800–57. NIST Special Publication **800**(57), 1–142 (2007)
3. Bellare, M., Hoang, V.T., Keelveedhi, S., Rogaway, P.: Efficient garbling from a fixed-key blockcipher. In: IEEE SP, pp. 478–492. IEEE (2013)
4. Carter, H., Amrutkar, C., Dacosta, I., Traynor, P.: For your phone only: custom protocols for efficient secure function evaluation on mobile devices. SCN **7**(7), 1165–1176 (2014)
5. Carter, H., Lever, C., Traynor, P.: Whitewash: Outsourcing garbled circuit generation for mobile devices. In: ACSAC, pp. 266–275. ACM (2014)

6. Carter, H., Mood, B., Traynor, P., Butler, K.: Secure outsourced garbled circuit evaluation for mobile devices. In: USENIX Security. USENIX (2013)
7. Costantino, G., Martinelli, F., Santi, P., Amoruso, D.: An implementation of secure two-party computation for smartphones with application to privacy-preserving interest-cast. In: PST, pp. 9–16 (2012)
8. Damgard, I., Geisler, M., Kroigard, M.: Homomorphic encryption and secure comparison. Int. J. Appl. Crypt. 1(1), 22–31 (2008)
9. De Cristofaro, E., Faber, S., Gasti, P., Tsudik, G.: Genodroid: are privacy-preserving genomic tests ready for prime time? In: ACM WPES. ACM (2012)
10. Demmler, D., Schneider, T., Zohner, M.: Ad-hoc secure two-party computation on mobile devices using hardware tokens. In: USENIX Security (2014)
11. Demmler, D., Schneider, T., Zohner, M.: ABY - a framework for efficient mixed-protocol secure two-party computation. In: NDSS (2015)
12. Erkin, Z., Franz, M., Guajardo, J., Katzenbeisser, S., Lagendijk, I., Toft, T.: Privacy-preserving face recognition. In: Goldberg, I., Atallah, M.J. (eds.) PETS 2009. LNCS, vol. 5672, pp. 235–253. Springer, Heidelberg (2009)
13. Erkin, Z., Veugen, T., Toft, T., Lagendijk, R.L.: Privacy-preserving user clustering in a social network. In: IEEE WIFS, pp. 96–100. IEEE (2009)
14. Erkin, Z., Veugen, T., Toft, T., Lagendijk, R.L.: Generating private recommendations efficiently using homomorphic encryption and data packing. IEEE Trans. Inf. Forensics Secur. 7(3), 1053–1066 (2012)
15. Franz, M., Deiseroth, B., Hamacher, K., Jha, S., Katzenbeisser, S., Schröder, H.: Towards secure bioinformatics services (Short Paper). In: Danezis, G. (ed.) FC 2011. LNCS, vol. 7035, pp. 276–283. Springer, Heidelberg (2012)
16. Goldreich, O., Micali, S., Wigderson, A.: How to play ANY mental game. In: ACM STOC, pp. 218–229. ACM (1987)
17. Huang, Y., Evans, D., Katz, J., Malka, L.: Efficient privacy-preserving biometric identification. In: NDSS (2011)
18. Huang, Y., Chapman, P., Evans, D.: Privacy-preserving applications on smartphones. In: USENIX HotSec. USENIX (2011)
19. Huang, Y., Evans, D., Katz, J., Malka, L.: Faster secure two-party computation using garbled circuits. In: USENIX Security. USENIX (2011)
20. Ishai, Y., Kilian, J., Nissim, K., Petrank, E.: Extending oblivious transfers efficiently. In: Boneh, D. (ed.) CRYPTO 2003. LNCS, vol. 2729, pp. 145–161. Springer, Heidelberg (2003)
21. Kerschbaum, F., Biswas, D., de Hoogh, S.: Performance comparison of secure comparison protocols. In: DEXA, pp. 133–136. IEEE (2009)
22. Kolesnikov, V., Sadeghi, A.-R., Schneider, T.: Improved garbled circuit building blocks and applications to auctions and computing minima. In: Garay, J.A., Miyaji, A., Otsuka, A. (eds.) CANS 2009. LNCS, vol. 5888, pp. 1–20. Springer, Heidelberg (2009)
23. Kolesnikov, V., Sadeghi, A.R., Schneider, T.: From dust to dawn: practically efficient two-party secure function evaluation protocols and their modular design. IACR Cryptology ePrint Archive (2010)
24. Kolesnikov, V., Schneider, T.: Improved garbled circuit: free XOR gates and applications. In: Aceto, L., Damgård, I., Goldberg, L.A., Halldórsson, M.M., Ingólfsdóttir, A., Walukiewicz, I. (eds.) ICALP 2008, Part II. LNCS, vol. 5126, pp. 486–498. Springer, Heidelberg (2008)
25. Kreuter, B., Shelat, A., Mood, B., Butler, K.R.: PCF: a portable circuit format for scalable two-party secure computation. In: USENIX Security. USENIX (2013)

26. Malkhi, D., Nisan, N., Pinkas, B., Sella, Y.: Fairplay - a secure two-party computation system. In: USENIX Security. USENIX (2004)
27. Naor, M., Pinkas, B.: Efficient oblivious transfer protocols. In: SODA, pp. 448–457. SIAM (2001)
28. Naor, M., Pinkas, B.: Computationally secure oblivious transfer. J. Cryptology 18(1), 1–35 (2005)
29. Paillier, P.: Public-Key Cryptosystems Based on Composite Degree Residuosity Classes. In: Stern, J. (ed.) EUROCRYPT 1999. LNCS, vol. 1592, pp. 223–238. Springer, Heidelberg (1999)
30. Rane, S., Boufounos, P.: Privacy-preserving nearest neighbor methods. IEEE Signal Process. Mag. 30(2), 18–28 (2013)
31. Schneider, T., Zohner, M.: GMW vs. Yao? efficient secure two-party computation with low depth circuits. In: Sadeghi, A.-R. (ed.) FC 2013. LNCS, vol. 7859, pp. 275–292. Springer, Heidelberg (2013)
32. Secomlib. http://cybersecurity.tudelft.nl/content/secomlib
33. Songhori, E.M., Hussain, S.U., Sadeghi, A.R., Schneider, T., Koushanfar, F.: Tiny-Garble: highly compressed and scalable sequential garbled circuits. In: IEEE SP. IEEE (2015)
34. Veugen, T.: Improving the DGK comparison protocol. In: IEEE WIFS. IEEE (2012)
35. Yao, A.: How to generate and exchange secrets. In: FOCS, pp. 62–167. IEEE (1986)
36. Zahur, S., Rosulek, M., Evans, D.: Two halves make a whole. In: Oswald, E., Fischlin, M. (eds.) EUROCRYPT 2015. LNCS, vol. 9057, pp. 220–250. Springer, Heidelberg (2015)
37. Ziegeldorf, J.H., Metzke, J., Henze, M., Wehrle, K.: Choose wisely: a comparison of secure two-party computation frameworks. In: IEEE SPW. IEEE (2015)

Outsourcing Secure Two-Party Computation as a Black Box

Henry Carter[1]([⊠]), Benjamin Mood[2], Patrick Traynor[2], and Kevin Butler[2]

[1] Georgia Institute of Technology, Atlanta, USA
carterh@gatech.edu
[2] University of Florida, Gainesville, USA
bmood@ufl.edu, {traynor,butler}@cise.ufl.edu

Abstract. Secure multiparty computation (SMC) offers a technique to preserve functionality and data privacy in mobile applications. Current protocols that make this costly cryptographic construction feasible on mobile devices securely outsource the bulk of the computation to a Cloud provider. However, these outsourcing techniques are built on specific secure computation assumptions and tools, and applying new SMC ideas to the outsourced setting requires the protocols to be completely rebuilt and proven secure. In this work, we develop a generic technique for lifting any secure two-party computation protocol into an outsourced two-party SMC protocol. By augmenting the function being evaluated with auxiliary consistency checks, we can create an outsourced protocol with low overhead cost. Our implementation and evaluation show that in the best case, our outsourcing additions execute within the confidence intervals of two servers running the same computation, and incur approximately the same communication cost. In addition, the mobile device itself requires minimal communication exchanged over a single round. This work demonstrates that efficient outsourcing is possible with any underlying SMC scheme, and implements an outsourcing protocol that is efficient and directly applicable to current and future SMC techniques.

1 Introduction

As the mobile computing market continues to grow, maintaining the privacy of user data stored on insecure or untrusted application servers is becoming more challenging. To better preserve privacy and functionality in these applications, secure multiparty computation (SMC) techniques offer protocols that allow application servers to process user data while it remains encrypted. Unfortunately, most existing SMC protocols require too much processing power and device memory to be practical on the mobile platform. Furthermore, the communication and power needed for SMC will always be a limiting requirement for mobile applications.

To bring SMC to the mobile platform in a more efficient way, recent work has focused on developing secure techniques for outsourcing the most expensive computation to an untrusted Cloud. A number of these protocols have been

© Springer International Publishing Switzerland 2015
M. Reiter and D. Naccache (Eds.): CANS 2015, LNCS 9476, pp. 214–222, 2015.
DOI: 10.1007/978-3-319-26823-1_15

specifically developed to outsource garbled circuit protocols [3,4,13], and are only proven secure for specific SMC constructions. As other constructions for SMC are developed, it is unclear whether these outsourcing protocols will be able to take advantage of the new developments.

In this work, we develop a technique for outsourcing secure two-party computation for *any* two-party SMC technique. To do this, we add a small amount of overhead to the underlying function being evaluated to ensure that none of the inputs are modified by malicious participants. This "augmented function" can then be evaluated using any SMC protocol that meets the standard definition of security. This protocol enables mobile devices to participate in *any secure two-party SMC protocol* with minimal cost to the device and with nominal overhead to the servers running the computation. Specifically, we make the following contributions:

- **Develop a black box outsourcing protocol:** We develop and prove the security of a novel outsourcing technique for lifting any two-party SMC protocol into the two-party outsourced setting. Unlike previous generic outsourcing approaches [12], this allows for *any* SMC protocol to be outsourced, not strictly reactive SMC protocols.
- **Implement and evaluate the overhead cost of the outsourcing operations:** Using the garbled circuit protocol of shelat and Shen [20], we implement our protocol and evaluate the overhead cost of outsourcing. Our results show that for large circuits, black box outsourcing incurs negligible overhead (i.e., the confidence intervals for outsourced and server only execution intersect) in evaluation time and communication cost when compared to evaluating the unmodified function. In the full version of this work [5], we demonstrate the practical use of our protocol with a mobile-specific facial recognition application based on the Scifi protocol [19].

2   Related Work

Since it was initially conceived in the early 1980's [21], secure multiparty computation has grown from a theoretical novelty to a potentially practical cryptographic construction. Since then, SMC protocols have been developed using homomorphic encryption [6], secret sharing [8], and garbled circuits [21]. While techniques developed in the semi-honest adversary model are relatively efficient [11], malicious secure SMC protocols [16,20] typically have significant overhead cost that makes them infeasible to execute without sizable processing, memory, and communication resources.

With smartphone applications retrieving private user data at an increasing rate, SMC could potentially offer a way to maintain privacy and functionality in mobile computing. However, the efficiency challenges of SMC are compounded when considered in the resource-constrained mobile environment. Previous work has shown that smartphones are generally limited to simple functions in the semi-honest setting [2,10]. Demmler et al. [7] showed how to incorporate precomputation on hardware tokens to improve efficiency on mobile devices, but still in the semi-honest setting. In addition to the cost of evaluating these SMC protocols, Mood et al. [18] and Kreuter et al. [15] demonstrated that even with significant optimization, the task of compiling circuits on the mobile device can also be quite costly.

Given these limitations, evaluating SMC protocols directly on mobile hardware does not seem possible in the immediate future. Because of this, mobile secure computation research has recently focused on applying techniques from server-assisted cryptography [1] to move the most costly cryptographic operations off of the mobile device and onto a more capable Cloud server. The first protocol to outsource a general SMC protocol was developed by Kamara et al. [13], which established a definition of security that assumes specific parties in the computation, while malicious, are not allowed to collude. Following this definition, several other protocols and efficiency improvements have been developed for the outsourced setting [3,4,17]. Unfortunately, these protocols are built on specific SMC constructions. With new techniques for SMC being developed at a rapid pace, it is unclear how to apply the outsourcing techniques used in these protocols to new schemes. In this work, we seek to develop a protocol that can lift *any* two-party SMC protocol into the outsourced setting with little overhead.

In recent work, Jakobsen et al. [12] develop a framework for outsourcing secure computation that is similar to our protocol. However, their protocol requires specific properties in the underlying SMC protocol, where our protocol is designed to be truly generic. Our implementation and empirical performance analysis demonstrate that the added circuit overhead required by our protocol does not significantly affect the execution time for large circuits, and allows for truly generic SMC outsourcing. We examine the tradeoffs between these two protocols in the full version of this work [5].

3   Protocol

3.1   Setting

Here we describe the protocol participants. As with the existing protocols in this setting, we assume that the application server and Cloud do not collude. We prove security in the full version of our work [5] using the definition set forth by Kamara et al. [13].

- SERVER: the application or web server participating in a secure computation with the mobile device. This party provides input to the function being evaluated.
- MOBILE: the mobile device accessing SERVER to jointly compute some result. This party also provides input to the function being evaluated.
- CLOUD: a computation provider that assists MOBILE in the expensive operations of the secure computation. This party executes any two-party SMC protocol with SERVER, but does not provide input to the function being evaluated.

3.2 Protocol Description

Common Input: All parties agree on a computational security parameter k, a message authentication code (MAC) scheme $(Gen(), Mac(), Ver())$, and a malicious secure two-party computation protocol $2PC()$. All parties agree on a two-output function $f(x, y) \rightarrow f_m, f_s$ that is to be evaluated.

Private Input: MOBILE inputs x while SERVER inputs y. We denote the bit length of a value as $|x|$ and concatenation as $x||y$.

Output: SERVER receives f_s and MOBILE receives f_m.

1. **Input preparation:** MOBILE generates a one-time pad k_{fm} where $|k_{fm}| = |f_m|$. Mobile then generates two MAC keys $v_s = Gen(k)$ and $v_c = Gen(k)$. Finally, MOBILE generates a one-time pad k_m where $|k_m| = |x| + |k_{fm}|$.
2. **Input delivery:** MOBILE encrypts its input as $a = (x||k_{fm}) \oplus k_m$. It then generates two tags $t_s = Mac(a||v_c, v_s)$ and $t_c = Mac(k_m||v_s, v_c)$. MOBILE delivers a, v_c, and t_s to SERVER and k_m, v_s, and t_c to CLOUD.
3. **Augmenting the target function:** All parties agree on the following augmented function $g(y, a, v_c, t_s; k_m, v_s, t_c)$ to be run as a two-party SMC computation:
   (a) If $Ver(a||v_c, t_s, v_s) \neq 1$ or $Ver(k_m||v_s, t_c, v_c) \neq 1$ output $\perp$.
   (b) Set $x||k_{fm} = a \oplus k_m$
   (c) Run the desired function $f_s, f_m = f(x, y)$
   (d) Set output values $o_s = f_s$ and $o_m = f_m \oplus k_{fm}$
   (e) Output $o_s||o_m$ to SERVER and o_m to CLOUD
4. **Two-party computation:** SERVER and CLOUD execute a secure two-party computation protocol $2PC(g(); y, a, v_c, t_s; k_m, v_s, t_c)$ evaluating the augmented function.
5. **Output verification:** CLOUD delivers its output from the two-party computation, o_m to MOBILE. SERVER also delivers the second half of its output o'_m to MOBILE. MOBILE verifies that $o_m = o'_m$.
6. **Output recovery:** SERVER receives output $f_s = o_s$ and MOBILE receives output $f_m = o_m \oplus k_{fm}$.

Security. Our protocol intuitively provides both correctness and privacy for the MOBILE input and output based on the underlying components. Privacy is achieved based on the security of the underlying SMC protocol as well as the input and output one-time pads. Correctness is based on three main points. The MAC evaluated within the circuit ensures that the MOBILE input is correct. The correctness of the circuit evaluation itself is guaranteed by the underlying SMC protocol. Finally, the correctness of the output is ensured by the security model assumption that at least one of the SERVER and CLOUD are behaving semi-honestly. Thus, any tampering with the MOBILE output by the malicious party will be detected when compared to the output provided by the semi-honest party. For a formal simulation proof of security, refer to the full version of this work [5].

4   Performance Evaluation

To demonstrate the practical efficiency of our black box outsourcing protocol, we implemented the protocol and examined the actual overhead incurred by the augmented circuit. We initially considered comparing our protocol to existing implementations of outsourcing protocols [3,4,13]. However, existing protocols are built on fixed underlying SMC techniques. As new protocols for two-party SMC are developed, the plug-and-play nature of our protocol allows for these new techniques to be applied, which would provide a different comparison for each underlying protocol. Instead, we chose to compare the overhead execution costs of our black box protocol to performing the same computation in the underlying two-party protocol. Because the MOBILE operations requires seconds or less to execute, we focus our attention on the cost at the two executing servers. This analysis demonstrates two key benefits of our protocol. First, it gives a rough overhead cost for outsourcing garbled circuit protocols. Second, it demonstrates that our outsourcing technique allows a mobile device with restricted computational capability to participate in a privacy-preserving computation in approximately the same amount of time as the same computation performed between two servers. Essentially, we show that our protocol provides a mobile version of any two-party SMC protocol with nominal overhead cost to the servers. This is a novel evaluation methodology not used to evaluate previous black box SMC constructions, and provides a baseline estimate for performance when applying a new underlying SMC construction.

4.1   System Design

Our protocol implementation uses the garbled circuit protocol developed by shelat and Shen [20] as the underlying two-party SMC protocol. We selected this protocol because it is among the most recently developed garbled circuit protocols and it has the most stable public release. We emphasize that it is possible to implement our outsourcing on *any* two-party SMC protocol, such as the recent protocols developed to reduce the cost of cut-&-choose [9,16]. We implement our MAC within the augmented circuit using AES in cipher-block chaining mode (CBC-MAC), as the AES circuit is well-studied in the context of garbled circuit execution. This MAC implementation adds an invocation of AES per 128-bit block of input. Using the compiler developed by Kreuter et al. [14], the overhead non-XOR gate count in the augmented circuit based on input size is $(\frac{|x|15686}{128})$ for input x. We provide exact gate counts with overhead measurements for each tested application in Table 1.

Testbed. Our experiments were run on a single server equipped with 64 cores and 1 TB of RAM. For each execution, the application server and cloud were run as 32 processes communicating via the Message Passing Interface (MPI) framework. The mobile device was a Samsung Galaxy Nexus with a 1.2 GHz dual-core ARM Cortex-A9 processor and 1 GB of RAM, running Android version 4.0.

Table 1. Comparing the original function size to the augmented outsourcing circuit. As the size of the circuit grows, the increase in gates incurred by outsourcing becomes vanishingly small.

Program name	SS13 total	BB total	Increase	SS13 Non-XOR	BB Non-XOR	Increase
Dijkstra10	259,232	456,326	1.8x	118,357	179,641	1.5x
Dijkstra20	1,653,542	1,949,820	1.2x	757,197	849,445	1.1x
Dijkstra50	22,109,732	22,605,018	1.0x	10,170,407	10,324,317	1.0x
MatrixMult3x3	424,748	1,020,196	2.4x	161,237	345,417	2.1x
MatrixMult5x5	1,968,452	3,360,956	1.7x	746,977	1,176,981	1.6x
MatrixMult8x8	8,069,506	11,354,394	1.4x	3,060,802	4,075,082	1.3x
MatrixMult16x16	64,570,969	77,423,481	1.2x	24,494,338	28,458,635	1.2x
RSA128	116,083,727	116,463,648	1.0x	41,082,205	41,208,553	1.0x

The mobile device communicated with the test server over an 802.11n wireless connection in an isolated network environment. We ran each experiment 10 times and averaged the results with 95 % confidence intervals.

We selected a representative set of test applications from previous literature [3,14,15,20] to measure the performance of our protocol over varying circuit and input sizes. We test multiplication of $n \times n$ matrices and 128-bit RSA as implemented by Kreuter et al. [14] and Dijkstra's algorithm for n-node graphs as implemented by Carter et al. [4].

4.2 Execution Time

With the mobile operations minimized to $O(|x| + |o_m|)$ symmetric key operations, our experiments showed a diminishing cost of server overhead as the size of the test application increased. Considering Dijkstra's algorithm in Fig. 1 shows that for a graph of 10 nodes, the outsourcing operations incur a 2.1x slowdown from running the protocol between two servers. However, as the number of graph nodes increases to 50, the confidence intervals for outsourced and server-only execution overlap, indicating a virtually non-existent overhead cost. When we compare these results to the gate counts shown in Table 1, we see that as the gate count for the underlying protocol increases, the additive cost of running the input MAC and output duplication amortize over the total execution time. This is to be expected from our predicted overhead of 15686 non-XOR gates for each CBC-MAC block in the input. However, since the mobile input for Dijkstra's algorithm is of a fixed size, we observe that increasing the application server input size does not add to the outsourcing overhead, showing the black box protocol to be more efficient for large circuit sizes with small mobile input.

When we consider a growing mobile input size, we observe the overhead cost of the MAC operation performed on the mobile input. In the matrix multiplication test program, we observed a 2.6x slowdown for the smallest input size of a 3×3 matrix (Fig. 1). As in the previous experiment, this overhead diminished to a 1.3x slowdown for the largest input size, but diminished at a slower rate when compared to the circuit size. This is a result of additional AES invocations to handle the increasing mobile input size. However, the reduction in overhead

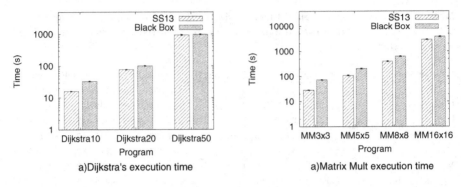

Fig. 1. Dijkstra and matrix multiplication execution time in seconds for $k = 80$. Note that the execution overhead diminishes even as the mobile input size increases.

Table 2. Comparing SS13 and Black Box execution time in seconds (ex) and communication cost in bytes (com). Note that as the circuit size increases, the increase in execution time and communication cost caused by outsourcing becomes insignificant.

Program name	SS13 (ex)	BB (ex)	Increase (ex)	SS13 (com)	BB (com)	Increase (com)
Dijkstra10	$16 \pm 1\%$	$33 \pm 1\%$	2.1x	2.44×10^9	3.87×10^9	1.6x
Dijkstra20	$77 \pm 1\%$	$100 \pm 1\%$	1.3x	1.52×10^{10}	1.73×10^{10}	1.1x
Dijkstra50	$940 \pm 2\%$	$980 \pm 2\%$	1.0x	2.02×10^{11}	2.05×10^{11}	1.0x
MatrixMult3x3	$28.6 \pm 0.8\%$	$73.2 \pm 0.5\%$	2.6x	3.43×10^9	7.66×10^9	2.2x
MatrixMult5x5	$110 \pm 2\%$	$200 \pm 2\%$	1.9x	1.57×10^{10}	2.56×10^{10}	1.6x
MatrixMult8x8	$400 \pm 2\%$	$627 \pm 0.9\%$	1.6x	6.43×10^{10}	8.73×10^{10}	1.4x
MatrixMult16x16	$2900 \pm 1\%$	$3800 \pm 2\%$	1.3x	5.11×10^{11}	6.01×10^{11}	1.2x
RSA128	$4700 \pm 2\%$	$4900 \pm 3\%$	1.0x	8.69×10^{11}	8.72×10^{11}	1.0x

shows that even as input sizes increase, the circuit size is still the main factor in execution overhead.

In our final experiment, we considered a massive circuit representing one of the most complex garbled circuit programs evaluated to date. When comparing the outsourced execution to a standard two-party execution, the overhead incurred by the outsourcing operations is almost non-existent, as shown in Table 2. This experiment confirms the trends of diminishing overhead cost observed in the previous two experiments. From this and previous work, we know that evaluating large circuits from mobile devices is *not possible* without outsourcing the bulk of computation. Given that many real-world applications will require on the order of billions of gates to evaluate, this experiment shows that our black box outsourcing technique allows mobile devices to participate in secure two-party computation at roughly the same efficiency as two server-class machines executing the same computation.

4.3   Communication Cost

Because transmitting data from a mobile device is costly in terms of time and power usage, we attempted to minimize the communication cost at the mobile device. Our protocol requires only $2(|x| + 2k) + 4(|o_m|)$ bits to be transmitted to and from the mobile, were x is the mobile input, o_m is the mobile output, and k is the security parameter. For the RSA circuit, this would amount to 136 bytes of data sent and received. To perform the same computation without outsourcing, Carter et al. [4] show that several gigabytes of data would be required if the mobile device possessed enough memory to perform the computation at all. Because our mobile communication is nearly minimal and easily calculated for any program, we focused our evaluation on measuring the communication overhead incurred between the application server and the Cloud.

As with execution time, Table 2 shows an inverse relation between circuit size and communication overhead. Theoretically, the communication overhead should approximately match the overhead in circuit size shown in Table 1. The experiments confirmed that the actual overhead was equal to or slightly larger than the overhead in non-XOR gates in the circuit. The reason for this correlation is twofold. First, the free-XOR technique used in the shelat-Shen protocol allows XOR gates to be represented without sending any data over the network. Thus, adding additional XOR gates does not incur communication cost. Second, in cases where the actual overhead is slightly larger than the circuit size overhead, we determined that the added cost was a result of additional oblivious transfers needed for longer inputs. These operations require the transmission of large algebraic group elements, so the test circuits which incurred increased overhead from the growth of the mobile input showed a slightly larger communication overhead as well. Ultimately, as in the case of execution time, our experiments demonstrate that black box outsourcing incurs minimal communication cost at the mobile device with diminishing overhead between the application server and the Cloud.

Acknowledgments. This work is based upon work supported by the U.S. National Science Foundation under grant numbers CNS-1540217 and CNS-1464088.

References

1. Beaver, D.: Server-assisted cryptography. In: Proceedings of the workshop on New security paradigms (NSPW) (1998)
2. Carter, H., Amrutkar, C., Dacosta, I., Traynor, P.: For your phone only: custom protocols for efficient secure function evaluation on mobile devices. J. Secur. Commun. Netw. (SCN) **7**(7), 1165–1176 (2014)
3. Carter, H., Lever, C., Traynor, P.: Whitewash: outsourcing garbled circuit generation for mobile devices. In: Proceedings of the Annual Computer Security Applications Conference (ACSAC) (2014)
4. Carter, H., Mood, B., Traynor, P., Butler, K.: Secure outsourced garbled circuit evaluation for mobile devices. In: Proceedings of the USENIX Security Symposium (2013)
5. Carter, H., Mood, B., Traynor, P., Butler, K.: Outsourcing secure two-party computation as a black box. Cryptology ePrint Archive, Report 2014/936 (2014). http://eprint.iacr.org/

6. Damgård, I., Pastro, V., Smart, N., Zakarias, S.: Multiparty computation from somewhat homomorphic encryption. In: Safavi-Naini, R., Canetti, R. (eds.) CRYPTO 2012. LNCS, vol. 7417, pp. 643–662. Springer, Heidelberg (2012)

7. Demmler, D., Schneider, T., Zohner, M.: Ad-hoc secure two-party computation on mobile devices using hardware tokens. In: Proceedings of the USENIX Security Symposium (2014)

8. Goldreich, O., Micali, S., Wigderson, A.: How to play any mental game. In: Proceedings of the Annual ACM Symposium on Theory of Computing (1987)

9. Huang, Y., Katz, J., Evans, D.: Efficient secure two-party computation using symmetric cut-and-choose. In: Canetti, R., Garay, J.A. (eds.) CRYPTO 2013, Part II. LNCS, vol. 8043, pp. 18–35. Springer, Heidelberg (2013)

10. Huang, Y., Chapman, P., Evans, D.: Privacy-preserving applications on smartphones. In: Proceedings of the USENIX Workshop on Hot Topics in Security (2011)

11. Huang, Y., Evans, D., Katz, J., Malka, L.: Faster secure two-party computation using garbled circuits. In: Proceedings of the USENIX Security Symposium (2011)

12. Jakobsen, T.P., Nielsen, J.B., Orlandi, C.: A framework for outsourcing of secure computation. In: Proceedings of the ACM Workshop on Cloud Computing Security (CCSW) (2014)

13. Kamara, S., Mohassel, P., Riva, B.: Salus: A system for server-aided secure function evaluation. In: Proceedings of the ACM Conference on Computer and Communications Security (CCS) (2012)

14. Kreuter, B., Shelat, A., Shen, C.: Billion-gate secure computation with malicious adversaries. In: Proceedings of the USENIX Security Symposium (2012)

15. Kreuter, B., shelat, A., Mood, B., Butler, K.: PCF: a portable circuit format for scalable two-party secure computation. In: Proceedings of the USENIX Security Symposium (2013)

16. Lindell, Y.: Fast cut-and-choose based protocols for malicious and covert adversaries. In: Canetti, R., Garay, J.A. (eds.) CRYPTO 2013, Part II. LNCS, vol. 8043, pp. 1–17. Springer, Heidelberg (2013)

17. Mood, B., Gupta, D., Butler, K., Feigenbaum, J.: Reuse it or lose it: More efficient secure computation through reuse of encrypted values. In: Proceedings of the ACM Conference on Computer and Communications Security (CCS) (2014)

18. Mood, B., Letaw, L., Butler, K.: Memory-efficient garbled circuit generation for mobile devices. In: Proceedings of the IFCA International Conference on Financial Cryptography and Data Security (FC) (2012)

19. Osadchy, M., Pinkas, B., Jarrous, A., Moskovich, B.: Scifi-a system for secure face identification. In: Proceedings of the IEEE Symposium on Security & Privacy (2010)

20. Shelat, A., Shen, C.H.: Fast two-party secure computation with minimal assumptions. In: Proceedings of the ACM Conference on Computer and Communications Security (CCS) (2013)

21. Yao, A.C.: How to generate and exchange secrets. In: Proceedings of the IEEE Annual Symposium on Foundations of Computer Science (1986)

Cryptography and VPNs

What Users Should Know About Full Disk Encryption Based on LUKS

Simone Bossi and Andrea Visconti$^{(\boxtimes)}$

Department of Computer Science, Università Degli Studi di Milano, Milan, Italy
simone.bossi2@studenti.unimi.it, andrea.visconti@unimi.it

Abstract. Mobile devices, laptops, and USB memory usually store large amounts of sensitive information frequently unprotected. Unauthorized access to or release of such information could reveal business secrets, users habits, non-public data or anything else. Full Disk Encryption (FDE) solutions might help users to protect sensitive data in the event that devices are lost or stolen. In this paper we focus on the security of Linux Unified Key Setup (LUKS) specifications, the most common FDE solution implemented in Linux based operating systems. In particular, we analyze the key management process used to compute and store the encryption key, and the solution adopted to mitigate the problem of brute force attacks based on weak user passwords. Our testing activities show that unwitting users can significantly reduce the security of a LUKS implementation by setting specific hash functions and aggressive power management options.

Keywords: LUKS · PBKDF2 · Full disk encryption · HMAC · Hash functions · Power management options

1 Introduction

Nowadays, mobile devices, laptops, USB memory are convenient and easy to use. They are fast becoming the preferred choice of companies, customers and employees, especially by those who are on the move. These devices usually store large amounts of sensitive information frequently unprotected. If such devices are lost or stolen, the risk of unauthorized disclosure of confidential, sensitive, or classified information is very high and the impact to the affected companies is potentially billions of dollars [13]. However computer users are not the only ones who do not pay attention to security when it comes to protecting sensitive data. Many operating systems store temporary files/swap partitions on hard drive and a number of problems arises when these files contain sensitive data [8].

A possible solution is to encrypt the whole hard disk. Full Disk Encryption (FDE) solutions, also known as "On-Disk Encryption" or "Whole Disk Encryption", work by encrypting every single bit of data that resides on a storage

---

S. Bossi—Part of this work was performed as part of the author's B.Sc. thesis, under the supervision of Dr. Andrea Visconti.

© Springer International Publishing Switzerland 2015
M. Reiter and D. Naccache (Eds.): CANS 2015, LNCS 9476, pp. 225–237, 2015.
DOI: 10.1007/978-3-319-26823-1_16

device — i.e., operating systems, applications, swap partitions, user's files, and so on. FDE solutions aim to provide data security, even in the event that an encrypted device is lost or stolen. All information is encrypted/decrypted on the fly, automatically and transparently. Without the encryption key, the data stored on the disk remains inaccessible to any users (regular or malicious).

One of the main issues facing Full Disk Encryption solutions is the password management. Indeed, the master key used to encrypt the whole disk is stored on it. A well-known solution to this problem, is to adopt a two level key hierarchy [14] but sometimes it is not enough (e.g. two level key hierarchy adopted by Android 3-4.3 [4]), and a number of questions arise. Could the choice of specific cryptographic parameters significantly reduce the security of a FDE solution? How should users choose cryptographic parameters that best meet security requirements? Could external factors (i.e. power management options) affect the security of a FDE solution?

In this paper we try to find answers to these questions, evaluating the level of security provided by Linux Unified Key Setup, the most common Full Disk Encryption specification implemented in Linux based operating systems. In particular, we analyze the key management process used to derive the encryption key, and how the choice of specific hash functions and aggressive power management options may affect the security of a FDE solution.

The remainder of the paper is organized as follows. In Sect. 2, we introduce the problems of managing passwords and the solution adopted. In Sect. 3 we describe the LUKS design. In Sect. 4 we analyze the key management process used by LUKS implementations, explaining the possible weaknesses found. Finally, discussion and conclusions are drawn in Sect. 5.

2   Password Management

An important problem to solve in FDE solutions is the password management. Users know they need to generate a strong password and change it frequently. But the process of changing encryption password brings with it a series of problems, indeed, if a FDE solution has been implemented using a master key which encrypts/decrypts the whole hard disk — i.e., single key schema — changing the master key means re-encrypt all the data with the new key. This process can be very time consuming and cause unacceptable unavailability of data.

A well-known solution to this problem, is to adopt a two level key hierarchy. A strong master key generated by the system is used to encrypt/decrypt whole hard disk. Such key have to be split, encrypted with a secret user key — each user has their own secret key — and stored on the device itself. The master key is unique but a number of encrypted master key are stored on disk, one for each user. This approach has a main advantage. If we set a new secret user key, the encrypted master key stored on disk changes but the master key does not. Hence, users can change password frequently without re-encrypting all the data.

But, what happens when a device is lost or stolen? Is the two level key hierarchy method strong enough to protect our sensitive data? When devices are lost or stolen, it is desirable that the master key cannot be decrypted by anyone. Unfortunately, master keys are protected with user keys which are usually short and lack entropy. Hence, an attacker would try to guess them constructing a list of possible passwords. A solution to this problem is described in [10]. Morris and Thompson suggest to combine a user password with a salt to generate a key. This approach allows to compute several possible keys for each user password. The effect is to discourage an attacker from precomputing a list of possible keys. Another solution described in literature [14] is to derive the key using a Key Derivation Function (KDF). This approach tries to slow down the computation of malicious users to mitigate the problem of brute force attacks. In particular, the KDF allows legitimate users to spend a moderate amount of time on key derivation, while inserts CPU-intensive operations on the attacker side.

To face the problems of password management described in this section, it is possible to adopt a solution based on a two level key hierarchy and protect the master key using both salt and key derivation function.

2.1 PBKDF2: A Key Derivation Function

PBKDF2 is a Password-Based Key Derivation Function described in PKCS #5 [11,14]. For providing better resistance against brute force attacks, PBKDF2 introduce CPU-intensive operations. These operations are based on an iterated pseudorandom function (PRF) which maps input values to a derived key. The most important properties to assure is that the iterated pseudorandom function is cycle free. If this is not so, a malicious user can avoid the CPU-intensive operations and, as described in [16], get the derived key by executing a set of functionally-equivalent instructions.

PBKDF2 inputs a pseudorandom function PRF, the user password p, a random salt s, an iteration count c, and the desired length len of the derived key. It outputs a derived key $DerKey$.

$$DerKey = PBKDF2(PRF, p, s, c, len) \qquad (1)$$

More precisely, the derived key is computed as follows:

$$DerKey = T_1 || T_2 || \ldots || T_{len} \qquad (2)$$

where

$$T_1 = Function(p, s, c, 1)$$
$$T_2 = Function(p, s, c, 2)$$
$$\ldots$$
$$T_{len} = Function(p, s, c, len).$$

Each single block T_i — i.e., $T_i = Function(p, s, c, i)$ — is computed as

$$T_i = U_1 \oplus U_2 \oplus \ldots \oplus U_c \qquad (3)$$

where

$$U_1 = PRF(p, s||i)$$
$$U_2 = PRF(p, U_1)$$
$$\cdots$$
$$U_c = PRF(p, U_{c-1})$$

The pseudorandom function applied to derive a key can be a hash function [12], cipher, or HMAC [1,2,9]. In the sequel, unless otherwise specified, by PRF we will refer to HMAC with the SHA-1 hash function, which is the default as per [7,14].

3   Linux Unified Key Setup

The Linux Unified Key Setup (LUKS) is a disk-encryption specification commonly implemented in Linux based operating systems. It is a platform-independent standard on-disk format developed by Clemens Fruhwirth in 2004 [6,7]. LUKS is based on a two level key hierarchy. It protects the master key using PBKDF2 as key derivation function. To solve the problem of data remanence — i.e., data continues to exist on hard disk even after it has been deleted — an anti-forensic splitter (AF-splitter) is adopted. This AF-splitter inflates and splits the master key before storing it on disk and, furthermore, uses a hash function as diffusion element.

A LUKS partition has a simple layout (see Fig. 1). It includes the partition header, the key material (KM_1, KM_2, ..., KM_8), and the user encrypted data.

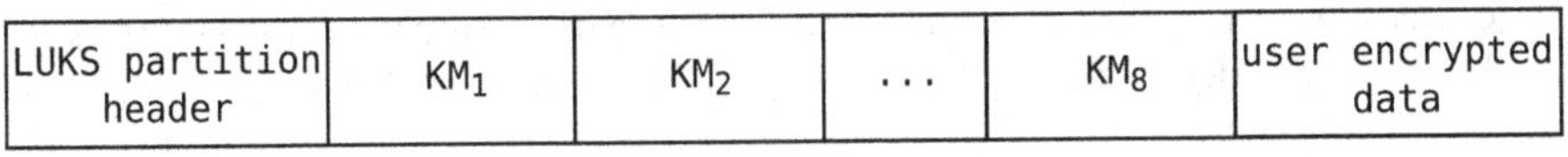

LUKS partition header	KM_1	KM_2	$\cdots$	KM_8	user encrypted data

Fig. 1. LUKS partition header

The partition header contains information about salt, iteration counts, key slots (eight), used cipher, cipher mode, key length, hash function, master key checksum, start sector of key material, and so on [6]. Among all these parameters, we look more closely at salt and iteration counts because they allow to mitigate brute force attacks. In particular, the salt is fetched from a random source [7], while the iteration counts are automatically computed by making some run-time tests when the encrypted partition is generated. Salt and iteration counts are stored in plain text in LUKS partition header.

In addition, the solution adopted by LUKS has as many user key as there are key slots. Therefore, the same master key can be encrypted with eight different user keys, and stored in one of the eight key material sections.

3.1 Master Key Recovery

In order to recover the master key, we need a valid LUKS partition header. When a user key is provided, it unlocks one of the eight key slots. As shown in Fig. 2, PBKDF2, an anti-forensic splitter, and a cipher are used to compute the master key. Such a key in turn will unlock the encrypted data.

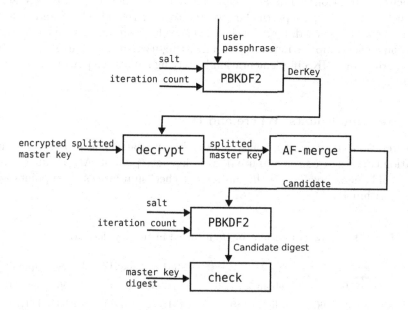

Fig. 2. Master key recovery process

More precisely, the following algorithm is processed:

Algorithm 1. Master key recovery process

---
1 Read the user password/passphare p;
2 Read salt s from active key slot;
3 Read iteration count c from active key slot;
4 Use PBKDF2 to compute derived key $DerKey$;
5 Read the start sector of key material from active key slot;
6 Read the split master key from key material;
7 Decrypt the split master key using derived key $DerKey$;
8 Merge the split encrypted master key and obtain a candidate master key;
9 Read the iteration count for computing the master key digest;
10 Use PBKDF2 to compute the candidate master key digest;
11 Compare such digest with those stored in the partition header;
12 If equal, the recovery is successful. Otherwise, the candidate is not the correct master key.

---

4   Analysis of a LUKS Implementation

In Linux world, LUKS implementations are based on cryptsetup and dm-crypt. In order to mitigate the problem of brute force attacks based on weak user passwords, LUKS combined the ideas of salt and key derivation function (i.e., PBKDF2). Because salt parameter is known and user password may be guessed, we focus on iteration counts and their ability to slow down a brute force attack as much as possible. In particular, we try to understand where and how the iteration counts are used, how the choice of specific hash functions may affect the iteration count computation, and how unwitting users might significantly reduce the security of a LUKS implementation by setting aggressive power management options.

4.1   Iteration Counts: Where and How

Two iteration counts are involved in the key management process. The first iteration count is used to compute derived key (see point 4, Algorithm 1), while the second one is involved in the master key checksum process (see points 9-10-11, Algorithm 1).

Table 1. Average iteration counts involved in the key derivation process

CPU	OS	sha1	sha512	sha256	ripemd160
Intel Atom z520	Debian 7.7 x86	31,035	7,019	18,567	29,491
Intel Core 2 Duo T6670	Kali 1.0 x86	151,772	22,821	67,634	111,791
Intel Pentium 3556U	Xubuntu 14.04 x64	126,617	50,082	77,379	103,287
Intel Core i3 2310M	Fedora 20 x64	136,375	50,107	77,682	111,536
Intel Pentium T4500	Ubuntu 12.04 x64	147,904	56,380	85,167	119,366
Intel Core i5 3320M	Debian 7.7 x64	232,203	88,843	139,985	196,209
Intel Core i7 2860QM	Kubuntu 14.04 x64	248,671	90,225	123,904	179,947
Intel Core i7 4710MQ	ArchLinux x64	588,761	302,148	392,916	350,378

Table 2. Average iteration counts involved in the master key checksum process

CPU	OS	sha1	sha512	sha256	ripemd160
Intel Atom z520	Debian 7.7 x86	7,826	1,702	4,668	7,327
Intel Core 2 Duo T6670	Kali 1.0 x86	37,761	5,752	27,498	16,764
Intel Pentium 3556U	Xubuntu 14.04 x64	31,419	12,406	19,318	25,659
Intel Core i3 2310M	Fedora 20 x64	33,903	12,657	19,307	27,718
Intel Pentium T4500	Ubuntu 12.04 x64	36,913	14,009	21,495	29,951
Intel Core i5 3320M	Debian 7.7 x64	58,218	22,026	34,802	49,138
Intel Core i7 2860QM	Ubuntu 14.04 x64	54,371	19,353	30,926	44,927
Intel Core i7 4710MQ	ArchLinux x64	147,727	75,570	98,929	87,572

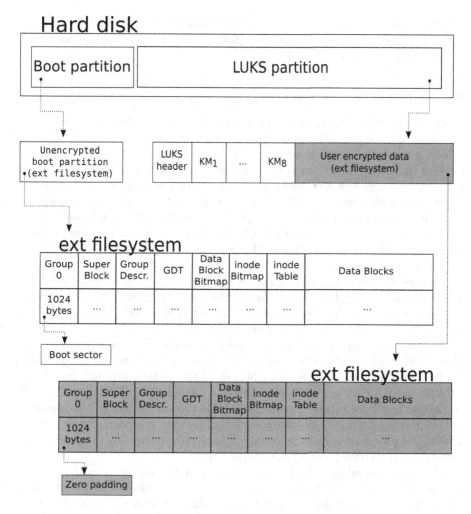

Fig. 3. The first 1024 bytes on EXT-family file systems

We experimentally observed that about 75–80% of the computational effort required to compute a derived key is generated by first iteration count (see Table 1), while the remaining 20–25% by second one (see Table 2). Unfortunately, the master key checksum process can be avoided exploiting the well known problem of file system structure. Indeed, on EXT-family file systems the first 1024 bytes are reserved for the boot sector (see Fig. 3, unencrypted boot partition). When unused — recall that a hard disk can contain several partitions, each with their own boot sectors — it is set to zeros (see Fig. 3, user encrypted data).

By decrypting the first bytes of the user encrypted data and checking if such bytes are zeros, we are able to understand if the candidate key is the correct master key or not. Hence, we substitute points 9-10-11 of Algorithm 1 with a decryption operation.

This means that, for all encrypted LUKS partitions the second iteration count can be avoided and the computational effort required to compute the master key can be reduced by about 20–25%.

4.2   Iteration Counts and Hash Functions

To better understand how the iteration counts are handled — recall that they are automatically computed by making some run-time tests — we experimentally[1] collected several partition headers related to a number of encrypted devices. To be sure that such values are not conditioned by external factors, e.g. running programs, we collected 3200 partition headers. More precisely, for each processor (eight) and each hash function (four) listed in Tables 1 and 2, we execute 100 runs for a total of $8 \times 4 \times 100 = 3200$ partition headers collected. Then, we read salt and iteration counts stored in each partition header. Tables 1 and 2 shown the average values collected. Notice that the variation across runs is observed to be less than 0.4 %.

As expected, devices with a different hardware configuration generate different iteration count values. For example, the values collected for SHA1 run on average between 588,761 (Intel Core i7 4710MQ) and 31,035 (Intel Atom z520), with higher values corresponding to a more powerful processor.

Surprisingly, even small changes in software, such as choose a different function of the SHA family, may considerably decrease the iteration count values. Notice the differences between 67,634 and 22,821 (Intel Core due duo T6670, SHA256 vs SHA512), or 18,567 and 7,019 (Intel Atom z520, SHA256 vs SHA512), or 139,985 and 88,843 (Intel Core i5 3320M, SHA256 vs SHA512). This abnormal behavior was not found in all cases tested. For example, it is partially mitigated in i7 4710MQ processor where the average values collected are 392,916 and 302,148 (Intel Core i7 4710MQ, SHA256 vs SHA512).

The approach adopted by LUKS in defining iteration count values does not always sound good. We found it curious that the iteration counts related to SHA-256/512 are considerably smaller than those of SHA-1. Although there is no reason why this should not happen when we talk about the security against password guessing, from an user's point of view, SHA-256 and SHA-512 are still considered more secure than SHA-1, therefore a FDE solution based on SHA-2 is expected to be stronger. We notice that the CPU time spent to compute a list of master key candidates based on SHA-256/512 costs less than one based on SHA-1. Hence, it is easier to attack a FDE solution which makes use of a safer hash function (e.g., SHA256 or SHA512) rather than one which uses a less secure function (e.g., SHA-1).

Furthermore, the computational time spent to compute a list of master key candidates does not only depend on the iteration count values. Even the number of fingerprints required to compute a single iteration affects the total execution time. Indeed, assuming that the decryption function involved in the master key

---

[1] 32-bit or 64-bit operating system and cryptsetup version 1.6.6 (the latest version available at the time of testing) were installed on our laptops.

recovery process is AES (i.e. the default choice), we need a 256 bits derived key. A SHA-1 fingerprint is only 160 bits in length and cannot be used as derived key. As described in Eq. 2, a second fingerprint is necessary — i.e., $DerKey = T_1 || T_2$. On the other hand, SHA-256 and SHA-512 generate enough bits to compute a derived key, hence $DerKey = T_1$. This means that, at equal iteration count values, a FDE solution based on HMAC-SHA1 slow down the brute force process better than one based on HMAC-SHA256 or HMAC-SHA512.

To point out this finding, we set the first iteration count to 500,000, and try to compute a list of 250,000 master key candidates using a number of hash functions. Figure 4 can help us to visualize the time necessary to execute a brute force attack on a i7 processor. Note that the gap between SHA-1, SHA-256, and SHA-512 hash functions is partially mitigated by compensatory mechanisms such as using a computationally more complex hash function.

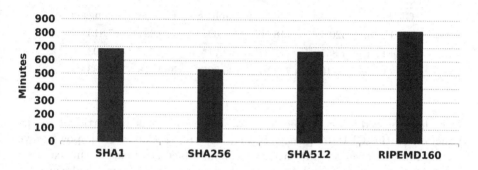

Fig. 4. Time spent to compute a list of 250,000 master key candidates

4.3 Iteration Counts and Power Management

Another important feature that users have to take into account during encryption operations are the power management options. A common way to increase the battery life of devices is to enable aggressive power saving policies. Such policies save power, but they also impact performance by lowering CPU clock speed. Hence, the iteration count values fall down even further.

Table 3. Maximum and minimum CPU frequency of some devices

CPU	OS	Max Freq (Plugged)	Min Freq (Unplugged)
Intel Atom z520	Debian 7.7 x86	1.33 GHz	0.80 GHz
Intel Pentium 3556U	Xubuntu 14.04 x64	1.70 GHz	0.80 GHz
Intel Core i7 4710MQ	ArchLinux x64	3.50 GHz	1.20 GHz

To better understand this behavior, we install a well-known Linux power management package (i.e., Laptop Mode Tools package version 1.66) and reduce the CPU frequency as much as possible (see Table 3). Then, we run a number of tests and experimental results are reported in Table 4.

Table 4. Power saving policies and their impact on the iteration count values

	SHA1		SHA512	
CPU	Plugged	Unplugged	Plugged	Unplugged
Intel Atom z520	31,035	18,693	7,019	4,288
Intel Pentium 3556U	126,617	62,969	50,082	25,161
Intel Core i7 4710MQ	588,761	202,143	302,148	104,216
	SHA256		RIPEMD	
CPU	Plugged	Unplugged	Plugged	Unplugged
Intel Atom z520	18,567	11,094	29,491	17,813
Intel Pentium 3556U	77,379	38,714	103,287	51,603
Intel Core i7 4710MQ	392,916	135,207	350,378	121,483

Note that the reduction of the iteration count values is proportional to the reduction of the CPU frequency. Indeed, for the i7 Core tested, power save settings imply a lowering of iterations by about a factor 3. Pentium, instead, has half the iteration counts, and Atom has about a third less. These results suggest that power saving policies might have an important impact on the iteration count values, hence, on the strength of the FDE solution adopted.

4.4   Testing

Our testing activity is not intended to decrypt a FDE solution — PBKDF2 can be parallelized on GPU architecture or specialized hardware (ASIC/FPGA) and interested readers can find more information about this topic in [3,5], and [15] — but only to evaluate how the choice of PBKDF2 parameters and power management options can affect the security of a full disk encryption solution.

We implemented a brute-force attack based on a password-list of 250,000 master keys. Cryptographic hash functions and PBKDF2 have been implemented using standard OpenSSL library. We run our code on a laptop equipped with an i7 4710MQ processor. No GPUs have been used. The brute force attack has been executed six times. For each CPU listed in Table 3, we target two LUKS partitions collected using the following configuration options:

1. default iteration count values, AES-256 XTS mode, HMAC-SHA1, laptop plugged in;
2. default iteration count values, AES-256 XTS mode, HMAC-SHA512, laptop unplugged;

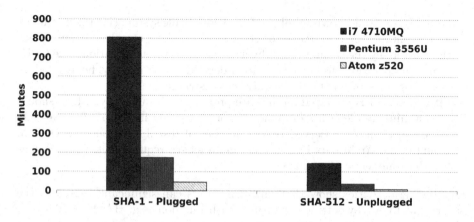

Fig. 5. A toy example: time spent attacking a FDE solution

Figure 5 visualizes the time spent attacking a FDE solution. Although this is a toy example — 250,00 master keys are an approximation of the size of a dictionary — we can easily identify the gap between different kinds of approach. The second approach abruptly reduce the timeframe for brute forcing, showing how the simple choice of configuration parameters may affect a FDE solution based on LUKS. Note that such an attack takes into account all the weaknesses described in Sects. 4.1, 4.2 and 4.3.

5   Discussion and Conclusions

In this paper, we addressed the security of a Full Disk Encryption solution based on LUKS specification. Such a solution aims to prevent data leakage even in the event that devices are lost or stolen. We analyzed the key management process used to compute and store the encryption key and how the problem of brute force attacks based on weak user passwords has been mitigated.

We identify a number of issues that should be assessed and faced when a full disk encryption is implemented.

- Firstly, the iteration count values are used to slow down a brute force attack, therefore, they should not be too small. Experimental results show that sometimes they are.
- Secondly, power management options should not affect the strength of a FDE solution. Testing results show that aggressive power-saving approaches may have a relevant impact on the iteration count values, hence, on the strength of the solution adopted.
- Thirdly, from an user's point of view a FDE solution based on HMAC-SHA256, or HMAC-SHA512, is expected to be much stronger than one based on SHA-1, and be far more resistant to brute-force attacks. Our testing disprove this.

- Fourthly, the well-known problem of EXT family file system (i.e. the first block group contains the boot record or is set to zero) allows attackers to substitute the master key checksum process by a simple decryption operation. The CPU-intensive operations used to compute a derived key should not be avoided by executing a set of functionally-equivalent instructions.
- Fifthly, master keys stored on disk are protected with user keys which should have a minimum length requirement in order to prevent a brute force attack. We experimentally observed that a number of distribution such as Debian, Ubuntu, and ArchLinux have no minimum length requirement, while Fedora has (but only eight characters).

Our testing activities show that unwitting users can significantly reduced the security of LUKS by setting "stronger" hash function (e.g. HAMC-SHA512 or HAMC-SHA256) and enabling aggressive power management options. Because attacks always get better and Moore's Law will continue to march forward, we strongly suggest to increase default iteration count values whenever a user key is defined. Unfortunately, the most common user approach is to leave the default values unchanged, although a number of parameters can be easily adjusted by user as desired.

References

1. Bellare, M., Canetti, R., Krawczyk, H.: Keying hash functions for message authentication. In: Koblitz, N. (ed.) CRYPTO 1996. LNCS, vol. 1109, pp. 1–15. Springer, Heidelberg (1996)
2. Bellare, M., Canetti, R., Krawczyk, H.: Message authentication using hash functions–the hmac construction. RSA Laboratories CryptoBytes **2**(1), 12–15 (1996)
3. Dürmuth, M., Güneysu, T., Kasper, M., Paar, C., Yalcin, T., Zimmermann, R.: Evaluation of standardized password-based key derivation against parallel processing platforms. In: Foresti, S., Yung, M., Martinelli, F. (eds.) ESORICS 2012. LNCS, vol. 7459, pp. 716–733. Springer, Heidelberg (2012)
4. Elenkov, N.: Android Security Internals. No Starch Press (2014)
5. Frederiksen, T.K.: Using cuda for exhaustive password recovery (2011). http://daimi.au.dk/~jot2re/cuda/resources/report.pdf
6. Fruhwirth, C.: New methods in hard disk encryption (2005). http://clemens.endorphin.org/nmihde/nmihde-A4-ds.pdf
7. Fruhwirth, C.: LUKS On-Disk Format Specification Version 1.2.1 (2011). http://wiki.cryptsetup.googlecode.com/git/LUKS-standard/on-disk-format.pdf
8. Gutmann, P.: Secure deletion of data from magnetic and solid-state memory (1996). https://www.cs.auckland.ac.nz/~pgut001/pubs/secure_del.html
9. Krawczyk, H., Bellare, M., Canetti, R.: Hmac: Keyed-hashing for message authentication. Internet RFC 2104 (1998)
10. Morris, R., Thompson, K.: Password security: A case history. Commun. ACM **22**(11), 594–597 (1979)
11. NIST: SP 800–132: Recommendation for password-based key derivation (2010)
12. NIST: FIPS PUB 180–4: Secure Hash Standard, March 2012. http://csrc.nist.gov/publications/fips/fips180-4/fips-180-4.pdf

13. Ponemon Institute: The billion dollar lost laptop problem (2010). http://newsroom.intel.com/servlet/JiveServlet/download/1544-16-3132/The_Billion_Dollar_Lost_Laptop_Study.pdf
14. RSA Laboratories: Pkcs #5 v2.1: Password based cryptography standard (2012)
15. Schober, M.: Efficient password and key recovery using graphic cards. Diploma Thesis, Ruhr-Universität Bochum (2010)
16. Visconti, A., Bossi, S., Ragab, H., Caló, A.: On the weaknesses of PBKDF2. In: Proceedings of CANS 2015 (2015)

Q-OpenVPN: A New Extension of OpenVPN Based on a Quantum Scheme for Authentication and Key Distribution

Aymen Ghilen[1]([✉]), Mostafa Azizi[2], and Ridha Bouallegue[3]

[1] ENIT, University of Tunis El Manar, Tunis, Tunisia
`ghilen06@gmail.com`
[2] Department of Computer Engineering ESTO,
University Mohamed Ist Oujda, Oujda, Morocco
`azizi.mos@gmail.com`
[3] Innovcom Laboratory, Higher School of Communications, Tunis, Tunisia
`ridha.bouallegue@gmail.com`

Abstract. Virtual Private Network (VPN) tunnels are cryptographic solutions that enable sensitive information to be transmitted over an untrusted environment, and ensure the most imperative security services such as confidentiality,integrity, and authentication. OpenVPN is an open source implementation of VPN. In the present work, we propose the deployment of a quantum protocol for cryptographic key exchange and authentication within OpenVPN between both sides of the tunnel. Our approach is a prominent step towards unconditional security based on the laws of quantum physics. Despite the huge progress in the quantum research field, quantifying the confidence and secrecy of the proposed scheme still remains a hard task. In this context, we adopt a probabilistic approach based on the technique of Model Checking, using the PRISM tool. We basically focus on two pioneering security properties: the ability to detect an eavesdropper independently of its computational power and the minimization of the amount of information gained by the eavesdropper about the secret key.

Keywords: Quantum cryptography · Authentication · Quantum key distribution · OpenVPN · Entanglement · Model checking · Prism

1 Introduction

Quantum computing [1] is a revolutionary field that combines the principles of computer science and the laws of quantum physics. The significant advance brought by the quantum effects consists substantially of protecting the quantum information from being intercepted, thanks to Heisenbergs Uncertainty Principle or the Bells inequalities. To guarantee an unconditional secure communication, any two endpoints are able to establish a secret random key which can be used for encrypting and decrypting message in a One-Time Pad (OTP) scheme.

© Springer International Publishing Switzerland 2015
M. Reiter and D. Naccache (Eds.): CANS 2015, LNCS 9476, pp. 238–247, 2015.
DOI: 10.1007/978-3-319-26823-1_17

This approach is called Quantum Key Distribution (QKD). One serious problem that all QKD protocols are confronted with is lack of an authentication mechanism. In other words, almost all the QKD algorithms are vulnerable against man-in-the-middle attacks. To overcome this shortcoming, an authentication must accompany or precede a QKD protocol, so that each one of the two parties of communication checks the identity of the other party. Several quantum authentication protocols were proposed [2]. The integration of a quantum algorithm for key establishment and authentication sounds to be a convenient solution to replace the whole classical structure of PKI in the existing security protocols. In particular, to securely transmit private communication data through public networking environment, VPNs have emerged as an excellent technological solution. This approach establishes an encrypted tunnel between two network nodes over an insecure data medium. OpenVPN is an open source VPN solution. Its core system is the SSL/TLS protocol which involves a mechanism of key generation/derivation for encryption and data integrity purposes. Our idea is to offer greater robustness and privacy by integrating a quantum protocol of authentication and key agreement to replace RSA/DiffieHellman exchange which is only computationally secure. In the new proposal Q-OpenVPN, no certificates are needed anymore. The authentication is reinforced by quantum means. As quantum phenomenon has a stochastic behavior, a probabilistic model-checking such as PRISM tool is a suitable technique for describing random processes and testing them to construct valuable proofs of correctness. The paper is organized as follows: in the second section, we introduce the OpenVPN technology. In Sect. 3, we review various related works and we examine the motivation behind integrating a quantum cryptography approach into OpenVPN tunnel. Then, a description of the quantum authentication with key distribution protocol is presented in Sect. 4. In Sect. 5, we introduce Q-OpenVPN, our quantum version of OpenVPN. A security analysis is developed in Sect. 6. We conclude in Sect. 7.

2   OpenVPN

The main idea behind VPN is to ensure safety and secrecy for transferred data by creating an encrypted tunnel over a public network between two hosts. Deploying a VPN solution in Wireless LAN will provide us a powerful protection against many threats. That is why VPN security implies many tools such as modern encryption algorithms, strong authentication techniques and even firewalls to protect the data traffic. Each VPN solution targets three important goals; firstly, the privacy of transmitted data must be ensured; secondly, the integrity of information between the sender and the receiver must be respected; thirdly, the data flow must be available when needed. OpenVPN was first published in 2001 as the most successful VPN implementation [3]. It offers much more pioneering features than other implementations, especially in terms of security and networking. The core cryptosystem of OpenVPN is based on SSL/TLS protocol. SSL/TLS consists mainly of two sub-protocols that efficiently provide security and data integrity, the record protocol and the handshake protocol. The first protocol enables encryption and transmission of data packets. The encryption key is derived from the second sub-protocol (handshake protocol). Figure 1 depicts the full handshake message flow of SSL/TLS handshake protocol. The protocol starts with exchanging two hello messages for parameters establishment. The two parties agree on the session ID, the encryption algorithm, the key exchange method (e.g. RSA/DH) as well as the Message Authentication Code (MAC) algorithm. Once an agreement is reached on all the cipher-suite elements, the server sends its certificate and optionally a key exchange message. The server may also request the client to send its certificate for client authentication. By *Server_Hello_Done* message, the server signals end of hello message. The client sends its *key_exchange* message, optionally accompanied by a certificate and a certificate verification. The purpose of *Client_Key_Exchange* is to establish a pre-master secret which will be used later for master key building. Finally, the client and the server exchange finished messages, in which a hashed MAC value is calculated at the two endpoints to make sure that both parties acknowledge that everything was exchanged correctly.

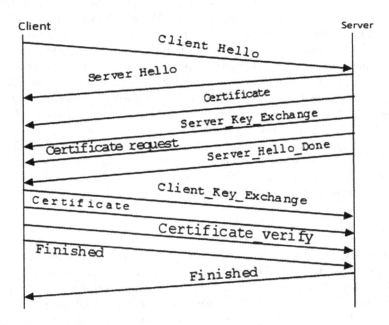

Fig. 1. SSL handshake protocol phases in OpenVPN

3 Related Works and Motivation

Many researches have focused on implementing more secure protocols by applying the Quantum Key Distribution approach within existing systems especially critical applications which need an extremely secure key transmission. Hence, by harnessing the laws of quantum physics, a tangible enhancement is observed on already existing properties and some features not feasible through classical means are provided henceforth. In paper [5], a quantum extension of EAP-TLS which enables a cryptographic key exchange with the authentication of a remote client peer, with absolute security, ensured by the laws of quantum physics. Papers [6, 7] present a methodology for incorporation of a QKD scheme to upgrade the security of IEEE 802.11 networks. Other approaches aim at introducing quantum cryptography into classical protocols such as CHAP, SSL and TLS [8, 9]. By combining OTP (One Time Pad) cipher and the key derived from the quantum protocol, the whole algorithm is unconditionally secure. Several quantum authentication protocols [2] are based on the entanglement property. In Open-VPN tunnels, the authentication mechanism is mainly based on certificates. The certificates make use of public cryptography to generate a pair of keys that are mathematically related to one another. The robustness of these cryptosystems relies on the difficulty to calculate the inverse of a one-way function or factorize a large number into prime integers. However, by relying on quantum cryptography, we make eavesdropping detection physically possible.

4   Quantum Authentication and Key Distribution Protocol

Many improvements are applied on [4] to enhance its security parameters. The proposed quantum algorithm exploits an unusual form of entanglement based on phase incompatibility. Lets consider the two qubits system described by:

$$\Phi = \frac{1}{2}(-|00> +|01> +|10> +|11>) \tag{1}$$

The four states $(|00>, |01>, |10>, |11>)$ are entangled. The two parties Alice and Bob need a unprotected classical channel and an array of N entangled qubit pairs denoted $(q_{1A}, q_{1B}), (q_{2A}, q_{2B}), ..., (q_{NA}, q_{NB})$ shared between Alice and Bob. The entanglement is of the form described by Eq. (1). Alice holds the first qubits $q_{1A}, q_{2A}, ..., q_{NA}$ of each pair, however, Bob holds the second qubits $q_{1B}, q_{2B}, ..., q_{NB}$. Before starting the algorithm, the two parties decide randomly which party performs measurements first. For instance, if we assume that Alice performs the first measurement, then for each pair(q_{iA}, q_{iB}), the algorithm runs as follows:

- If $q_{iA} = 0$, then Bobs qubit will be $q_{iB} = \frac{1}{\sqrt{2}}(-|0> +|1>)$. If $q_{iA} = 1$, Bobs qubit $q_{iB} = \frac{1}{\sqrt{2}}(|0> +|1>)$.
- Bob applies the operator M on his qubit and reads the result $M(q_{iB})$. Table 1 summarizes the correlation between the two readings of Alice and Bob:
  Where $M = \frac{1}{\sqrt{2}} \begin{pmatrix} -1 & 1 \\ 1 & 1 \end{pmatrix}$. M is an unitary operator decomposable to

$$M = X.Z.H \text{ where } X = \begin{pmatrix} 0 & 1 \\ 1 & 0 \end{pmatrix} \text{ and } Z = \begin{pmatrix} 1 & 0 \\ 0 & -1 \end{pmatrix} \text{ and } H = \frac{1}{\sqrt{2}} \begin{pmatrix} 1 & 1 \\ 1 & -1 \end{pmatrix}.$$

Table 1. Correlation between measuring results of Alice and Bob

Alices qubit q_{iA}	Bob's qubit q_{iB}	$M(q_{iB})$	Classical state of $M(q_{iB})$
0	$q_{iB} = \frac{1}{\sqrt{2}}(-|0> +|1>) = M(|0>)$	$|0>$	0
1	$q_{iB} = \frac{1}{\sqrt{2}}(|0> +|1>) = M(|1>)$	$|1>$	1

Upon applying the operator M, Bob reads exactly the same binary number as Alice. If Bob performs the first measurement, then Alice applies the operator M on his particle and likewise he obtains $M(q_{iA}) = q_{iB}$. After browsing all the set of the qubit pairs, Alice and Bob obtain two identical binary strings. Alice and Bob sacrifice $2m$ qubits from the N qubit pairs array to construct their protected public keys. Alices public key consists of the first m qubits. Alice publishes her public key that will be seen by Bob who compares it to his own measured qubits. If the two binary numbers match, then Bob becomes certain of the identity of his interlocutor. Hence, Alice is authenticated. Bobs public key is established by the same procedure using the second m sacrificed qubits. This step perfectly authenticates Bob. In case of any mismatch throughout the $2m$ qubits, the two parties abort the protocol and launch a new session. The secret key consists of the remaining $n = N - 2m$ qubits. We call it K. Consequently, by processing the N pairs, and with no interference from any eavesdropper, Alice and Bob are able to establish their public keys and then authenticate each other. More interestingly, they will share an authenticated key K that will be used later in deriving the pre-shared secret as well as the master secret and the rest of the keys hierarchy.

5   The Quantum Version of OpenVPN: Q-OpenVPN

Instead of certificates, the quantum scheme generates two public keys which perfectly authenticate their holders as shown in Fig. 2. By comparing them, the two parties authenticate each other. Furthermore, if we set
pre_master secret = K, then the master secret takes the form:

$$master\_secret = PRF(K, \text{``}mastersecret\text{''}, ClientHello.random$$
$$+ServerHello.random) \quad (2)$$

The resulting secret key K is essential to calculate the master secret which will be used in deriving the encryption keys and the MAC keys. The two finished messages are a second level of authentication besides the quantum authentication carried out by the quantum scheme presented in Sect. 4. They are calculated by the expression:

$$Finished = PRF(master\_secret, finished\_label, hash(handshake\_messages)) \quad (3)$$

According to our new proposal, the classical authentication ensured by Finished messages depends on the key generated by the quantum algorithm. The two Hello messages should be used in agreeing on the quantum algorithm parameters such as N, m and n. An unconditional secure *pre_master* secret is generated through a quantum algorithm. It authenticates perfectly its holders. The Public Key Infrastructure (PKI) is replaced by a quantum scheme to authenticate the two parties and agree on a secret. The proposed protocol is more efficient, for which, the security relies on quantum effects to build a quantum framework that make the certificates not necessary any more. A second session of authentication besides the quantum one is performed by exchanging the Finished messages. If the quantum authentication succeeds, the two endpoints will share the same secret K which is useful in calculating the Finished messages.

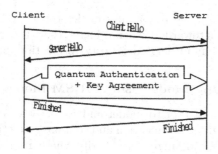

Fig. 2. Q-OpenVPN handshake protocol

6   Security Analysis

6.1   Eavesdropping Capabilities

We basically focus on the man-in-the-middle attack against the quantum algorithm in which Eve sends a classical 0 to Alice and $M(|0>)$ to Bob. In other words, $q_{iA} = |0>$ and $q_{iB} = M(|0>)$. All the other man-in-the-middle attacks are equivalent to this one or less advantageous than it. We suppose that the two endpoints of the quantum channel have the option of selecting randomly a measurement basis between diagonal basis ($|+>, |->$) and rectilinear basis ($|0>, |1>$). In Tables 2 and 3, we explain the relation between measuring results when Alice starts the first measurement and when Bob starts the first measurement. For instance, if we assume that Alice makes the first measurement, and if both Alice and Bob choose Z basis, then their readings will match, which means that the eavesdropper is not detected.

In Table 4, we explore the security properties of the quantum algorithm. Eve is detected only if they obtain different measuring results. For a key K of size n bits:

$$P_{det}(n) = 1 - (\frac{3}{8})^n \tag{4}$$

Table 2. Relation between measuring results when Alice is first

Chosen basis	q_{iA}	$M(q_{iB})$
X basis	$\frac{1}{\sqrt{2}}(\lvert+>+\lvert->)$	$\frac{1}{\sqrt{2}}(\lvert+>+\lvert->)$
Z basis	$\lvert 0>$	$\lvert 0>$

Table 3. Relation between measuring results when Bob is first

Chosen basis	q_{iB}	$M(q_{iA})$
X basis	$-\lvert->$	$-\lvert->$
Z basis	$\frac{1}{\sqrt{2}}(-\lvert0>+\lvert1>)$	$\frac{1}{\sqrt{2}}(-\lvert0>+\lvert1>)$

where P_{det} expresses the probability of detecting an eavesdropper. As we can observe, P_{det} tends towards 1 when n increases. Although these preliminary results are promising, an automated security verification must be developed.

6.2   Analysis of M_{QA} Model Using PRISM Model Checker

PRISM is an automated tool to model and formally verify whether the proposed model meets a given specification and computes exactly the corresponding probability [10]. In PRISM language, to verify whether a model M_{QA} satisfies a property p, we compute the probability:

$$Pr\{M_{QA} \models p\} \tag{5}$$

where p is a PCTL (Probabilistic Computation Tree Logic) formula and corresponds to a security specification. Our model M_{QA} is composed of 3 modules: Alice (peer), Bob (AP) and a third one for the channel. A module represents a party involved in the protocol and contains a set of local variables and a series of actions to be executed. A typical action takes the form of a guarded command:

$$[action]g \rightarrow a_1 : (x_1' = val_1) + a_2 : (x_2' = val_2) + \ldots$$
$$+a_N : (x_N' = val_N) \tag{6}$$

x_i' is an updated version of x_i that changes to val_i with probability a_i. We will focus on reviewing the following security property: the protocol must detect the presence of any intruder trying to retrieve information about the key. Especially, our model will evaluate the probabilities:

Table 4. Review of some security properties

Probability of	Our quantum scheme
Same readings	37.5
Detecting Eve	$\frac{5}{8}$

$$P_{det}(n) = Pr\{M_{QA} \models p_{det}\} \tag{7}$$

6.3 Expression of P_{det} and Property Verification

Eve applies a man-in-the-middle attack by sending fake particles to both parties. She sends $q_{iA} = |0>$ to Alice and $q_{iB} = M(|0>)$ to Bob. According to Tables 2 and 3, to detect Eve, the two readings must disagree. The following code line computes P_{det}:

$$[Bob\_get]((b\_st = 3)(b\_qbit! = a\_qbit))|((b\_st = 4)(b\_qbit! = a\_qbit)) \to (b\_st' = 7); \tag{8}$$

where b_st, b_qbit, and a_qubit denote respectively Bobs state, Bobs qubit and Alices qubit. Consequently, the corresponding PCTL formula is:

$$P_{det} = \{TRUE \bigcup (b\_st = 7)\}; \tag{9}$$

Let P_Z be the probability to choose the rectilinear basis. If we vary the key length n, we obtain the curve $P_{det}(n)$ which depends on the choice of the measurement basis. Figure 3 shows a comparison between the probabilies of detecting Eve for a scheme with a randomly chosen basis ($P_Z = 0.5$) and another scheme with only Z basis ($P_Z = 1$).

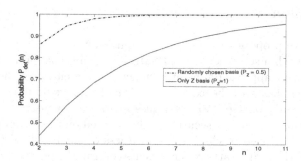

Fig. 3. Probabilities of detecting Eve as a function of n if only Z basis is used

According to the results depicted in Fig. 3, we conclude that our protocol becomes less vulnerable against man-in-the-middle attacks if the legitimate users choose randomly their measurement bases. The review of Fig. 4 highlights that the best performance is reached if the rectilinear and the diagonal bases are equiprobable. Another interesting result is that the security properties of our proposed scheme are independent of the one who starts the measurement. If n increases, the probability to detect Eve increases and tends towards 1:

$$lim_{N \to \infty} P_{det}(N) = 1 \tag{10}$$

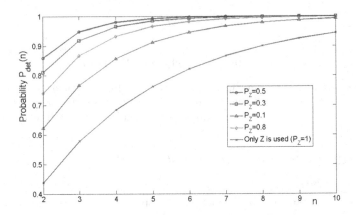

Fig. 4. Probability of detecting Eve for different values of P_Z

Moreover, if we increase the length of the key, we systematically improve the capability to prevent man-in-the-middle attacks. By the same way, we decrease exponentially the amount of valid information that a spy gains on the secret key. Consequently, our proposal is unconditionally secure and satisfies the expected security properties, especially if a sufficiently long key is considered.

7 Conclusion

In this work, we propose to incorporate a quantum algorithm to authenticate users and establish a secret key within SSL/TLS handshake protocol for Open-VPN tunnels. Our approach aims at enhancing the security of the VPN technique and it complies with the explosive growth of wireless networks market. We focused particularly on OpenVPN because of its compatibility with the most modern operating systems. A security analysis based on the technique of Model Checking was developed to check the robustness of our proposed Q-OpenVPN against man-in-the-middle attack. The results confirm the proof of unconditional security. Furthermore, if our solution is adopted, we systematically guarantee both key establishment and users authentication without exchanging certificates or any PKI. The security of the resulting keys within SSL/TLS handshake for OpenVPN technique was prominently strengthened.

References

1. Peikert, C.: Lattice cryptography for the internet. In: Mosca, M. (ed.) PQCrypto 2014. LNCS, vol. 8772, pp. 197–219. Springer, Heidelberg (2014)
2. Ghilen, A., Belmabrouk, H., Bouallegue, R.: Classification of quantum authentication protocols and calculation of their complexity. In: Proceedings of 15th International Conference on Sciences and Techniques of Automatic Control & Computer Engineering-STA, December 2014

3. OpenVPN. http://openvpn.net/
4. Nagy, N., Akl, S.G.: Quantum authenticated key distribution. In: Akl, S.G., Calude, C.S., Dinneen, M.J., Rozenberg, G., Wareham, H.T. (eds.) UC 2007. LNCS, vol. 4618, pp. 127–136. Springer, Heidelberg (2007)
5. Ghilen, A., Azizi, M., Belmabrouk, H.: Incorporation and model checking of a quantum authentication and key distribution scheme in EAP-TLS. In: Proceedings of Mediterranean Conference on Information & Communication Technologies 2015, MedICT 2015, May 2015
6. Priyanka, B., Ronak, S.: Framework for Wireless Network Security Using Quantum Cryptography, (IJCNC), vol. 6(6), pp 45–61, November 2014
7. Premlata, S., Leena, R.: Quantum Cryptography with Key Distribution in Wireless Network. IJACTE 6(2), 74–79 (2013)
8. Elboukhari, M., Azizi, M., Azizi, A.: Improving the security of CHAP protocol by quantum cryptography. In: Essaaidi, M., Malgeri, M., Badica, C. (eds.) Intelligent Distributed Computing IV. SCI, vol. 315, pp. 241–245. Springer, Heidelberg (2010)
9. Faraj, S.T.: Integrating quantum cryptography into SSL. UbiCC Journal, vol. 5, special Issue of Ubiquitous Computing Security Systems, pp. 1778–1788 (2010)
10. Kwiatkowska, M.: Probabilistic model checking with PRISM. In: POPL 2015 Tutorial, Mumbai, January 2015

An LTE-Based VPN for Enhancing QoS and Authentication in Smallcell Enterprise Networks

Maroua Gharam, Meriem Salhi$^{(\boxtimes)}$, and Noureddine Boudriga

Communication Networks and Security (CNAS) Research Laboratory,
University of Carthage, Tunis, Tunisia
Mariem.slh@gmail.com

Abstract. In this paper we deal with VPN implementation in Smallcell enterprise networks. Equipped with USIM cards, these access points represent the end points of communication tunnels. First, an authentication scheme is proposed. It reduces the exchanged messages between users and the LTE core and permits to avoid unnecessary LTE re-authentication. Also, an aggregation mechanism using LTE features is proposed reducing the communication costs.

Keywords: VPN · LTE-smallcells · Enterprise network · QoS · Authentication

1 Introduction

Nowadays the enterprise environment is characterized by a multiplication of the mobile devices in the workplace, a proliferation of real-time multipmedia applications as well as more stringent requirments in terms of reliability and data rates. The fourth generation (4G) Smallcells represent an attractive solution for that since they are able to afford high speed wireless access with high Quality of Service (QoS) support together with reduced power consumption and operating costs. In addition to that, a critical necessity for the enterprise consists in ensuring a secure and reliable communication platform to handle its private connections between either sites of its wide area network. In this context, Virtual Private Networks (VPN) represent the best approach ensuring the continuity and flexibility of business procedures in a secure, reliable and cost-efficient manner. Its incorporation in 4G-networks increases the supported level of data protection.

There are different types of remote access VPN [1] where each one operates on different layer of the Open Systems Interconnection (OSI) model, for example Point to Point Tunneling Protocol (PPTP) and Layer Two Tunneling Protocol (L2TP) operate over layer 2 whereas Internet Protocol Security (IPsec) and Multi Protocol Label Switching (MPLS) operate over layer 3, and Secure Socket Layer (SSL) operates over the higher-layer. The most prominent technique for deploying VPN across IP networks is the IPsec standard [2], which is able to

© Springer International Publishing Switzerland 2015
M. Reiter and D. Naccache (Eds.): CANS 2015, LNCS 9476, pp. 248–256, 2015.
DOI: 10.1007/978-3-319-26823-1_18

guarantee the security and privacy of any type of carried services. However, it presents several limits where the major drawback consists on the lack of QoS guarantee. In [3], authors studied the effect of IPsec tunneling on the QoS for video and voice traffics and concluded that latency and packet loss are affected because of traffic load and encryption process. More importantly, IPsec on itself makes QoS provisioning very complex since packets are encapsulated inside the tunnel. To solve this problem, there have been some efforts to propose QoS enhancements for IPsec such as in [4] where a priority scheduling algorithm, that takes into account the QoS requirements of traffic flows, is integrated in IPsec. Another major drawback of IPsec is its limited scalability related to the need of maintenance of security associations which makes the dynamic adaptation of mobile VPNs inappropriate. To solve this issue authors in [5] proposed a distributed VPN auto-configuration. In [6], authors propose a real time scheduling algorithm with optimization of security service according to network dynamics, thus reducing the overhead.

Over the last few years Long Term Evolution (LTE) has gained a great interest as a prominent access technology with great enhancements in the system architecture as well as the communication features. It can be viewed as a generic architecture permitting the interconnection of various types of access networks. The main goal of this paper is to promote the establishment of a QoS-guaranteed VPN over the fourth generation cellular technology. First, a novel architecture is considered. It enhances the role of Smallcells for VPN establishment and includes a local authentication center for security functions. Second, an authentication mechanism, which is compliant to the standard LTE authentication procedure, is proposed. Third, a QoS guaranteed tunneling framework employing a smart aggregation mechanism is build upon the LTE bearer model, in order to ensure the reliability and cost savings of the VPN connections. The remainder of the paper is organized as follows. Section 2 gives the VPN network architecture. Section 3 details the proposed authentication mechanism. Section 4 describes the proposed smart aggregation mechanism. After that, the performance evaluations are given in Sect. 5. Finally, Sect. 6 concludes the work.

2   Proposed VPN Architecture

In this work we are concerned with an enterprise with multiple distributed local networks using the LTE Smallcell as an access technology. The backbone for this architecture consists of the LTE core network and the public internet (or IMS system). As depicted in Fig. 1 each local network includes three main entities:

- UE: The User Equipment is a smart device equipped with an Universal Subscriber Identity Module (USIM) to enable users attach to the LTE system. It allows them to communicate with each other in the local network or through the backbone for classical LTE communication.
- Smallcell: It is the radio access point in the LTE network system intended to serve the enterprise users. Furthermore, in our architecture, the Smallcell is equipped with a set of external USIM cards enabling it to perform additional

functionalities. At least one of those cards is dedicated for coordination tasks inside the same local network and with distant enterprise local networks, we refer to it by coordination agent (COR-Agent). The other cards enable VPN communication and are named communication agents (COM-Agents).

- L-AuC: The Local Authentication Center is a central entity in the enterprise site. It works together with the Smallcell node to ensure the local administration of enterprise's communications. The main function of L-AuC consists in the local authentication of UEs when requesting for VPN communication. To do this, it holds a local security table containing three parameters related to the UEs who are initially authenticated by the LTE core network, namely: Mobile Station International Subscriber Directory Number (MSISDN), Globally Unique Temporary Identity (GUTI) and IP address.

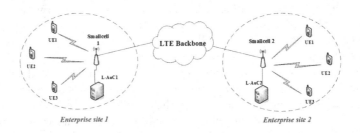

Fig. 1. LTE-VPN architecture

3   Proposed Authentication Mechanism

3.1   Initial User Authentication

According to the 3GPP LTE, when the UE is powered on, it invokes the attach procedure to access the LTE network by sending the International Mobile Subscriber Identity (IMSI) number as the identity to provide mutual authentication and key agreement with the evolved packet system (EPS) [7] known as AKA EPS authentication. After a successful AKA EPS authentication, the local registration of the UE is performed as shown in Fig. 2. In fact, the Smallcell node registers the parameters of the authenticated users (GUTI, IP address) in the local authentication center (L-AuC) in order to be used later for local authentication procedure as explained in the next paragraph. Then, the L-AuC requests from the UE the MSISDN corresponding to the registered GUTI. The UE sends an additional information response to the L-AuC. Finally, the user's basic information are stored in L-AuC. It is noteworthy to mention that the GUTI number is used for the local re-authentication procedure whereas the MSISDN is used for the VPN service request procedure as it will be described in the next section.

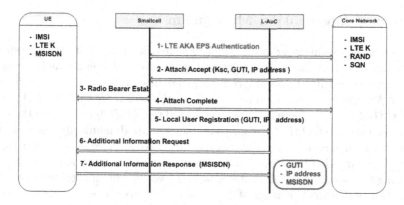

Fig. 2. LTE authentication procedure

3.2 Local User Authentication

Once the employees of the enterprise are attached to the LTE network, only the enterprise local network is responsible for the local authentication and the verification of users based on the temporary identity GUTI which is obtained during the attach procedure. We mention that when an LTE UE switches to idle mode its identification parameters (MSISDN, GUTI, IP address) still available in the core network. Thus, in order to avoid unnecessary re-authentication to the core network, we propose a local authentication procedure as described in Fig. 3. Firstly, the UE sends a service request to the Smallcell which forwards it transparently to the L-AuC in order to verify the existence of GUTI number. Then, the L-AuC generates a local Key using the GUTI and a random number (RAND). This local key will be used temporary to secure the wireless link between the UE and the Smallcell node. This local authentication procedure is advantageous since it reduces the delay of the user's LTE core network authentication and avoids the overhead related to LTE re-authentication.

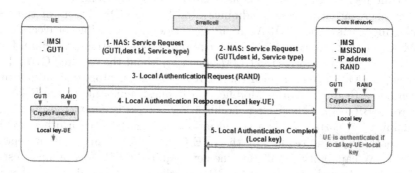

Fig. 3. Local authentication procedure

4   Smart Aggregation Mechanism

The tunnel management procedure includes creating a new tunnel between two communicating parts as well as aggregating the user's traffic through an established tunnel according to the smart aggregation mechanism described in the next section. A tunnel is represented by a set of entities which are the $COM\text{-}Agent_{src}$ and $COM\text{-}Agent_{dest}$, the set of users connected to $COM\text{-}Agent_{src}$ and the set of those connected to $COM\text{-}Agent_{dest}$ these two sets are dynamically updated, furthermore a tunnel is characterized by a specific class of service. Also, before tunnel creation, we note that a destination discovery function is performed. It consists on localizing the destination UE at the Smallcell level within an enterprise site. The description of this function is out of the scope of this paper. Conforming to the LTE technology, the enterprise user's traffic is routed along a set of bearers traversing the backbone part. In fact, a bearer can be either Guaranteed Bit Rate (GBR) guaranteeing a bit rate level by reserving some capacity along the transmission path, or Non-Guaranteed Bit Rate (N-GBR). In this work, we consider only GBR applications (e.g. conversational voice, conversational video and buffered streaming). Also, we assume that only one tunnel can be established per COM-Agent.

According to the LTE 3GPP standard, when a COM-Agent is already attached to the LTE core, it can request bearer resource modification procedure for an E-UTRAN [7]. This permits to the agent to request for an increase or decrease of GBR. Consequently, in addition to the metrics previously defined, a tunnel is also characterized by three additional parameters, namely: the reserved GBR, the effective GBR which consists in the bit rate that is actually used, and the maximum bit rate (MBR) which is the value that the reserved GBR cannot exceed. We note that the value of the two first parameters may change along the lifetime of the tunnel, whereas the third remains unchanged. In this work, we propose to take advantage of the bearer modification procedure in order to aggregate multiple users' traffics in the same tunnel. Obviously, traffics aggregated in the same tunnel should have the same QoS class. Each new traffic has a certain GBR, we call it user GBR. Also we define the effective GBR as the sum of the user GBRs of all users associated to the same tunnel.

The aggregation process is administrated by the COR-Agents of the communicating parts. The COR-Agent in each side is responsible of electing the COM-Agent that will trigger the bearer resource modification procedure. First, the $COM\text{-}Agent_{src}$ informs the $COM\text{-}Agent_{dest}$ about the required GBR. Then the elected COM-Agents launch the GBR modification process simultaneously by sending a Bearer Resource Modification Request indicating to the PGW the required GBR value. The bearer modification process is completed only if the communicating parts receive a confirmation message from each other proving the acceptance of the request by the LTE Core. In fact, this decision depends on the PGW capability of carrying the new required GBR. At the initial establishment of a tunnel the reserved GBR is initiated to a certain value denoted GBR_i depending to the QoS class. Whenever a new traffic is aggregated in the tunnel, if the sum of the effective GBR and the new user GBR is lower than the reserved GBR, then the reserved GBR will remain the same, otherwise it will be augmented following equation (1): $GBR(t+1) = GBR(t) + (1+\alpha)GBR_i$ (1) In fact, a high augmentation step (i.e. high value of α) leads to a wastage of the reserved resources since it increases the gap between the reserved GBR and the effective GBR. On the other hand, a low augmentation step results in higher overhead, because in that case the bearer modification procedure would be triggered more frequently. As previously mentioned, one of the important objectives of our VPN tunneling protocol is to minimize the communication costs which is directly related to the reserved GBR. Subsequently, the higher is the augmentation step, the higher would be the cost. Thus, an accurate value of α is required to guarantee a trade off between the two aforementioned constraints. At the reception of a new VPN service request from an enterprise user, the Smallcell node performs the tunnel management procedure as detailed in Algorithm 1.

Algorithm 1. Tunnel Management Algorithm

%Inputs: set Ω_c of established tunnels of service class c; set S_f of inactive COM.Ag%
%Initialization%
User u Requests a Service of class c $\neq$ {}
COR-Ag selects the COM-Ag-A from the set Ω_c with the minimun number of associated users
if $GBR_{newuser} > GBR_{reserved}$ - $GBR_{effective}$ **then**
    COR-Ag triggers the COM-Ag-A to launch GBR modification procedure
    COM-Ag-A launches the Bearer Resource Modification
    if Bearer modification is successful **then**
        Aggregate traffic
        Update Tunnel parameters (set of users, effective GBR, reserved GBR)
    else Delete from the set Ω_c the COM-Ag-A
    end if
else Aggregate traffic; Update Tunnel parameters(users, effective GBR);
end if
if $\Omega_c =$ {} **then**
    if $S_{f-src} \neq$ {} **then** COR-Ag_{src} selects a COM-Ag_{src} from S_{f-src} randomly
        COR-Ag_{src} informs the COR-Ag_{dest} about the selected COM-Ag_{src}
        $COR.Ag_{dest}$ selects a COM-Ag_{dest} from S_{f-dest} randomly
        COR-Ag_{dest} associates the UE_{dest} to $COM - Ag_{dest}$
        COR-Ag_{src} associates the UE_{src} to the COM-Ag_{src}
    else%User is blocked;
    end if
end if

---

5 Performance Evaluation

In this section, we give numerical results aiming to study the dimensioning characteristics of the proposed platform in relation to the Smallcell density, the number of COM-Agents per Smallcell, and different classes of service. The considered network is composed of two distant enterprise sites each consisting of one

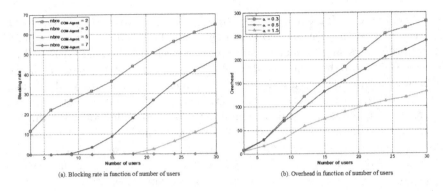

(a). Blocking rate in function of number of users   (b). Overhead in function of number of users

Fig. 4. The blocking rate and overhead in function of number of users

Smallcell node. We consider three classes of service each characterized by two specific values user GBR and MBR, namely: voice call (GBR, MBR=60 kbps), conversational video (GBR=120 kbps, MBR=700 kbps), and streaming video (GBR=180 kbps, MBR=1200 kbps). We note that traffic for conversational video and voice is bidirectional, whereas for streaming video it is unidirectional (downlink). The number of users for each class is approximately the same, and the inter-arrival time is constant; however the sequential arrival events in terms of the type of service is random. To evaluate the performance of our platform, we study first the blocking rate in function of the number of users. A user is blocked when there is no available COM-Agents to be associated with, this is due to the limited number of COM-Agents in the Smallcell. Figure 4(a) gives the variation of the experienced blocking rate for different number of COM-Agent with a specific number of users (30 users). This figure illustrates the resulting blocking rate showing that it decreases rapidly when the number of COM-Agents increases. We varied the number of available COM-Agents in the Smallcell from 2 to 7 for a constant Smallcell load (30 UEs), and we see that for 7 COM-Agents the blocking rate is approximately null. In fact, the adding of one COM-Agent reduces the blocking rate since it permits to serve multiple UEs requiring the same class of service. Figure 4(b) gives the variation of the overhead when the Smallcell density increases with 5 COM-Agents per Smallcell. This overhead refers to the number of messages exchanged between the source and destination enterprise sites when a new user requires a VPN connection, more precisely: messages exchanged over the LTE core system for new tunnel establishment or GBR modification. The overhead increases when the GBR augmentation step α decreases. In fact, the smaller the augmentation step is the smaller is the difference between the effective and reserved GBR which results in increasing the number of triggered GBR updates until reaching the MBR. Figure 5(a) illustrates the ratio between the effective GBR and the reserved GBR showing that it increases when the GBR augmentation step α decreases. In fact, when a new user requests a VPN communication, the COM-Agent tries to associate it to an established tunnel with the minimum effective GBR in order to avoid GBR update. We conclude

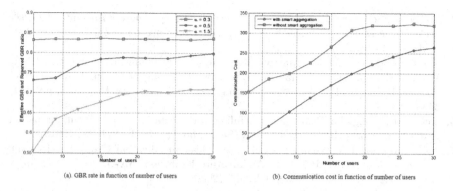

(a). GBR rate in function of number of users   (b). Communication cost in function of number of users

Fig. 5. The GBR rate and communication cost in function of the number of users

that the more α is important and the MBR associated to the tunnel is not yet reached the more new users can be associated to that tunnel. Figure 5(b) gives the variation of the communication cost for the proposed method with smart aggregation and for the method without smart aggregation. We remark that the first method offers a lower cost compared to the second method. In our scheme the communication cost is related to the reserved GBR which i adapted to the communication needs. It is also related to the new establishment of tunnels. On the other hand, for the method without smart aggregation the communication cost augments whenever a new tunnel is established. The cost per tunnel in this method is fixed from the beginning and is related to the MBR of the desired service.

6   Conclusion

In this paper, we first proposed a local authentication mechanism for LTE-based VPN platform based on the initial LTE authentication. Our scheme permits to avoid unnecessary LTE re-authentication, thus reducing the related overhead. Also, we developed an aggregation mechanism based on the LTE-bearer modification concept that permits to guarantee QoS of tunneled traffic and at the same time reduce communication costs.

References

1. Jaha, A.A., Ben Shatwan, F., Ashibani, M.: Proper Virtual Private Network (VPN) solution In: Proceedings of International Conference on Next Generation Mobile Applications, Services, and Technologies (2008)
2. Paterson, K.: A cryptographic tour of the IPsec standards. Inf. Secur. Tech. Rep. **11**(2), 72–81 (2006)
3. Perez, J.A., Zarate, V., Montes, A., Garcia, C.: Quality of service analysis of IPSec VPNs for voice and video traffic. In: Proceedings of International Conference on Internet and Web Applications and Services (2006)

4. Volker, L., Scholler, M., Zitterbart, M.: Introducing QoS mechanisms into the IPsec packet processing. In: Proceedings of IEEE Conference on Local Computer Networks, October 2007

5. Rossberg, M., Schafer, G., Martius, K.: Automatic configuration of complex IPsec-VPNs and implications to higher layer network management. In: Pohlmann, N., Reimer, H., Schneider, W. (eds.) Securing Electronic Business Processes, pp. 334–342 (2011)

6. Saleh, M., Dong, L.: Real-time scheduling with security enhancement for packet switched networks. IEEE Trans. Netw. Serv. Manage. **10**(3), 271–285 (2013)

7. 3rd Generation Partnership Project, "Technical Specification Group Services and System Aspects", 3GPP System Architecture Evolution (SAE), Security architecture (Release 9) 3GPP TS 33.401 V9.4.0 (2009)

Author Index

Printed in the United States
By Bookmasters